dc Talk

TOBY MAC AND MICHAEL TAIT

with WallBuilders

DER

GOD

COMPILED BY

LeAnna Willis

BETHANYHOUSE
MINNEAPOLIS, MINNESOTA

UNDER GOD

by Toby Mac and Michael Tait of dc Talk with WallBuilders

Copyright © 2004 by Bethany House Publishers
Manuscript prepared by LeAnna Willis and David R. Long.
Research by Scott Kaste.
Additional contributions by Amanda Clawson, Kyle Duncan, Dan Pitts, and Natasha Sperling.

Design by Lookout Design Group, Inc.

Published by Bethany House Publishers
11400 Hampshire Avenue South
Bloomington, Minnesota 55438
www.bethanyhouse.com

Bethany House Publishers is a division of
Baker Publishing Group, Grand Rapids, Michigan.

Printed in the United States of America.

Library of Congress Cataloging-in-Publication Data

Tobymac, 1964-
  Under God / DC Talk's Toby Mac And Michael Tait with WallBuilders ; compiled by LeAnna Willis.
    p. cm.
  Includes bibliographical references and index.
  ISBN 0-7642-0008-9 (pbk. with flaps)
  1. United States—Church history. I. Tait, Michael. II. Willis, LeAnna. III. WallBuilders (Organization) IV. Title.

BR515.T63 2004
277.3--dc22

2004018669

First Edition

Contents

Introduction 7

1. Bulletproof: The French and Indian War—
   Account of a British Officer 11

   Worship in the Capitol 14

2. A Declaration of Dependence...Upon God:
   The Signing of the Declaration of
   Independence 15

3. A Time for War: Peter Muhlenberg 20

   "Give 'Em Watts, Boys!" 24

4. His Sons—Captured!: Abraham Clark . . . 25

   *Anthony Benezet—Father of American
   Abolitionism* 28

5. Benjamin Who?: Benjamin Rush 29

6. Saved by the Fog: Evacuation of Long
   Island 31

   George Duffield, Patriot Preacher 33

7. Giving Credit Where It's Due:
   Robert Morris 34

   *Samuel Adams—A Man Devoted
   to a Cause* 38

8. Gifted: Phillis Wheatley 39

9. Into the Presence:
   First Continental Congress 43

10. Out of the Jaws of the Wicked:
    William and Ellen Craft 48

    The History of Juneteenth 53

11. "Unless You Kill Me":
    John Prentiss "Print" Matthews 54

12. Pirating the *Planter*: Robert Smalls 58

    Henry Highland Garnet 62

13. Tired of Giving In: Rosa Parks 63

14. In a Class of Only One: Ruby Bridges . . 68

    The Road to Desegregation 75

15. A Special Instrument Sent of God:
    Tisquantum—"Squanto" 76

*Native American Contributions to the
Government* 81

16. A Covenanted People: The Pilgrims'
    Landing at Cape Cod 83

    Jamestown 89

17. Government by the Gospel:
    Plymouth, Massachusetts 91

18. No Justice: C. J. Miller 94

    The Jim Crow Era and Black Codes . . . 99

19. Innocent Blood Cries Out:
    Ida B. Wells-Barnett 102

    *Lynchings by Race and Year
    (1882–1960)* 108

20. Freedom's Railroad: Harriet Tubman . . 109

    The Underground Railroad 115

21. "Don't Let Them Have Him!": Charles
    Nalle and Harriet Tubman 116

22. Begin Again: Bridget "Biddy" Mason . . . 119

    Revivals in War and Peace 125

23. Crazy Bet: Elizabeth Van Lew 126

24. They Tried to Forget:
    Duluth, Minnesota 132

25. The Holy Experiment: William Penn . . 139

    State Constitutions 143

26. Defender of the Union: Daniel Webster . 144

    The Star-Spangled Banner 150

27. One Life to Lose: Nathan Hale 151

    Did You Know? and Laus Deo 154

28. Empowered to Persuade: Patrick Henry . 156

29. With Regrets: Benedict Arnold 161

30. The United Cry of the Nation:
    Abraham Lincoln 165

    The Gettysburg Address 170

31. Turning Point: Isabella Baumfree—
    "Sojourner Truth" 172

    Three Remarkable Women 177

32. Denise. Carole. Cynthia. Addie Mae: Birmingham Bombing of the Sixteenth Street Baptist Church 180

33. Stand Up: Martin Luther King Jr. 186

   Chinese Labor and the Transcontinental Railroad 190

34. When a Sport Is Something More: Jackie Robinson. 191

35. Lifting a People: Richard Allen. 198

   Negro Spirituals 205

36. The Birth and Second Coming of a Message of Hate: Ku Klux Klan 206

37. "It Is All So Terribly True": Woodrow Wilson and *The Birth of a Nation* 212

38. "God Save These People": John Witherspoon. 216

39. The Strong Voice of Freedom: Theodore Weld. 220

   The Missouri Compromise and the Fugitive Slave Law 225

40. The Repentant Slaveholder: Angelina Grimké 226

41. "As a Mother...As a Christian": Harriet Beecher Stowe 230

   The Power to Get Wealth 236

   Inspiration From a Slave 237

42. A Cycle of Service and Love: John Perkins. 238

   1857–1858 Noonday Prayer Meetings . . . 243

43. "An Impassioned Defense": John Quincy Adams and the *Amistad* 244

   A Father's Advice 248

44. The Dark Side of Lincoln's Home: Springfield Riot 249

   The Price of Fear 253

45. The Right Man at the Right Time: Dwight D. Eisenhower 255

   The Pledge of Allegiance 260

46. "We Need the Storm, the Whirlwind, and the Earthquake": Frederick Douglass . . 262

   First African Americans in Congress . . 269

47. What Four Hundred Dollars Can Buy: George and Lewis Latimer 270

   Their Contributions Many 275

48. Forever Fourteen: Emmett Till. 279

   Medgar Evers 285

49. A Legacy of Freedom: John Jay 286

   Robert Gould Shaw and the 54th Massachusetts 289

50. "I Will Fight No More Forever": Chief Joseph and the Nez Percé War . . 290

   America's First Nations People 295

51. The Smuggled Patriot: John Adams . . . 298

   Fifty Years Later 305

52. "Remember the Ladies": Abigail Adams 307

   The Construction of the U.S. Capitol. . . 312

53. The Voice of Reason: Roger Sherman . . 313

54. "Turned Loose to the Whirlwind": Compromise of 1877. 317

55. A Purposeful Life: George Washington Carver 322

   Forty Acres and a Mule 329

   Remembering Everyone at the Alamo . . 330

56. A Soldier's View: The Sand Creek Massacre 331

   Mexican-American Pioneer: Mariano Guadalupe Vallejo 336

57. A Growing Awareness: Benjamin Franklin 337

58. "Before We Proceed to Business": Congressional Prayer 343

   What Happened to the Signers of the Declaration of Independence? 345

59. The Interesting Narrative: Olaudah Equiano 349

60. Kettle Prayers: Lake Providence, Louisiana 353

   America's Underground Church 360

What Is Freedom For? 361

Closing Thoughts From Toby and Michael. . 363

A Call to Prayer. 366

Timeline. 372

Bibliography. 376

Index 379

For More Information 384

Introduction

On July 4, 1776, the forefathers of our nation set upon a course and forged a direction that would reverberate throughout the world and lead this nation to offer unforeseen levels of hope, prosperity, and freedom to an amazing tapestry of people. The American Revolution was truly revolutionary.

"Government of the people, by the people, for the people" was a very radical concept. No one could have dreamed the impact it would have. In our founding document, the Declaration of Independence, one of the most profound ideals set forth was that "all men are created equal." Today, it is hard to truly understand how radical the introduction of that concept was. It helps to go back to the eighteenth century and gain a greater understanding of what the world was like. Kings and queens were the rulers and conquerors of the day. Justice and wealth was held in their hands. Our forefathers sought to take some of that tightly bound power and distribute it so that many who could never dream of hope and opportunity would find peace and prosperity through a freedom that was built upon the principles of God. In 1776, and for basically the next two hundred years, however, for some who lived in America, this concept of "all men are created equal" was more authentic in word than it was in deed.

Two enormous tragedies that occurred through Europe's colonization of America are found in the stories of Native Americans (or the Host Peoples) and the descendants of Africa. Slavery, the great scourge of our national history, became a gaping wound of injustice from the very outset of our nation's birth. As well, as white settlers moved west in search of a better life, the Native American peoples were decimated and expelled from their lands. It is important to grasp that these two people groups —Native Americans and blacks— did not come to America seeking the American Dream. It is probably more accurate to say that they lived the American nightmare. What is often lost in all this, however, are the amazing contributions they made to this great country. Every step of the way as our nation developed, they were right there making major contributions.

While our forefathers set forth the ideal of what this nation could become, it was immensely more difficult to carry out and ensure this ideal for all men and women. It is a profound task that continues to this very day. Here is where we see the greatness of the American Revolution: A foundation was laid that would allow for change, and this foundation could be built upon to lift this nation higher toward its grand ideal. Our forefathers cautioned, however, that if we were to lose our religion and morality, our foundation would surely crumble.

This is a glimpse into the battle that started roughly five hundred years ago when the first European explorers came to this land. Some have called it our "dual heritage." To help give a framework for examining this heritage, we can look at two of the earliest settlements—Jamestown and Plymouth. Jamestown, Virginia, was a colony primarily formed as a business venture by investors to obtain wealth. In contrast, Plymouth, Massachusetts, was a colony established by Pilgrims primarily to further the Gospel. The Protestant Reformation was a powerful force that fueled the vision of the Pilgrims.

If you study these two settlements in any kind of depth, you will find some interesting observations. Plymouth centered around covenanting with God and with one another. While they were not perfect, by any means, over and over the Pilgrims seemed to encounter divine providence at just the right times. Jamestown, on the other hand, centered primarily on the acquisition of gold and the building of capital. While there were some redemptive elements in the colony, the settlers seemed to encounter much fighting and bickering and failure.

Many people came to America. Many came seeking wealth. Many came seeking religious freedom.

When studying the founding of the United States, one thing that you can't help but encounter is the faith of our forefathers. Time and time again our forefathers recognized God's hand in the shaping of this nation. You will find Him mentioned repeatedly in their words and documents. Amazingly, hardly any of this factual history is taught today, whereas it was common public school teaching material seventy-five years ago. It is important to note, though, that while our forefathers were great men who did great things, they were also just men. Fallible. Imperfect.

When we decided to embark upon creating this book, we decided to use King David from the Bible as our model. He was a man after God's own heart, but he was also a murderer and adulterer. And though David repented of his errors, they haunted him the rest of his life. In the same way, our forefathers left some things undone, and along the way our nation plunged into some dark traditions.

Ours is a heritage of light and ours is a heritage of darkness.

This book is a collection of short stories about our heritage. Each short story could have—and has had—entire books written about its subject. Our collection of stories is by no means exhaustive. We have left out many great ones. But it is our hope that these accounts will ignite a passion and inspire you to learn more about the great heritage you have and to seek out the unfinished work left to do. It is our hope that you enjoy reading these stories as much as we did discovering them.

TOBY and MICHAEL

Bulletproof
The French and Indian War:
Account of a British Officer

JULY 9, 1755

The American Indian chief looked scornfully at the soldiers on the field before him. How foolish it was to fight as they did, forming their perfect battle lines out in the open, standing shoulder to shoulder in their bright red uniforms. The British soldiers—trained for European warfare—did not break rank, even when braves fired at them from under the safe cover of the forest. The slaughter at the Monongahela River continued for two hours. By then 1,000 of 1,459 British soldiers were killed or wounded, while only 30 of the French and Indian warriors firing at them were injured.

Not only were the soldiers foolish, but their officers were just as bad. Riding on horseback, fully exposed above the men on the ground, they made perfect targets. One by one, the chief's marksmen shot the mounted British officers until only one remained.

"Quick, let your aim be certain and he dies," the chief commanded. The warriors—a mix of Ottawa, Huron, and Chippewa tribesmen—leveled their rifles at the last officer on horseback. Round after round was aimed at this one man. Twice the officer's horse was shot out from under him. Twice he grabbed a horse left idle when a fellow officer had been shot down. Ten, twelve, thirteen rounds were fired by the sharpshooters. Still, the officer remained unhurt.

The native warriors stared at him in disbelief. Their rifles seldom missed their mark. The chief suddenly realized that a mighty power must be shielding this man. "Stop firing!" he commanded. "This one is under the special protection of the Great Spirit." A brave standing nearby added, "I had seventeen clear shots at him . . . and after all could not bring him to the ground. This man was not born to be killed by a bullet."

As the firing slowed, the lieutenant colonel gathered the remaining troops and led the retreat to safety. That evening, as the last of the wounded were being cared for, the officer noticed an odd tear in his coat. It was a bullet hole! He rolled up his sleeve and looked at his arm directly under the hole. There was no mark on his skin. Amazed, he took off his coat and found three more holes where bullets had passed through his coat but stopped before they reached his body.

Nine days after the battle, having heard a rumor of his own death, the young lieutenant colonel wrote his brother to confirm that he was still very much alive.

> *As I have heard since my arrival at this place, a circumstantial account of my death and dying speech, I take this early opportunity of contradicting the first and of assuring you that I have not as yet composed the latter. But by the all-powerful dispensations of Providence I have been protected beyond all human probability or expectation; for I had four bullets through my coat, and two horses shot under me yet escaped unhurt, although death was leveling my companions on every side of me!*

The battle on the Monongahela, part of the French and Indian War, was fought on July 9, 1755, near Fort Duquesne, now the city of Pittsburgh. The twenty-three-year-old officer went on to become the commander in chief of the Continental Army and the first president of the United States. In all the years that followed in his long career, this man, George Washington, was never once wounded in battle.

Fifteen years later, in 1770, George Washington returned to the same Pennsylvania woods. A respected Indian chief, having heard that Washington was in the area, traveled a long way to meet with him.

He sat down with Washington, and face-to-face over a council fire, the chief told Washington the following:

> *I am a chief and ruler over my tribes. My influence extends to the waters of the great lakes and to the far blue mountains. I have traveled a long and weary path that I might see the young*

warrior of the great battle. It was on the day when the white man's blood mixed with the streams of our forests that I first beheld this chief [Washington].

I called to my young men and said, "Mark yon tall and daring warrior? He is not of the red-coat tribe—he hath an Indian's wisdom and his warriors fight as we do—himself alone exposed. Quick, let your aim be certain, and he dies."

Our rifles were leveled, rifles which, but for you, knew not how to miss—'twas all in vain, a power mightier far than we shielded you.

Seeing you were under the special guardianship of the Great Spirit, we immediately ceased to fire at you. I am old and shall soon be gathered to the great council fire of my fathers in the land of the shades, but ere I go, there is something bids me speak in the voice of prophecy:

Listen! The Great Spirit protects that man [pointing at Washington], and guides his destinies—he will become the chief of nations, and a people yet unborn will hail him as the founder of a mighty empire. I am come to pay homage to the man who is the particular favorite of Heaven, and who can never die in battle.

★ ★ ★

This story of God's divine protection and of Washington's open gratitude could be found in many school textbooks until the 1930s. Now few Americans have read it. Washington often recalled this dramatic event that helped shape his character and confirm God's call on his life.

Though a thousand fall at your side,
though ten thousand are dying around you,
these evils will not touch you.
PSALM 91:7 NLT

Worship in the Capitol

Thanks to the constitutional mandate of Article I, Section 5, Paragraph 3, every debate and every vote that has taken place in Congress from 1774 to the present is recorded in the public records. As a result of this mandate, the American people are able to read exactly what happened when Congress first moved into the Capitol.

On December 4, 1800, just a few weeks after moving into the building, Congress decided that the Capitol would also serve as a church building. This fact is not only recorded in the Annals of Congress but also confirmed in the journals of various representatives and senators serving at that time.

For example, Senator John Quincy Adams recorded on October 30, 1803:

Attended public service at the Capitol where Mr. Ratoon, an Episcopalian clergyman from Baltimore, preached a sermon.

Just a week earlier he'd written:

Religious service is usually performed on Sundays at the Treasury office and at the Capitol. I went both forenoon and afternoon to the Treasury.

Thus began the longstanding—and congressionally sanctioned—practice of using government buildings as houses of worship.

2. A Declaration of Dependence...Upon God

The Signing of the Declaration of Independence / SUMMER 1776

Thomas Jefferson stretched and yawned loudly. He was completely drained of thought and empty of rhetoric, but he was finished writing the Declaration of Independence. He smiled proudly; he was very pleased with the final draft. In fact, the whole process had been amazing. It was as if he were a container that had been filled over the years with bits and pieces—a phrase here, a concept there. And all of it had been waiting, waiting for this moment. When he sat down to write, the words began to flow out. Majestic, powerful, poetic words— words that would change all history. He had such a sense of purpose, of destiny, as he wrote. He lost track of time. Someone had brought him food—and he had eaten—but all he could remember were the beautiful words coming out of the depths of his being.

He extinguished the lamp and went to sleep.

The next day Thomas approached the other four committee members chosen by the Continental Congress to work on the Declaration of Independence. He could hardly wait to show them the genius of his workmanship. At first, they were amazed that he had finished the draft so quickly. Then they were amazed at what he had written. It was magnificent!

When in the course of human events . . .

"Perfect!"

We hold these truths to be self-evident, that all men are created equal. . . .

"This is good!"

Governments are instituted among men, deriving their just powers from the consent of the governed. . . .

"I wouldn't change a word."

Thomas Jefferson closed his eyes, basking in the praises of the older statesmen. It was the highlight of his life.

Then the congressman from Massachusetts broke his reverie. "I would like to add the words, 'They are endowed by their Creator with certain unalienable Rights,'" said John Adams.

"Where?" Thomas asked.

"Right after 'all men are created equal.'"

Benjamin Franklin nodded in agreement. "Oh, that's good. Yes! And what about toward the end—let's insert 'with a firm reliance on the protection of Divine Providence.'"

Thomas was offended. Government by committee was an exciting concept, but writing by committee left a lot to be desired. The committee of five continued to work together, making small changes until they agreed the Declaration of Independence was ready to present to the Continental Congress—if Congress was finally ready to declare independence!

They would soon know. Their draft would be presented when the delegates reconvened on July 1, 1776. Then they would vote on whether to break with Great Britain.

The choice was not a decision that our Founding Fathers made lightly—in fact, they had tried everything else first. A year earlier, on July 5, 1775, Congress had sent the "Olive Branch Petition" directly to King George III, asking for his help in making peace. But the king refused to even look at it.

Famous British parliamentarians argued for America's cause, but none of their arguments moved King George. In his eyes there was only one way to deal with rebellion: crush the rebels by military force. He declared war.

But never in Britain's history was recruiting volunteers so difficult. The recruiting officers were tarred and feathered in Wales and stoned in Ireland; in the previous war three hundred thousand men had volunteered, now not even fifty thousand had come forward. King George was forced to hire mercenaries from Germany who were willing to fight the Americans.

Despite the fact that England had declared war, many congressional delegates were still hoping for a way to reconcile. Only eight of the thirteen colonies had voted to declare independence.

Then, on June 7, 1776, news came that King George's hired mercenaries were coming to America to fight. In response, Richard Henry Lee of Virginia formally proposed to Congress that the colonies declare their independence. Congress postponed its decision until July, so those delegates who were uncertain could check with the people they represented.

When they reconvened, the Resolution for Independence was adopted by twelve of the thirteen colonies, with New York abstaining. Congress then began to discuss the wording of the Declaration. The changes demonstrated Congress's strong reliance upon God—as delegates added the words "appealing to the Supreme Judge of the World for the rectitude of our intentions."

In the center section are the complaints against King George that made independence necessary. Surprisingly, the reason given by modern history books—"taxation without representation"—is not at the top of the list. In fact, it was seventeenth in a list of twenty-seven grievances, including eleven points on abuse of representative powers, seven on abuse of military powers, and four on abuse of judicial powers.

The revisions continued into the late afternoon of July 4, when, at last, church bells rang out over Philadelphia; the Declaration had been officially adopted.

One of the most widely held misconceptions about the Declaration is that it was signed on July 4, 1776, by all the delegates in attendance. In fact, it wasn't officially signed until August 2.

On that day, John Hancock, the president of Congress, was the first to sign. He signed with a flourish, using a big, bold signature centered below the text.

Then, one by one, the other delegates were called upon, beginning with the northern-most states. Each man knew what he risked: To the British this was treason, and the penalty for treason was death by hanging. Benjamin Franklin said, "Indeed we must all hang together. Otherwise we shall most assuredly hang separately."

William Ellery, a delegate from Rhode Island, inched his way to stand near the desk where the delegates were signing their names. He was curious to see their faces as each committed this supreme act of courage. Ellery later reported that he was not able to discern real fear on anyone's face. One man's hand shook badly: Stephen Hopkins, also from Rhode Island, was in his sixties and was quick to explain, "My hand trembles, but my heart does not."

A pensive and awful silence filled the room, as one delegate after another signed what many at that time believed to be their own death warrants. The only sound was the calling of the names and the scratch of the pen.

Then the silence and heaviness of the morning were interrupted by the tall, sturdily built Colonel Benjamin Harrison of Virginia, who told the slender Elbridge Gerry of Massachusetts, "I shall have a great advantage over you, Mr. Gerry, when we are all hung for what we are now doing. With me, it will all be over in a minute, but you, you'll be dancing on air an hour after I'm gone."

In the end, no signer was hung for treason, though many suffered greatly for their stand. For these men, who mutually pledged to each other their lives, their fortunes, their sacred honor, this was more than a declaration. It was more than a document. It was a covenant, the most solemn, the most sacred of human agreements. They understood that God himself was a witness of their actions that day.

In declaring their independence from earthly power and authority, our Founding Fathers declared their dependence upon Almighty God: "with firm reliance on the protection of divine Providence." Like the Pilgrims before them, they fully expected God to keep His side of the covenant as they obeyed His Word and followed His Spirit.

They were not disappointed.

★ ★ ★

I am well aware of the toil and blood and treasure
that it will cost us to maintain this Declaration,
and support and defend these States.
Yet through all the gloom I can see rays of ravishing
light and glory. I can see that the end
is worth more than all the means.
—JOHN ADAMS

We have this day restored the Sovereign,
to Whom alone men ought to be obedient.
He reigns in heaven and . . .
from the rising to the setting sun,
may His Kingdom come.
—SAMUEL ADAMS

A Time for War
Peter Muhlenberg
JANUARY 21, 1776

Pastor Muhlenberg stood in the vestry of his church, putting on his traditional pastoral robes as he had on so many other Sunday mornings. A sense of destiny filled the air around him. This was the last time he would enter his pulpit, the last time he would open the Bible and share the words of life with his congregation.

He knew the sermon he had to preach—yet he knew that some of his people would not understand or accept his position. He himself had wrestled with it for months: How involved should a pastor be in the affairs of government? Didn't Jesus say, "Render unto Caesar the things that are Caesar's and unto God the things that are God's"? Would Christ get involved? Would He run to the battle? It was hard to imagine Jesus carrying a weapon. But it was equally hard to imagine Him not taking a stand.

"To every thing there is a season, and a time to every purpose under heaven," Pastor Muhlenberg proclaimed, reading from Ecclesiastes 3. "A time to be born, and a time to die. . . . A time to weep, and a time to laugh. . . . A time of war, and a time of peace." He stopped and looked at the people God had put in his care—hardworking farmers and their wives, merchants, recent immigrants. The tiny town of Woodstock, Virginia, was a long way from the fighting in the colonies of New England. And the Blue Ridge Mountains had kept its citizens from hearing the news of events in their own state in early January 1776.

"It is a time for war!" Pastor Muhlenberg declared. "And not only in New England. War has come to Virginia! The British have marched on our own city of Williamsburg, seizing our supply of gunpowder and munitions. Soldiers are entering private homes, homes just like ours.

"It is time for war! 'We are only farmers,' you may say. Patrick Henry has rallied five thousand men—farmers just like you—to fight back and drive the British out. It is time to act! Many of us came to this country to practice our religious freedoms. It is time to fight for those freedoms that we hold so dear. It is time for war!

"Let us pray." With that, Pastor Muhlenberg bowed his head and offered the traditional closing prayer. Then, breaking with all tradition, while still standing in the pulpit, he began to remove his pastor's robes and vestments. "I am a clergyman, it is true. But I am also a patriot—and my liberty is as dear to me as to any man. Shall I hide behind my robes, sitting still at home, while others spill their blood to protect my freedom? Heaven forbid it!

"I am called by my country to its defense. The cause is just and noble. I am convinced it is my duty to obey that call, a duty I owe to my God and to my country."

With that, he threw off the final layer of his robes—and now stood before his stunned congregation in the full uniform of an officer of the Continental militia. He marched to the back of the church, declaring to all, "If you do not choose to be involved, if you do not fight to protect your liberties, there will soon be no liberties to protect!"

Pastor Peter Muhlenberg had a brother, Pastor Frederick Muhlenberg. At first, Frederick criticized Peter for getting involved in the war, saying that a minister of the gospel should not be involved in politics. But when the British arrived in New York City in 1777, they drove Frederick from his own church and then desecrated the building. Frederick rethought his position and joined in the fight for liberty. In 1789, he became America's very first Speaker of the House of Representatives. In fact, his signature is one of only two on the Bill of Rights.

Just outside the church army drummers waited. At Pastor Muhlenberg's command, they began to beat out the call for recruits. God's conviction fell on the men of the congregation. One by one they rose from their pews and took their stand with the drummers. Some three hundred men from the church joined their pastor that day to fight for liberty.

★ ★ ★

Pastor Muhlenberg and his men became the Eighth Virginia Regiment, who fought valiantly in many of the battles of the Revolutionary War. During the war, Muhlenberg was promoted to major-general. After the war he was a hero second only to General George Washington among the Germans of his native state of Pennsylvania. In 1785 he became vice-president of Pennsylvania (Benjamin Franklin was president). He worked hard to influence others to adopt the Federal Constitution in 1787 and served in the First U.S. Congress in 1789–91.

A Time for Every Purpose

To everything there is a season,
A time for every purpose under heaven:
A time to be born, and a time to die;
A time to plant, and a time to pluck what is planted;
A time to kill, and a time to heal;
A time to break down, and a time to build up;
A time to weep, and a time to laugh;
A time to mourn, and a time to dance;
A time to cast away stones, and a time to gather stones;
A time to embrace, and a time to refrain from embracing;
A time to gain, and a time to lose;
A time to keep, and a time to throw away;
A time to tear, and a time to sew;
A time to keep silence, and a time to speak;
A time to love, and a time to hate;
A time of war, and a time of peace.
What profit has the worker from that in which he
labors? I have seen the God-given task with which the
sons of men are to be occupied. He has made everything
beautiful in its time. Also He has put eternity in their
hearts, except that no one can find out the work that
God does from beginning to end.
ECCLESIASTES 3:1–11 NKJV

"Give 'Em Watts, Boys!"

Another minister-leader in the Revolution was the Reverend James Caldwell. His church, the First Presbyterian Church of Elizabethtown, New Jersey, counted among its members such noted men as William Livingston, the governor of the state; Elias Boudinot, Commissary General of Prisons and President of the Congress; Abraham Clark, one of the signers of the Declaration of Independence; and more than forty commissioned officers of the Continental Army. In 1776 Caldwell was named chaplain of the regiment that was largely composed of members of his church. Later he became Assistant Commissary General.

Known among the troops as the "Soldier Parson," Caldwell was a zealous proponent of the patriots' cause. During one particular battle, near a battered Presbyterian church, the Americans had run out of wadding for their guns—a problem just as serious as having no ammunition. Rev. Caldwell recognized the perfect solution; he ran inside the church and returned with a stack of Watts' *Psalms and Hymns*—one of the strongest doctrinal hymnals of the Christian faith. (Isaac Watts authored hymns like "O God Our Help in Ages Past," "Joy to the World," "Jesus Shall Reign," and other classic hymns.) Distributing the Watts hymnals among the soldiers served two purposes: First, its pages would provide the needed wadding; second, it carried a symbolic message. In fact, Rev. Caldwell took that hymn book—the source of great doctrine and spiritual truth—raised it up in the air, and shouted to the Americans, "Give 'em Watts, boys!", the famous cry that inspired a painting of the same title.

His Sons—Captured!
Abraham Clark
1781

"We have captured your sons!" The British officer's words hung in midair.

Abraham Clark staggered backward at the news. Three British soldiers stood on his front porch; two were armed with muskets. The third man, an officer, paused to let his words sink in, then continued. "Your sons are prisoners of the Crown, locked away in our prison ship, the *Jersey*. They will surely die there, unless you repent of this foolish rebellion against the king."

The officer took a rolled-up letter out of his jacket and held it out to the stunned father. "Sign this paper. Admit you were wrong, Mr. Clark, and your sons go free!"

Clark turned his head away to hide his confusion. His sons—captured? Held as prisoners of the Crown? How could this be? They had done no wrong. He was the one who had taken a stand, who had signed the Declaration of Independence. He was the one who had pledged his honor, his property, and his life for the cause of liberty. But not his sons.

"Shoot me!" Clark begged the armed soldiers. "I'm the one you want! Shoot me and let my sons go free. They are so young. Their lives are still before them."

The officer's eyes gleamed. So far, the British had been unable to break the resolve of any of the signers of that accursed document. Perhaps this father would be the first one to crack under pressure—to give up the cause for the love of his sons.

"No. Your sons remain our prisoners until you sign the paper."

Clark closed his eyes. How could he choose his country over his own sons? It was a choice no father should ever have to make.

Pressing the advantage, the British officer thrust the letter in Clark's face. "This rebellion is a lost cause. You backwoods colonists can never stand against the power of the British Empire. Don't be a fool," he sneered. "Your sons' lives—their freedom—is at stake!"

The officer's words cut through Clark's indecision.

He suddenly knew what he must choose. It was for freedom's sake that he had taken this stand for independence, so his sons could live free—free from tyranny and oppression.

Before God and man, Clark had pledged to stand with the others, to stand united for this cause, and he would not back down. He knew others had been attacked, captured, and tortured. He knew the British were trying hard to force Clark and the others to break the pledge they had made with one another. If just one man gave in, others might also. Clark knew then that, despite the terrible price he must pay—the lives of his sons—he could not back down. He was a link in a long chain, and he determined he would not be the link that broke under pressure.

★　★　★

It was safer for an American soldier to be on the battlefield facing British muskets than to be captured and placed in a British prisoner-of-war camp. Thousands more Americans died as prisoners of war than from British bullets.

Abraham Clark's sons were held in a British prison boat known as the "hell ship" *Jersey*. During the course of the war, eleven thousand American captives died there. Because their father was a signer of the Declaration of Independence, the Clark sons received especially harsh treatment, including solitary confinement with no food for one of them. They did, however, survive and eventually regain their freedom.

The signers all knew the penalty for instigating rebellion against the Crown was death. Yet many of them believed in a divine purpose and God's timing behind their actions. Thus they wrote: "With a firm reliance on the protection of divine Providence, we mutually pledge to each other our Lives, our Fortunes, and our sacred Honor."

Before God, I believe the hour has come. My judgment
approves this measure, and my whole heart is in it.
All that I have, and all that I am, and all that I hope in this
life, I am now ready here to stake upon it. And I leave off
as I began, that live or die, survive or perish, I am for the
Declaration. It is my living sentiment, and by the blessing
of God it shall be my dying sentiment, Independence now,
and Independence for ever.

—JOHN ADAMS,

in a Speech to the Continental Congress, July 1, 1776

Gentlemen, New Jersey is ready to vote for independence.
In our judgment, the country is not only ripe
for independence, but we are in danger of becoming
rotten for the want of it, if we delay any longer.

—JOHN WITHERSPOON,

in a speech to the Continental Congress, July 1, 1776

I am well aware of the toil and blood and treasure
that it will cost us to maintain this Declaration,
and support and defend these States. Yet through all
the gloom I can see rays of ravishing light and glory.
I can see that the end is worth more than all the means.

—JOHN ADAMS,

in a letter to Abigail Adams, July 2, 1776

We have this day restored the Sovereign,
to Whom alone men ought to be obedient.
He reigns in heaven and . . .
from the rising to the setting sun,
may His Kingdom come.

—SAMUEL ADAMS,

in a speech to the Continental Congress, July 4, 1776

Anthony Benezet—
Father of American Abolitionism

Anthony Benezet was born in 1713 in tumultuous times in Catholic France. His parents, Protestant Huguenots, lost all they had and were forced to flee, eventually ending up in England. At the age of eighteen, Anthony and his family immigrated to Pennsylvania, where they became Quakers.

Known for his humility and devotion to the education and betterment of Philadelphia's black citizens, Benezet was known as "the single most prolific antislavery writer and the most influential advocate of the Negro's rights on either side of the Atlantic." Though abolitionist pioneers such as William Wilberforce and John Wesley are better known, it was Benezet who was a major influence upon these men and other famous abolitionists.

But unlike most abolitionists of his day, Benezet did more than campaign for the blacks—he worked and taught among them. Upon his arrival to Philadelphia in 1731, Benezet became a schoolmaster, teaching a Quaker school by day and tutoring both free and slave blacks the same subjects by night. He was one of the few white men of his generation—even among abolitionists—who did not believe blacks to be inferior, nor did he view Africa as a barbaric continent.

Along with friend and fellow Quaker John Woolman, Benezet convinced the Philadelphia (Quaker) Yearly Meeting to take an official position against the practice of buying and selling slaves. In 1775 Benezet issued the call for the first meeting of the Pennsylvania Abolition Society, whose leaders, including Ben Franklin, were strongly influenced by Benezet's letters and petitions. When Benezet died in 1783, more than four hundred black Philadelphians came to pay their respects.

With a pure heart and a steadfast belief in the equality of all men, Anthony Benezet helped set the tone of equality embedded in the Declaration of Independence and, eventually, the emancipation of all slaves some eighty years after his death.

Benjamin Who?
Benjamin Rush
1743–1813

Who is Benjamin Rush? Today, it could well be a two-thousand dollar question on *Jeopardy!*

When Dr. Benjamin Rush died in 1813, he was considered one of America's three most notable founders, ranking up there with George Washington and Benjamin Franklin. But today, Dr. Rush and his contributions to our country are almost completely forgotten.

As a patriot, Dr. Rush was a signer of the Declaration of Independence. Many of the delegates were disappointed with the number of compromises that had been made in writing the Constitution. But Dr. Rush saw the solid structure that had been achieved: the genius behind the system of checks and balances between the legislative, executive, and judicial branches; the creativity of having two bodies of Congress—the Senate with two votes per state and the House with votes based on population. He pronounced it "a masterpiece of human wisdom."

As a physician, Dr. Rush has been called the most eminent American physician of his generation. He served as physician-general of the Continental Army. He also heroically attacked a deadly yellow fever epidemic in Philadelphia in 1793 that claimed over four thousand lives in one hundred days. By studying old manuscripts, he rediscovered a cure that saved six thousand lives.

He was also the medical adviser/trainer to Meriwether Lewis before Lewis and William Clark embarked on their quest to explore the Northwest Territories. Dr. Rush spent two weeks training Lewis for medical emergencies that he might encounter on the expedition.

As an educator, Dr. Rush served as professor of medicine at the University of Pennsylvania. He helped establish five universities and colleges. In 1791 he founded the First Day Society, an early form of today's Sunday schools. He also helped start America's first Bible society.

Known as the Father of Public Schools, he called for free public education supported by a property tax. He wrote a pamphlet giving twelve reasons why the Bible needs to be the central textbook in schools. In his concluding remarks, he states, "I lament that we waste so much time and money in punishing crimes and take so little pains to prevent them. . . . We neglect the only means of establishing and perpetuating our republican forms of government; that is, the universal education of our youth in the principles of Christianity by means of the Bible . . . equality among mankind. . . respect for just laws . . . and sober and frugal virtues."

As an abolitionist, Dr. Rush was one of the black community's strongest white allies. He worked alongside Anthony Benezet to organize the Pennsylvania Society for Promoting the Abolition of slavery, and later served as its president. He also wrote a scathing pamphlet exposing the evils of the entire institution of slavery.

In 1787 Dr. Rush had a dream in which he was on a beach with a group of Africans who had been relating stories about the horrors of slavery, when the ghost of Benezet (who had died in 1784) came walking down the beach to meet with them. Rush awoke determined to continue Benezet's work and dedicated himself afresh to the cause of his "black brethren." Though still a slave owner himself, he promised freedom to his slave, William Grubber.

Rush was heavily involved in promoting the African Methodist Episcopal (AME) Church in Philadelphia. Richard Allen, founder and first bishop of the AME Church, acknowledged his great debt to Dr. Rush in his memoirs: "[He] espoused the cause of the oppressed and aided us in building the house of the Lord for the poor Africans to worship in."

When Benjamin Rush died in 1813, Thomas Jefferson wrote to John Adams: "Another of our friends of [1776] is gone, my dear Sir. . . . And a better man than Rush could not have left us, more benevolent, more learned, of finer genius, or more honest." Adams wrote in reply, "I know of no character living or dead, who has done more real good in America."

Dr. Benjamin Rush was a man who profoundly respected and honored God, putting Him first in everything he did. Though well-known and greatly respected, he never separated himself from the cause of the common man. Throughout his life, he diligently served others—as a patriot, a physician, an educator, and an abolitionist. May his name never be forgotten among us.

Saved by the Fog
Evacuation of Long Island
SUMMER 1776

"We are expecting the final attack at any moment. Our men are surrounded and outnumbered almost four to one." Just returning from headquarters to the trenches, Major Benjamin Tallmadge spoke softly to his fellow officers so as not to be overheard by the soldiers around them. "We are low on powder—as always—and the British fleet is even now preparing to sail up the East River to cut off any chance of retreat."

It was August 27, 1776, only six weeks after the Continental Congress had voted to accept the Declaration of Independence, and things were not looking good for the Continental army. To fight would mean defeat. And surrender was out of the question.

"What are we going to do, then?" a lieutenant asked.

"Firmly rely on the protection of Divine Providence," was General George Washington's reply. "God has not brought us this far to desert us." Little did the officers know they were about to see the most amazing episode of divine intervention in the Revolutionary War.

The Americans waited all afternoon—and no attack came. The night passed quietly. They waited all the next day as well. Why had the British not attacked? They clearly outnumbered the Americans. Perhaps they were waiting for the winds to change so their warships could join in the battle.

While General Washington waited, he was inspired with a daring plan. By night, they would secretly evacuate the entire army—eight thousand men—across the East River. It was a desperate move. The East River was a mile wide. And wouldn't the British see them in the moonlight or hear the splashing of their oars—not to mention the sounds that eight thousand men would make, no matter how quiet they tried to be?

Was it a coincidence that just the day before, a regiment of Massachusetts fishermen had come over to reinforce Washington's army?

They were joined by equally skilled mariners from Salem. Together they would gather the necessary row boats, and then all night long they would make the dangerous two-mile round trip, rowing expertly and soundlessly, back and forth, their boats loaded with men, supplies, cannons, carts, cattle, and horses.

But as the next day dawned, the retreat was far from complete. At least three more hours were needed. Major Tallmadge's unit was among those who remained. They watched—silent but anxious—knowing that without the cover of night they would be exposed to certain discovery and fierce attack.

Major Tallmadge described the scene: "At this time, a very dense fog began to rise out of the ground and off the river, and it seemed to settle in a peculiar manner over both encampments. I recollect this providential occurrence perfectly well, and so very dense was the atmosphere that I could scarcely discern a man at six-yard distance. . . . We tarried until the sun had risen, but the fog remained as dense as ever."

Against all odds, the fog remained until the last boat, with General Washington in it, had left the shore. As the fog lifted, the British were shocked to find the American trenches empty. They ran to the shore and started firing on the last four boats, which were now out of range of their guns. By the time the British were able to move their cannons into position, the Americans had completely escaped.

★ ★ ★

No people can be bound to acknowledge
and adore the invisible hand which conducts the affairs
of men more than the people of the United States.
Every step by which they have advanced to the
character of an independent nation seems to have been
distinguished by some token of providential agency.
—PRESIDENT GEORGE WASHINGTON,
Inaugural Address

George Duffield, Patriot Preacher

From 1772 to 1790, Rev. George Duffield was pastor of Pine Street Presbyterian Church in Philadelphia, attended by such patriots as John Adams. In May 1776, Adams heard a sermon by Duffield that compared the way King George III treated the colonists to how Pharaoh treated the Israelites. Duffield personally believed that God intended for the Americans to be liberated, just as He intended the Israelites to be set free.

So inspired was Adams that on May 17 he wrote to his wife, Abigail:

> *Is it not a saying of Moses, Who am I that I should go in and out before this great people? When I consider the great events which are passed, and those greater which are rapidly advancing, and that I may have been instrumental in touching some springs, and turning some small wheels, which have had and will have such effects, I feel an awe upon my mind, which is not easily described. Great Britain has at last driven America to the last step, complete separation from her; a total, absolute independence.*

Duffield, who also served as chaplain of the Continental Congress and of the Pennsylvania militia during the war, had a profound influence on many patriots, according to J. T. Headley:

> *In a discourse delivered before several companies of the Pennsylvania militia and members of Congress, four months before the Declaration of Independence, he took bold and decided ground in favor of that step, and pleaded his cause with sublime eloquence, which afterwards made him so obnoxious to the British that they placed a reward of fifty pounds for his capture.*

Later on in that sermon, Duffield delivered a prophetic word that is as immediate today as it was then:

> *Whilst sun and moon endure, America shall remain a city of refuge for the whole earth, until she herself shall play the tyrant, forget her destiny, disgrace her freedom, and provoke her God.*

Giving Credit
Where It's Due
Robert Morris
1734–1806

"It's Robert Morris," mumbled the sleepy voice. A loud pounding at their door had awakened the couple from a sound sleep. "I wonder what he could need so urgently at this hour of the morning."

His wife yawned. "Especially on New Year's Day. I hope nothing has happened to his family."

The two quickly dressed and went downstairs to let Robert in. "Are you well, Robert? Is your family well?"

"Yes, yes, we are fine. But I have something of the greatest urgency to discuss with you. Have you heard of our splendid victory at Trenton? General Washington has proven to all that with God's help, the Continental army is well able to defeat the British."

Robert held out a letter. "It is on behalf of General Washington that I have come today. He writes that many of his soldiers will not reenlist unless they can be paid. Their families are in dire distress. The men will not accept the worthless paper bills issued by the Continental Congress. General Washington needs fifty thousand dollars in gold and silver most urgently."

Sensing his friends' hesitation, Robert continued. "We must follow up on the success won at Trenton. We have the British on the run. If we don't pursue them at this time, in all probability the American cause will be lost. I beg you, give what you can. We must not let General Washington down!"

Going from one wealthy friend to another, Robert Morris collected and sent the entire amount in "hard money" to the man he called "the greatest man on earth."

Robert Morris was a warm and generous man with a talent

for earning money. He was a partner in one of the top business houses in Philadelphia and owned a fleet of trading ships. His many, many friends were among the most famous American patriots, including Alexander Hamilton, John Jay, and George Washington. Called the Financier of the Revolution, Morris also had a God-given knack for raising funds. Historians have said, "Had it not been for Robert Morris's services in raising funds, it is hard to see how the Revolution could have succeeded."

Time and again, General Washington would let Robert know about a pressing need, and Robert would be able to come up with the amount. Once, the British came so close to Philadelphia that the Congress fled to Baltimore. Washington was almost in despair and wrote to Robert, saying that to make any successful movement, he would need an almost impossible amount of money. Mr. Morris left the office feeling utterly hopeless and headed for home.

On the way he met a wealthy Quaker—and promptly asked him for help.

"What security can you give?" asked the Quaker.

"My note and my honor," replied Robert.

The Quaker said, "Robert, you shall have it."

The money was immediately sent to Washington. Without Robert's help at this crucial moment, Washington would not even have been able to hold his starving troops together. But with the money Robert raised, Washington made a surprise attack on Trenton, New Jersey, that resulted in a much-needed victory.

Another time Washington wrote Robert that the army needed bullets. Every scrap of lead the Colonists could find had already been used for the cause—even the weights of clocks and the downspouts of houses had been used. Even so, the army scarcely had enough bullets to fight a single battle. At just this critical moment, one of Robert Morris's ships arrived, loaded down with ninety tons of lead. Robert immediately hired one hundred men to mold bullets, and within two days Washington had the ammunition he so desperately needed.

In 1781 Robert agreed to serve as Superintendent of Finance, or "the financier" of the government, on condition that no more paper money be issued. He explained, "The United States may command everything I have except integrity, and the loss of that would effectually disable me from serving them now."

It was true: Many who did not trust Congress to make good on its promises to pay believed that the word of Robert Morris was as good as gold. When Robert took over as financier, the treasury had more than two and a half million dollars worth of past due accounts. For three years Robert worked night and day to raise the money his country needed to continue to operate. At one time he had borrowed a total of $600,000 on his own credit. He also sent every dollar of his own that he could lay his hands on to help the suffering Continental army.

By August 14, 1781, the war had been dragging on for six long years. General Washington was preparing to attack the British in New York when he got news from French Admiral Count de Grasse that the French fleet—all twenty-nine ships and three thousand soldiers—had changed plans. They were no longer headed for New York to help Washington, as promised, but were instead headed for Virginia. Robert Morris was at headquarters that day and saw how bitterly disappointed General Washington was at this news.

But Washington's despair was short-lived. Almost immediately Robert saw Washington's face brighten with sudden inspiration. He would attack General Cornwallis and his troops at Yorktown instead. Robert watched in silent awe as Washington quickly outlined the campaign that would soon result in Cornwallis's surrender and the end of the war.

Washington turned to Judge Richard Peters, at that time secretary to the board of war. "What can you do for me?" he asked.

"With money, everything. Without it, nothing," Judge Peters replied, looking anxiously at Robert Morris.

"Let me know the sum you desire," Robert replied. Before noon, General Washington had completed his plan and had estimated the cost, an amount Robert readily promised. He unhesitatingly risked his property and his reputation to ensure liberty for his fellow Americans. The campaign that virtually won the war was waged solely on Robert Morris's financial credit.

Robert was one of the signers of the Declaration of Independence. But July 4, 1776, was not the first time Robert had committed his all to his country. On the night of the Battle of Lexington, he was at a dinner party when news of the battle came. Most of the party guests soon left, but a few stayed and discussed the great question of American freedom. That night Robert and these few men, by a solemn vow, dedicated their lives, their fortunes, and their honor to the sacred cause of the Revolution.

By the end of the war, Robert Morris had given much of his fortune to his country. But his business ventures were so successful that he was soon once again one of the wealthiest men in America. Robert continued to serve his country as a member of the Congress that framed the Constitution, and he later served in the first Senate.

★ ★ ★

After the surrender at Yorktown, General Washington acknowledged the many providential events of the battle. He declared the day after the surrender to be a day of thanksgiving, and his troops were directed to attend religious services. On November 15, 1781, Washington wrote to the president of Congress: "I take particular pleasure in acknowledging that the interposing hand of Heaven, in the various instances of our extensive preparations for this operation, has been most conspicuous and remarkable."

Samuel Adams—A Man Devoted to a Cause

In 1765, the British Parliament imposed a tax on printed paper used by Americans, including legal documents, licenses, newspapers and other publications, and even playing cards. This Stamp Act was viewed as an attempt by England to raise money in the colonies without the approval of colonial legislatures. Though the actual costs of the Stamp Act were relatively small, this tax could open the door for far more troublesome taxation in the future. Samuel Adams publicly opposed the law and encouraged citizens to do the same. He instigated the Stamp Act riots to intimidate potential tax agents.

A few years later, when Parliament placed a tax on imported products such as glass, lead, paints, paper, and tea, Adams protested and soon had all Americans boycotting the new tax. An angry British government retaliated by sending soldiers to Boston to collect the money. Tauntings between the British and Americans were frequent, and one riotous afternoon in 1770, five colonists were killed. Samuel Adams dubbed the event the Boston Massacre. Though the incident was not a massacre at all, the highly volatile name promoted anti-British sentiments.

One of the most famous demonstrations against the British occurred when Adams, the leader of the Sons of Liberty, a secret patriot society, encouraged the group to board British ships and dump hundreds of chests of tea into the harbor as a protest of the tax on tea— the Boston Tea Party, as it came to be known.

In addition to his devotion to the independence of the colonies, Samuel Adams was also a devout Christian. William Allen, a biographer of Adams and other founding fathers, wrote of Adams' faith:

> Mr. Adams . . . early approached the table of the Lord Jesus, and the purity of his life witnessed the sincerity of his profession. On the Christian Sabbath he constantly went to the temple, and the morning and evening devotions in his family proved, that his religion attended him in his seasons of retirement from the world. The last production of his pen was in favor of Christian truth. He died in the faith of the Gospel.

Gifted
Phillis Wheatley
1753–1784

Susannah Wheatley's *eyes kept going back to the frail little girl, wrapped in a piece of carpet, trying to stay warm. She stood quietly with the other slaves who had just arrived from Africa on the slave ship. They waited for their future to be decided on the auction block.*

Although the poor child was shivering from the cold, she was gracious and eager to do what she was told. She smiled up at the auctioneer. It was the toothless grin of a child who had just lost her baby teeth.

Mrs. Wheatley was torn to the heart. She and her husband, a prosperous Boston tailor, had come to the slave market to get a personal servant for her, someone in her midteens who could take care of Mrs. Wheatley, both now and in her old age.

But the minute she saw little Phillis, she knew God wanted her to help this girl. Mr. Wheatley sensed it too and raised his hand to bid. In a moment, Phillis was theirs!

★ ★ ★

Phillis Wheatley's hands shook as she opened the delicate envelope. A letter from General George Washington? He must have received her poem after all! Four months earlier, during the siege of Boston, Phillis had written a poem to encourage the American commander in chief. With excitement she opened the letter and read what the most important man in America had written to her.

Washington started by apologizing for the delay in his response, saying, "A variety of important occurrences" had distracted him. He then thanked Phillis for the poem, praised her poetic talents, and explained that he had decided not to publish the poem because her words were so superlative that people might accuse him of vanity. He then invited her to his headquarters, saying he would be happy to see a person "to whom Nature has been so liberal and beneficent in her dispensations."

No question about it, Phillis was extremely gifted. Kidnapped in Senegal, Africa, at age seven, she crossed the Atlantic on a slave ship bound for Boston. Put up for bid at a slave auction, the frail, young girl attracted the attention of the Wheatley family. Moved with compassion, John Wheatley purchased Phillis as a personal servant for his wife.

The Wheatley family, including two older children, Mary and Nathaniel, was delighted with Phillis. She quickly won their hearts with her gentle temperament, affectionate nature, and pleasant ways. Phillis was never given menial tasks to do as originally planned. Instead she was treated with great kindness, as though she were a daughter of the family, and given the family name.

Susannah and Mary soon discovered Phillis was both quick to learn and perceptive. They taught her to read the Bible and to write. Within sixteen months Phillis mastered English and was able to read even the most difficult parts of the Bible with ease—to the great astonishment of those who heard her. Mary then taught her astronomy, geography, ancient history, the Latin classics, and the English poets.

Soon Phillis began to make up rhymes, and by age thirteen she wrote her first poetic verses. At sixteen she wrote her most famous elegy, a poem titled "On the Death of Mr. George Whitefield," the English evangelist so instrumental in the Great Awakening. Whitefield's preaching had a profound effect on Phillis, and in her unusual poem, Whitefield dramatically speaks from heaven in rhymed verse. The poem won Phillis international attention and was published in both England and America.

The Wheatley family encouraged Phillis and took pride in her writing. She accompanied the family on various social occasions, where she so impressed the Boston intellectual community that they considered her a child wonder. Clergymen, scholars, and patriots, including Benjamin Franklin, came to visit her.

As patriotic fervor continued to grow in Boston in the late 1760s and early 1770s, Phillis embraced the cause of American liberty. Freedom was a topic that often appeared in her poetry. Poems of this period include "On America," "On the Death of Master Snider" (Phillis counted Snider "the first martyr" of the Revolution), "On the Arrival of the Ships of War and Landing of the Troops," and "On the Affray in King Street on the Evening of the 5th of March," a poem about the Boston Massacre. Phillis's poems greatly encouraged patriots throughout the region and remained popular for generations after her death. She is remembered as America's first black female poet.

When she was seventeen, Phillis was allowed to join the Old South Church, breaking a tradition that excluded slaves. Her faith in God gave her an optimism that colored her outlook on life. Although she described slavery as "an impossible condition for any human being," she was grateful to God that she had been brought to a place where she could hear the Gospel. In her poem "On Being Brought From Africa to America," she wrote:

'Twas mercy brought me from my Pagan land
Taught my benighted soul to understand
That there's a God, that there's a Savior too:
Once I redemption neither sought nor knew.
Some view our sable race with scornful eye,
"Their colour is a diabolic die."
Remember, Christians, Negroes, black as Cain,
May be refin'd, and join th' angelic train.

Phillis was never very strong, and in 1773 her health began to fail. Doctors recommended a sea voyage, so she traveled with Nathaniel Wheatley to England. Her elegy on Rev. Whitefield had attracted the attention of the Countess of Huntingdon, a wealthy philanthropist who soon paid to have a book of Phillis's poems published. The young slave girl caused a sensation among the

English royalty. In addition to her gift for writing, she was a brilliant conversationalist and quite charming. Her popularity was immediate and great. English friends invited Phillis to the royal court to be presented to the king.

Suddenly word came that Susannah Wheatley, the only mother Phillis had ever known, was deathly ill. Phillis left immediately, arriving back in America just in time to see Susannah before she died. Soon after she returned from England in 1773, John Wheatley granted Phillis her freedom.

It was just after this that Phillis received her letter from George Washington. Later in 1776, General Washington passed Phillis's poem on to a friend, who quickly arranged to have it printed several times to help further the patriotic cause. Phillis took General Washington up on his invitation to visit him at his army headquarters. History does not record what they spoke about, but Washington was able to spend an eye-opening thirty minutes with this remarkable black woman of faith—who had challenged her generation's preconceived ideas of racial limitations while she had blessed so many with her charm, creativity, intelligence, and kindness.

A selection of Phillis's poems published in America around 1770 caused a controversy, as a number of people did not believe they could have been written by her. The publisher settled the dispute by having eighteen well-known citizens, including John Hancock and the governor of Massachusetts, certify that "Phillis, a young Negro Girl, who was, but a few Years since, brought, an uncultivated Barbarian, from Africa, and has ever since been, and now is, under the disadvantage of serving as a Slave in a family in this town. She has been examined by some of the best judges, and is thought qualified to write them."

9 Into the Presence
First Continental Congress
SEPTEMBER 7, 1774

The fifty-six men had come together from all thirteen colonies. A collection of the most gifted, virtuous, and wealthiest men upon the continent, they had come together with a strong spirit of unity. Moving with secrecy and with great deliberation, they knew what they were planning would ultimately lead to treason in the eyes of the British. Yet they were not afraid.

The Founding Fathers were not ashamed to admit that they were openly relying on God. At the first meeting of Congress, it was suggested that they open with prayer. The motion was opposed at first, not because the delegates didn't believe in God but because they were from such varied religious backgrounds—there were Episcopalians, Quakers, Anabaptists, Presbyterians, and Congregationalists—that some thought they could not join in the same act of worship.

Then Samuel Adams stood to address the assembly. "I am no bigot. I could hear a prayer from a gentleman of piety and virtue, who was at the same time a friend to his country. I am a stranger in Philadelphia, but I have heard that Mr. Jacob Duché, an Episcopal clergyman, well fits that description. I move that Mr. Duché be asked to read prayers to the Congress tomorrow morning."

The motion was seconded and passed. If Mr. Duché was good enough for Samuel Adams, he would do! Mr. Duché was promptly contacted and eagerly accepted the invitation. He appeared the next morning in his pastoral robes and vestments. Using the Collect, a book of prayers and daily Scripture readings, he read several formal prayers before coming to the Scripture for the day, Psalm 35.

That Psalm seemed peculiarly appropriate, for an express message had just arrived from Israel Putnam of Connecticut with a dreadful rumor. Boston, the colonies' most patriotic city, had been bombarded by the British and inhabitants murdered by British soldiers. The delegates could only imagine the scenes of distress, terror, and confusion that would result from this horrible catastrophe. John Adams wrote, "The effect of the news we have both upon the Congress and the inhabitants of this city was very great— great indeed! Every gentleman seems to consider the bombardment of Boston as the bombardment of the capital of his own province."

The bells of Philadelphia were muffled and tolled in token of this great sorrow.

It was in this setting that Mr. Duché read the Scripture of the day, which was a fervent prayer of David:

> *Plead my cause, O Lord, with them that strive with me: fight against them that fight against me. Take hold of shield and buckler, and stand up for mine help. Draw out also the spear, and stop the way against them that persecute me: say unto my soul, I am thy salvation.—Psalm 35:1–3 KJV*

As Mr. Duché reverently read the Word of God, the delegates felt deep feelings of grief, yes, but also the amazing sense that the God who sees all and knows the future had seen ahead to this day of destiny and wanted to comfort them. As Mr. Duché read, it seemed as if God himself were speaking to the men assembled there, saying to each patriot present, "I am your deliverance, your salvation!" They felt God was assuring His chosen leaders that He would fight their battles for them.

As Mr. Duché continued to read, the Holy Spirit anointed his words, the powerful presence of God increasing with every verse:

> *Let them be confounded and put to shame that seek after my soul: let them be turned back and brought to confusion that devise my hurt. Let them be as chaff before the wind: and let the angel of the Lord chase them. Let their way be*

dark and slippery: and let the angel of the Lord persecute them. . . . And my soul shall be joyful in the Lord: it shall rejoice in his salvation. All my bones shall say, Lord, who is like unto thee, which deliverest the poor from him that is too strong for him. —Psalm 35:4–6, 9–10a KJV

Renewed hope and strength came to the delegates. They had been struggling with the thought that to keep their precious freedoms they—a poor colony with no army and no navy—would be forced to take on Great Britain, the mightiest empire in the world. They sensed God's words of encouragement through this sweet psalm, and it brought renewed hope to their spirits.

John Adams later wrote, "I never saw a greater effect upon an audience. It seemed as if Heaven had ordained that Psalm to be read on that morning."

But that was not the end of the prayer meeting. Mr. Duché surprised everyone present by striking out in extemporaneous prayer, which was most unusual for that era. His prayer was so pertinent, affectionate, and devout that every heart was moved:

Be Thou present O God of Wisdom, and direct the counsel of this Honorable Assembly; enable them to settle all things on the best and surest foundations; that the scene of blood may be speedily closed; that Order, Harmony and Peace may be effectually restored, and that Truth and Justice, Religion and Piety, prevail and flourish among the people. Preserve the health of their bodies, and the vigor of their minds, shower down on them, and the millions they here represent, such temporal blessings as Thou seest expedient for them in this world, and crown them with everlasting Glory in the world to come. All this we ask in the Name and through the merits of Jesus Christ, Thy Son and our Savior, Amen.

John Adams said it "filled the bosom of every man present. I must confess I never heard a better prayer . . . such fervour, such ardor, such earnestness and pathos, and in language so elegant and sublime—for America, for the Congress, for the Province of Massachusetts Bay, and especially the town of Boston. It has had an excellent effect upon everybody here."

God met the members of Congress that day and put His seal on their dreams of freedom for this nation. By the simple act of opening their day with prayer, they had acknowledged their need for His guidance and His protection, and God flooded in on them with great comfort, destiny, and purpose.

Artist Harrison Tompkins Matteson depicted the events of that day in a life-sized painting titled "The First Prayer in Congress." A stained-glass representation of the painting hangs in the Liberty Window of Christ Church, Philadelphia. Half of the delegates have fallen to their knees, and several are weeping. Silas Deane verifies that this time of prayer and Scripture reading in Congress was so powerful that "even Quakers shed tears."

When the extended prayer was over, something else amazing happened. Another messenger came from Boston—this time with the news that the first report had been a mistake. There had been no bombardment and murdering in Boston. Imagine the joy the delegates felt! Their praises filled the hall again: "Great is the Lord!"

John Adams wrote to his wife, Abigail, describing what had happened. Then he exhorted her: "I must beg you to read that Psalm .... Read this letter and the 35th Psalm to [your friends]. Read it to your father."

By His Word the Lord brought fresh confidence to the delegates at the first Continental Congress, and they sensed that they were on the right path. In the dark hours that were ahead in their fight for freedom, they would need that assurance. Those present would never forget the day.

★ ★ ★

[God] Himself has said, "I will never leave you nor forsake you."
HEBREWS 13:5 NKJV

Now therefore, I pray, if I have found grace in Your
sight, show me now Your way, that I may know You and
that I may find grace in Your sight. And consider that
this nation is Your people.
EXODUS 33:13 NKJV

If God be for us, who can be against us? The enemy [the
British Army] has reproached us for calling on His name
and professing our trust in Him. They have made a mock
of our solemn fasts and every appearance of serious
Christianity in the land. . . . May our land be purged from
all its sins! Then the Lord will be our refuge and our
strength, a very present help in trouble, and we will have
no reason to be afraid, though thousands of enemies set
themselves against us round about.

—REVEREND SAMUEL LANAGDON,
President of Harvard College, *in an address to the Provincial
Congress of Massachusetts, May 31, 1775*

Out of the Jaws of the Wicked

10

William and Ellen Craft

DECEMBER 1848 AND OCTOBER 1850

The Baltimore stationmaster was insistent with the elderly gentleman: "I will not let you on this train unless you show me proof that you own that slave!"

"Oh, but you must let us on!" the frail voice answered. "I have to get to Philadelphia quickly. And I cannot travel without the help of my manservant."

"I say no. And without my permission, even President Polk cannot get on that train!" So many slaves were escaping to the North that officials in the South had cracked down on all blacks traveling without proper documents. "Times have changed, old man."

Seeing that the stationmaster was not to be moved by human sympathy, the elderly gentleman tried a different approach. Mustering all the indignation he could, he waived his tickets to Philadelphia in the stationmaster's face. "Here are our tickets! You have no right to keep us here in Baltimore just because we don't have some newfangled paper work you need."

The stationmaster did not budge. "Right or no right, I will not let you go!"

The two travelers fervently prayed in their hearts. Unless God did something quickly, all would be lost. But they had come so far, through so many narrow escapes—surely God would not abandon them now!

For the "elderly gentleman" was not really a gentleman at all, but a light-skinned slave woman named Ellen Craft, and her "manservant" was her husband, William. The two had devised a daring plan to escape from their home plantation in Macon, Georgia, to the North—and freedom. They had saved for years—any money or tips they received had gone into their travel fund. Finally, they had saved enough.

On December 21, 1848, William and Ellen blew out the lights in their little cabin, knelt down, and prayed, "Heavenly Father, help us as you did your people of old, to escape from cruel bondage. Lead us, guide us. We put our trust in you."

Ellen, disguised as the elderly "William Johnson," bought their train tickets to Savannah without a problem. The real William helped her into her compartment and went to his. Then, just before the train was scheduled to pull out of the station, William spotted the cabinetmaker his master had hired him out to work for. He was going from car to car searching for William. William's heart cried out, "Help, Lord!" Then, just before the man looked into William's compartment, the bell rang, alerting nonpassengers that the train was about to leave. The cabinetmaker turned and got off the train.

Meanwhile, Ellen discovered she was sitting next to Mr. Cray, an old friend of her master who had known Ellen since childhood and had dined with her master's family just the day before. Ellen was terrified—and prayed fervently.

Mr. Cray spoke to her.

What should I say, Lord? Suddenly, it occurred to her to pretend to be deaf. It worked! Mr. Cray turned to another passenger, and for the rest of the trip, they talked about slaves, cotton, and the abolitionists.

Once they arrived in Savannah, Ellen bought tickets for them on a steamship to Charleston. During the pleasant trip, a young army officer approached the "elderly gentleman" and chatted with her briefly as William stood silently by. That same officer would soon prove to be a godsend.

When they reached Charleston, Ellen bought tickets to Wilmington. As they boarded, a crewman asked her to sign the ledger. William and Ellen had prepared for such a moment. Since Ellen could neither read nor write, they had put her right arm in a sling so she would not be expected to sign. "Young man, would you mind doing it for me?" she asked, pointing to her arm.

To her surprise, he said, rather loudly, "No, sir. That would be against regulations." Everyone looked in their direction. The ship's captain came over to see what the trouble was. The two travelers again prayed fervently.

At that moment the army officer she had chatted with earlier came up and vouched for her. The ship captain's manner instantly changed; he personally signed the ledger for Ellen and her servant. Later, as they traveled to Wilmington, the army officer explained to Ellen, "They make it a rule to be very strict at Charleston." He shook his head. "If they were not very careful, any d——n abolitionist might take off with a lot of valuable n——rs."

They continued on without a problem to Wilmington, Fredericksburg, Washington, D.C., and Baltimore. It was in Baltimore, on the final stretch of their long journey to freedom, that they were stopped by the unyielding stationmaster.

William later told friends, "We felt as though we had come into deep waters and were about to be overwhelmed. In our hearts we cried out to Him who is ever ready and able to save."

The bell rang, signaling that the train was leaving the station. As the stationmaster looked at the "old gentleman" again, his face softened. He said to the other officer, "I really don't know what to do." He paused. "I suppose it's all right." He told his subordinate, "Run and tell the conductor to let this gentleman and his slave pass. As he's not well, it's a pity to stop him here. We will let him go."

"Thank you kindly," Ellen said. She and William hurried to the platform as best they could while keeping up the pretense that she was an invalid gentleman. William helped her into one of the best carriages and hopped into his own, just as the train was gliding off.

On the train, William met a free black man who gave him the address of a Philadelphia boardinghouse, run by an abolitionist, where they would be safe. When they reached the boardinghouse, they realized it was Christmas Day. They knelt down and poured out their heartfelt gratitude to God. "You are our shield, God! Thank you for your goodness to us. Thank you for helping us through so many difficulties. We have escaped out of the jaws of the wicked."

They spent three weeks in Philadelphia with a Quaker farmer and his family. Finally the Crafts arrived in Boston. They had traveled more than one thousand miles.

Soon William found work as a cabinetmaker and Ellen worked as a seamstress. They boarded at the home of Lewis Hayden, an African American who owned a boardinghouse that often served as a rendezvous for fugitive slaves on the Underground Railroad. There, they joined wholeheartedly in the satisfying work of helping other slaves find their way to freedom.

Two years later, in September of 1850, Congress passed the Fugitive Slave Act, requiring that fugitive slaves be returned to their masters in the South and that federal marshals and private citizens were legally bound to help capture the fugitives.

The abolitionists in Boston were furious! In protest, they immediately organized the League of Freedom, electing Lewis Hayden as president and William Craft as vice-president. This organization soon merged with the Boston Vigilance Committee, designed "to secure the colored inhabitants of Boston from any invasion of their rights."

Then came October 20, 1850. As William walked home from work, he was intercepted by Lewis Hayden with bad news: "William, you must not go home. Two slave catchers from Georgia are here in Boston looking for you and Ellen. We've moved Ellen to a safe place already. We will find you someplace as well—"

"I don't want to run," William interrupted. "I will stay and fight with you and the others."

"Good," answered Lewis. "We are boarding up the windows now. That house will soon be a veritable fortress! And I vow to you that I will blow up my entire residence rather than surrender a single fugitive within my care."

As soon as members of the Vigilance Committee learned of the slave catchers, they began to relentlessly harass them. Members confronted them as they walked down the streets. Their every move was documented in the popular *Liberator* magazine. Flyers were posted denouncing the slave catchers in the strongest of words. William's pastor, Theodore Parker, led a committee to the slave catchers' hotel room, where he demanded that they leave town. They refused and were subsequently arrested and rearrested by sympathetic law officers on charges ranging from slander to attempted kidnapping, carrying concealed weapons, smoking on the streets, and "profane cursing and swearing."

Finally the slave catchers ran out of funds and left, vowing to return. Abolitionists in Bristol, England, had heard of William and Ellen's plight and offered refuge. The Crafts lived in England until after the Civil War, when it was safe to come home.

★ ★ ★

The Crafts' daring escape became one of the most celebrated stories of its kind in Boston, and it set a precedent for the militant activism of black and white abolitionists of the 1850s. Their well-coordinated efforts show the power of a community in the face of an unjust law.

Blessed be the Lord,
Who has not given us as prey to their teeth.
Our soul has escaped as a bird from the snare of the fowlers;
The snare is broken, and we have escaped.
Our help is in the name of the Lord,
Who made heaven and earth.
PSALM 124:6–8 NKJV

The History of Juneteenth

What day comes to mind when you hear the word *independence*? For most Americans the answer would be the Fourth of July. However, for African Americans of the nineteenth century, realization of independence came not on the fourth of July, but on the nineteenth of June, 1865. But theirs was a different word: emancipation.

On September 22, 1862, President Lincoln issued the Emancipation Proclamation that freed the slaves of the rebellious Confederate states. However, the only thing that was going to actually free every slave was complete military victory. Finally, after four bloody years, the Civil War came to a close at Appomattox Courthouse on April 9, 1865. Slavery was abolished—in deed, more than just word.

But for slaves in east Texas, word traveled slowly. Finally, on June 19, 1865, nearly three years after the Emancipation Proclamation, Union General Gordon Granger landed in Galveston with the news that the war was over. The slaves were free! Some blacks reacted in stunned silence while others celebrated in jubilation.

Over the proceeding decades, June 19, or "Juneteenth," came to be known as African-American independence day and a time of celebration, prayer, and festivities. Though this wonderful holiday nearly faded away during the early part of the twentieth century, today it has made a resurgence and is now celebrated widely across the country. In fact, on January 1, 1980, through the efforts of African-American legislator Al Edwards, Juneteenth became an official Texas state holiday.

July 4, 1776, was an important milestone in our nation's history, and a worthy cause for celebration. However, it would be another eighty-nine years before blacks in this nation would truly gain their independence.

This year, let's start our Fourth of July celebrations a couple of weeks early—on June 19.

"Unless You Kill Me"
John Prentiss "Print" Matthews
1840–1883

11

The violent chain of events began two weeks before election day. Print Matthews, a white man, and his supporters, both black and white, were completely unprepared for what was to happen.

Their Fusion Independent Party, a coalition of blacks and white farmers, had been successful in previous elections. But this year the militant white Democrats had decided that "incendiary speeches have but one counter-irritant—lead." Starting on October 25, 1883, 150 armed Democrats mounted their horses and started "The Procession" into the heavily black precincts of Copiah County, Mississippi. Every night until election day, they galloped along the dirt roads by moonlight, firing a small canon and stopping to pay "surprise visits" to the cabins of African-American families. The riders were not your usual lawless troublemakers, but rather were among the most respected men in the county, a good many of them planters and professionals.

Tom Wallis, a black farmer, was a friend and supporter of Print Matthews and took a good deal of interest in politics. Members of the procession entered Wallis's home, dragged him from bed, and tried to put a rope around his neck. They probably intended to threaten him with death and whip him to teach him not to meddle with politics, as they had one of his neighbors earlier that night. But Wallis fought back, and the intruders shot and killed him.

The terror continued almost nightly until the election, although no one else was killed until election day. Numerous black men were threatened with death and forced to swear they would either vote the Democratic ticket or stay away from the polls. Many of their families spent the last few days and nights before the election hiding in the nearby forest. Several white families who supported Matthews' party joined them.

Why was Print Matthews and his Fusion Independent Party the source of such hatred? Because they had successfully defied the will of the some of the white power structure in the county. They proved that blacks and whites could work together to bring change to the status quo.

Print, the unlikely leader of the coalition, was from a wealthy white family known for not conforming to the society around them. Throughout the Civil War, Print was a known Union sympathizer. During Reconstruction he was elected county sheriff. A man with a reputation for personal charm, generosity, and honesty, he steadfastly maintained that African Americans were "entitled to all the rights, privileges, and immunities of American citizens." Local blacks ranked him alongside Abraham Lincoln. The integrity of his party also won the loyalty of more than six hundred white owners of small farms who had grown tired of being victims of the Democratic aristocracy. As a result, his interracial coalition carried the majority of the voters in the county and could win in an honest election.

Print's son, John Prentiss Matthews Jr., was only fifteen when Print was killed. He carried on his father's legacy and became a Republican leader in Mississippi. President Benjamin Harrison appointed Print Jr. postmaster of Carrollton, Mississippi, a town 130 miles north of Hazlehurst. White Democrats there resolved "that no Republican should hold that office." On Christmas Day, 1890, Print Jr. was shot and killed on the streets of Carrollton, just a week after his twenty-second birthday. He was buried next to his father at the Matthews family home in Hazlehurst.

But elections were not free in Mississippi during the 1870s and 1880s. In 1881 Print lost reelection to the sheriff's office by eighty-four votes. The Democrats threw the election, claiming a hungry mule thrust his head through a window and ate the ballots in the nearly all-black precinct of Mount Hope. Still, Print's party won the majority of the seats on the powerful Copiah County Board of Supervisors. The Democrats swore this would not happen again.

By election day 1883, it was obvious that voters favoring Print's Fusion Independent Party were too terrified to come to the polls. Print himself was handed a written warning to stay at home. As a point of personal honor, he decided to ignore it. His wife and daughters listened as he told the messenger, "I think I have as much right to vote as any of you. I have never done any of you any harm. I have tried to be useful to society in every way that I could. . . . You have got it in your power to murder me, I admit. But I am going to vote tomorrow, unless you kill me."

The next morning Print walked to the polling place across the street from his home. He walked past several Democrats standing by the door with shotguns. Inside, he saw Ras Wheeler, the precinct captain and a family friend, and went over to sit next to him. The two talked in low voices for a minute. Wheeler said, "Print, I would not vote today if I were you."

Print rose, walked over to an election official, and handed him his ballot. As he was folding it, Wheeler picked up a double-barreled shotgun and, taking quick aim, fired both barrels. Print Matthews died instantly.

Print was not buried in the Hazlehurst town cemetery, but in a single grave on his own property. A white-dominated jury found Wheeler innocent, and Democrats appointed him city marshal of Hazlehurst. It was even suggested he run for state governor. The day after the murder, white Democrats passed the following resolution: "Henceforth no man . . . shall organize the Negro race against the whites in this county, and if the same shall be attempted in the future we hereby give notice that it shall be at the peril of the person attempting so to do."

In 1890 the final hope of interracial and antiracial idealism was also snuffed out. National Republicans were not able to get their Fair Elections bill through Congress. Mississippi passed its notorious Constitution of 1890, which "legally" prevented African Americans from voting. By 1907 all the Southern and border states had copied Mississippi in their voting laws.

* * *

Greater love has no one than this,
that he lay down his life for his friends.
JOHN 15:13 NIV

Pirating the *Planter*
Robert Smalls
1839–1915

12

R o b e r t   S m a l l s looked out over the lights of Charleston Harbor. Tonight was the night he had waited for all his life. In a few more hours he would no longer be a slave—he would be a free man!

For weeks Robert and his crew of slaves on the *Planter* had been planning a daring escape. The *Planter*, the fastest and most valuable of the Confederate ships in Charleston Harbor, was big enough to transport one thousand armed men at once. In return for their freedom, Robert and his crew planned to turn this prize ship over to the U.S. gunboats that were stationed to blockade Charleston Harbor.

On the night of May 12, 1862, they realized their moment of opportunity had come. The white officers of the *Planter* had entrusted the 150-foot-long steamer to the black crew while they went into town on an unauthorized leave. As prearranged, Robert and his men sprang into action. Several left to round up the wives and children of the crew. Others started up the boilers. Robert went to the captain's quarters and put on the captain's uniform and cap. Of mixed heritage, Robert hoped his skin was light enough to pass for white. Looking in the mirror, he thought, "Not perfect. But it's a dark night and the sentries are far away on the shore. With God's help, it will work!"

Robert and his crew were taking a big risk—but it was worth it to be free. Robert and his mother, Lydia, were always treated with kindness and given quite a bit of freedom by their master. But Lydia wanted her son to understand the fate of African Americans within the system of slavery. She took young Robert to slave auctions and made him watch slaves being beaten in the front yard of Beaufort jail.

Robert never forgot he was a slave—and he worked day and night to purchase freedom for himself, his wife, and his daughter. He made arrangements with his master to hire himself out after hours. Of the sixteen dollars he earned each week, he sent fifteen to his master to buy his freedom. He worked first at the Planter's Hotel, then as a lamplighter for the city of Charleston, and later as a sailor and sailmaker before getting his job on the *Planter*.

As it turned out, Robert didn't finish paying his master— God had other plans for him. But looking back, Robert saw how God had prepared him for this night and this daring escape: The skills he had learned as he had worked so hard to purchase his freedom would soon prove essential.

It wasn't long before all the families were on board and everything was ready: The boilers were fired, the steam up, the mooring ropes cast off, and the anchor hauled aboard. The *Planter* slipped away from the dock. Robert expertly guided the ship through the tricky currents and channels of the harbor. He had learned to pilot the vessel by watching every move the captain and the two mates made. He had been sailing in Charleston Harbor for years and knew every current and every sandbar.

Tonight, however, the problem was not the currents or the sandbars. It was getting past the other Confederate ships and the forts and on out to sea without having their plan discovered. They sailed past each of the fortresses in Charleston Harbor without a glitch. At each stop Robert, dressed as the captain, gave the proper signal and the *Planter* was allowed to proceed.

Robert knew the hardest part would be getting past the sentries at Fort Sumter, the last of the fortifications. Wouldn't the sentries wonder why the *Planter* was going out to sea at this hour?

As they neared the fort, there was complete silence on board, except for Robert's quiet prayer: "Oh, Lord, we entrust ourselves into thy hands. Like thou didst for the Israelites in Egypt, please stand over us to our promised land of freedom."

Robert stood tall in the cockpit. He gave the captain's signal. He waited for a long minute. "Help, Lord!" he prayed. Would they notice his darker skin? Or the lack of the two white mates? If discovered, the crew and their families had all agreed to set the ship on fire, hold hands, and jump into the ocean rather than be captured and returned to slavery.

At last the signal came, "Pass the *Planter*." Everyone breathed a sigh of relief. They had made it past Fort Sumter!

Full steam ahead, the *Planter* sailed out of Charleston Harbor and into the Atlantic Ocean. As soon as the ship was out of sight and out of the range of Fort Sumter's guns, Robert pulled down the Confederate flag and hoisted a white sheet of surrender.

Robert set his course for the nearest gunboat, the U.S.S. *Onward*. The crew on the *Onward* were startled by the fast-approaching ship and prepared their guns to fire. Just before they did, a sailor noticed the white flag and called out, "Hold your fire!"

Captain Nicholas was suspicious. He told his men, "This could be some kind of Confederate trick. Ensign, take ten men, board the *Planter*, and bring the officers to me. Let's hear their story." After hearing Robert's report, he was not convinced. "It still sounds strange to me. Ensign, go back on the *Planter* again and search it thoroughly." When the searchers found only five women and three children on board, Captain Nicholas referred Robert to Admiral Du Pont. The admiral was delighted to receive such a worthy ship and her cargo of Confederate artillery. Robert and his black crew were welcomed as heroes.

Once an obscure slave, Robert had suddenly become a national hero, with his story and picture appearing in *Harper's Weekly*, the leading magazine of the day. He was invaluable to the navy because he was familiar with the channels and bays of South Carolina, Georgia, and Florida. He convinced Union naval officers to immediately attack Cole's Island, as its cannons had recently been sent to Charleston. Within the week Union gunboats seized the fort without a fight and had a valuable base of operations for the rest of the war.

At first Robert could not be enlisted directly into the navy as an officer—the navy only used blacks as ship laborers—so he served on the ship as an army officer. Then, in December 1863, the *Planter* was fired upon as she sailed through the Stono River near Folly Creek. The white commanding officer, Captain Nickerson, panicked and hid in the coal bunker of the ship. Robert took control of the ship and brought the vessel out of firing range and safely back to port.

Later, President Lincoln received Robert Smalls in Washington and rewarded him and his crew for their valor. Robert received a promotion due to his heroism at Folly Creek. He became the first African-American captain in the U.S. Navy. Given official command of the *Planter*, Robert served in this position throughout the war. In all, Robert fought in seventeen battles.

At the end of the war, Smalls bought his former master's home, including the slave quarters where he was born, and lived there for the rest of his life.

Robert's service to his country did not end with the war. As a war hero, he was one of the most prominent men in South Carolina. Building upon this, Robert entered politics and served his state and his country for twenty-five more years, first as a state representative and later for five terms as a congressman in the U.S. House of Representatives. He worked hard to secure basic human rights for his people, including equal travel accommodations for black Americans and for the civil and legal protection of children of mixed parentage. Education for African-American children was one of Robert's great passions, as he felt education was the key to his race's advancement, and it became one of his greatest crusades. He introduced legislation that established free public schools in South Carolina and instituted many social reforms.

Robert had the following words inscribed on his gravestone:

My people need no special defense,
for the past history of them in this country
proves them to be the equal of any people anywhere.
All they need is an equal chance in the battle of life.

Henry Highland Garnet

After being led out of slavery in 1824, Henry Highland Garnet began his life as a strong-willed abolitionist, independent in forming his own views and bold in expressing them.

Around 1833 Garnet joined the Sunday school of the First Colored Presbyterian Church in New York, where he worked for minister and noted abolitionist Theodore Sedgewick Wright, the first black graduate of Princeton's Theological Seminary. Wright brought about Garnet's conversion and encouraged him to enter the ministry.

In 1840 Garnet settled in Troy, New York, where he worked toward the full establishment of black congregations and eventually became the first pastor of the Liberty Street Presbyterian Church.

Following his residency in Troy, Garnet was invited to Great Britain by the Free Labor Movement, an organization opposing the use of products produced by slave labor. After two years of a rigorous schedule of engagements, the United Presbyterian Church of Scotland sent Garnet to Jamaica as a missionary. He remained there for only a few years before a serious illness sent him back to the United States. Upon returning, Garnet became the successor of his mentor, Theodore S. Wright, at the Shiloh Church in New York. Garnet's reputation as an orator and spokesperson preceded him, and he quickly had a once-jeopardized church flourishing again.

In 1859 Garnet founded the African Civilization Society, an organization that encouraged black missionary work and entrepreneurship in Africa. With the outbreak of the Civil War in the early 1860s, Garnet joined other blacks in organizing black troops for the North. During the draft riots in 1863, white working-class mobs rioted in New York City and targeted blacks and leading abolitionists. Garnet was run out of town, but shortly thereafter became the pastor of the Fifteenth Street Presbyterian Church of Washington, D.C. There he became the first African American to deliver a sermon in the House of Representatives.

Tired of Giving In
Rosa Parks
1913—PRESENT

Rosa Parks was tired, so tired that she decided to take the bus home. She had been pressing slacks all day at her job. Her feet hurt and her back and shoulders ached. The first bus that came past had standing room only, so she decided to wait for the next bus in hopes of getting a seat. During her wait, she remembered why she often walked home—riding the bus took its toll on her dignity.

The segregation laws in force in 1955 Montgomery, Alabama, seem unbelievable today, but they were a reality for thousands of blacks in the South. Take the restrictions on riding the bus, for instance. Even though the majority of bus passengers were people of color, the front four rows of seats were always reserved for white customers. It was common to see people standing in the back of the bus while the first four rows remained empty. Behind the reserved-for-whites section was a middle section where African Americans could sit if the seats were not needed by white customers. If just one white customer, however, needed a seat in this center section, all those already seated had to move.

Even getting on the bus was an elaborate process for black people. They would pay their fare in the front, exit, and then reboard the bus at the back. Rosa died a little each time she found herself face-to-face with this kind of discrimination. In fact, Rosa had once been thrown off a bus for refusing to reboard at the back door.

Finally a second bus came, and to Rosa's joy, there were a few seats available in the middle section—"no-man's land." Rosa climbed the stairs, put her dime in the fare box, climbed back down the stairs, hurried to the back door of the bus, climbed up the stairs, and made it through the aisle in time to find there was still a seat available. She sat down in the row just behind the white section. What a relief to relax for a minute!

The bus picked up more riders and the front section of the bus filled up. When the driver noticed a white man standing in the aisle, he ordered four people, including Rosa, to give up their seats. At first no one moved.

The bus driver said, "You all better make it light on yourselves and give me those seats." The other three riders did as they were told, but Rosa knew that to do so would be wrong—and she quietly refused to get up. "I'm gonna call the police," the bus driver threatened.

"Go ahead and call them," said Rosa. She was tired, true—but even more, she was tired of giving in. It wasn't just the bus. It was the "whites only" restaurants, the drinking fountains and elevators marked "Colored," and the unspoken intimidation that were all a part of daily life in a place that did not treat all its citizens as equals. Rosa remembered, "I was tired of seeing so many men treated as boys and not called by their proper names or titles. I was tired of seeing children and women mistreated and disrespected because of the color of their skin. I was tired of legally enforced racial segregation. I thought of the pain and the years of oppression and mistreatment that my people had suffered. . . . Fear was the last thing I thought of that day. I put my trust in the Lord for guidance and help to endure whatever I had to face. I knew I was sitting in the right seat."

Rosa later wrote, "I felt the presence of God on the bus and heard His quiet voice as I sat there waiting for the police to take me to the station. There were people on the bus that knew me, but no one said a word to help or encourage me. I was lonely, but I was at peace. The voice of God told me that He was at my side."

As Rosa waited for the police to come, she thought about her life in the segregated South. Born in 1913, she had grown up on a farm with her mother, her brother, and her grandparents. They were very poor and worked hard to raise enough food to feed themselves. Rosa's mother, a schoolteacher, taught whenever she could but also took in sewing and worked as a hairdresser. Rosa's grandparents picked corn, peanuts, and sweet potatoes on nearby plantations—with little Rosa working alongside them. It was so common for African-American children to work all day in the fields that Rosa's school closed three months earlier than the school for white children. And unlike the white children's school, Rosa's school was little more than a shack, without windows or desks and with only a few books.

Rosa was raised as a devout Christian. She grew up attending a church where her uncle served as a preacher. She recalled reading the Bible with her grandmother and their daily devotions before heading to the cotton fields. Prayer and the Bible became a part of her everyday thoughts and beliefs. Rosa learned to put her trust in God and to seek Him as her strength.

Rosa remembered how, as a young girl walking through a white neighborhood in Montgomery, she was pushed from behind by a white boy. Instead of walking on, pretending nothing had happened—which was the expected behavior—Rosa turned around and pushed the boy back. His mother was shocked. "How dare you touch a white boy!"

The city bus where Rosa Parks refused to give up her seat was found in a backyard in Montgomery, Alabama, where it had been gutted and used as a trailer for thirty years. After old No. 2857 was confirmed as authentic by a dispatcher's scrapbook, an intense bidding war started between several institutions, including the Smithsonian. The winner was the Henry Ford Museum in Dearborn, Michigan, which paid $492,000 for the bus. The museum has since restored it—and then aged it—to look the way it would have in 1955. Every detail is historically accurate, right down to Montgomery's distinctive red dirt on the wheel wells and tire treads.

Rosa replied, "I don't want to be pushed by your son or anyone else," and calmly walked away.

She had tried to work within the system. She remembered her struggles to help African-American citizens get registered to vote. She remembered her years as a youth adviser for the National Association for the Advancement of Colored People (NAACP).

Remembering these things put a determination within Rosa. She had never been one to ignore acts of injustice. What was going on was not fair. Not in the eyes of man, and not in the eyes of God. It was time for action.

When the police arrived, Rosa calmly asked, "Why do you push us around?"

The officer replied, "I don't know, but the law is the law and you're under arrest." When the officers asked her to stand up and get off the bus, Rosa quietly obeyed. They drove her to the police station and fingerprinted her as though she were a criminal. Before they put her in a jail cell, they allowed her one phone call. She called a prominent member of the NAACP, who called a lawyer. The two bailed Rosa out of jail for one hundred dollars and suggested that Rosa appeal her case to challenge the segregationist law that had led to her arrest. Rosa's husband and her mother had some real concerns about Rosa's personal safety, but they all agreed that it was time to act. Rosa later recalled, "As I sat in that jail cell, behind bars, I felt as if the world had forgotten me. But I felt God's presence with me in the jail cell."

The ministers of the city's African-American congregations lent their support. Dr. Martin Luther King Jr. made seven thousand leaflets encouraging African Americans to boycott the Montgomery city bus system on Monday, December 5. A community meeting that night drew an overflow crowd numbering in the thousands.

What began as a one-day boycott lasted for 381 days. Continuing the boycott was neither comfortable nor convenient: Some people walked miles to work, others rode bikes or shared rides. For more than a year—in the cold, pouring rain and in the blistering heat of summer—the black community worked together, giving their 100 percent cooperation. They were determined to pay the price to see change. As the months went by, Rosa's case went all the way to the U.S. Supreme Court—and Rosa won. On December 21, 1956, Rosa sat in the front row of a newly integrated city bus.

Both Rosa and her husband lost their jobs and were considered unemployable as a result of their part in the boycott. They were also harassed with phone calls, letters, verbal threats, and intimidation. The family moved to Detroit, Michigan, in 1957, and for the next eight years they struggled financially, until Rosa was hired as a staff assistant to a U.S. congressman.

In later years Rosa was hailed as the mother of the civil rights movement and received many awards and honors. Among them was a seventy-seventh birthday celebration in the nation's capitol in 1990, which was attended by government dignitaries, prominent entertainers, and a host of notable African-American leaders. Here Rosa was praised for her "beautiful qualities [of] dignity and indomitable faith that with God nothing can stop us." In 1999 President Clinton awarded Rosa the Congressional Gold Medal, the nation's highest civilian honor.

★ ★ ★

Our country is the model for every other developing country in the world for achieving justice and equality for its citizens. Our Constitution has lasted longer than any other constitution in modern history.
We cannot take these blessings for granted. We must share these gifts from God. Whether we are thirteen or eighty-three, we must show the world that we are able to correct our mistakes—including homelessness, poor race relations, and violence—and move forward to a better society. I know that we can. This nation has always overcome the obstacles it has faced.
— ROSA PARKS

I have learned that in order to bring about change, you must not be afraid to take the first step. We will fail when we fail to try. Each and every one of us can make a difference.
— ROSA PARKS

In a Class of Only One
Ruby Bridges
1960

It was the morning of November 16, 1960. Two big, black limousines pulled up in front of the William T. Frantz Elementary school in New Orleans, where a large, angry crowd had gathered. Four husky U.S. federal marshals got out. Then, while sheltering her from the crowd with their own bodies, they helped a tiny black girl in a starched white dress get out of the car. Putting her carefully on the sidewalk, they turned her around, and with two marshals in front of her and two behind her, the procession climbed the steps and entered the school.

It was Ruby Bridges' third day at her new school. On the first day her mother, Lucille, had gone with Ruby and the federal marshals. The night before, she had told Ruby, "There might be a lot of people outside the school, but you don't need to be afraid. I'll be with you." Ruby saw the barricades and heard the people shouting but thought it was the Mardi Gras carnival that takes place in New Orleans every year.

That whole first day, Ruby and her mother sat behind the glass window of the principal's office and waited. No one spoke to them—but all day they watched as white parents came in and dragged their children out of the school. Finally it was three o'clock and time to go home. The crowd outside was even bigger and louder than it had been that morning, but the marshals helped them get through it safely.

That first afternoon Ruby taught a friend a chant she had learned: "Two, four, six, eight, we don't want to integrate." Neither of the little girls knew what the words meant, but they began to jump rope to it every day after school.

On the second day Ruby, her mother, and the marshals went to school again, marching together past the noisy, angry crowd. When they finally got into the building, Ruby's new teacher, Mrs. Henry, was there to greet them. Ruby noticed that the halls were quiet and asked if she was early, but Mrs. Henry said, "No, you are right on time." Ruby later learned that the white children were not coming to school that day.

Mrs. Henry escorted Ruby and her mother to a classroom on the second floor. There were lots of desks in the room but no other children. Ruby's mother took a seat in the back, Ruby took a seat up front, and Mrs. Henry started to teach Ruby the alphabet. Mrs. Henry was young and white, and Ruby was uneasy at first—she had never spent time with a white person before. She spent the whole day in the classroom with Mrs. Henry. She couldn't go to the cafeteria or outside for recess. Federal marshals sat outside the door, guarding and protecting them.

On the third morning Ruby's mother told her she couldn't go to school with her. She had to work and look after Ruby's brothers and sister. Ruby remembers her mother assuring her, "The marshals will take good care of you, Ruby Nell. And remember, if you get afraid, say your prayers. You can pray to God anytime, anywhere. He will always hear you."

One of the federal marshals, Charles Burks, remembers those days: "For a little girl six years old going into a strange school with four strange deputy marshals, a place she had never been before, she showed a lot of courage. She never cried. She didn't whimper. She just marched along like a little soldier. We were all very proud of her."

Although the Supreme Court had outlawed school segregation in *Brown v. Board of Education of Topeka, Kansas*, in May 1954, the schools in the South had never complied with the new order. Finally, a federal judge decreed that Monday, November 14, 1960, would be the day black children in New Orleans would go to school with white children.

Six first graders were chosen to integrate the city's public school system. Three were assigned to McDonogh School No. 19. The two others assigned to Ruby's school decided to stay in their old segregated schools, so Ruby would be going to William T. Frantz alone. Ruby's family knew it would not be easy. They discussed it for weeks, they prayed about the decision, and in the end, they decided that despite the risks, they had to take this step forward, not just for their own children, but for all black children.

An article in the November 28, 1960, issue of *U.S. News & World Report* gave the following statistics: "On November 17, three Negro girls and one white child were the only pupils present at McDonogh School No. 19, which normally has 467 pupils. The other 'integrated' Negro [Ruby] had the company of only three white children in William T. Franz School, which normally has 576 pupils." A few white families braved the protests and kept their children in school. Like Ruby, they had to walk through a mob of white people screaming obscenities, yelling threats, and waving their fists at them. But they weren't in Ruby's class, so she didn't see them.

The first few days of integration were tense. Militant segregationists did not just protest at the schools. They took to the streets in protest, and riots erupted all over the city. Whites assaulted blacks in broad daylight and the blacks fought back, even though the NAACP urged them not to. Extra police were called in. Finally, by the end of the week, the worst of the street riots were over.

Ruby's father, Abon, was fired from his service station job because customers were threatening to boycott the business if he remained there. But financial help was on the way. People from around the country who'd heard about Ruby on the news sent letters, gifts, and money. A neighbor gave Abon a job painting houses. Others baby-sat for the family and watched their house to keep away troublemakers. Ruby's family couldn't have made it without the help of their friends and neighbors.

Mrs. Henry tried to explain integration to Ruby and why some people were against it. "It's not easy for people to change once they have gotten used to living a certain way. Some of them don't know any better and they're afraid. But not everyone is like that."

Ruby now recalls:

Even though I was only six, I knew what she meant. The people I passed every morning as I walked up the school's steps were full of hate. They were white, but so was my teacher, who couldn't have been more different from them.

She was one of the most loving people I had ever known. The greatest lesson I learned that year in Mrs. Henry's class was the lesson Dr. Martin Luther King, Jr., tried to teach us all: Never judge people by the color of their skin. God makes each of us unique in ways that go much deeper.

About this time, Dr. Robert Coles, a trained child psychiatrist who specialized in helping children under stress, offered to help Ruby and her family during the most stressful time in their lives. He was amazed to find that Ruby and her family were upheld and sustained by a very real and profound peace. Dr. Coles marveled at Ruby's ability to withstand this kind of treatment and wondered where she got her emotional strength. Every week he would come to Ruby's home to visit and draw with her, and then he would ask her about her drawings.

One day, Mrs. Henry, who always watched Ruby walk into the school, told Dr. Coles that Ruby had stopped and talked to the people in the street. When Dr. Coles asked Ruby about this, she said, "Oh, yes. I told her I wasn't talking to them. I was just saying a prayer for them."

Usually Ruby prayed in the car on the way to school, but that day she had forgotten until she was in the middle of the crowd. Her mother had taught her that every time she felt afraid she should pray. With childlike obedience, when Ruby felt afraid that morning, she stopped right where she was and said a prayer.

Dr. Coles was amazed that Ruby would pray for people who were so hateful to her. He asked her, "Ruby, you pray for the people there?"

"Oh, yes."

"Why do you do that?"

"Because they need praying for," Ruby replied.

"Ruby, why do you think they need you to pray for them?"

"Because I should."

Ruby's mother heard this exchange and explained, "We tell Ruby that it's important that she pray for the people."

Dr. Coles asked Ruby what she prayed.

Ruby answered, "I pray for me, that I would be strong and not afraid. I pray for my enemies, that God would forgive them.

"Jesus prayed that on the cross," she told Coles, as if that settled the matter. "Forgive them, because they don't know what they're doing."

For the rest of the year, Mrs. Henry stubbornly taught her class of one. Mrs. Henry said, "I grew to love Ruby and to be awed by her. It was an ugly world outside. . . . Neither of us ever missed a single day of school that year. It was important to keep going."

Sometime in the spring, Mrs. Henry was stunned to find out four other first graders had been coming to the school for a while. She immediately told the principal she wanted Ruby and the other first graders to be together, as it was cruel to keep Ruby by herself for so long. She said, "By law, you have to integrate this school. Integration means putting black and white children in the same classroom. As I see it, you are breaking the law by keeping them separate." The principal would not force the other first grade teacher to include Ruby in her class. Instead, the white children came into Mrs. Henry's classroom for part of each day. Mrs. Henry said, "It was progress."

It was from these children that Ruby finally learned about racism and integration.

I had picked up bits and pieces over the months from being around adults and hearing them talk, but nothing was clear to me. The light dawned one day when a little white boy refused to play with me.

"I can't play with you," the boy said. My mama said not to because you're a n——r."

At that moment, it all made sense to me. I finally realized that everything had happened because I was black. I remember feeling a little stunned. It was all about the color of my skin.

I wasn't angry at the boy, because I understood. His mother had told him not to play with me, and he was obeying her. I would have done the same thing. If my mama said not to do something, I didn't do it.

By late spring the crowd outside dwindled to just a few protestors. Instead of the federal marshals, a taxi driver was sent to pick Ruby up every morning. Before she knew it, it was June.

When Ruby went back to school in September, everything was different: There were no marshals, no protestors. There were other kids—even some other black students—in her second-grade class. It was odd, but it was almost as if that first year of school integration had never happened. No one talked about it. Everyone seemed to have put that difficult time behind them.

★ ★ ★

Today Ruby Bridges lives in New Orleans with her husband, Malcolm Hall, and four sons. In the early 1990s, Ruby volunteered to work at the same William Franz Elementary School she had "integrated" as a child. It had since become an inner-city school with mostly African-American students—so the children were segregated once again. Eventually, Ruby established the Ruby Bridges Foundation to help schools succeed.

Ruby often speaks to audiences across the U.S., telling them that every child is a unique human being fashioned by God, and that schools can be a place to bring kids together from all races and backgrounds:

If kids of different races are to grow up to live and work together in harmony, then they are going to have to begin at the beginning—in school together.

People are touched by the story of the black child who was so alone.... In all of this, I feel my part is just to trust in the Lord and step out of the way. For many years, I wasn't ready to be who I am today, but I've always tried not to lose my faith. Now I feel I'm being led by just that— faith.... I don't know where events will go from here, but I feel carried along by something bigger than I am.

Ruby had been called by her country to perform
an act of profound bravery, to become the [only] black
child in an all-white school. By her simple act of courage,
Ruby moved the hearts and opened the minds
of millions of people.
—A CIVIL RIGHTS WORKER

There is no easy way to create a world where men
and women can live together, where each has his own
job and house and where all children receive as much
education as their minds can absorb. But if such a world
is created in our lifetime, it will be done in the United
States by Negroes and white people of good will.
It will be accomplished by persons who have the courage
to put an end to suffering by willingly suffering
themselves rather than inflict suffering upon others.
It will be done by rejecting the racism, materialism,
and violence that has characterized Western civilization
and especially by working toward a world of
brotherhood, cooperation, and peace.
—DR. MARTIN LUTHER KING JR.

Racism is a grown-up disease and we must stop
using our children to spread it.
—RUBY BRIDGES

The Road to Desegregation

The Supreme Court's *Brown v. Board of Education* decision in 1954 did not abolish segregation in all public areas, such as restaurants and rest rooms, nor did it require desegregation of public schools by a specific time. It did, however, declare the segregation that existed in twenty-one states unconstitutional. While the *Brown v. Board* case was a giant step toward complete desegregation of public schools, even partial desegregation was still very far away.

By 1957 Little Rock, Arkansas, had already desegregated its public buses, the zoo, the library, and the park systems. Working toward the desegregation of the entire city, the Little Rock school board had made plans to integrate the high school that year, followed by the junior high the next year, and the elementary schools in the following year. It seemed the process would go smoothly, since seven of Arkansas' eight state universities had desegregated, a law school had been integrated since 1949, and blacks had been appointed to state boards and elected to local offices. But a smooth transition of integration for the state's school system was not to be.

On September 3, when nine black students arrived at Little Rock Central High School, a group of National Guard members turned them away, a direct order from Arkansas governor Orval Faubus in an effort to protect citizens and property from the violence of protestors. The Guard was withdrawn a few weeks later, and on September 23, the nine black students were quietly ushered in a side door of the school building while a mob of a thousand people waited outside the front of the school. When the mob learned that the students had entered the school, shouts of challenges and threats forced the fearful police to remove the students from the school. Two days later the nine black students reentered the school under the protection of one thousand members of the United States Army.

The year that followed was intense for Little Rock Central High School. Most of the students, faculty, and administration not only accepted desegregation as the law but also accepted the black students among the white. Although the black students suffered physical and verbal assaults, commencement ceremonies in May successfully graduated Ernest Green, the school's first black graduate.

A Special Instrument Sent of God

15

Tisquantum—"Squanto"

WINTER 1620

"I'm finally home!" Squanto's heart beat fast with excitement as he reached the section of shore that is now known as Plymouth Bay. It had been years since he had laid eyes on this beautiful coast. The thought of returning had sustained him through many hardships. It was just as he remembered it: a rocky shoreline with trees growing down to the sparkling water.

But as he approached his village, he noticed everything was strangely silent. Getting closer, he could now see the dwellings were all in ruins—the sticks and branches used for walls had rotted, and the mats used for roofs had caved in. He entered one *wetu*, then another. In every place he found skulls and bones—entire families had died suddenly, with no one to bury them.

It was the most tragic blow of his life. He wandered through the empty fields where he had played as a child, through forests where he had learned to hunt deer and wild turkey. Fond memories flooded his mind—only to be dashed once again by the realization that all who were dear to him were now dead, and with them his hopes for the future. The mighty Patuxet band of the Wampanoag tribe was gone.

The last fifteen years had not been easy for Squanto. He and four other braves had been kidnapped in 1605 by Captain George Weymouth, who was exploring the New England coast. The five were taken to England and taught English so they could answer the explorer's questions about the New World.

After spending nine years in England, Squanto met Captain John Smith (of the Virginia colony), who took him back to his home in New England.

But Squanto did not get to stay with his people long. He was soon kidnapped again, along with twenty-six others—this time by Captain Thomas Hunt, who intended to sell them as slaves in Spain. But Squanto escaped and found his way back to England again, where he joined the household of a wealthy merchant in London.

Finally in 1619 he was able to make arrangements to sail for home with Captain Dermer. That's when he found his village devastated. He soon learned a plague had wiped out everyone in his tribe, and he was the sole survivor. In despair, he asked for shelter with Massasoit, the chief of a neighboring tribe, who understood his circumstances and took pity on him.

But life no longer had meaning for Squanto. For fifteen years his only goal had been to return home. But now there was no home to return to. For six months he merely existed.

Then one day a friend named Samoset came with interesting news. Samoset had also been kidnapped by Englishmen and learned to speak English. He had met Squanto on Captain Dermer's ship.

Samoset had just discovered that a small settlement of peaceful English families were trying to farm Squanto's tribal lands. "I walked in on a meeting in their common house. I stood there in silence for a while to make them wonder. When I said, 'Welcome,' they were so surprised they didn't know what to do. A Native American who could speak English? They had never heard of such a thing! Finally someone answered, 'Welcome.'

"My friend, you should have seen their faces when I asked, 'Have you got any beer?' They were astounded! They were out of beer but offered me brandy, a biscuit, some pudding, and a piece of roast duck. After I finished eating, they started asking me questions about nearby native tribes.

"Of course I told them about the fierce and fearless Patuxets, and how bravely your tribe defended their homeland against all invaders. I told them about the deadly plague. I told them how the neighboring tribes think it was the work of a great supernatural spirit and how they now shun your lands out of fear that the same thing might happen to them."

While he spoke, Samoset kept his eyes on Squanto. Samoset was not sure how his friend would take the news that people were settling in his village. As he listened, Squanto seemed to come alive with purpose. But what purpose? Would he savagely defend his tribal lands? Would he begin planning how he would destroy the small settlement?

Samoset added quickly, "These families are kind and generous and treated me with respect. But they probably won't live on your land for long."

Squanto asked, "What do you mean?"

"They have little food with them, and the only seeds they have to plant are English wheat and barley. They will soon starve to death."

"I want to meet these people," said Squanto.

Within a few days Samoset, Squanto, Chief Massasoit, and all sixty of his warriors went to visit the colony at Plymouth. The Pilgrims welcomed them with courtesy and fanfare—complete with trumpet and drum, which pleased the chief immensely. With Squanto's aid as an interpreter, the Pilgrims and Chief Massasoit successfully negotiated a treaty of mutual aid and assistance.

When Massasoit and the others left, Squanto stayed. Finally he had a reason for living! His homeland would once again be populated and prosperous. He showed the settlers how to survive in the wild: how to plant corn and pumpkins, how to catch eels and fish, how to stalk deer, how to find herbs for food and medicine.

At the same time, he watched the Pilgrims, noting how they treated one another with love and respect. He went to their prayer meetings and saw the way God answered their prayers. He listened as the Bible was read each morning and evening. Before long Squanto asked Jesus, the Savior of the Pilgrims, to be his Savior too.

One evening at supper, as Squanto looked around at the English faces he had grown to love, he started thinking about how his life was nothing like the life he had planned as a young Patuxet warrior. But if he had never been kidnapped and taken to England, he never would have learned English. If he hadn't been kidnapped a second time, he would have died of the plague with the rest of his tribe. If he hadn't sailed with Captain Dermer, he never would have met Samoset. If Samoset hadn't discovered the settlement when he did, the Pilgrims would have missed the time for planting corn. How would they have survived another winter?

The things that had happened to Squanto were evil. But now he began to see how God could take the evil things people had done and bring good out of it.

Governor William Bradford had called Squanto "a special instrument sent of God for [our] good beyond [our] expectation." Bradford showed Squanto a story in the Bible about how God's redeeming power helped a young man named Joseph save a nation. Men had done evil to him too, but Joseph told them, "You intended to harm me, but God intended it for good to accomplish what is now being done, the saving of many lives" (Genesis 50:20 NIV).

For two years Squanto lived with the Pilgrims, teaching them things they would need to know to survive in their wild new land. Then, in November 1622, while serving as guide and interpreter for Bradford as he explored the shores of Cape Cod, Squanto fell sick "of an Indean feavor." Within a few days it became obvious that he was dying. He called for the governor, as many might call for their pastor: "Please pray for me, Governor, that I might go to the Englishmen's God in heaven." Then, one by one, he bequeathed his various possessions to his English friends—his new family—as remembrances of his love.

It was a great loss for the Pilgrims. But with the skills Squanto had taught them, not only did the Plymouth colony survive, but it prospered and grew. Through the hand of God, the Pilgrims did not share the fate of other English colonies in the New World, which were wiped out by hostile natives. The peace treaty designed by Chief Massasoit and Governor John Carver would last for forty years and was a model for many such peace treaties to come. Massasoit was probably the only chief on the northeast coast of America who would have welcomed the white man as a friend. And the Pilgrims were careful to treat the chief and his people in a way that demonstrated the love of Christ.

* * *

Take courage, all you people still left in the land,
says the Lord. Take courage and work,
for I am with you, says the Lord Almighty.
My Spirit remains among you, just as I promised when
you came out of Egypt. So do not be afraid. . . .

I am giving you a promise now while the seed is still
in the barn, before you have harvested your grain and
before the grapevine, the fig tree, the pomegranate, and
the olive tree have produced their crops. From this day
onward I will bless you.

HAGGAI 2:4–5, 19 NLT

Native American Contributions to the Government

Americans tend to overlook the origin of so many aspects of the world provided by Native American cultures. The American Indians introduced to the world much more than the many varieties of food so highly recognized every year on Thanksgiving. The Indians are responsible for being the first to mine gold and silver in the New World, which helped start the industrial revolution that spread to Europe and eventually around the world. America's Indians supplied materials like cotton, rubber, and dyes that fed the new system of production, and they discovered the healing powers of many substances, helping to lead the way to today's use of modern medicine.

Native Americans also helped influence the democracy and political system used throughout the world today, making themselves true colonizers of America. When the Founding Fathers were deciding how to make one country from thirteen states, the Iroquios chief Canassatego suggested the colonies form a union like the Indians had done with the League of the Iroquois, a constitution known as the Great Law of Peace. The league united six Indian nations, each of which elected a council to represent their tribe. The six councils, each with equal authority, met at least once every five years to discuss issues of common concern. The league successfully blended the differences of several nations into one government.

Benjamin Franklin, who printed many records and speeches of the various Indian assemblies, advocated the Indians' political structure for use in the colonies. The model of several units united into one government was adopted by the New England government, and a variation is used throughout the United States today. It is known as the federal system, in which each state retains power over internal affairs and the national government regulates affairs common to all.

The Americans continued to adopt many other governmental ideas from the Native Americans, including retaining the purpose of a debate to be to persuade and educate, not to confront, as the European parliaments had been wont to do. While the Europeans got together and spoke over one another to be heard, the Indians' system maintained that no man could speak while another was already being heard, and a moment of silence followed every speaker, in case he wanted to revise or add anything to his original comment.

Perhaps one of the most important political institutions borrowed from Native Americans was the caucus, a word derived from the Algonquian word *caucauasu*, meaning "counselor." This informal meeting to discuss issues is much like the Indians' traditional powwows. The informality of this kind of meeting made political decisions less combative. The caucus became such an important aspect of American politics that it is used in the nomination of presidential candidates.

A Covenanted People
The Pilgrims' Landing at Cape Cod
NOVEMBER 1620

"**Land ho!**" The cry rang out.

Land? Had the *Mayflower* reached land at last? For seven weeks at sea, through storm after storm, the Pilgrims had waited for this moment. They had reached the New World!

They rushed up to the main deck. Such an overflow of thanksgiving followed as men, women, and children all poured out the gratitude of their hearts toward God, their Protector and Provider. The giving of thanks continued for so long that Captain Jones finally had to order the Pilgrims back down to the tweendecks so the sailors could maneuver the ship.

The Pilgrims had to content themselves with posting a few watchmen to look out the hatch and report to the others what they saw. As they grew closer, the watchmen saw a land that was already in the first stages of winter. The delays in leaving England had cost them almost two months of mild autumn weather. It would soon be bitterly cold. And how wild it looked. The long sandy beach was covered with dune grass and scrub pine—and not a single trace of humanity.

Where were they? How far had the storms blown them off course?

Finally news came back that they were at a place fishermen called Cape Cod. Amazingly enough, they were only a few hundred miles north of their original destination at the mouth of the Hudson River, the northern-most point of what was then the Virginia colony. Within a week they would arrive at their new home. There was more rejoicing!

They started south but soon encountered dangerous shoals, riptides, and roaring breakers as they tried to pass around the point of the cape. Had they come this far to see the *Mayflower* broken on the rocks? The farther they went, the more treacherous it became. The Pilgrims began to fervently pray for the safety of their ship.

The leader of the group, Elder William Brewster, called John Carver, William Bradford, and Edward Winslow aside. "Sirs, I am sensing there is more here than meets the eye. What is the Lord saying to you?"

Carver paused a moment and then answered, "The farther we go, the greater the sense of dread I feel. I wonder if God really wants us to go south to Virginia as originally planned."

They looked to Bradford. "When I looked out at the coast near Cape Cod, I felt a strange warming in my heart. I thought it was because I was so grateful to see land again. But now, I too am beginning to see that it was something more."

Brewster added thoughtfully, "In the Scripture, Paul and Silas wanted to preach in Asia, but God hindered them. He prevented them from doing what they had planned and sent them to Macedonia instead. Perhaps we were blown off course because God has something better in mind for us."

Winslow nodded. "What if God had us blown to Cape Cod because He wants us to settle at Cape Cod?"

Just then Captain Jones approached the three leaders. "The wind is very strong this time of year, and when we try to sail south around the cape, it blows mightily against us. It's too dangerous to sail this close to shore. Our only choice is to head back out to sea and wait a day to see if the wind will change."

Brewster spoke up. "Captain, before you head back to sea, permit us an hour to speak with the others."

At length, after much prayer and further discussion, the Pilgrims unanimously decided on their course of action. Brewster instructed Captain Jones to turn back toward Cape Cod. On November 11, they dropped anchor in a natural harbor on the inside of the cape.

What a joyful celebration they had. Bradford wrote in his journal, "They fell upon their knees and blessed the God of heaven, who had brought them over the vast and furious ocean, and delivered them from all the perils and miseries thereof, again to set their feet on the firm and stable earth, their proper element. And no marvel if they were thus joyful . . ."

Because the *Mayflower* was blown off course, there was a further delay before the passengers could go ashore. Since this was unfamiliar territory, they needed to send men to explore the coast and decide on the best place to put their new settlement.

Being blown off course caused another problem. Since the Pilgrims would be settling outside the boundaries of the Virginia colony, they would not be governed by Virginia's charter. In fact, they would have no charter at all. Brewster called the leaders together to discuss it. "Brothers, we must pray and ask the Lord what we should do about the government."

Winslow was puzzled. "What government? There is no government here! No kings, no bishops, no sheriffs . . ."

"Exactly," Brewster replied. "No laws—and no one to enforce them if there were. And we know how corrupt human beings are. I am not worried about our Pilgrim families. But the "strangers" outnumber us. I heard one boast about what he planned to do once he got to shore. With nothing to limit their behavior, we could soon have serious problems."

"I see what you mean," Bradford replied. "If we don't establish a civil government with a firm Christian base before leaving the ship, we will soon have mutiny and anarchy. We must pray!"

The leaders raised their voices in one accord and began to seek the Lord for wisdom.

Before long Bradford spoke up. "Brothers, I know why God wanted us to return to this bay. He didn't want us to settle in Virginia because he doesn't want us to be governed by Virginia's charter. He wants to do a new thing—He wants all men to see what He can do with a people who totally rely on Him for everything—including their government."

Brewster caught Bradford's excitement. "Just like Jesus said: 'You are the light of the world. A city set on a hill cannot be hid.'"

"Yes!" Bradford said.

"Listen—God has prepared us for this!" Brewster exclaimed. "Remember when we were still in Holland, how Pastor Robinson studied the Bible to discover God's pattern for church government?"

Bradford smiled. "How could we ever forget? I can hear him now: 'The self-governing Christians of the New Testament churches are the perfect model for church government. The Lord Jesus is King of His Church and holds all power in heaven and earth. Christ the Lord gives each Christian the power of self-government. Christians then elect representatives, or elders, from among themselves to serve them and be examples to them.'"

"So we take what we've learned about church government and use it to write a covenant for civil government," Bradford added. "The scriptural model is the same."

The Pilgrims knew the value of becoming one body, of submitting to one another in love. Pastor Robinson had warned them that the very survival of their little settlement would depend upon the depth of their covenant relationship with one another.

In signing the Mayflower Compact, the members of the Plymouth Colony chose to relinquish their individual independence, and as a covenanted people, "to enact . . . just and equal laws . . . from time to time . . . for the general good of the colony. Unto which we promise all due submission and obedience." The Mayflower Compact became one of the pillars of American constitutional government. It marked the first time in recorded history that free and equal men had voluntarily covenanted together to create their own new civil government.

★ ★ ★

Is there any encouragement from belonging to Christ?
Any comfort from his love? Any fellowship together in
the Spirit? Are your hearts tender and sympathetic?
Then make me truly happy by agreeing wholeheartedly
with each other, loving one another, and working
together with one heart and purpose.

Dearest friends, you were always so careful to
follow my instructions when I was with you.
And now that I am away you must be even more
careful to put into action God's saving work in your
lives, obeying God with deep reverence and fear.
For God is working in you, giving you the desire to
obey him and the power to do what pleases him.

In everything you do, stay away from complaining
and arguing, so that no one can speak a word of blame
against you. You are to live clean, innocent lives
as children of God in a dark world full of crooked
and perverse people. Let your lives shine
brightly before them.
PHILIPPIANS 2:1-2,12-15 NLT

The moral principles and precepts contained in
the Scripture ought to form the basis of all our civil
constitutions and laws. All the miseries and evil men
suffer from vice, crime, ambition, injustice, oppression,
slavery, and war, proceed from their despising or
neglecting the precepts contained in the Bible.
—NOAH WEBSTER

We have no government armed in power capable of
contending with human passions unbridled by morality
and religion. Our Constitution was made only for a
religious and moral people. It is wholly inadequate
for the government of any other.
—JOHN ADAMS

The Mayflower Compact

In the name of God, Amen. We, whose names are underwritten, the Loyal Subjects of our dread Sovereign Lord, King James, by the Grace of God, of England, France and Ireland, King, Defender of the Faith, e&.

Having undertaken for the Glory of God, and Advancement of the Christian Faith, and the Honour of our King and Country, a voyage to plant the first colony in the northern parts of Virginia; do by these presents, solemnly and mutually in the Presence of God and one of another, covenant and combine ourselves together into a civil Body Politick, for our better Ordering and Preservation, and Furtherance of the Ends aforesaid; And by Virtue hereof to enact, constitute, and frame, such just and equal Laws, Ordinances, Acts, Constitutions and Offices, from time to time, as shall be thought most meet and convenient for the General good of the Colony; unto which we promise all due submission and obedience.

In Witness whereof we have hereunto subscribed our names at Cape Cod the eleventh of November, in the Reign of our Sovereign Lord, King James of England, France and Ireland, the eighteenth, and of Scotland the fifty-fourth. Anno Domini, 1620.

Jamestown

In stark contrast to the Pilgrims' constant reliance upon God's guidance was the settlement of Jamestown, Virginia, in 1606, thirteen years earlier.

With the tragedy of the lost colony of Roanoke less than a generation behind them, British enthusiasm for New World adventures was still significantly dampened. But the promise of wealth was enough for some, and the Virginia Company was formed. When the partners had difficulty finding investors to fund a new expedition, some of them presented it as an evangelistic outreach to the Indians, and soon had clergy endorsing the endeavor—and investors lining up. Even the Company's charter stated its purpose of "propagating [the] Christian religion to such people as yet live in darkness and miserable ignorance of the true knowledge and worship of God."

What was so nobly pledged in word, however, was only halfheartedly carried out in deed. Among the 144 men enlisted for the first expedition, only one, Robert Hunt, was a minister. And upon arrival, despite Hunt's efforts, there was little interest in seeking God's will for the colony.

A pattern of taking the "easy way" began with the very location of Jamestown. They had landed on a small, low-lying peninsula that was heavily wooded, had no fresh water, and was surrounded by fetid swamps. But rather than find a more suitable spot, the men chose to settle where they were.

During their first year, they survived only on the corn they could buy, beg, or steal from the Indians. The following spring, when a gift of corn arrived from the Indians, they found an easy excuse to delay the planting of their own crops. Mortality, from a multitude of diseases and ailments, soared and seemed obviously attributable to their horrible location, but the settlers decided that moving and starting over seemed infinitely more difficult than simply rebuilding. They even maintained their codes of conduct forbidding a gentleman from any sort of manual labor, even when faced with his own death. Chopping wood for warmth, digging a well for fresh water—it was all beneath them; many died rather than be dishonored.

Word began to return to England about the terrible state of the settlement, but rather than admit the truth and request help, the Company tried to whitewash over the truth. Sermons lauding the work being done were published and more investors were duped by the release of John Smith's *True Relations.* Others were not so easily fooled, however, and in the wake of mounting criticism, the Company turned on the last surviving member of the original ruling Council. John Smith was removed from leadership, the Council was dissolved, and a governor, Thomas Gates, was appointed by the king—bringing with him an enlarged charter for the colony.

Their goal was still to return the investment of all their partners in England. Their first plan was to mine the region's deep veins of gold—which turned out to be pyrite, or fool's gold. Later, the colony turned its eye to the fortune that could be made harvesting tobacco. Large tracts of land were parceled out to the non-indentured men and the crop soon became a harvest of cash. And in choosing this path, Virginia also chose a darker path, because by 1619—thirteen years after being started—the first African slaves arrived. No single family could tend such large fields; thus slavery became a tenable solution. So it would come to pass that almost 250 years later—with the outbreak of the Civil War—the country would be torn apart by the bitter fruit sown in places like Jamestown, Virginia.

Government by the Gospel
Plymouth, Massachusetts

SPRING 1623

Susanna Winslow, walking down the dirt road that served as the main street of Plymouth, Massachusetts, was lost in thought. Walking toward the common cornfield, she thought of the past winter, when food was in such short supply that the Pilgrims had been reduced to a daily ration of five kernels of corn apiece.

"Lord, I'm still amazed that we made it through that winter. How could we have lived on five grains of corn a day? Yet not one of us died. You, Lord, are a great miracle-worker!"

Even though it was still spring, Susanna was concerned that the coming winter of 1624 would be a repeat of that time of hunger. With the additional settlers who had come, she knew they would need at least twice the harvest. She had noticed that the new settlers, sent as replacements by the trading company, were not hard workers like the Pilgrims. In fact, many had been shipped off to the colony fresh from the debtors' prisons of England.

Most of the time, the newcomers sat and grumbled—they wanted more privileges, more food, and less work. Their complaining was taking its toll on the morale of the entire colony, so much so that even the hard-working Pilgrims seemed less energetic.

"Lord, please help us. I know you have the answer!" Susanna continued to pray the whole morning as she removed weeds from among the corn plants.

Meanwhile, as was his custom every morning, young William Bradford, Plymouth's new governor, was reading from the Bible. He, too, was worried about the colony. He knew that even with every man, woman, and child carrying their own weight, there would be little surplus this winter. But with the newcomers doing little more than lying around and eating up the meager reserves, the whole group could easily starve in the harsh New England winter. He also knew that the compassionate Pilgrims would want to give food to the lazy ones—even if it worked against their very survival.

Fortunately, Governor Bradford was convinced that the answer to every problem facing mankind was to be found in the Word of God. "The Bible is a book about government," he would often say. "When we don't know what to do, we should look in its pages." That morning as he read the Bible, he was looking for answers. And he was not disappointed—there, in the Scriptures, was the perfect solution! Taking a pen and paper, he carefully wrote a verse that would be the basis of a new policy—a policy that would have a profound effect on the colony and ultimately on the nation.

Walking outside, he shouted for the Pilgrims and the newcomers to meet him at the meeting hall. Once the crowd assembled, Governor Bradford read his verse: "'If any man would not work, neither should he eat'—the Second Epistle of Paul the Apostle to the Thessalonians, chapter three, verse ten."

Then he continued, "This is a command in the Word of God. From now on, this will be the rule of our community.

"Those who believe in the Holy Scriptures are bound to obey its teachings. Those who do not are to be bound by its consequences."

Governor Bradford assigned the single men in the colony to live with Pilgrim families. Then he temporarily divided the common cornfield into small tracts, giving a tract to each family. Corn grown on each family's tract would be for that family's private use.

At first the sluggards tested the Pilgrims—would they really let them go hungry if they didn't work? They soon found that the Pilgrim families were resolved to obey the Word of God and refused to let them eat if they did not work. After experiencing several days of hunger, even the laziest among them began to pull his own weight.

Bradford's new policy was a success. He later wrote in his journal, "Any general want or suffering hath not been among them since this day."

The next year Bradford divided the land permanently and told the families they could keep all they produced, except for the tenth they would pay to the trading company. The opportunity to own their own land was beyond their wildest dreams in England. The colonists worked even harder, the colony prospered, and government according to the Scriptures was established as a principle.

* * *

Indeed, it is an indisputable fact that all the complex and horrendous questions confronting us at home and worldwide have their answer in [the Bible].
—RONALD REAGAN

No Justice
C.J. Miller

JULY 5–7, 1893

Of course John Ray wanted justice. His little girls were dead. The young white sisters, Mary, age sixteen, and Ruby, age twelve, had gone to pick berries near their home on Wednesday morning, July 5. They never returned. They were found lying near each other, their throats slashed with a razor. Doctors who examined the girls said they had both been raped.

People had come from miles around to the little town of Bardwell, Kentucky, to help catch the murderer. Neighbors reported they had seen a light-skinned man, possibly of mixed race, running from the scene. Two members of the search party had seen a man—white, or nearly so—run into a cornfield. They fired their guns at him, but he got away.

A bloodhound tracked the fugitive to the eastern bank of the Mississippi River. When they found a fisherman who said he had rowed a man—white or very light—across the wide river, they put the dog in the boat and took him across to the Missouri shore. The hound immediately ran to the nearby house of a white farmer and refused to search any further.

The search was called off until the next morning, when they got a report from officials in Sikeston, Missouri, some thirty miles away. They had arrested a young black man, identified as C. J. Miller, for hitching a ride on a freight train. The telegraph said the prisoner wore a blue vest and pants, which might match the blue coat found at the scene of the crime. And in his pocket were two gold rings with the names of the girls inscribed inside.

John Ray's blood boiled. He couldn't wait to get his hands on the man who had raped and murdered his daughters. Justice would be served!

A train was chartered, and Thursday night at nine o'clock, a large group was on its way to Sikeston, including two sheriffs, two witnesses, and thirty armed and determined men who had pledged themselves to bring the prisoner back to Bardwell if he proved to be the guilty man.

But the group from Bardwell was surprised when they finally saw C. J. Miller. He was very dark skinned, yet all of their reports had indicated the murderer was a light-skinned person. The two witnesses said they could not be sure Miller was the same man. Plus, Miller wore light pants and coat—which did not correspond to the blue coat found near the slain girls. The rings turned out not to have any names inscribed on them at all, and John Ray said they did not belong to his daughters.

Despite the growing evidence that Miller was not guilty, the sheriff at Sikeston turned him over to the mob to be taken back to Bardwell for further investigation.

John Ray was not satisfied that they had the right man and protested, "I thought we were looking for a white man." But his logic was lost on those who had come with him.

By the time their train arrived back in Bardwell at eleven o'clock Friday morning, hundreds of people from the surrounding countryside had arrived in town. As the deputies protected the prisoner, John Ray spoke to the crowd, asking that the sheriff be allowed more time to investigate the case. He promised they would complete the investigation by three o'clock that afternoon. The crowd was armed and could have seized Miller at any time, but they honored the grieving father's request and settled in to wait until the appointed time.

The prisoner then made his own appeal to the crowd: "My name is C. J. Miller of Springfield, Illinois. My wife lives at 716 North Second Street. I am here among you, a stranger; am looked on by you as the most brutal man that ever stood on God's green earth. I am standing here, an innocent man, among men excited, and who do not propose to let the law take its course. I have committed no crime, and certainly no crime gross enough to deprive me of my life or liberty to walk upon the green earth. I am not guilty."

A hurried investigation began. Police telegraphed Springfield to verify Miller's story, but officials there said they had no such record. Different witnesses gave conflicting testimony—but most pointed to Miller's innocence. Miller was taken back to jail, where he was stripped of his clothes and examined again. On his shirttail they found a dark reddish spot about the size of a dime. Miller said, "That's paint! You take the clothes to any expert. If the spot is shown to be blood, you can do anything you wish with me." They took his clothes and were gone for a while. But evidently it was not blood, because they threw it back into the cell instead of keeping it as evidence.

Miller asked for a priest, but none could be found. He then asked for a Methodist minister, who came, prayed with the doomed man, and baptized him. The pastor pleaded with Miller to confess his sin before he died. But Miller resolutely proclaimed his innocence, saying, "Burning and torture here lasts but a little while, but if I die with a lie on my soul, I shall be tortured forever. I am innocent."

Still, the rumor went out to the mob that Miller had confessed, which stirred them up all the more.

While the minister was in with Miller, the townspeople were erecting a large pile of wood in the center of town. Its purpose? To burn Miller to death. The mob, which had grown from hundreds of people to thousands, was growing impatient with the delay and demanded that John Ray honor the deadline he had set.

"We want justice," they shouted. "Burn him! Burn the murderer!"

John Ray shuddered. He wanted justice too. But this felt wrong. He knew in his heart that this man was innocent. The mob demanded a life for a life. Taking this man's life would serve no purpose. And it would not bring his daughters back.

He wanted to do the right thing—but in the face of this mob, so determined to see vengeance, what could he do?

He faced the impassioned crowd, who quieted to hear his words. "I am not convinced this is the culprit who murdered my little girls. Please, do not torture this man. You must not burn him alive."

The crowd was still for a moment. John Ray wondered, *Is it possible they will honor my wishes and let this innocent man go free?*

A voice broke the silence. "Hang him." Immediately hundreds of other voices joined in the chorus. "Hang him! Hang him!"

John Ray staggered backward from the force of their violent cries. His grief and the strain of the last three days were beginning to take their toll on him. He had said his piece, had done his best. A mob set in motion rarely reversed its course. He resigned himself and nodded his agreement. There would be no justice that day in Bardwell.

There was a loud yell, and a rush was made for the prisoner. Miller's clothes were torn from his body, his shirt tied around his loins. A log-chain, nearly a hundred feet long and weighing more than one hundred pounds, was wrapped around his neck and body. He was led, then dragged through the streets to the crude platform where they had intended to burn him.

The chain was fastened around his neck, the other end fastened to the crossarm of a telegraph pole. He was lifted up several feet from the ground and then let to fall. The first fall broke Miller's neck, but the body was repeatedly raised and lowered while men in the crowd shot Miller full of holes. The corpse hung there for two hours while it was photographed again and again. Miller's fingers and toes were cut off for souvenirs. Finally the chain was released and the body of an innocent man fell into the fire that had been lit below.

★ ★ ★

Soon afterward, a telegram came from officials in Springfield, Illinois. A man named Miller and his wife did live at the address the prisoner had given in his speech. But it came too late to help.

John Ray, troubled by what had occurred, came forward four years later with evidence that the murderer was a white man living in Missouri. There is no record of whether John Ray ever had a chance to investigate his hunch, as the case was never officially reopened.

★ ★ ★

If you fail under pressure, your strength is not very great. Rescue those who are unjustly sentenced to death; don't stand back and let them die. Don't try to avoid responsibility by saying you didn't know about it. For God knows all hearts, and he sees you. He keeps watch over your soul, and he knows you knew! And he will judge all people according to what they have done.

PROVERBS 24:10–12 NLT

LYNCHED AN INNOCENT MAN

WRONG NEGRO HANGED BY THE BARDWELL, KY., AVENGERS.

Discovery Soon After the Death that the Victim Was Guiltless of the Murder of the Ray Girls—There Was Doubt Before the Lynching and for that Reason it Was Decided Not to Burn the Man at the Stake, as Originally Intended—Mr. Ray Superintends the Lynching.

CAIRO, Ill., July 7.—Charles F. Miller, a mulatto, who it was thought murdered the two Ray Girls near Bardwell, Ky., Wednesday, was hanged this afternoon and his body burned. The only evidence against Miller was circumstantial, and a strong plea made by him when it was decided to burn him at the stake convinced many that they might not have the right man, after all.

It was decided that it would be less terrible to hang an innocent man than to burn him.

The mob hanged the wrong man. He made a statement to show an alibi, which was proved to be true after he was hanged. The people say they think it was better to have hanged him than to have burned him, under the circumstances.

Miller was captured just across the Kentucky State line in Missouri last night. He was to-day taken to Wickliffe, the county seat of Carlisle, for examination. The evidence against him seemed conclusive, though he protested his innocence.

He was taken to Bardwell, the scene of the crime, at 11 o'clock this morning. The fact that he had been arrested had been telegraphed ahead and the people could

At the Bardwell station and stretched along the railway for a quarter of a mile was seen a mass of humanity with expectancy depicted on every countenance. As the train drew into the station the mob became impatient to see the victim, and yelled for him. He was in the custody of the Sheriff, John Hudson, and in the last car.

Alongside the station stood piles of bridge timber ten feet high. These were to form the funeral pile, for the verdict of all the Bardwell people was to burn him.

While the mob was looking through the first cars the Sheriff and his posse slipped out of the end car and hurried the negro across the back street in order to escape the fury of the populace, but they were not quick enough.

A cry was taken up which could be heard for miles, and then began the rapid tramp of thousands of feet through the dusty street, and the dust stirred up was a cloud that completely enveloped the mass of struggling people.

Into every street poured the mob, yelling at the top of their voices. They met the column marching rapidly down the street and headed them off. The Sheriff saw that it was useless to resist longer, so he agreed to take the negro to the place where the platform had been erected.

The prisoner was made to climb upon the platform, followed by the Sheriff and guard. Immediately the great mob surrounded the platform until there were fully 5,000 people in the vicinity shouting and yelling for the negro's death.

When he reached the top he raised his shackled hands high above his head, as if to implore mercy. Mr. Ray, the murdered girls' father, called on the Cairo and Wickliffe people that he had promised Cairo and Wickliffe people that he would let them know before they

"I want you to set the time," said Ray. Cries of "Set your own time, but put it off too long," were the answers.

"Well, say we put it at 3 o'clock," said Ray.

"All right," shouted the crowd. "Make him stay on the platform until that time."

"Where will we burn him?"

"Right here; right here."

After a time order was restored and cries for the negro to speak prevailed.

He came with a firm step and confided air to the edge of the platform and said:

"Please be quiet, everybody. My name is C. J. Miller. I am from Springfield. I and my wife lives at 716 North Second Street. I am here among you to-day looked upon as one of the most brutal men before the people.

"I stand here surrounded by men who are excited, men who are not willing to let the law take its course, and as far as the crime is concerned, I have committed no crime, and certainly no crime gross enough to deprive me of my life or liberty.

"I had some rings which I bought in Bismarck of a Jew peddler. I paid him $4.50 for them. I left Springfield July 4 and came to Alton. From Alton I went to East St. Louis, from there to Jefferson Barracks, thence to De Soto, thence to Bismarck and to Piedmont, thence to Poplar Bluff, thence to Hoxie and to Jonesborough, then on a local freight to Walden, from there to Sikeston July 5.

"The day I was supposed to have committed the offense I was at Bismarck."

The Sheriff then stepped to the front and said:

"For God's sake, gentlemen, I must take this man to jail. I am bound by my oath to deliver him at the jail."

The mob had become somewhat quiet by this time, and one man shouted:

"Yes, take him to jail until 3 o'clock; then we want him!"

The prisoner was helped off the pile of inflammable material and taken to jail. The crowd dispersed soon after, and all that could find dinners did so, but thousands could not be accommodated. Farm wagons and vehicles of every description could be

★ 98 ★

The Jim Crow Era and Black Codes

The Jim Crow Era has been described by some experts as being "worse than slavery." After the Civil War, the old system of chattel slavery was now against the law and new forms of bondage and oppression developed. The Southern white Democratic aristocracy who feared losing their power waged a vicious war against the two groups that were a threat to their former way of life: Southern blacks and white Republicans. Secret organizations like the Ku Klux Klan were created to systematically terrorize and forcefully control those who were in opposition. The press played a key role in fostering mob violence, which left little room for justice. During Reconstruction, which lasted from 1866 to 1876, the federal government sent troops in to protect the civil rights of African Americans and their sympathizers. They achieved some success and African Americans made some great gains, but the overall resistance was too great and injustice began to take hold and strengthen its grip.

The wheels of segregation were set in motion immediately after the Civil War. Newly elected President Andrew Johnson enabled the Southern state legislatures to ignore many of the civil rights laws passed by the pro-abolitionist Congress over the preceding years. State bureaucracies began passing a new series of laws that were meant to dictate the newly freed blacks' civil and legal rights, but the laws inhibited the rights of blacks more than anything else. The Southern white Democrats were fearful that freed blacks, who outnumbered the whites, would take too many liberties with their new freedom, and the laws, called the Black Codes, were a way to prohibit African Americans from the freedoms that had been won.

In 1865 the Radical Republicans—a group of Republicans who were not only in favor of abolition but believed freed slaves should have rights the same as white citizens—attempted to pass the Civil Rights Bill, a law in favor of protecting freed slaves from Southern Black Codes. The Codes, passed by Southern states, prohibited freed slaves—tax-paying citizens—from their right to vote and forbid interracial marriage, carrying weapons in public places, and working in certain occupations.

These Black Codes were so successful that by 1960 in the state of Mississippi only 5 percent of eligible black voters were registered. Laws were different for every state, but most incorporated the same kinds of restrictions. Commonly, the Black Codes forced freedmen to work. In many states unemployed African Americans faced the threat of arrest, and those who did work had their days regulated, as the Codes dictated the hours and duties. In some states blacks had to obtain a special certificate from a judge in order to work in any occupation other than agriculture or domestic work. Other states enforced laws where blacks needed permission from their employers to visit town.

When the U.S. Supreme Court declared the Civil Rights Act of 1875 unconstitutional, most of the Southern states passed discrimination laws against blacks in order to retain the segregation of public emporiums such as schools, theaters, hotels, trains, and buses. The Jim Crow Laws, as they became known, were created due to the Southern white power structure's fears that blacks were gaining confidence, a result of their earned freedom. Jim Crow spanned nearly a century until 1954, when *Brown v. Board of Education of Topeka, Kansas*, declared separate public schools unconstitutional.

With the Compromise of 1877, the federal government agreed to pull its troops out of the South and basically abandon the cause of freedom for nearly half its Southern citizens. The Jim Crow Era now blossomed. With the ability to operate unchecked, terror and injustice reigned.

In the newly cash poor Southern economy, and with blacks yearning for equality, sharecropping developed as one way to replace slave labor. The new system allowed blacks to rent a plot of land and pay for it with a percentage of the crop. Sharecropping seemed to be a good deal for the ex-slaves, since blacks could work independently and freely, but the arrangement was quickly found to be disastrous for the workers of the land. After borrowing tools, animals, fertilizer, seeds, and food from the landlord's store—which then charged the black workers incredibly high interest rates—most croppers ended each season in debt. While some blacks were able to escape the horrible conditions of the South and settle in the North, others were thrown off the land they had been working when machines became the primary work source for cotton picking.

Two other horrific systems that sought to replace slave labor were convict leasing and peonage. With peonage, former slaves would be thrown in jail on trumped-up charges and be fined maximum amounts. Many times if they could not find work they would be arrested for vagrancy or for being idle. Their former masters would then pay their fines, and they would be released to work off their debt. They would be held on the plantation in appalling conditions as long as the plantation owner so desired. The police, the judges, and the plantation owners all conspired together.

Convict leasing was just as dreadful. A loophole in the law allowed slavery as legal punishment for a crime. Prisoners were leased out to plantations and businesses with no government overseers. Prisoners who were leased out had a death rate ten times higher than other prisoners. Many of these prisoners were falsely imprisoned. Many were children who committed minor offenses but were sentenced to years in prison. This was big business throughout the South, and it was done on a mass scale. In 1898 convict leasing brought in 73 percent of Alabama's total revenue.

Although sharecropping, peonage, and convict leasing were created as replacements for slavery and the slave labor conditions, the new systems essentially ensured that freed slaves would remain poor and locked out of any opportunity for land ownership or basic human rights.

It is evident that the purpose of Jim Crow and the Black Codes was so fearful white citizens could legally control and inhibit the freedom of exslaves. Almost every aspect of blacks' lives was regulated, including the freedom to roam. The creators of the Codes did not try to hide the obvious bias and prejudice. It would be years before blacks would taste equality in its fullest measure—a struggle that still continues for many.

Innocent Blood Cries Out

Ida B.Wells-Barnett

1862–1931

Ida B. Wells, an African-American woman, was co-owner, editor, reporter, and publisher for the *Free Speech*, a weekly newspaper in Memphis. Ida was in Natchez, Mississippi, covering a story when she heard the news: Thomas Moss had been brutally killed. Lynched! Thomas and his family were her closest friends. Ida was devastated.

As she heard the details, she went from being devastated to being incensed. Thomas and two partners, Calvin McDowell and Lee Stewart, were successful young businessmen and leading citizens in Memphis. Honorable, reliable, and peaceable men, they owned and operated the large and prosperous People's Grocery Store located outside the Memphis city limits—and beyond police protection. Across the street was another grocery store, owned and operated by a white man.

A dispute started by the white store owner resulted in a late-night shootout at Thomas's grocery store in which three white men were wounded. A number of black men were randomly arrested, and the three black store owners were jailed and charged with wounding white men—even though they were attempting to defend their own property.

By law, the three would be given a fair trial, in which it would be decided if they shot in self-defense or not. Even if found guilty, they would not receive a death sentence, as the white men had not been seriously wounded and no one was killed.

Unfortunately, the only law in force was the lynch law.

Three or four nights later, at three o'clock in the morning on March 9, 1892, a mob of almost a dozen men appeared at the jail. The police did not try to stop them as they removed Thomas, Calvin, and Lee from their cell, put them in a railroad car, carried them a mile north of town, and riddled their bodies with bullets.

As Ida listened to the heart-wrenching tale, her eyes were suddenly opened to the truth about lynchings. She later wrote,

> *I have always abhorred lynchings. But like so many others, I believed the lie that such violence, such passion, resulted from the horror of rape. I thought it was because a Negro man assaulted a white woman. I thought lynchings happened in remote places where there was no law and order, that people whose loved ones had been violated had no choice but to take the law into their own hands. . . .*
>
> *But now my eyes are opened, and I see it all so clearly. Lynching is not a spontaneous punishment for a horrible crime. It is a deliberate act of terror.*
>
> *Thomas Moss, Calvin McDowell, and Lee Stewart were lynched in Memphis, one of the leading cities of the South. No lynching has ever taken place here. Yet they were murdered as brutally as any other victim of mob rule. They had committed no crime against white women. This is what opened my eyes to what lynching really is: an excuse to get rid of Negroes who are acquiring wealth and property. The goal is to keep the race terrorized and "keep the n——r down."*

As Ida grieved the death of her friend, Memphis simply gave the lynchings a passing glance—then looked the other way. The police knew the men who committed these brutal murders, and yet not the first step was ever taken to bring them to justice. The official report said the three were killed "by hands unknown."

Driven by a passion for justice, Ida dedicated herself to the fight against mob violence. She began to collect data on other lynchings and to keep what she called "The Red Record." Within eleven days of the lynching of her friend, Ida reported on the lynchings of eight more African Americans in four Southern states.

By inviting her readers to look past the lies and pay attention to the facts, Ida worked to change the perceptions of the South. Known for stating her case simply and directly, she did not mince words. Her articles were extraordinarily bold and courageous for an African-American woman at that time.

Soon after her articles were published, the offices of her newspaper in Memphis were demolished by white hoodlums and she was driven from the city. Undeterred, Ida continued to write for a New York paper about the injustices she saw, informing northerners about the catastrophic situation of lynching. During the next few years, she published a series of eye-opening pamphlets such as *Southern Horrors: Lynch Law in All Its Phases*; *A Red Record: Tabulated Statistics*; and *Alleged Causes of Lynching in the United States, 1892, 1893, and 1894*.

She proved with statistics that the "protection of white womanhood," as the South claimed, was not the basis for lynchings, since in no given year had even half of the Negroes who were lynched been charged with rape or attempted rape and that in 1900 less than 15 percent of those lynched had been so suspected.

Ida's antilynching campaign had a great and immediate impact on public opinion. In 1894, just two years after her friend was murdered, Memphis was rocked again by brutal murders. Six African-American men, suspected of burning down a building, were arrested. Ida wrote:

> *They were handcuffed and chained together by the officers of the law, loaded into a wagon, and deliberately driven into an ambush where a mob of lynchers awaited them. . . . The wagon was halted and the mob fired upon the six manacled men, shooting them to death as no humane person would have shot dogs. Chained together as they were, in their awful struggles after the first volley, the victims tumbled out of the wagon upon the ground and there in the mud, struggling in their death throes, the victims were made the target of the murderous shotguns, which fired into the writhing, struggling, dying mass of humanity, until every spark of life was gone. Then the officers of the law who had them in charge drove away to give the alarm and to tell the world that they had been waylaid and their prisoners forcibly taken from them and killed.*

But this time the eyes of the civilized world were upon the citizens of Memphis. There was a public outcry against the violence. The governor of Tennessee and the judge who had jurisdiction over the crime took prompt and vigorous steps to capture the murderers connected with the lynchings. Ida's hard work at exposing the evils of lynching had paid off.

Ida B. Wells was born a slave in Mississippi, six months before the Emancipation Proclamation. Her father became active in politics and education, while her mother insisted the children accompany her to church. Ida read through the Bible many times, as she loved to read and this was the only book her mother would allow her children to read on Sunday.

When Ida was about sixteen, her parents and three of her siblings died in a yellow fever epidemic. Determined to keep the rest of the family together, Ida, the oldest child, arranged her hair to look older and, putting on a long dress, was able to convince local school officials that she was eighteen and old enough to teach. She continued to teach to support the family until 1891, when she became a full-time journalist.

In 1895 Ida married Ferdinand L. Barnett, a successful attorney and newspaperman in Chicago, and she bought his newspaper, the *Chicago Conservator*. She became increasingly active in organizing associations for political action, including cofounding the Negro Fellowship League—to protest against racism—and the Alpha Suffrage Club—which dealt with women's issues. Ida also became chairperson of the Anti-Lynching Bureau of the National Afro-American Council and a famous speaker at home and abroad on Negro rights. One of only two women to sign the petitions that led to the birth of the NAACP, Ida was asked to join the fledgling organization. But when she learned the leaders were white, she left in protest.

In January 1922 Ida took up the cause of twelve black prisoners sentenced to death in Little Rock, Arkansas. Snuck in undercover, she interviewed these men who were wrongly accused of leading what would be called the Arkansas Race Riots. Black sharecroppers in

Phillips County, Arkansas, had joined together in a union and demanded better prices for their cotton. Area whites were outraged. Armed gangs came from three neighboring states and murdered dozens of the poor black farmers.

But instead of arresting the murderers, police arrested hundreds of blacks, both men and women, for planning a revolt and plotting to kill white people. The "trial" lasted only a few minutes—an all-white jury sentenced sixty-seven blacks to long years in prison and twelve to death. Once behind bars, the men lived in constant torment. They were beaten and tortured with electrical shocks in an attempt to force them to confess their alleged plot to murder whites. A lynch mob tried to seize them. Three times they were saved from execution by last-minute appeals to the courts.

When Ida had completed her interviews, the twelve men sang for her, beautiful songs about heaven and the wonderful life that awaited them. When they finished, they smiled at Ida, waiting for her approval. But instead she moved close to their cells and told them in a low voice, "I have listened to you for nearly two hours. You have talked and sung and prayed about dying, and forgiving your enemies, and of feeling sure you are going to be received in heaven. But why don't you pray to live and ask to be freed? . . . If you believe God is all-powerful, believe He is powerful enough to open these prison doors. . . . Pray to live and believe you are going to get out!"

Ida turned her notes from the interview into a pamphlet, *The Arkansas Race Riot*, which she sent to influential people in Arkansas. Thanks in part to her work, the U.S. Supreme Court ruled in 1923 that the twelve men had not received a fair trial and released them from prison.

★ ★ ★

Ida B. Wells-Barnett faithfully played the role of watchman and persistently warned a nation of its wicked ways. And fortunately our nation did change, making the violence of the lynch mob largely a thing of the past.

★ ★ ★

You, son of man, are the watchman. . . . The minute
you hear a message from me, warn them.
If I say to the wicked, "Wicked man, wicked woman,
you're on the fast track to death!" and you don't speak up
and warn the wicked to change their ways,
the wicked will die unwarned in their sins and
I'll hold you responsible for their bloodshed.
But if you warn the wicked to change their ways
and they don't do it, they'll die in their sins well-warned
and at least you will have saved your own life.

EZEKIEL 33:7–9 THE MESSAGE

THE SHAME OF AMERICA

Do you know that the United States is the Only Land on Earth where human beings are BURNED AT THE STAKE?

In Four Years, 1918-1921, Twenty-Eight People Were Publicly
BURNED BY AMERICAN MOBS

3436 People Lynched 1889 to 1922

For What Crimes Have Mobs Nullified Government and Inflicted the Death Penalty?

The Alleged Crimes	The Victims
Murder	1288
Rape	571
Crimes against the Person	615
Crimes against Property	333
Miscellaneous Crimes	453
Absence of Crime	176
	3436

Why Some Mob Victims Died:

Not turning out of road for white boy in auto
Being a relative of a person who was lynched
Jumping a labor contract
Being a member of the Non-Partisan League
"Talking back" to a white man
"Insulting" white man.

Is Rape the "Cause" of Lynching?

Of 3,436 people murdered by mobs in our country, only 571, or less than 17 per cent., were even accused of the crime of rape.

83 WOMEN HAVE BEEN LYNCHED IN THE UNITED STATES

Do lynchers maintain that they were lynched for "the usual crime"?

AND THE LYNCHERS GO UNPUNISHED

THE REMEDY

The Dyer Anti-Lynching Bill Is Now Before the United States Senate

The Dyer Anti-Lynching Bill was passed on January 26, 1922, by a vote of 230 to 119 in the House of Representatives

The Dyer Anti-Lynching Bill Provides:

That culpable State officers and mobbists shall be tried in Federal Courts on failure of State courts to act and that a county in which

The Senate has been petitioned to pass the Dyer Bill by—
29 Lawyers and Jurists, including two former Attorneys General of the United States
19 State Supreme Court Justices
24 State Governors

★ 107 ★

Lynchings by Race & Year (1882–1960)

After the Civil War, some whites turned to lynching—death by hanging at the hands of a mob that has taken the law into its own hands—to maintain power over African Americans. Many of the hangings were for unproven or invented offenses. Families were often in attendance and newspapers carried advance notice. Lynchings, which increasingly included burning, torture, and dismemberment to prolong suffering, in many cases became a social recreation rather than a punishment for crime.

Mississippi recorded the greatest number of deaths by lynching, with 539 black victims and 42 white victims in a span of eighty years. Georgia held the second-greatest number of lynchings, with the deaths of 492 blacks and 39 whites. While the number of lynchings declined in the twentieth century, unusually riotous years accounted for an increased number of hangings. These statistics do not tell the entire story, however, as many lynchings were never reported.

Year	Whites	Blacks	Total
1882	64	49	113
1883	77	53	130
1884	160	51	211
1885	110	74	184
1886	64	74	138
1887	50	70	120
1888	68	69	137
1889	76	94	170
1890	11	85	96
1891	71	113	184
1892	69	161	230
1893	34	118	152
1894	58	134	192
1895	66	113	179
1896	45	78	123
1897	35	123	158
1898	19	101	120
1899	21	85	106
1900	9	106	115
1901	25	105	130
1902	7	85	92
1903	15	84	99
1904	7	76	83
1905	5	57	62
1906	3	62	65
1907	2	58	60
1908	8	89	97
1909	13	69	82
1910	9	67	76
1911	7	60	67
1912	2	61	63
1913	1	51	52
1914	4	51	55
1915	13	56	69
1916	4	50	54
1917	2	36	38
1918	4	60	64
1919	7	76	83
1920	8	53	61
1921	5	59	64
1922	6	51	57
1923	4	29	33
1924	0	16	16
1925	0	17	17
1926	7	23	30
1927	0	16	16
1928	1	10	11
1929	3	7	10
1930	1	20	21
1931	1	12	13
1932	2	6	8
1933	4	24	28
1934	0	15	15
1935	2	18	20
1936	0	8	8
1937	0	8	8
1938	0	6	6
1939	1	2	3
1940	1	4	5
1941	0	4	4
1942	0	6	6
1943	0		
1944	0	2	2
1945	0	1	1
1946	0	6	6
1947	0	1	1
1948	1	1	2
1949	0	3	3
1950	1	1	2
1951	0	1	1
1952	0	0	0
1953	0	0	0
1954	0	0	0
1955	0	3	3
1956	0	0	0
1957	1	0	1
1958	0	0	0
1959	0	1	1
1960	0	0	0
Totals	1294	3441	4735

Freedom's Railroad
Harriet Tubman
1820–1913

It was now or never. It had been decided: Tomorrow—or the next day at the latest—Master Brodas would sell Harriet Tubman and her three older brothers to a plantation far to the south in Georgia. Harriet knew that the farther south they lived, the more impossible it was for them to escape. She had heard about the Underground Railroad that took slaves to freedom in the Northern states. She convinced her brothers to come with her, that this was the night they had to make their escape to the North—and freedom.

Harriet did not dare tell the rest of her family they were leaving. She had once talked with her husband about running away, and he had threatened to tell her master. And her mother was an expressive sort—if Harriet told her, everyone on the plantation would soon know. So off they went without a word, leaving behind everything and everyone.

The Maryland woods seemed especially dark that night as Harriet led her brothers through the trees. The farther they went, the more fearful Harriet's brothers became—afraid of the bloodhounds used by the patrollers to capture escaping slaves, of being whipped for running away, of being sold even farther south if they were caught. The brothers decided to turn back—but Harriet refused.

"You can't go alone," they told her.

"I can't go back," she said. "And I'm not alone. Jesus is here with me."

She later said, "I had reasoned this out in my mind: there was one of two things I had a right to, liberty or death; if I could not have one, I would have the other; for no man should take me alive; I should fight for my liberty as long as my strength lasted."

Harriet's father had taught her how to make her way silently through the woods. And that is what she did. A white Quaker woman who lived in a nearby town had once told her, "If you ever need help, come to me." The woman guided Harriet to the next "station" on the Underground Railroad. Harriet traveled only at night, following the North Star and using all her knowledge of the woods to avoid being discovered.

Every time she was afraid or did not know what to do next, she prayed the same simple prayer: "Lord, I'm going to hold steady on to you. You've got to see me through." Every time she asked for help, God answered. This was the beginning of Harriet's adventures in being guided step-by-step in a supernatural way. She hid in a haystack, in a root cellar, and in an attic. She traveled in a wagon, hidden under a load of vegetables. Once she found the next "station" along the way, friendly people would feed her, hide her, and tell her how to find her next stop. In all, Harriet walked a total of ninety miles.

At the end of her trip, she was given new shoes, fancy women's clothes and, since she couldn't read, a paper with the word *Pennsylvania* written on it so she could recognize the sign when she crossed the state line.

Finally she made it—Pennsylvania and freedom! What a wonderful feeling. Harriet said, "There was such a glory over everything, the sun came like gold through the trees and over the fields, and I felt like I was in heaven. I looked at my hands to see if I was the same person now that I was free."

With the experience of freedom came a new realization—Harriet had escaped only to find herself alone in a strange city. She remembered: "Oh, how I prayed then, lying on the cold, damp ground, 'Oh, dear Lord, I ain't got no friend but you. Come to my help, Lord, for I'm in trouble!'" She missed her family, who were all still slaves in the South. She came to a solemn resolution: She would make a home for her family in the North and, with the Lord's help, bring them there. "I was free, and my family should be free also."

She stayed in Philadelphia for the rest of the year, working night and day as a cook and a maid. She saved every extra penny, and when she had enough, she started making frequent trips to the South to lead other slaves to freedom. Her first trips were to

Baltimore, to help her half-sister, her two nieces, her brother John, and two other slaves.

After two years she was ready to risk going farther south—all the way to the plantation where she grew up. She knocked on the door of her cabin, hoping that her husband would agree to return north with her. But she was startled to find he had remarried. Then and there she decided, "I will forget John Tubman forever." By midnight Harriet had gathered ten others who wanted to escape, and she headed north with them, guided by the North Star and constant prayer.

Harriet made trip after trip to the South. But it was growing more and more dangerous. The government passed the Fugitive Slave Act of 1850, a law that made it illegal to help slaves escape. Anyone who led slaves to freedom or even sheltered them could lose everything they owned—house, fields, farm animals. If they were African-American, they could even lose their lives. Along the "railroad" there were always slave catchers and spies.

But those who helped the slaves worked together and devised countless ways to disguise the slaves and outwit the slave catchers. Harriet quickly learned how to avoid all the cunning traps. Even so, she had dozens of narrow escapes.

One night she was escaping with a group of ten runaways, including babies given strong medicine to keep them asleep. It was almost dawn when the weary slaves arrived at the next "station." Harriet gave the familiar knock at the door, but there was no answer.

She knocked again and a voice said, "Who is it?"

"A friend with friends," said Harriet, giving the password.

A frightened voice answered, "Slave catchers searched my house yesterday. Go away! Quick now!"

Harriet looked at the ten slaves standing on the country road. She had to do something—and fast. She prayed her familiar prayer, "Lord, I'm going to hold steady on to you. You've got to see me through." Suddenly she remembered an island in a nearby swamp. No one would think to look for them there. She hurried the group along, carrying the babies herself. They waded through the water and crawled under the bushes just before full daylight. They were so tired and hungry—but Harriet couldn't leave them in order to get food.

Over and over again she prayed. As night fell, they heard someone coming. The others shrank back in the bushes while Harriet moved closer to hear. The man was muttering as though to himself: "My wagon stands in the barnyard across the way. The horse is in the stable. The harness hangs on a nail." Still muttering, he soon was gone.

Harriet silently thanked God—once again He had made a way. As soon as it was dark, she crept to the barnyard. There stood a wagon loaded with blankets and baskets of food. Harriet quickly harnessed the horse and drove the wagon back to the swamp. Her passengers greeted her with joyful whispers.

Over the years Harriet experienced many more narrow escapes, but the Lord always sent help. Sometimes deliverance came through a friend on the Underground Railroad, while other times God would warn her and instruct her on exactly what to do.

Once, a premonition warned her she must immediately leave the path she was on and cross a swollen stream. Not knowing how deep the river was, the men with her hesitated. Harriet stepped in the water boldly and found it never came above her chin. When the men saw she was safely across, they followed her. Later Harriet learned that a group of men had been waiting just ahead to seize them. If she had not obeyed the whisper of warning in her mind, she would have been captured.

Harriet always gave God the credit for her escapes. Sarah Bradford, a white schoolteacher in Auburn, New York, who helped Harriet write the story of her life, recalled, "Sudden deliverance never seemed to strike her as at all mysterious; her prayer was the prayer of faith and she expected an answer." Whenever Sarah expressed surprise at Harriet's courage and daring or at her unexpected deliverance, Harriet would always reply, "Didn't I tell you, Missus. It wasn't me. It was the Lord!"

Harriet made nineteen dangerous trips back to Maryland, risking her life countless times to help others. She led more than three hundred slaves to freedom, including her elderly parents and all of her living brothers and sisters. During this period she became known as the "Moses" of her people. Like the biblical Moses, who led the Israelites out of slavery in Egypt, Harriet led so many out of bondage in the American South.

Harriet always carried a pistol at her side. She would not hesitate to use it in self-defense, neither did she hesitate to point it at any "passenger" who wanted to turn back. If captured, they could do great harm: The slave catchers would force them to reveal the people who had helped them. Her go-on-or-die philosophy worked—no matter how tired or afraid they were, her passengers invariably went on. Timid slaves seemed to find courage in her presence; no one ever betrayed her.

While Harriet became a hero to her people, she was a threat to the slave owners. Posters with her picture could be seen all over Maryland: "Wanted: Harriet Tubman—dead or alive! Reward $40,000." Still, no one ever caught her. Her skills became legendary— it was said she could see at night like an owl and smell danger like a deer. Slaves began to believe she could never be caught. She totally trusted in God, and He protected and helped her every step of the way.

During the Civil War Harriet served with the Union army, first as nurse and later as a scout and spy. Harriet's expertise with disguises and her ability to move around unnoticed were a great help behind enemy lines. Slaves were often as afraid of the Yankees as they were of their own masters and would not talk to other spies, but they would talk with Harriet. With her songs and cheerful words she would coax them to reveal important information.

In 1863 she led a band of former slaves under Colonel James Montgomery on a successful raid into enemy territory. More than eight hundred slaves were freed. An official dispatch about the incident said, "She became the only woman in American military history ever to plan and conduct an armed expedition against enemy forces." She was never paid for her efforts. In fact, Congress jeered at an attempt to award her a pension. Harriet spent the next thirty years petitioning the government to receive a twenty-dollars-a-month pension, which was finally granted in 1897.

Harriet spent her last years helping others and the cause of her people. She worked to raise money for freedmen's schools and to improve the plight of destitute children. She cared for her aging parents. With the help of the American Methodist Episcopal Zion Church, she founded the Harriet Tubman Home for Aged and Indigent Colored People, which she managed until her death in 1913. She was buried with full military honors.

Harriet spent her entire life working to correct injustices and give dignity to her people. After her death, the citizens of Auburn celebrated her life with these words: "With implicit trust in God, she braved every danger and overcame every obstacle. Withal she possessed extraordinary foresight and judgment so that she truthfully said, 'On my Underground Railroad I never ran my train off the track, and I never lost a passenger.'"

★　★　★

I would have lost heart, unless I had believed that I would see the goodness of the Lord in the land of the living. Wait on the Lord; be of good courage, and He shall strengthen your heart; wait, I say, on the Lord!
PSALM 27:13–14 NKJV

The Underground Railroad

The Underground Railroad was the term given to the system by which African Americans fled a life of slavery in the South to a life of freedom in the North. Opponents of slavery began using their homes and other resources to quietly and quickly get fugitive slaves to safe territory. Though there were many people willing to help the fugitives, escape for the slaves was always very difficult. Sleep occurred during the day, since movement between stations happened at night, and it was not unheard of for guides, or conductors, and runaways to walk twenty miles or more before coming to the next station. Safety, not speed, was the main concern, as it was necessary for the guides to lead the slaves on bad roads and through deep mud, zigzagging often, so as not to meet up with any slave catchers stationed along the way. Some guides and fugitives even hid in bushes and swamps for many days until it was safe to continue on.

Levi Coffin was just one of many conductors on the Underground Railroad. Risking their own safety countless times, Levi and his wife opened their home to fugitive slaves, offering food and shelter to the weary travelers. The Coffins discovered that as more slaves stopped at their house, the more the number of slaves seeking refuge increased. Coffin noted that the Underground Railroad business came with heavy expenses, but his own profitable affairs blessed him with enough means to continue working through the dangerous conditions.

The passing of the Fugitive Slave Act in 1850 made escape from the South even more difficult. Under the new law, a federal marshal who did not arrest a runaway slave could be fined, anyone aiding a fugitive slave could be fined and imprisoned, and the slaves themselves could be returned to their masters and subjected to severe punishment. The Fugitive Slave Act failed to stop the Underground Railroad, however, and from 1810 to 1850, an estimated one hundred thousand slaves were led to freedom.

"Don't Let Them Have Him!"

21 Charles Nalle and Harriet Tubman

SPRING 1860

"So this is how it ends," thought Charles Nalle. A fugitive slave, Charles had enjoyed two years of freedom before a slave catcher found him in Troy, New York. He was arrested and brought to trial to determine if he could remain free or if he would be returned to slavery. As Charles waited in the courtroom, the judge delivered his decision: Charles would be returned to slavery in Virginia.

After the sentencing Charles looked out the second-story window at the street below, where a large group of antislavery protestors had gathered. Suddenly a plan came to mind: He would jump into the arms of the crowd below and escape to freedom. He scrambled out onto the window ledge, but before he could jump, the officers grabbed him and pulled him back inside.

Charles didn't know it, but at the back of the courtroom, disguised as an elderly black woman carrying a food basket, was Harriet Tubman. Harriet was in Troy visiting a cousin, and when she heard of Charles' trial, she knew she had to do what she could to help.

As she waited she prayed silently, and a plan popped into Harriet's head—but she was a visitor and didn't know if the good people of Troy would help Charles escape. It was a good sign that Charles had tried to jump into the arms of the crowd. It showed that Charles was courageous and committed to escaping and that he had confidence that the crowd would help him. Harriet's escape plan was risky but worth trying.

A police wagon was waiting to carry Charles away. The large, angry crowd had the officers worried, though, so they waited for it to disperse. Instead it kept growing bigger. After a long wait they announced, "If you will clear the stairs and make a path to the wagon, we will bring the prisoner down the front way."

Harriet found a spot at the bottom of the stairs. Charles walked past her, handcuffed, with guards on either side. Instantly the frail, elderly woman transformed herself. Taking the guards by surprise, she grabbed hold of Charles and ran into the crowd. She was struck—again and again. An eyewitness reported, "She was repeatedly beaten over the head with policemen's clubs, but she never for a moment released her hold . . . until the police were literally worn out with their exertions." The two were knocked to the ground by one of the marshals. They got up, only to be knocked down again. With his wrists bound, Charles was all but helpless. Blood streamed from his head.

"Drag us out," Harriet shouted to the crowd. "Take him to the river. Don't let them have him!" The crowd swept the pair away from the marshals and toward the river. Charles was rowed across. Harriet followed in a ferry boat, accompanied by almost four hundred abolitionists, dedicated to keeping Charles from being recaptured.

But the rescue was not over. The police on the other side had been alerted by telegraph and were waiting for the rowboat. They grabbed Charles and took him into police custody, locking him upstairs in the judge's office. Harriet and her followers mobbed the building, throwing rocks at the policemen posted at the entrance and at every window. The police shot back in response, aiming over the heads of the crowd. The crowd fell back.

Suddenly a big, strong black man broke from the crowd and dashed toward the building. He slammed his shoulder into the door and broke it open. In a moment he was knocked down by a deputy with a hatchet. Badly wounded, the man's body blocked the door so that it could not be shut.

A dozen men poured into the building. As they tried to go up the stairs, the police fired down on them. Before the police could reload, Harriet and other black women rushed past the wounded men, grabbed Charles, carried him outside, and put him in a wagon. Suddenly Charles was on his way to Canada and freedom.

In their reports on the incident, one local paper said, "The rescuers numbered many of our most respectable citizens—lawyers, editors, public men and private individuals. The rank and file, though, were black, and African fury is entitled to claim the greatest share in the rescue."

Another paper reported, "This incident has developed a more intense Anti-slavery spirit here than was ever known before."

Working together, the people of Troy had won a great victory over an unjust system and struck a blow for freedom.

★ ★ ★

This is my command: Love one another
the way I loved you. This is the very best way to love.
Put your life on the line for your friends.
JOHN 15:12–13 THE MESSAGE

UNVEIL "TUBMAN" MEMORIAL.

Auburn, N. Y.—Impressive ceremonies were held at the Fort Hill Cemetery by the Harriet Tubman Club of New York City, assisted by Empire State Federation of Women's Clubs at the grave of Harriet Tubman, the late famous conductor of the underground railway.

The "Civil War heroine" died last year at the age of ninety-six.

Harriet Tubman, who was born in slavery, fled to the North, and after regaining her freedom in this manner assisted 400 slaves to freedom. John Brown commissioned her "General Tubman and Congress gave her a pension.

The monument is a shaft of handsome design, one of the principal figures being three oak logs out of which flowers are growing. This monument was made in the city of New York, the design was the work of Mrs. Jackson Stuart. The following inscription appears on the stone: "In memory of Harriet Tubman-Davis, heroine of the underground railroad, nurse and scout in the Civil War. Born in Maryland about 1820. Died at Auburn, March 10, 1913. Servant of God well done. Erected by the Harriet Tubman Club of New York City, assisted by the Empire State Federation of Women's Clubs, Monday, July 5, 1915, at 4 P. M."

Rev. C. A. Smith of Auburn offered a short invocation, after which Mrs. Frances Smith, first president of the Home, gave a short address on "Harriet Tubman as I Knew Her." The presentation of the stone was made by Mrs. H. T. Johnson of Auburn, proxy for Mrs. M. J. Stuart,

Begin Again
Bridget "Biddy" Mason
1818–1892

22

"**We are free!** We are really free!" Biddy Mason's three daughters, ages seventeen, eleven, and seven, were laughing and dancing for joy. Just a few hours earlier, a district judge had decided that Biddy and her children were being illegally kept as slaves—and therefore set them free.

Now, as they celebrated their newfound freedom at the home of their friend Robert Owens and his family, they realized that on this day, January 21, 1856, their lives had changed forever.

As Biddy sat at Robert's kitchen table, surrounded by people, she was lost deep in thought. She had, of course, dreamed of freedom for herself and her family, but she had never thought her dream would come true. After a lifetime of always doing what she was told to do, she was suddenly on her own. "Biddy," she told herself, "this is your chance to really begin again." Now she could decide for herself where she would live, what sort of work she would do, and what she would accomplish with her life.

In a way, starting over in a new place was nothing new for Biddy Mason. As a slave, she had been moved from place to place all her life. She had been separated from her parents as a child and sold several times, working on plantations in Georgia, Mississippi, and South Carolina. When she was eighteen, her master gave her to his cousin, Robert Smith, as part of a wedding present. She lived in Mississippi for twelve years.

Then Smith packed up his family and headed west to Utah. Biddy and her children, ages ten, four, and four months at the time, walked with the other slaves driving the livestock behind the wagon train. In seven months they traveled more than two thousand miles, walking every step of the way. The little group followed the Overland Trail through Tennessee, Kentucky, Missouri, Iowa, Nebraska, and Wyoming. Several babies were born during the trip, and Biddy, an experienced midwife, helped deliver them all. Several years later the Smith family moved again to San Bernardino, California, more than seven hundred miles away. Biddy and the other slaves once again walked behind the wagon train.

But unknown to Biddy's master, California had joined the Union in September 1850 as a free state. Slave owners who had arrived in California before 1850 could keep their slaves as indentured servants, but any slaves arriving in California after that date were required by law to be set free.

Smith, his family, and his slaves arrived in 1851, but he never gave his slaves their freedom. As antislavery sentiment grew stronger in California, Smith decided to move to Texas, a slave state where he could legally keep his slaves. He hurriedly packed up his family, his slaves, and his possessions and headed to the Santa Monica Mountains, where he planned to hide out until the boat that would take them to Texas docked in Los Angeles.

But God had different plans.

While in California, Biddy and her girls had become friends with some free blacks. When Biddy's friends heard of Smith's intentions, they devised a bold rescue scheme. They asked Robert Owens, a famous black cowboy, to persuade the county sheriff to rescue Biddy and her daughters and keep Smith from taking his slaves out of the state.

The sheriff agreed, and he, Owens, and ten of Owens' fellow black cowboys searched the hillsides until they finally found Smith's camp in a hidden canyon. The sheriff took the women and children into protective custody, escorting them back to Los Angeles and giving them shelter in the county jail. Owens then filed a legal petition claiming that Smith was breaking the law by owning slaves in a free state.

Biddy's case was to become one of the landmark civil rights trials in history. Smith claimed Biddy, her children, and the other slaves were not slaves at all, but members of his family. The judge who heard the case, however, decided in favor of the African Americans.

And now Biddy and her family were free. They would never have to be uprooted again. But Biddy needed to get a job and find a place to live. Like most slaves, Biddy had never been allowed to learn to read or write. But unlike most slaves, Biddy had learned a valuable profession and knew her skill as a midwife would help her get a job. Still, she had never looked for a job before. How should she begin?

Just then Robert Owens interrupted her thoughts. "Biddy, my wife and I would like for you and the girls to stay here with us for as long as you want. And tomorrow, we'll see if we can get you a job."

Biddy soon found her skills as a midwife were in great demand. She delivered hundreds of babies for women of all races and social classes, working in the grandest Victorian homes and the lowliest of hovels. For those who could not pay, she worked for free. During a smallpox epidemic, she nursed many people at the risk of her own life.

She had two goals during this time—to help others and to buy her own land. Earning $2.50 a day, a good wage for an African-American woman at that time, in ten years she was able to save $250. On November 28, 1866, Biddy bought two lots bounded by Spring, Fort (now Broadway), Third, and Fourth Streets on the outskirts of the city. She was one of the first black women to buy property in the United States.

Biddy kept improving her property, first building small rental houses and then a commercial building. Selling and buying pieces of real estate, she began to build a fortune, which she used to help her community. A devout Christian, Biddy's passion was helping others in need. She gave money and land to schools, where the poorest and most needy children could be taught. In 1872 she and her son-in-law, Charles Owens, formed the First African Methodist Episcopal Church in Los Angeles, building the first black church in the city on land Biddy provided. She helped establish day-care centers, stores,

The First African Methodist Episcopal Church, Los Angeles, which Biddy founded, is still going strong in the heart of downtown L.A. Today the congregation tops 17,300 members. The church's inspiring ministry still reaches out beyond the walls of the church, enriching thousands of lives with some forty task forces for ministry in the community, including a unique prison ministry, adoption/foster care programs, and numerous children's ministries offering tutoring, Bible studies, and college preparation workshops.

They also sponsor FAME Renaissance, a faith-based ministry that helps minority businessmen grow their companies. The church was recognized by President George H. W. Bush, who declared it a Point of Light for its courageous outreach in community services.

The famous Azusa Street Revival, a major outpouring of the Holy Spirit, occurred in Los Angeles in the early 1900s. It began at 216 Bonnie Brea Street, through the ministry of black evangelist William Seymour.

The revival later moved to the old First African Methodist Episcopal Church building that Biddy Mason and Charles Owens had founded and built.

and eleven convalescent homes. After floodwaters destroyed sections of Los Angeles in the 1880s, Biddy went to a local grocer and set up open-ended accounts so people who lost their homes and jobs could get food and necessities. Biddy quietly paid the bills, helping people of all races. To Biddy there were no differences.

Biddy did not just give money and land. She also visited the poor, the sick, prisoners in jail, and the elderly. A godly woman, Biddy taught her children the virtues of generosity and Christlike love. Her life demonstrated the biblical principle that if you give, it will be given to you, and that giving to others always brings back more than you gave.

In the same way Robert Owens had helped her get started, Biddy also helped many hard-working African-American families who had left farms to make a better living in the city get established in Los Angeles.

The city continued to grow, and within twenty-five years the main financial district of the city was just a block away from Biddy's property. By the late 1800s Biddy's shrewd investments had made her one of the wealthiest African-American women in Los Angeles.

On a beautiful morning in downtown Los Angeles, Biddy Mason looked out her window at the needy people who had come to "Grandma Mason's" homestead for help. Although it was still early, the line already stretched out for a ways along Spring Street. Biddy smiled. She had come a long, long way from her life as a little slave girl in Georgia. God had led her and guided her and blessed her in so many ways, and she was happy to share with others—neighbors as well as newcomers to the city—the blessings she had received. Biddy knew firsthand how it felt to be poor and alone in a strange place.

Her life preached a sermon to all around her.

★ ★ ★

Then these righteous ones will reply, "Lord, when did
we ever see you hungry and feed you? Or thirsty and
give you something to drink? Or a stranger and show
you hospitality? Or naked and give you clothing? When
did we ever see you sick or in prison, and visit you?
And the King will tell them, "I assure you, when you
did it to one of the least of these my brothers and
sisters, you were doing it to me!"

MATTHEW 25:37–40 NLT

Is this not the fast that I have chosen:
To loose the bonds of wickedness,
To undo the heavy burdens,
To let the oppressed go free,
And that you break every yoke?
Is it not to share your bread with the hungry,
And that you bring to your house the poor who are cast out;
When you see the naked, that you cover him,
And not hide yourself from your own flesh?
Then your light shall break forth like the morning,
Your healing shall spring forth speedily,
And your righteousness shall go before you;
The glory of the Lord shall be your rear guard.

ISAIAH 58:6–8 NKJV

Revivals in War and Peace

For anyone familiar with America's eighteenth- and nineteenth-century revivals, George Whitefield, Jonathan Edwards, Charles Finney, and D. L. Moody are probably familiar names. How about George B. McClellan, Oliver O. Howard, Robert E. Lee, and Thomas "Stonewall" Jackson? If you guessed Civil War generals, you are correct. But did you know that these men of the Union and Confederate armies helped facilitate spiritual revival among their troops?

General George McClellan decreed that the North's "holy cause" required regular Sunday services every week, military conditions permitting. Union General Oliver Howard was commonly referred to as "the Christian General," and would preach in a pinch if a chaplain were unavailable. In the western theater, Union General William Rosecrans, a devoted Catholic, refused to fight on the Sabbath. At the battle of Stone's River, Tennessee, he fought on Saturday, and then reputedly called a halt to the fighting on Sunday for Christian observances; by Monday, the Confederates had withdrawn.

The Confederacy boasted its own set of Christian generals. Lee and Jackson, the heart and soul of the Confederate army, were ardent believers in divine providence. When asked why he was so fearless and unflappable in battle, "Stonewall" Jackson replied, "I feel as safe in battle as in bed. God has fixed the time for my death."

From the late fall of 1863 through the spring and summer of 1864, a revival reached its peak as it swept through both armies in the military theaters of Virginia and Tennessee. For the Confederates, Bibles and tracts were in such great demand that they were snatched up "as if they were gold guineas for free distribution," according to Civil War chaplain and author J. William Jones. It is calculated that as many as 100,000 Confederate soldiers and between 100,000 to 200,000 Union soldiers came to Christ during the war.

War is horrible—conservatively, about 500,000 men died during the Civil War. That is more than all other American wars combined. Yet in the midst of this grand darkness, God brought light where there otherwise would have been little.

Crazy Bet

Elizabeth Van Lew

1818–1900

"Miss Lizzy, Miss Lizzy!" Mary, a former slave, ran up the steps of the mansion on top of the hill. Breathlessly, she burst in on Elizabeth Van Lew, sitting on the veranda having tea with her mother. "Sorry, ma'am." The girl nodded to the older Mrs. Van Lew. "Miss Lizzy, the soldiers are coming again to get your horse. They know you hid him in the smokehouse last time. What you gonna do?"

Elizabeth shut her eyes for a moment, praying silently. Then she rose from the table. "Excuse me, Mother. Mary, I've got a plan. We're about to have a new guest in the upstairs library. Quick, tell Peter to bring the horse to the back door, and then have Henry get some straw and put it on the floor. The soldiers will not get my horse. We need him too badly for our work!"

As the Civil War wore on, horses for the Southern army were in short supply. Soldiers had already confiscated almost all the horses in Richmond, Virginia. Elizabeth—who believed in Providence, not accidents—had now on two occasions been warned in time to hide her horse. "Thank you, Lord, for the warning," she prayed. "And thank you for your plan."

Meeting Peter at the back door, Elizabeth took the horse's bridle and led him through the house. They clattered past chandeliered parlors with silk brocade wall coverings and mantels of imported marble, then up the stairs to the library. The horse behaved as though he completely understood what was happening. He never stomped or neighed while the soldiers thoroughly searched the barns, the gardens, and the grounds. Finally they gave up and left. "You are a good, loyal horse," Elizabeth told him as she led him down the stairs. "What would we do without you?"

In fact, the mobility her horse provided was a key part of the work Elizabeth Van Lew and her mother did in Richmond during the Civil War. Among the wealthiest families in the capital city of the newly formed Confederate States of America, the two women did not share the views of most of the citizens around them. In the face of strong persecution, public criticism, and personal threats, they opposed both slavery and the Civil War. "I am not a Yankee," Elizabeth once said. "I am only a good Southerner, holding to an old Virginia tradition of opposition to human bondage. I am the loyal one. Those who oppose the Union are the traitors."

Elizabeth, a devoted Quaker, had felt great compassion for the sufferings of the slaves even as a child. As a young woman, she freed all the family servants, most of whom stayed on in their jobs. And whenever she heard that the children or relatives of a former Van Lew slave were to be sold by their owners, she bought them and set them free as well.

As the state of Virginia prepared to secede from the Union, Elizabeth prayed, "Lord, help us." On April 17, 1861, when she saw the first Confederate flag flying over Richmond, Elizabeth turned to her mother and said, "It is a sad day for those with loyalty in their hearts." That night there was a great celebration in the streets of her city. Through tears, Elizabeth watched the torchlight procession. She fell to her knees, praying and weeping for her nation. As she prayed, a sense of awe came upon her and with it a sense of purpose and duty. She remembered that moment for the rest of her life, saying, "Never did a feeling of more calm determination and high resolve for endurance come over me."

That "calm determination" would show up again and again as Elizabeth walked the path set before her. She made it clear her sympathies were with the Union. While every "true" Southern woman was making shirts or knitting socks for their troops, Elizabeth and her mother steadfastly refused. Only when personally threatened did they agree to help—by offering to take Bibles and religious books to the soldiers.

Three months later, the South beat the North at Manassas, the first battle of the Civil War. Elizabeth watched as wagonloads of Union army prisoners, many of them injured, were brought to Richmond's Libby Prison. A plan began to form in her heart. She approached her mother and announced, "Mother, I have found a way to help the Union."

"My dear! What can you do?"

"I have heard how the war prisoners are suffering. I want to be their nurse."

"Oh, Elizabeth! I've heard the stories too—the conditions at Libby Prison are very grim. But you are not accustomed to such hard work. And you are so tiny and frail. How can you do it?"

"Mother, God has put this in my heart, and He will help me." As it turned out, even getting into the prison to help was difficult. The prison keeper could not believe she wanted to nurse the Yankees. But Elizabeth did not give up. She kept talking to officials until she finally got her pass. From that day until the end of the war, Elizabeth was a regular visitor at the prison, pouring out money and energy to assist and comfort the Union soldiers. She convinced Confederate doctors to transfer the sick prisoners to hospitals. She took clothes, bedding, medicine, food, books, and stationery for letters home. On special occasions she took in warm, home-cooked meals.

It wasn't long before Elizabeth discovered an additional way to serve her country. The prisoners understood the meaning of Confederate troop movements, and they could pick up hints from the soldiers and guards. Elizabeth became a dedicated and resourceful spy, a trusted channel to get military information to the Union generals. The roads in and out of the capital were guarded. But the Van Lews had a small vegetable garden out of town which gave her servants a ready-made excuse to freely travel back and forth on horseback with messages hidden in a basket of eggs or the sole of a muddy boot.

It was Elizabeth's very outspokenness of being pro-Union and antislavery that was her "cover" for her activities as a spy. Instead of being secretive about her actions and hiding her true sentiments, as is expected of a spy, she let everyone know right where she stood. As a result, she suffered "the threats, the scowls, the frowns of an infuriated community. . . . I have had brave men shake their fingers in my face and say terrible things."

At one point it got so bad that Elizabeth boldly went to Jefferson Davis, the president of the Confederacy, to request protection. Then she had an even better idea. The new prison keeper at Libby Prison was a man with a family. The war had caused a severe housing shortage, and they needed a place to stay. Elizabeth invited them to stay with her in her mansion . . . and the Van Lews were left in peace.

Soon after this, Elizabeth contacted her friend Mary Bowser, a black slave who had once belonged to the Van Lew family. After Elizabeth had set her free, the Van Lews paid for her to attend school in Philadelphia. At Elizabeth's request, Mary returned to Richmond and worked closely with Elizabeth in her espionage activities. Mary became the new house servant for Confederate President and Mrs. Jefferson Davis, which enabled her to obtain Confederate secrets firsthand. As a maid, Mary was ignored as she served meals and overheard conversations. She was also able to read documents she found. Periodically Mary and Elizabeth would meet after dark near the Van Lew farm. For such trips Elizabeth played the part of a poor country woman driving around in her horse and buggy. A huge bonnet, leather leggings, and a canvas coat completed her disguise.

It was about this time that Elizabeth took advantage of the fact that Richmond had long regarded her as a trifle odd. She began to play up the part. She would walk down the street, dressed in her oldest clothes and a battered bonnet, having a mumbled conversation with herself. Townspeople would look away and shake their heads. The prison guards gave her a new name, "Crazy Bet."

But Elizabeth was not crazy. She had enlisted the help of a number of farmers, storekeepers, and factory workers. She also had clerks in the rebel war and navy departments who gave her confidential information. With cool daring she operated right under the noses of Confederate officials to get the necessary information to federal spies and scouts and to help prisoners of war escape.

It was dangerous work, but God always gave Elizabeth a creative way around any obstacle. God also protected her from being discovered—sometimes a friend would "accidentally" hear something, other times her own heart would warn her. One time a new agent came to Richmond and was scheduled to meet Elizabeth, but she was filled with suspicion and anxiety. Suddenly the agent rushed into Confederate headquarters, where he sold out the Union sympathizers. At least two Union agents went to prison. For hours Elizabeth worried that she, too, would be turned in, but nothing happened.

By the time General Ulysses S. Grant moved toward Richmond, Elizabeth's network was well established. Grant asked repeatedly for specific information, and she steadily conveyed it to him. Finally the day came when General Robert E. Lee's line of defense around Richmond broke and General Grant was marching toward the city. Elizabeth had been waiting for this moment to make a grand gesture. She had ordered a big American flag and had it smuggled through the lines. Now she and her servants scrambled to the roof and unfurled the first Union flag to wave again in the Confederate capital.

The residents of Richmond were furious. A mob gathered, shouting, "Burn the place down!" Elizabeth confronted the angry men and called out their names: "I know you and you and you. . . . General Grant will be here in an hour. You do one thing to my home, and all of yours will be burned before noon!" Convinced she would back up her threat, the men backed away.

Later that day, a special guard sent by General Grant to protect Elizabeth found her in the Confederate capitol building, searching among the ashes of the archives for remains of secret documents that might prove helpful to the Union. Elizabeth had given herself one final assignment before she retired from her career as a spy.

General George Sharpe of the Army Intelligence Bureau declared, "The Van Lews' position, character and charities gave them a commanding influence, and many families of plain people were decided and encouraged by them to remain true to the flag.... For a long, long time, she represented all that was left of the power of the United States government in the city of Richmond."

After the fall of Richmond, Elizabeth was visited by General Grant, and they had a cup of tea together on her veranda. Grant expressed the nation's gratitude for her help, telling her, "You are the one person who has sent me the most useful information I have received from Richmond during the war."

For the next thirty-five years, Elizabeth lived in her family's mansion in Richmond. She was shunned by white society for her loyalty to the Union. Having spent most of the family fortune on her wartime activities, she died in miserable poverty. After her death, her neighbors tore her house down so there would be no memory of her in Richmond. Not one white Southerner came to her funeral.

A Union soldier from Massachusetts, whom Elizabeth had cared for during the war, sent a huge tombstone that can still be seen at her gravesite. It has the following inscription on it:

She risked everything that is dear to man—friends,
fortune, comfort, life itself, all for the one absorbing desire
of her heart, that slavery might be abolished and
the Union preserved.

THIS BOULDER FROM THE CAPITOL HILL IN BOSTON
IS A TRIBUTE FROM MASSACHUSETTS FRIENDS.

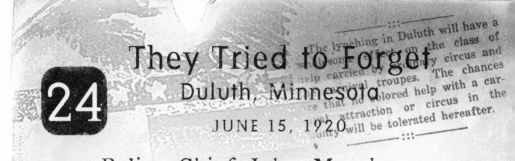

24 They Tried to Forget

Duluth, Minnesota

JUNE 15, 1920

Police Chief John Murphy looked at the white teenage couple—then back at the long lineup of young black circus workers. It was hard to know what to believe. The teenagers reported they had been out necking in a field near the circus site when they were attacked by a gang of "circus n———rs." They claimed six black men had held them at gunpoint and raped the young woman. Chief Murphy's instincts told him something was not quite right about the teenagers' story, and there were several contradictions in it. But with racial tensions growing in Duluth, he also knew he would have to process the case with the utmost care.

Like many Northerners, Chief Murphy had grown up hearing about race-based violence in the Southern states. He was glad that Duluth, Minnesota, one of the northern-most cities in the United States, did not have a history of racial problems. But veterans return-ing from Europe after World War I were upset to find their job oppor-tunities limited. Not only had Duluth's steel plant imported African Americans from the South as cheap labor, they were now using them as strikebreakers against the labor unions. Racial tensions mounted. Recently the police had received reports of Ku Klux Klan meetings and of crosses burning on the heights overlooking the city. The investiga-tor nodded to himself—this case would attract a lot of public interest.

The chief turned to the young couple and asked, "Do you rec-ognize any of the men who assaulted you?" The circus, which had arrived in town for a one-day performance on June 14, had brought with it more than a hundred young black men to serve as roustabouts, haulers, and unskilled workers. The police lineup was made up of thin, muscular fellows in their late teens or early twenties. To the chief, all of them looked virtually identical.

After a long pause, the woman replied, "It was so dark. I can't really recognize any of their faces. . . ."

The chief was just beginning to hope that the case could be dropped when the young man spoke up. "Isn't that one of them?" he asked, pointing to a black teenager who was a little taller than the others.

"Yes," the woman said. "One was a little taller."

The minutes passed. Somehow the young couple managed to identify six men as the ones who assaulted them. These six young black men were immediately arrested and put in the Duluth jail.

By midmorning a doctor's report indicated the young woman had not been raped after all. Investigators had found no evidence to link the young circus workers to the time or the place of the assault.

The circus moved on to a neighboring town, but tensions continued to grow. The police chief and several other top officials left Duluth, following the circus to interview other circus workers and additional suspects, hoping to discover the truth.

Then, around suppertime, one of the junior officers came into police headquarters with a disturbing report. A rumor was spreading that the young woman was dead because of injuries due to the alleged rape.

A man in a passing car had stopped and asked her mother how the girl was doing. The mother replied, "She's in bed."

But the man heard, "She's dead." Gossip spread like wildfire, and soon the town was in an uproar. By nightfall a frenzied mob numbering over five thousand people had gathered outside the jail. Armed with sticks and bricks, they began to shout, "We want justice! We want justice!"

The police sergeant, as the highest-ranking officer at the jailhouse that night, went out to address the crowd, but the mob never allowed him to speak.

Someone in the crowd shouted, "Lynch the n——rs!" The chant was taken up by others. Soon thousands of men, women, and children were shouting and waving sticks and clubs at the policeman. A brick was thrown, then another. The sergeant ducked back inside the jailhouse just in time, locking the door behind him.

The mob then stormed the police station, throwing bricks through the windows. Using rails and heavy timbers, they broke down the front door of the brick building. A wave of humanity pushed through, past the counter and back to the cells where the prisoners were kept. They tore off the doors to the cells and seized three of the thirteen young men—Elias Clayton, nineteen, Elmer Jackson, nineteen, and Isaac McGhie, twenty. As the three were pulled from their cell, each began to loudly proclaim, "I am innocent!"

The police officers had been ordered not to use their guns. The sergeant pushed his way through the crowd. "I cannot let you take these prisoners. They are innocent until proven guilty. It is my sworn duty to protect them until they can have their trial. You are breaking the law."

A burly man said, "Someone shut the cop up." Three men grabbed the officer, allowing another to punch him until he was unconscious.

The mob dragged the prisoners out to the porch of the jailhouse, where they proceeded to have a "vigilante trial." A judge spoke up from the crowd: "As a judge in this town, I assure you, you don't want to do this. You do not want to take the law into your own hands. This is America, a land of law and order. Our legal process is for our protection—so that citizens can live in safety, free from fear. Justice is always best served in an orderly process, not by mob rule."

The burly man answered, "Sorry, judge. We want justice and we want it now. We need to show these n——rs that they can't rape our women. I say, 'Let the lynch law rule.'"

The mob started to chant again, "Lynch the n——rs!"

Rough hands grabbed Isaac, the oldest of the three, and dragged him to a lamppost a block away. Isaac pleaded for his life the whole way, saying repeatedly, "I didn't do it. I am innocent!" As they put the lynch rope around his neck, a Catholic priest spoke up: "Good men! Think about what you are doing! The command of the Lord is 'Thou shalt not murder.' The blood of an innocent man will be upon your souls forever. I beg you, in the name of Christ, don't do this."

Once again, the burly man replied, "Yeah? My Bible says 'an eye for an eye and a tooth for a tooth.'" He jerked the noose tight around Isaac's neck. "I say a life for a life." Many hands lifted the young man up to a makeshift platform, then pushed him off. His neck broken, he died instantly, soon followed by Elmer and then Elias, who pleaded with the mob, "Please, oh God, don't kill me! I am innocent."

Photographers preserved the image of the young black men hanging from a single lamppost in the center of downtown Duluth. On either side of the dead youths are the men responsible for their deaths. Posing for the photographer, members of the mob crowded in and craned their necks to be included in the photo next to their shameful handiwork. These photos were printed and sold as postcards.

As news of the Duluth lynching spread, the state and the nation were shocked.

This is a crime of a Northern state, as black and ugly as any that has brought the South in disrepute. The Duluth authorities stand condemned in the eyes of the nation.
—THE CHICAGO EVENING POST

The sudden flaming up of racial passion, which is the reproach of the South, may also occur, as we now learn in the bitterness of humiliation in Minnesota.
—MINNEAPOLIS JOURNAL

Duluth has suffered a horrible disgrace, a blot on its name that it can never outlive.
—MILTON W. JUDY,
a prominent black Duluthian

In the following weeks, seven blacks were indicted by a grand jury for the crime of rape. Charges were dismissed for five of them. The remaining two, Max Mason and William Miller, were tried for rape. William Miller was acquitted. Max Mason was convicted and sentenced to serve seven to thirty years in prison.

The grand jury issued thirty-seven indictments for whites who took part in the lynch mob: twenty-five for rioting and twelve for the crime of murder in the first degree. Some people received indictments for both offenses. Eight whites were tried. Four were acquitted and one trial resulted in a hung jury. Three of the whites—Louis Dondino, Carl Hammerberg, and Gilbert Stephenson—were convicted for rioting. Each served less than fifteen months in prison. Not one was convicted of murder.

This attempt at justice did nothing to remove the guilt or soothe the conscience of the city. Ashamed of what had taken place, the city of Duluth burned the court records about the incident. People refused to talk about the lynching.

Duluth tried to forget.

Just one year before the Duluth incident, a rash of lynchings and race rioting erupted in twenty-five cities throughout the country, including the midwestern cities of Omaha and Chicago. Named the "Red Summer" of 1919, fifteen whites and twenty-three blacks were killed in the Chicago riots alone. From 1889 to 1918 at least 3,224 people were lynched nationwide, 79 percent of them black. The events in Duluth shocked many, but lynching was hardly new to the North. From 1889 to 1918, at least 219 people were lynched in Northern states. There have been at least twenty lynching deaths in Minnesota history. Of this number, the only black victims were the three men killed in Duluth on June 15, 1920. The shock of the lynchings spurred Minnesota's black community to press for a state antilynching bill. Nellie Francis, a prominent black activist from St. Paul, led the campaign. Signed into law on April 21, 1921, the bill provided for the removal of police officers negligent in protecting persons in their custody from lynch mobs. The bill also stipulated that damages be paid to the dependents of the person lynched. Antilynching bills existed in several other states. Despite many efforts, however, a national antilynching bill was never passed.

Eighty-three years later, in 2003, a large crowd gathered once again in downtown Duluth. They had come to remember what happened there on June 15, 1920—and to dedicate themselves to work for understanding and compassion between the races so nothing like that would ever happen again.

Two thousand people marched and sang songs of freedom and songs of faith. City leaders unveiled a monument with giant bronze statues of the three lynching victims. An account of the events leading to their deaths was inscribed in stone nearby. Quotations from philosophers, poets, authors, and civil rights activists were etched into stone as well.

The $267,000 monument was impressive and demonstrated the importance this project held in the hearts of the city leaders. But the most touching part of the day came near the end of the two-hour program, when Warren Read of Kingston, Washington, took the podium to address the crowd.

Read's great-grandfather, Louis Dondino, was one of several people imprisoned in the 1920s for inciting the riot that led to the lynchings. Read told the audience that he and his mother didn't know about Dondino's role in the hangings until two years earlier, when he was researching his family's history on the Internet. Read said he was stunned when he learned of his great-grandfather's role in what happened. His voice breaking, Read expressed his heartfelt apology to the victims and their families and to a community that had suffered with the memories. As he sat down, the crowd stood and applauded his courage for admitting that his grandfather had done wrong and his determination to right that wrong. And they applauded his compassion for their pain. Something profound happened in the hearts of many people that day. As shameful deeds were brought to light, forgiveness came in and lit the dark recesses where fear had lurked.

Jim Soderberg, a Duluthian participating in the event, commented, "If two thousand people had shown up eighty-three years ago to say no, [the lynchings] may not have happened."

★ ★ ★

Make this your common practice: Confess your sins to each other and pray for each other so that you can live together whole and healed. The prayer of a person living right with God is something powerful to be reckoned with.
JAMES 5:16 MESSAGE

On the ten-foot wall that surrounds the park and the monument in downtown Duluth are powerful, thought-provoking quotations. Here are a few:

An event has happened, upon which it is difficult to speak and impossible to remain silent.
—EDMUND BURKE

The world is a dangerous place, not because of those who do evil, but because of those who look on and do nothing.
—ALBERT EINSTEIN

There may be times when we are powerless to prevent injustice, but there must never be a time when we fail to protest.
—ELIE WIESEL

He who is devoid of the power to forgive is devoid of the power to love.
—MARTIN LUTHER KING JR.

The Holy Experiment
William Penn
1644–1718

For those in England, the colonies represented one thing: promise. To the entrepreneurial, it beckoned with the siren call of great wealth; to the destitute and desperate, America seemed to welcome them with a chance for a new beginning. The persecuted saw freedom. The wealthy saw dominion. William Penn, thirty-seven years old, saw the rarest of opportunities to attempt something amazing. Owed a familial debt by the Crown, Penn received a charter from King Charles for an expanse of land between the established colonies of New York and Maryland. In this "sylvan" spread of oak, maple, birch, and elm, Penn foreswore to carry out "a holy experiment"—establishing a model state built on the principles of godliness, tolerance, and liberty. Pennsylvania was conceived with nearly unattainable expectations—unattainable, that is, without divine favor.

The morning of September 3, 1682, broke with all the subtlety of a blacksmith's forge. To the east the sun rose, molten and fierce, as Penn stood starboard on his passage across the Atlantic to finally see the land he'd received a charter for over a year ago. Salt spray stung his face, and though the cool wind should have been bracing, he yawned despite himself. He'd stayed up late that evening penning a response to a friend who inquired to his motives with the colony. The words still remained with him:

> *For my country, I eyed the Lord in the obtaining of it, and more was I drawn inward to look to him and to owe it to his hand and power, than to any other way. I have so obtained it, and desire that I may not be unworthy of his love, but do that which may answer his kind providence, and serve his truth and people; that an example may be set up to the nations; there may be room there, though not here, for such an holy experiment.*

He could only imagine his friend's reply. "A Quaker serving as governor of an entire colony? What folly!" Penn chuckled to himself. It was an absurdity. And yet William knew, despite being so drawn to the teachings of the Friends, or Quakers, that he'd never be their truest disciple, their model adherent.

He'd come to the Friends through a message he'd heard delivered by Thomas Loe. At home unexpectedly at his father's estate in Ireland in 1665, Penn heard the words that would become his guiding principle in life: "There is faith that overcometh the world, and there is faith that is overcome by the world." It was a paradoxically strong message to have been preached by the fundamentally meek Quaker, and Penn saw the transcendent power of living a life of submission to God's will in sacrifice, gentleness, and humility. The practice of such a life proved much more difficult.

"It's like watching a lion playing at being a dormouse," a friend teased, and Penn's prowling nature soon found ample room to roam.

The Act of Uniformity, passed by Parliament in 1662, established Anglicanism as the religion of the land and made a gathering of more than five people of any faith illegal and subject to disbanding by force. The Quakers chose to continue meeting and were often fined or even imprisoned for their lawlessness. But where the Friends often bore their punishments in humble acceptance, Penn would not be silenced. His words, his writings such as *The Sandy Foundation Shaken*, and his unceasing efforts to worship as God led landed him, time and again, in prison—time he used merely to further hone his religious and political sensibilities in works like *No Cross, No Crown*, a text replete with calls to honest, unfettered faith.

"And if they couldn't silence me in the Tower [of London], they thought best to place the wide Atlantic between us," Penn noted dryly, his sleepiness finally sloughing off. Terns and gulls cawed about the mast far above, and for a few minutes he watched transfixed as a pod of porpoises dove and danced with playful grace, racing the ship as she rushed to the New World.

The 1682 trip was the first of two voyages he'd make to the colony he governed, the second taken in 1699. Even then he was well at work on the *Frames of Government*, the founding document that would rest at the heart of Pennsylvania's developing constitution and serve as a template for the expression of all the colonists and Founding Fathers' purest dreams.

Governments, like clocks, go from the motion men give them; and as governments are made and moved by men, so by them they are ruined too. . . . Let men be good, and the government cannot be bad; if it will be ill, they will cure it.

He would never spend as much time in America as he wanted, only four years in the two trips, but in his time he accomplished much. He purchased land for his estate from the Leni-Lenape Indians and signed a treaty of friendship with the Delaware Indians. On his second return, he freed all his slaves at his estate, allowing them to remain as tenants on the land. And his *Frames of Government* offered a strong beginning for the freedoms—freedom of speech and religion, the right to self-government—that would continue to be valued so highly in the coming push toward independence.

★ ★ ★

Did Penn's "holy experiment" work? Perhaps not to his wildest imaginings. It was never paradise on earth. But his guiding sense and call to sincere and godly living affected the colony and the world profoundly. Penn himself christened Philadelphia the "City of Brotherly Love"—which later became the anvil on which an unbroken chain of patriots would be forged. His legacy surges forward, like the prow of a ship headed toward destiny, in every faith that dares to overcome the world. In quiet sacrifice. In raucous challenge. Or in the vision to point to God's everlasting truth and say, "We are all part of this holy experiment."

I love America because America is not just a country, it's an idea. You see my country, Ireland, is a great country, but it's not an idea. America is an idea, but it's an idea that brings with it some baggage, like power brings responsibility. It's an idea that brings with it equality, but equality even though it's the highest calling, is the hardest to reach. The idea that anything is possible, that's one of the reasons why I'm a fan of America. It's like hey, look there's the moon up there, lets take a walk on it, bring back a piece of it. That's the kind of America that I'm a fan of.

In 1771 your founder Mr. Franklin spent three months in Ireland and Scotland to look at the relationship they had with England to see if this could be a model for America, whether America should follow their example and remain a part of the British Empire. Franklin was deeply, deeply distressed by what he saw. In Ireland he saw how England had put a stranglehold on Irish trade, how absentee English landlords exploited Irish tenant farmers and how those farmers in Franklin's words "lived in retched hovels of mud and straw, were clothed in rags and subsisted chiefly on potatoes." Not exactly the American dream … So instead of Ireland becoming a model for America, America became a model for Ireland. . . .

—BONO, LEAD SINGER OF U2,

in his commencement address to the 2004 University of Pennsylvania graduating class on May 17, 2004

State Constitutions

It's not just the Declaration of Independence and the U.S. Constitution that call on the name of the Almighty for divine guidance in governing the nation. In fact, the preambles—or in some cases the first chapter, part, or article—to the constitutions from every state in the Union include similar acknowledgments.

This is true for the first state in the Union, Delaware: *Through Divine goodness, all men have by nature the rights of worshiping and serving their Creator according to the dictates of their consciences. . . .*

It's true for the last state admitted to the Union, Hawaii: *We, the people of Hawaii, grateful for Divine Guidance . . . do hereby ordain and establish this constitution for the State of Hawaii.*

For the upper Pacific West, Washington: *We, the people of the State of Washington, grateful to the Supreme Ruler of the Universe for our liberties, do ordain this constitution.*

The deep Atlantic South, Florida: *We, the people of the State of Florida, being grateful to Almighty God for our constitutional liberty. . . do ordain and establish this constitution.*

And the geographic center of the country, Kansas: *We, the people of Kansas, grateful to Almighty God for our civil and religious privileges, in order to insure the full enjoyment of our rights as American citizens, do ordain and establish this constitution of the state of Kansas. . . .*

Every state in the country that you set foot in has, at its core, a recognition of the importance of God in daily life and especially in the decisions that will govern us as people. From Maine to California, Minnesota to Louisiana, we are truly a nation under God.

To read the portions of all fifty state constitutions that acknowledge God, visit *www.undergodthebook.com.*

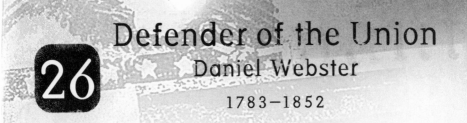

Defender of the Union
Daniel Webster
1783–1852

26

The year was 1820 and the place was Plymouth Rock. A large crowd had come to celebrate the two-hundredth anniversary of the Pilgrims' landing and to hear Daniel Webster's inspiring words. They were not disappointed.

Daniel gave honor, respect, and reverence to his Pilgrim forefathers, for their sufferings, their labors, their virtues and godliness, and "those principles of civil and religious liberty, which they encountered the dangers of the ocean, the storms of heaven, the violence of savages, disease, exile, and famine, to enjoy and to establish."

He then challenged his own generation "to transmit the great inheritance unimpaired," to do their part to ensure that the freedom and blessings they now enjoyed would be preserved for their children. And that a hundred years from now, "on the morning of that day. . . the voice of acclamation and gratitude, commencing on the Rock of Plymouth, shall be transmitted through millions of the sons of the Pilgrims, till it lose itself in the murmurs of the Pacific seas."

The crowd rose to its feet; many were touched deeply. Daniel smiled. He enjoyed the thrill of moving an audience with his words. John Adams later wrote concerning Daniel's Plymouth Rock speech: "If there be an American who can read it without tears, I am not that American. It ought to be read at the end of every year, forever and ever."

Daniel's skills in speaking and debate soon won him first place among American orators. But Daniel had not always enjoyed public speaking. As a child he was brilliant, and from an early age he loved to read. He later recalled, "I do not remember when or by whom I was taught to read, because I cannot recall a time when I could not read the Bible." In the schools near the frontier town of Salisbury, New Hampshire, where Daniel grew up, he often knew more than the teachers in charge.

When Daniel was fourteen, his father was able to send him to Phillips Exeter Academy. But ashamed of his rough clothing and frontier manners, Daniel became painfully shy. He did well with his studies—except for public speaking. Week after week his teacher would call his name to speak before the group.

"Mr. Daniel Webster."

Week after week Daniel prepared his message carefully. On Monday he would tell himself, "I'm going to do it this week!" By Tuesday he would have his topic prepared. On Wednesday, he would begin to practice it to perfection. But Thursday night he couldn't sleep. And Friday he couldn't eat breakfast or lunch. And every Friday afternoon, it would happen again. Daniel later said, "I could never command sufficient resolution to leave my seat!"

At age fifteen Daniel entered Dartmouth College. Before his first year at Dartmouth was over, he won his battle with shyness—and began to make a name for himself as a powerful debater. A classmate remembered, "In his movements, he was rather slow and deliberate—except when his feelings were aroused. Then his whole soul would kindle into a flame. . . . No one ever thought of equaling the vigor and flow of his eloquence." Later, in his career as a lawyer, Daniel's skills were so exceptional that attorneys would sometimes withdraw from a case rather than face Webster's genius.

Daniel carefully prepared both his arguments and his voice. His wonderful intonation was low and musical when he was simply talking, but in passionate debate it became resonant and loud, the high tones clear as a trumpet, the low ones rumbling like a pipe organ.

Webster believed that to become a great orator one must study the Word of God, and he regularly practiced his own oratory by reciting the Bible aloud. Visitors often gathered just to hear Daniel Webster read the Bible.

The crowd's favorite was to hear him read from the book of Job, for Webster would read that book dramatically, first taking the part of Job and then answering as one of Job's friends. At the end of the book, when God entered the debate, Webster's voice would thunder and boom, and it seemed as if the doors would rattle off their hinges as he recited the words spoken by the Almighty. "Then the Lord answered Job out of the whirlwind, and said, Who is this that darkeneth counsel by words without knowledge? Gird up now thy loins like a man; for I will demand of thee, and answer thou me. Where wast thou when I laid the foundations of the earth?"

Daniel served his Union, first representing New Hampshire in the House of Representatives between 1813 and 1816, and then representing Massachusetts in the Senate beginning in 1827.

The focus of his legal and political career was his great love for the Constitution of the United States. The man who would become famous as the leading defender of the Constitution and the Union found his specialty early. When he was eight, he used his life savings to buy a cotton handkerchief on which was printed the Constitution of the United States. He studied it thoroughly, later recalling, "There is not an article, a section, a phrase, a word, a syllable, or even a comma of that Constitution that I did not study and ponder in every relation and in every construction of which it was susceptible."

Again and again, Daniel would be unanimously chosen as the right man at the right place at the right time to defend the Union and the Constitution. Perhaps the best-known occurrence happened by "coincidence." Although Daniel was a senator from Massachusetts, he had been deeply involved in arguing a case before the Supreme Court and had not been following the Senate's debate. But the Supreme Court had adjourned early that afternoon, and Daniel "just happened" to stop by the Senate chambers. As he listened to Senator Hayne from South Carolina, he became alarmed. The real issue being debated here was one of tremendous importance. Behind the issues of "state rights" and "nullification," the real question was: Could a state decide which federal laws they would obey—and which they wouldn't?

Although Daniel was unprepared—and Senator Hayne had had months to prepare his message—Daniel felt equal to the task of defending the Union. During the next two days, Senator Hayne gave one of the greatest speeches ever heard in the Senate chambers. His magnificent delivery, combined with his logic and the progression of his reasoning, impressed everyone who heard him.

Gloom descended on Daniel's supporters. Hayne had outdone himself, and Daniel had only one evening to prepare his rebuttal. Still, Daniel did not seem anxious. When Supreme Court Justice Joseph Story stopped by to offer his assistance, Webster smiled and shook his head. "Give yourself no uneasiness, Judge Story: I will grind him as fine as a pinch of snuff." God had seen ahead and provided: Daniel had already prepared detailed notes on the subject for another purpose. Webster later said, "If Hayne had tried to make a speech to fit my notes, he could not have hit it any better."

The Senate chamber was filled to capacity the next morning. When Daniel rose to speak, an expectant hush fell over the room. He began to speak calmly and with great strength. Eyewitnesses later remarked, "A deep-seated conviction of the extraordinary character of the emergency, and of his ability to control it, seemed to possess him wholly."

Daniel reminded his audience that the power behind the Constitution did not come from the various state legislatures, but from

"We, the people of the United States." He showed the absurdity of having the laws of our national government subject to twenty-four state governments, "each at liberty to decide for itself, and none bound to respect the decisions of others, and each at liberty, too, to give a new construction on every election of its own members."

In closing, he turned and looked at our flag. "Behold the gorgeous ensign of the republic, now known and honored throughout the earth. . . not a stripe erased or polluted, not a single star obscured, bearing for its motto, no such miserable interrogatory as 'What is all this worth?' nor those other words of delusion and folly, 'Liberty first and Union afterwards'; but everywhere, spread all over in characters of living light, blazing on all its ample folds, as they float over the sea and over the land, and in every wind under the whole heavens, that other sentiment, dear to every true American heart, 'Liberty and Union, now and for ever, one and inseparable!'"

Daniel sat down to complete silence. An observer remarked, "The feeling was too overpowering to allow expression by voice or hand. It was as if one was in a trance, all motion paralyzed." Under God's grace Daniel presented the real issues so plainly and eloquently that no one could argue or misunderstand. Webster's oration dramatically affected many Americans, reminding them of the value and sacredness of union.

Despite Daniel's historic speech, the nullification issue continued to gain momentum. In 1832 South Carolina nullified the Tariff of 1832, and President Andrew Jackson threatened to send in troops to enforce the law. John Calhoun and Henry Clay achieved a compromise tariff that pacified both sides and put off the question of nullification, which was ultimately decided by the Civil War.

Many thought Daniel Webster should be elected president, but it was not to be. In 1852 he retired to his beloved home on the Massachusetts coast. For nine miles before he entered its gates, friends scattered flowers in front of his carriage to honor him and welcome him home. Just before he died, this great defender of the Union whispered, "My wish has been to do my Maker's will. I thank Him now for all the mercies that surround me."

* * *

Posterity—you will never know how much
it has cost my generation to preserve your
freedom. I hope you will make good use of it.
—JOHN QUINCY ADAMS

Our ancestors established their system of government
on morality and religious sentiment. . . . Whatever makes
a man a good Christian also makes a good citizen.
—DANIEL WEBSTER

The Star-Spangled Banner

Born in Maryland in 1779, Francis Scott Key was greatly influenced by the Christian example of his grandmother. As he grew into adulthood, Key held fast to his faith, and he never failed to conduct family prayers in his home twice a day. Through his involvement in the American Sunday School Union, Key was instrumental in planting thousands of Sunday schools in settlements throughout the Midwest.

Two years into the War of 1812, after a British attack on Washington, D.C., Key—now a well-respected lawyer with a thriving practice—was called to Baltimore to arrange the release of a civilian prisoner on the British flagship *Tonnant*. He took with him Colonel John Skinner, an experienced negotiator. Their timing couldn't have been worse. Once aboard ship, they overheard the British military's plans to attack Baltimore's Fort McHenry. Even though Key and Skinner had successfully negotiated the prisoner's release, the three men were detained.

Key and his companions were helpless to do anything as the attack began on the morning of September 13, 1814. For twenty-five hours the bombardment continued. During a brief break in the shellfire, at twilight on September 14, Key spotted the magnificent, thirty-by-forty-two-foot, fifteen-star flag of the United States, flying high over Fort McHenry. And when the attack resumed, as long as Key could see and hear the fireworks, he knew Fort McHenry had not surrendered. But then, well into the night, an almost eerie silence descended upon the harbor. Had Fort McHenry fallen? In the predawn darkness Key anxiously awaited any news, any sign of his countrymen's survival. Finally, as dawn broke, Key could see that the flag was still there!

An amateur poet, and so inspired by the glorious sight before him, Key began to write. Originally published as "The Defense of Fort McHenry," Key's poem was set to the English drinking tune "To Anacreon in Heaven" and instantly resonated with Americans. For more than one hundred years "The Star-Spangled Banner" was simply one of many popular patriotic airs, until finally, in 1931, the stirring song was officially adopted as our national anthem.

One Life to Lose
Nathan Hale

1755–1776

27

"I only regret that I have but one life to lose for my country."
Tradition states that Nathan Hale said this before his hanging on September 22, 1776. Unfortunately, he himself didn't write it down. It was passed on secondhand, thirdhand, cousin-of-an-uncle-of-a-friend-of-a-brother-style until it made it into the annals of history.

"I only regret that I have but one life to lose for my country."

If Hale did say it, he was likely quoting act 4 of a popular 1773 play by Joseph Addison titled *Cato*, about the life of the great Roman Stoic Cato the Younger. If it was attributed to Hale by someone paying him honor, then they were borrowing the phrasing.

The proof isn't in the words themselves, but in the life that led up to the words. That phrase, no matter how pithy, would have been meaningless in the mouth of Benedict Arnold. Instead, it came from a talented, whip-smart, devoted young man who sacrificed everything for the cause of freedom.

"I only regret that I have but one life to lose for my country."

It doesn't matter if the words weren't original to Nathan Hale. More important, he lived them.

Hale attended Yale College, graduated with the intent of eventually heading to seminary, but first took up teaching at a boy's grammar school in Connecticut. With a liberality that belied the times, he also offered classes to the sisters of his students in the name of better educating the women of the country. Those classes started very early, yet they were always filled, partly because of the astounding opportunity and partly, it is assumed, because Nathan was young, single, and apparently quite handsome.

New England sat at the epicenter of revolutionary rumblings and flare-ups, though, and it was not long before he enlisted to play his part. He served as a first lieutenant, and then after General Washington's reorganization, as captain, with many of his men choosing to stay under him. Finally in September 1776, Hale joined the "Knowlton Rangers," a special-ops group of only the finest men. It was to these men that General Washington turned for a dangerous mission.

New York City was about to be lost to the British. Worse, Washington had no idea at all about the size of the British troops or any information about an attack that would help defend what would remain. He wanted a spy to infiltrate and report.

Nathan Hale became that spy. Against the counsel of friends, he crossed over in a longboat to Long Island in early September dressed as a British citizen. He carried a notebook for his observances, which he scribbled in Latin, and his diploma. He was pretending to look for work as a teacher. The plan was to stay for about two weeks and then meet the boat again on September 20.

Hale passed the wary fortnight with success, and he had gathered a parcel of crucial information by the time he was to cross back to safety. The night broke cool and brought in with it mist. Hale slipped from the crowds milling about near the shore and found his way to a rough path that traced along the bay. He found the rock where he'd disembarked, pulled a lantern from his satchel, and readied his signal. The darkness pulled in at him. Frogs croaked with last desperation before winter. Otherwise all was silent. Finally, when it seemed he could wait no longer, there was the splash of oars off in the mist. In a minute the dusky shadow of a boat emerged, and Hale raised the blind off his lantern, the prearranged signal. He waited for a reply.

There was none. The boat beat on, turning now toward shore. Toward him. In a minute he saw his horrible mistake. It was a landing boat off a British schooner. Two men pulled at the oars and a third stood at the bow, ready to leap. Hale's suspicious signal had been enough cause for them to pursue him, and now he ran, confirming his guilt. They gave chase and soon apprehended him.

His notes, still on him, condemned him.

On the day of his execution, he asked to speak to a pastor and was denied. He asked to see a Bible but was denied.

That evening, he was hung.

★ ★ ★

"I only regret that I have but one life to lose for my country."

Those may have been Hale's final words—or not. But that shouldn't be his legacy. It shouldn't be what he means to us. Instead, we should see a young man who counted sacrifice an honor and put the call of a nation in front of himself. Nathan Hale was saying he would have done *exactly* the same thing again if given the chance. That is Nathan Hale's story. Whether he said it or not.

> Those who sacrifice essential liberty for temporary
> safety are not deserving of either liberty or safety.
> —BENJAMIN FRANKLIN

Did You Know?

* A paid minister, whose salary has been paid by taxpayers since 1789, opens every session of Congress with prayer.

* Bible verses are etched in stone all over the federal buildings and monuments throughout Washington, D.C.

* Fifty-two of the fifty-five founders of the Constitution were members of the established orthodox churches in the colonies.

* Thomas Jefferson worried that the courts would overstep their authority and instead of interpreting the law would begin making law—an oligarchy, the rule of few over many.

* The very first Supreme Court Justice, John Jay, said, "Americans should select and prefer Christians as their rulers."

Laus Deo

* The Washington Monument in Washington, D.C., is topped by an aluminum cap, upon which are etched two words: *Laus Deo*. What do they mean? "Praise be to God."

* On the 140-foot landing of the monument, a memorial stone is inscribed with a prayer from the city of Baltimore: "May Heaven to this union continue its beneficence; may brotherly affection with union be perpetual; may the free constitution which is the work of our ancestors be sacredly maintained and its administration be stamped with wisdom and with virtue."

* Inscribed in a memorial stone on the 220-foot landing is a eulogy of George Washington, presented by Christians from Ningpo, Chekiang Province, China.

* On the 260-foot landing, memorial stones presented by Sunday school children from New York and Philadelphia quote Proverbs 10:7, Proverbs 22:6, and Luke 17:6.

* Within the cornerstone, laid on July 4, 1848, rests the Holy Bible, presented by the Bible Society.

In a letter to the governors of the thirteen states, upon the close of the Revolutionary War, George Washington offered the following benediction:

I now make it my earnest prayer that God would have you, and the State over which you preside, in his holy protection; that he would incline the hearts of the citizens to cultivate a spirit of subordination and obedience to government, to entertain a brotherly affection and love for one another... and finally that he would most graciously be pleased to dispose us all to do justice, to love mercy, and to demean ourselves with that charity, humility, and pacific temper of mind, which were the characteristics of the Divine Author of our blessed religion, and without an humble imitation of whose example in these things, we can never hope to be a happy nation.

Empowered to Persuade
Patrick Henry
1736–1799

28

Patrick Henry had experienced this incredible feeling before. As he sat in his pew at Saint John's Church in Richmond, Virginia, listening to the other honored delegates selected to speak at the Second Revolutionary Convention of Virginia, he once again felt the fire in his bones, the tingle on his skin, and the urgency in his heart.

The first time he had experienced this, his life was changed forever. Before that moment, Patrick was a young man of fine Christian character, the best fiddler, the best storyteller in the county—but he could not earn a living for his wife and children. He tried storekeeping and farming but failed repeatedly.

At age twenty-three Patrick studied law and passed the state examinations to be a lawyer, but he was still unknown—and poor. Finally he landed a case no one else wanted. Virginia had passed a law limiting the salaries of clergymen—to discourage "professional churchmen" who were just in it for the money. But the king of England declared Virginia's law "null and void." The professional churchmen then sued the tax collectors for back pay—which meant that the land owners would have to pay more taxes.

Patrick stood before the court, shabby, timid, and awkward, speaking slowly, almost stopping at times. His clients, the land owners, hung their heads; the judge, Patrick's own father, covered his face with his hand.

Then, in a flash, the "feeling" hit. Patrick stood tall; his words rang out, clear and strong. "This case is not about clergymen who don't care for their congregations. It is about the rights of a people to govern themselves." With patriotic fervor Patrick thundered, "When a king overturns such beneficial laws, he degenerates into a tyrant and forfeits all right to his subjects' obedience." For several minutes he spoke on freedom and government and America. He held his listeners spellbound—tears streamed down their faces. When he stopped, the jury went out to deliberate, only to return in five minutes to award to the greedy churchmen damages...of only one penny. The crowd cheered and carried Patrick out on their shoulders.

That evening Patrick tried to explain to his wife what had happened to him. "It was as when Samson battled a thousand Philistines with the jawbone of a donkey. Or when Peter spoke on Pentecost, or Stephen spoke to the Jewish council. I was more than myself, more than just Patrick Henry. God's power came upon me." That night in their devotions, the family gave God heartfelt thanks. And Patrick dedicated himself anew to follow after God's will, both for himself and for his country. Patrick Henry had discovered his purpose, his destiny.

During his career as a lawyer, Patrick Henry developed the custom of spending one hour each day in prayer. This hour—at sunset—was sacred, never to be intruded upon. This time was followed by devotions with his family. On Sunday evenings he would read aloud from a book of sermons, and then the family would sing hymns together, accompanied by Patrick on his violin. He continued these customs until the closing days of his life, when, due to weakness, he could no longer lead his family in worship. Instead he lengthened his hour of prayer at sunset. In his will Patrick wrote, "This is all the inheritance I can give to my dear family. The religion of Christ can give them one which will make them rich indeed."

Suddenly he was in demand as a lawyer—and as a politician. He was elected to Virginia's House of Burgesses, where he experienced God's power on his words for the second time. He electrified the assembly by boldly affirming Virginia's right to set her own taxes. At the end he exclaimed, "Caesar had his Brutus, Charles the First his Cromwell, and George the Third—"

"Treason! Treason!" shouted the king's friends.

"And George the Third may profit by their example!" He folded his arms and stood tall. "If that be treason, make the most of it!"

As Virginia's representative to the First Continental Congress, God's power—evident in Patrick's words of unity—thrilled the delegates as Patrick declared, "The distinctions between Virginians, Pennsylvanians, New Yorkers, and New Englanders are no more. I am not a Virginian, but an American!"

Over the years Patrick had grown to understand how God moved through him and how to yield to the Holy Spirit to say what God wanted said when He wanted to say it.

Now, sitting among the delegates at the Second Revolutionary Convention, Patrick knew it was time to speak. As he rose to his feet, there was a stir among his listeners. By custom, he addressed himself to the Convention's president, Peyton Randolph of Williamsburg. First acknowledging the great patriotism and abilities of those who argued that war with Britain may still be prevented, Patrick then stated:

> *Mr. President . . . Should I keep back my opinions at such a time, through fear of giving offense, I should consider myself as guilty of treason towards my country, and of an act of disloyalty toward the Majesty of Heaven, which I revere above all earthly kings.*
>
> *Sir, we have done everything that could be done to avert the storm which is now coming on. There is no longer any room for hope. If we wish to be free . . . we must fight! An appeal to arms and to the God of hosts is all that is left us!*
>
> *They tell us, sir, that we are weak. . . . Sir, we are not weak. . . . The millions of people, armed in the holy cause of liberty, and in such a country as we possess, are invincible by any force which our enemy can send against us.*
>
> *Besides, sir, we shall not fight our battles alone. There is a just God who presides over the destinies of nations. . . . The battle, sir, is not to the strong alone; it is to the vigilant, the active, the brave. Besides, sir . . . it is now too late to retire from the contest. There is no retreat but in submission*

and slavery! . . . The war is inevitable—and let it come! I repeat it, sir, let it come. . . .

. . . The next gale that sweeps from the north will bring to our ears the clash of resounding arms! Our brethren are already in the field! Why stand we here idle? What is it that gentlemen wish? What would they have? Is life so dear, or peace so sweet, as to be purchased at the price of chains and slavery? Forbid it, Almighty God! I know not what course others may take; but as for me, give me liberty or give me death!

The delegates' response was instant and wholehearted. They voted to take their place by Massachusetts in the fight for freedom.

Patrick Henry served as a delegate to the Second Continental Congress and as governor of Virginia for three terms. Then, his health failing, he retired to his plantation at Red Hill.

Patrick Henry was to experience the power of God moving through him to set the course for his country once more before he died. In 1799 George Washington wrote to him, asking for his help. Virginia was protesting laws passed by Congress, declaring that a state could accept or reject the federal laws at will. Washington asked him to speak on behalf of a strong union. The whole countryside came to hear him speak on the Charlottesville courthouse steps.

He began his speech as a bent old man who spoke with a cracked, shrill voice. Then the power of God took hold of him, and by the end his head was erect, his blue eyes flashed, and his clear voice rang out over the thousands of listeners. His theme was "Let us preserve our strength united against whatever foreign nation may dare to enter our territory." At the end of his speech, he was carried—half-fainting—into the courthouse. He returned home never to leave again.

Listen as wisdom calls out!
Hear as understanding raises her voice!. . .

"I, Wisdom, live together with good judgment.
I know where to discover knowledge and discernment.
. . . Good advice and success belong to me. Insight and
strength are mine. Because of me, kings reign,
and rulers make just laws. Rulers lead with my help,
and nobles make righteous judgments.

"I love all who love me. Those who search for me will
surely find me. Unending riches, honor, wealth, and
justice are mine to distribute. My gifts are better than
the purest gold, my wages better than sterling silver!
I walk in righteousness, in paths of justice. Those who
love me inherit wealth, for I fill their treasuries. . . .

"Happy are those who listen to me, watching for me
daily at my gates, waiting for me outside my home!
For whoever finds me finds life and wins approval
from the Lord. But those who miss me have injured
themselves. All who hate me love death."
PROVERBS 8:1, 12, 14–21, 34–36 NLT

29

With Regrets
Benedict Arnold
1741–1801

Benedict Arnold lay dying on his bed in England, filled with sadness as he reviewed his life. Once, he was the talk of the nation for his boldness in battle. Known for attacking the British against overwhelming odds—and winning—he was an American Revolutionary War hero second only to George Washington himself. Courageous and daring, his name had once struck terror in the hearts of British soldiers.

Now his name had come to mean "traitor" to a whole nation. *How has it come to this?* The old man recalled the events as though it were yesterday. . . .

He had been promoted to general and given command of West Point, one of the most strategic American strongholds in the Revolutionary War. On September 21, 1780, Arnold slipped out of the fort to meet with British Major John André at a spot between the American and British battle lines. There, he gave André—who was dressed as a civilian—complete drawings of West Point and detailed plans that would guarantee a victorious British attack on the fort. All was settled, and Arnold was promised twenty thousand pounds for his treachery. The two went their separate ways. But André discovered the British ship that had brought him north to West Point had been attacked by the Americans and forced to turn back toward New York. He was stranded miles from the British lines. He was able to pass through several roadblocks of American guards using a pass given him by General Arnold, but two days later, he was still in the saddle, trying to get back to his countrymen.

At last he saw them in the distance—the familiar red coats could not be mistaken. With great relief he rode toward the British line, only to be stopped by a patrol of three young militiamen.

Supposing them to be loyalists, André stopped to chat and let it be known that he was a British officer in disguise.

To his dismay, he discovered the militiamen were Americans. They immediately ordered André searched and found the detailed drawings of West Point and the pass signed by General Arnold in his shoe. They took him to their commanding officer, who planned to send him back to West Point so General Arnold could question him.

Fortunately, Major Benjamin Tallmadge, General Washington's chief of intelligence, happened to be in the area. When he heard about the capture of the spy, he immediately figured out what was going on, for he had long suspected General Arnold of selling secrets to the British. When he questioned André, the truth came out. It was too late to stop the news of André's capture from reaching General Arnold, who was able to escape. But West Point was saved.

Arnold recalled as he had countless times before: His carefully laid plan had almost worked. They had been so close! What if the young militiamen hadn't been there to stop André? What if André hadn't let it slip that he was a British officer? What if Tallmadge, the only man who suspected Arnold was a traitor, had not been passing through the area? The British would have attacked, and West Point would have fallen. The American army would have been divided and conquered. The Revolutionary War would have been an unsuccessful colonial revolt against the most powerful empire in the world. The colonial leaders would be hung as traitors. Arnold would be known around the world as a great British war hero who had single-handedly turned the course of the war! He could well be living in luxury as governor of the once-again-peaceful American colonies instead of in this hovel in England, despised by both Americans and Englishmen.

Where had he gone wrong?

He remembered all the reasons he'd turned against the colonists. In 1775 he had used his own personal savings and credit to fight in Massachusetts, but the colony refused to reimburse him. This was so unfair that Congress, with all its poverty, voted to pay him eight hundred dollars. Then in 1777 Congress insulted him by promoting five less-experienced men to the rank of major general. He would have resigned if General Washington had not personally begged him to stay. Washington, the only one who believed in him and valued his bravery, immediately demanded an explanation from Congress and emphasized Arnold's extraordinary leadership.

Arnold's face softened when he thought of General Washington, who had been like a father to him. Washington believed that with God on their side, nothing was impossible—not even taking on the entire British Empire. To be around Washington was to catch his infectious faith in the American cause.

Then, sorrow upon sorrows, Arnold remembered how he had betrayed Washington. He was not able to live on the small salary of a Continental officer, and his debts were piling up. He had diverted food and supplies bound for the starving, dying soldiers at Valley Forge and sold it, keeping the money. His cheeks flushed with shame.

Once he had started down that path, Arnold found it became easier and easier to act against his conscience. It was a small step from embezzling American supplies to offering to sell military secrets to the British. Arnold knew General André from a time when they had both lived in Philadelphia. He approached the British officer—and soon Arnold and his wife were both spying for America's enemy.

Arnold had turned against the Colonists because he had lost faith that America could win.

Yet against all odds, they had.

I have lived with regrets; I will die with regrets.

It was too late to apologize for his betrayal—Washington had died two years earlier. It was too late to make things right with his country—Arnold was dying and he knew it. Suddenly he remembered his godly mother and the lessons she had taught him as a child. His face brightened. It was not too late to make things right with God. He shut his eyes and prayed. In a moment, the regrets of twenty years lifted.

When he opened his eyes, he knew it was true: Benedict Arnold was forgiven. The sins of the past were forgotten, as though they had never happened. Arnold experienced a peace he had never known. It was time to celebrate! But how? He was dying.

Suddenly he remembered a trunk he had brought with him across the ocean when he returned to England. He had kept it all these years, although shame had prevented him from ever opening it and looking inside. Suddenly he knew why he had never sold it— even when his family was desperate for cash. He had saved its cherished contents for this very moment.

"Margaret," he called to his wife, "get my colonial uniform out of the trunk. I wish to die an American."

★ ★ ★

General Washington called the discovery of Arnold's plot to turn West Point over to the British "a combination of extraordinary circumstances." He added, "In no instance since the commencement of the War has the interposition of Providence appeared more conspicuous."

In Washington's message to his troops concerning Arnold's treason and its discovery, he said: "Treason, of the blackest dye, was yesterday discovered. General Arnold, who commanded at West Point, lost to every sentiment of honor, of public and private obligation, was about to deliver up that important post into the hands of the enemy. . . . Happily the treason has been timely discovered, to prevent the fatal misfortune. The Providential train of circumstances which led to it affords the most convincing proof that the liberties of America are the object of Divine Protection."

On October 18, 1780, Congress set apart a national day of thanksgiving and prayer to call for America's "devout and thankful acknowledgments, more especially in the late remarkable interposition of [God's] watchful providence, in rescuing the person of our Commander in Chief and the army from imminent dangers, at the moment when treason was ripened for execution."

The United Cry
of the Nation
Abraham Lincoln

30

JULY 1863

Things were not going well for the Union armies on July 1, 1863. President Lincoln could not find a general who would fight. The North kept losing battles, even when they outnumbered the Southern soldiers two to one. On June 28, Lincoln had made General George Meade the commander of the Army of the Potomac—making him the fifth general to command the Union army since the outbreak of conflict.

Robert E. Lee, a brilliant military man, had been Lincoln's first choice to be the general-in-chief of the Union army, but Lee had turned him down, choosing to fight for his beloved state of Virginia. Now General Lee and his Army of Northern Virginia were marching toward Washington, D.C. Lee was still undefeated in battle, and everyone in the U.S. capital was worried about what the future might hold.

But Abraham Lincoln was not a man to worry—he was a man who prayed and trusted God. After he was elected president, on the day he left for Washington, D.C., he told friends, "Unless the great God who assisted Washington shall be with me and aid me, I must fail; but if the same Omniscient Mind and Mighty Arm that directed and protected him shall guide and support me, I shall not fail. . . . Let us all pray that the God of our fathers may not forsake us now."

Being the leader of so great a nation in such a time of terrible conflict had pushed Lincoln into an even deeper relationship with God. He wrote, "I have been driven many times upon my knees by the overwhelming conviction that I had nowhere else to go. My own wisdom, and that of all about me, seemed insufficient for that day."

So with General Lee marching toward the capital and a new commander in charge of its defense, Lincoln prayed. He humbled himself before "the Almighty God, the beneficent Creator and Ruler of the universe," and prayed for his country.

His prayers were answered: Lee was stopped at Gettysburg, the battle that marked the turning point of the war.

Immediately following the battle, Union General Daniel Sickles asked President Lincoln, "Were you anxious about the battle at Gettysburg?"

President Lincoln replied that he was not worried and then explained: "In the pinch of your campaign up there, when everybody seemed panic-stricken, and nobody could tell what was going to happen . . . I went to my room one day, and I locked the door, and got down on my knees before Almighty God, and prayed to Him mightily for victory at Gettysburg.

"I told Him that this was His war, and our cause His cause, but we couldn't stand another Fredericksburg or Chancellorsville. And I then and there made a solemn vow to Almighty God, that if He would stand by you boys at Gettysburg, I would stand by Him.

"And after that . . . soon a sweet comfort crept into my soul that God Almighty had taken the whole business into His own hands and that things would go all right at Gettysburg. And that is why I had no fears about you."

Lincoln was not the only one praying. He had proclaimed April 30, 1863, to be a national day of fasting, humiliation, and prayer. He requested that "all the people abstain on that day from their ordinary secular pursuits and unite . . . in keeping the day holy to the Lord."

Here is part of Lincoln's Presidential Proclamation:

We know that by His divine law, nations . . . are subjected to punishments . . . in this world. May we not justly fear that the awful calamity of civil war which now desolates the land may be a punishment inflicted upon us for our presumptuous sins, to the needful end of our national reformation as a whole people?

We have been the recipients of the choicest bounties of heaven; we have been preserved these many years in peace and prosperity; we have grown in numbers, wealth and power as no other nation has ever grown.

But we have forgotten God. We have forgotten the gracious hand which preserved us in peace and multiplied and enriched and strengthened us, and we have vainly imagined, in the deceitfulness of our hearts, that all these blessings were produced by some superior wisdom and virtue of our own. . . . We have become too self-sufficient to feel the necessity of redeeming and preserving grace, too proud to pray to the God that made us.

It behooves us, then, to humble ourselves before the offended Power, to confess our national sins, and to pray for clemency and forgiveness. . . .

All this being done in sincerity and truth, let us then rest humbly in the hope authorized by the divine teachings, that the united cry of the nation will be heard on high, and answered with blessings no less than the pardon of our national sins, and the restoration of our now divided and suffering country to its former happy condition of unity and peace.

The "united cry of the nation" that Lincoln asked for was heard by God. A chain of events was set in motion that would turn the tide of war in favor of the North.

Two months later, July 1–3, 1863, General Lee's army was stopped at Gettysburg, a major victory for the North.

The day after that, on July 4, 1863, Vicksburg, the last Confederate stronghold on the Mississippi River, surrendered to General Ulysses S. Grant and the Army of the West. With the Union now in control of the Mississippi, the Confederacy was cut off from its western allies and effectively split in two.

On July 15, 1863, President Lincoln asked for a day of national thanksgiving, praise, and prayer, exhorting citizens to thank "the Divine Majesty for the wonderful things He has done in the nation's behalf, to invoke the influence of His Holy Spirit to subdue the anger which has produced...a needless and cruel rebellion, to guide the counsels of government, and to visit with tender care and consolation all those who [because of the war] suffer in mind, body, or estate."

A man of prayer himself, Lincoln set the example for the whole nation. During his presidency, which lasted only four years and six weeks, Lincoln called for a total of three days of national humiliation and prayer and six days of national thanksgiving, praise, and prayer.

★ ★ ★

Another Day of Prayer

Eighty-eight years earlier, another day of prayer resulted in turning the tide of war. On April 18, 1775, British General Thomas Gage secretly planned a raid on the patriots' ammunition stores at Concord, Massachusetts. Providentially, Dr. Joseph Warren heard of the general's plans and sent Paul Revere and William Dawes to ride through the countryside that night to sound the alarm.

The Battle of Lexington took place the next morning. The farmers' brief battle with the British was over quickly, but it bought time for the patriots at Concord to hide their guns and ammunition and gather the minutemen. The Concord farmers defended themselves well. They forced the British into retreat while the Americans shot at them from behind the cover of stone walls, hedges, and trees. By the time their reinforcements came, the British were exhausted and nearly out of bullets. They lost 273 men on that day; the Americans lost 93. The victory clearly and gloriously belonged to the Americans.

The people in Lexington and Concord believed that the providential hand of God had moved for them—in the discovery of the British plot, in the warnings delivered, in the timing of the battles, in God's protection. What they probably did not know was that the entire colony of Connecticut was praying for them. Governor Jonathan Trumball had proclaimed that very day, April 19, 1775, as a day of prayer and fasting for all the colonies. His proclamation asked that God "would restore, preserve, and secure the Liberties of this and all the other British American colonies and make the Land a mountain of Holiness and Habitation of Righteousness forever."

★ ★ ★

Declare a holy fast, call a special meeting, get the leaders together, Round up everyone in the country. Get them into God's Sanctuary for serious prayer to God.

JOEL 1:14 THE MESSAGE

If my people, which are called by my name, shall humble themselves, and pray, and seek my face, and turn from their wicked ways; then will I hear from heaven, and will forgive their sin, and will heal their land.

2 CHRONICLES 7:14 KJV

My great concern is not whether God is on our side. My great concern is to be on God's side.

—ABRAHAM LINCOLN

The Gettysburg Address

As the train left Washington, the author was still immersed in the contents of his impending speech. He read it and reread it. "Is it too short?" he wondered. And how could he possibly do honor to the tens of thousands of men who had spilled their blood on that historic ground? As the travelers reached the battlefield—now quiet and peaceful, belying the violence and death that had prevailed upon its soil just over four months before—the tall, gaunt figure walked slowly to the podium. Hesitantly, willing himself to push aside his insecurity about the quality of his speech, he began:

Four score and seven years ago our fathers brought forth on this continent a new nation, conceived in liberty and dedicated to the proposition that all men are created equal. Now we are engaged in a great civil war, testing whether that nation or any nation so conceived and so dedicated can long endure. We are met on a great battlefield of that war. We have come to dedicate a portion of that field as a final resting-place for those who here gave their lives that that nation might live. It is altogether fitting and proper that we should do this. But in a larger sense, we cannot dedicate, we cannot consecrate, we cannot hallow this ground. The brave men, living and dead, who struggled here have consecrated it far above our poor power to add or detract. The world will little note nor long remember what we say here, but it can never forget what they did here. It is for us the living, rather, to be dedicated here to the unfinished work which they who fought here have thus far so nobly advanced. It is rather for us to be here dedicated to the great task remaining before us—that from these honored dead we

take increased devotion to that cause for which they
gave the last full measure of devotion—that we here
highly resolve that these dead shall not have died in
vain, that this nation, under God, shall have a new
birth of freedom, and that government of the people, by
the people, for the people shall not perish from the earth.

Lincoln delivered his two-minute Gettysburg Address on November 19, 1863, at the dedication of the cemetery at Gettysburg, the site of the battle that arguably turned the tide of the Civil War in favor of the Union. So short was his message that many in the crowd did not even realize he was speaking until he was done. But so powerful were the words that shone a new light on the Declaration of Independence, a document espousing equality for all people. Just ten months before, on January 1, 1863, Lincoln's Emancipation Proclamation had declared freedom for the slaves. And whereas the Declaration of Independence put forth freedom for all as an *idea*, the Gettysburg Address was a bold step toward making a "new birth of freedom" for all, including the slaves, a *reality*.

The last written draft of the Gettysburg Address contained 265 words. However, as Lincoln stood to deliver the address, he added two words on the spur of the moment: *under God*. Lincoln's eloquent address is considered one of the finest speeches ever delivered by an American, and the addition of just two words reminds us of a truth that we must not subtract from America's equation: Our future will be assured and secured only as we remain under God, in His grace and guidance.

Turning Point

31
Isabella Baumfree—
"Sojourner Truth"
1797–1883

Faneuil Hall, Boston, was packed. Frederick Douglass, a well-known black abolitionist and one of the chief speakers, had been describing the wrongs done to the black race. The longer he spoke, the more excited he became. By the time he reached his conclusion, he was passionate: "Our race has no hope of justice from the whites. We have no possible hope except in our own right arms. It must come to blood! We must fight for ourselves! We must redeem ourselves, or it will never be done."

As he sat down, the crowd pondered his words in silence. Would there *have* to be violence and bloodshed before things changed? Had it come to this? Few in the audience wanted to take this step. Hopelessness filled the hall.

Sojourner Truth was sitting, tall and dark, on the very front seat, facing the platform. In the hush of deep feeling after Douglass finished, she spoke out in her deep, peculiar voice. "Frederick, is God dead?"

The effect was perfectly electrical and flashed through the entire house, changing the whole feeling of the audience. Sojourner did not need to say another word; it was enough.

Few human beings have ever had the power to turn a whole audience by a few simple words the way Sojourner Truth could. Uneducated by the world's standards, she was extremely gifted by God. He would often give her words to speak "in season," and she would boldly speak them out with a power and authority that would turn a situation completely around.

She was born into slavery and named Isabella Baumfree. Describing herself as "the pure African," she was an imposing woman, standing six feet tall with thick, muscular arms. By law, on July 4, 1827, slaves in New York were to be freed. Isabella's master had promised to free her family one year earlier than the legal deadline. When he didn't keep his promise, Isabella left anyway.

That same year, Isabella had a profound encounter with God that changed her life forever:

> *God revealed Himself to me, with all the suddenness of a flash of lightning, showing me that He pervaded the universe. Conscious of my great sin, I wanted to hide, but I plainly saw there was no place, not even in hell, where He was not. I exclaimed aloud, "Oh, God, I did not know You were so big."*
>
> *I desired to talk to God, but my vileness utterly forbade it. I began to wish for someone to speak to God for me. At length a friend appeared to stand between myself and an insulted Deity.*
>
> *"Who are you?" I asked, as the vision brightened into a form distinct, beaming with the beauty of holiness, and radiant with love.*
>
> *"It is Jesus."*
>
> *Before this event, I had heard Jesus mentioned, but thought that He was like any other eminent man, like a Washington or a Lafayette. Now He appeared to my delighted mental vision—and He loved me so much! How strange that He had always loved me, and I had never known it! And how great a blessing He conferred, in that He should stand between me and God!*
>
> *My heart was now as full of joy and gladness, as it had been of terror and despair. The very air sparkled as with diamonds and smelled like heaven.*

After this overwhelming experience, Isabella was always aware of God and totally committed to do His will. She began attending church and, not long afterward, moved to New York City and soon began preaching at camp meetings throughout the city.

In 1843 Isabella had another profound religious experience. The Lord called her to serve Him by traveling around the United States and preaching against greed, alcohol, and other sins so prevalent in the city. It was at this time that Isabella received her new name. In her autobiography she explained: "I went to the Lord and asked him to give me a new name. And the Lord gave me Sojourner [which means 'wanderer'], because I was to travel up and down the land, showing the people their sins, and being a sign unto them." She later said that when she asked God for a new last name, "I heard the word 'Truth'—because I was to declare the truth to the people." From then on, Isabella was known as Sojourner Truth.

For months Sojourner wandered throughout Long Island, New York, Connecticut, and Massachusetts. She finally chose to settle down in a Utopian colony in Northampton, Massachusetts, where she became friends with well-known abolitionists such as William Lloyd Garrison and Frederick Douglass.

In 1850 Sojourner began to travel again throughout the North—this time giving speeches on civil rights for African Americans and women. She consistently pointed her audiences to God—knowing that the only way people can solve such complex problems is to turn to Jesus Christ for the answer.

In 1851, at a women's rights convention in Akron, Ohio, Sojourner gave her most famous speech (see sidebar). In four minutes she refuted every point put forth by male speakers at the convention, who argued that women should not have equal rights because they needed men's protection and because Eve, the first woman, had caused mankind to be expelled from Paradise. Sojourner's "Ain't I a Woman?" speech was the turning point of the convention and became one of the most quoted pieces of oratory in American history.

Later that year, while speaking at Union Village, New York, Sojourner made another famous speech in her unique style:

> *While others have been talking about the poor slave . . . I am going to talk about the poor slave holder. What will happen to him? I'm afraid that he is going to hell unless he changes.*
>
> *My home is open to the man who had held me as a slave and who had so wronged me. I would feed him and take care of him if he was hungry and poor.*

O friends, pity the poor slave holder, and pray for him. It troubles me more than anything else, what will become of the poor slave holder, in all his guilt and all his impenitence. God will take care of the poor trampled slave, but where will the slave holder be when eternity begins?

In 1863 Sojourner traveled to Washington, D.C., to help freed slaves while working with the federal government's Freedmen's Bureau. She taught domestic skills, visited in homes and hospitals, and distributed supplies.

In her years of speaking and public service, Sojourner became one of the most famous black women of the nineteenth century. Blacks and whites both admired her courage, and people repeated lines from her speeches, words that cut through all the rhetoric and went right to the heart of what God wanted to say to keep this nation—a nation under God—on track.

★ ★ ★

But you prophets who have a message from me—
tell it truly and faithfully. What does straw
have in common with wheat?
Nothing else is like God's decree.
Isn't my Message like fire? . . . Isn't it like
a sledgehammer busting a rock?
JEREMIAH 23:28–29 THE MESSAGE

God means what he says. What he says goes.
His powerful Word is sharp as a surgeon's scalpel,
cutting through everything, whether doubt
or defense, laying us open to listen and obey.
HEBREWS 4:12 THE MESSAGE

Ain't I a Woman?

by Sojourner Truth

Well, children, where there is so much racket there must be something out of kilter. I think that 'twixt the negroes of the South and the women at the North, all talking about rights, the white men will be in a fix pretty soon. But what's all this here talking about? That man over there says that women need to be helped into carriages, and lifted over ditches, and to have the best place everywhere. Nobody ever helps me into carriages, or over mud-puddles, or gives me any best place! And ain't I a woman? Look at me! Look at my arm! I have ploughed and planted, and gathered into barns, and no man could head me! And ain't I a woman? I could work as much and eat as much as a man—when I could get it—and bear the lash as well! And ain't I a woman? I have borne thirteen children, and seen most all sold off to slavery, and when I cried out with my mother's grief, none but Jesus heard me! And ain't I a woman? Then they talk about this thing in the head; what's this they call it? [A member of the audience whispers, "Intellect."] That's it, honey. What's that got to do with women's rights or negroes' rights? If my cup won't hold but a pint, and yours holds a quart, wouldn't you be mean not to let me have my little half measure full? Then that little man in black there, he says women can't have as much rights as men, 'cause Christ wasn't a woman! Where did your Christ come from? Where did your Christ come from? From God and a woman! Man had nothing to do with Him. If the first woman God ever made was strong enough to turn the world upside down all alone, these women together ought to be able to turn it back, and get it right side up again! And now they is asking to do it, the men better let them. Obliged to you for hearing me, and now old Sojourner ain't got nothing more to say.

Three Remarkable Women

Clara Barton's extensive list of occupations is impressive: nurse, teacher, education superintendent, U.S. Patent Office copyist, Civil War relief worker, lecturer. . . But she is best known for her work to establish the American Red Cross.

Born on Christmas Day, 1821, in Massachusetts, Clara Barton had the advantage of a middle-class upbringing under the tutelage of four much older siblings. Her soldier father taught her army lore and the belief that "next to Heaven our highest duty is to. . . serve our country and. . .support its laws." For two years Clara nursed an invalid brother, acquiring additional skills that would serve her well.

After a teaching career of eighteen years, Clara moved to Washington, D.C., where she found work in the U.S. Patent Office. Clara began Civil War relief work in 1861 and continued to serve throughout the War and afterward.

In the late 1860s and early 1870s, Clara took her nursing and relief work skills to Europe, joining the International Red Cross in the Franco-Prussian War. She returned home in 1873, bringing with her the vision for the American Red Cross.

The Geneva Convention of 1864 had called for the creation of an international relief organization, but the United States had not yet ratified the treaty. In 1877 Clara began a campaign to raise awareness of the need for such an organization in the U.S. by visiting senators and congressmen, lecturing, even enlisting the help of the Associated Press to generate publicity for her cause.

Finally, in 1882, the U.S. adopted the Geneva Convention, and Clara was able to establish the first American chapter of the Red Cross, of which she became the first president.

Mary McLeod Bethune, known for more than thirty years as the most influential black woman in the United States, made many advances toward the improvement of education for blacks and especially for black women.

Born in 1875, the fifteenth of seventeen children to former slaves, Mary McLeod began her education at a black mission school in South

Carolina. She proved to be a quick study and at age thirteen earned a scholarship to Scotia Seminary, a Presbyterian school for black girls in New Hampshire, where Mary studied to become a teacher.

After holding a series of teaching positions from 1895 to 1903, Mary moved to Daytona Beach, Florida, and in 1904 established the Daytona Normal and Industrial Institute for black girls—which she modeled after Scotia Seminary. The school opened with only five students, but it grew quickly and within two years reached 250 students. Stressing religious and industrial education, Mary also taught the duties and privileges of citizenship—encouraging her students and their families to vote and participate in the social and political issues of the day. Even the Ku Klux Klan could not deter her from leading a successful black voter registration drive in 1920.

In 1923 the Daytona Institute merged with the all-male Cookman Institute of Jacksonville, becoming a coeducational school that in 1929 would be renamed Bethune-Cookman College and retains that name to this day. Mary continued on as the school's president until 1942.

In 1898 Mary had met and married Albertus Bethune, and a year later she gave birth to their only child, Albert. Albertus did not share the missionary goals of his wife, however, and the two separated when Mary moved to Daytona.

During the 1930s and 1940s, Mary assisted both the Roosevelt and Truman administrations, serving on the National Advisory Committee to the National Youth Administration (NYA) and heading up Negro Affairs within the NYA, representing African-American interests, and consulting on civil rights matters. She was also founder and president of the National Council of Negro Women and commander of the Women's Auxiliary Corps of the U.S. Army.

Mary retired in Daytona in 1944, continuing to fight for racial equality until her death in 1955.

Sarah Breedlove—aka Madame C. J. Walker.

At age twenty, Sarah Breedlove found herself a widowed single mother with limited education. Born to a poor Mississippi sharecropping family in 1867, Sarah was orphaned by the death of her parents at age seven. Taken in by her older sister, Sarah endured intolerable cruelty at the hands of her brother-in-law and escaped the oppressive situation at age fourteen by marrying Moses McWilliams. She was eighteen when her daughter, Lelia, was born, and two years later her husband was killed. Knowing there would be more job opportunities in an urban area, Sarah took Lelia to St. Louis, Missouri, where Sarah found work as a cook and washerwoman.

Soon after her move to St. Louis, Sarah's hair began to fall out—a common result of the harsh hair-care routines among African-American women of her day. In an act of desperation, after trying every product she could find, Sarah prayed to God to save her hair. He answered in the form of a dream, in which she received the instructions for preparing a remedy. Some of the ingredients had to be ordered from Africa, but Sarah was determined to follow through. Within a few weeks of first applying the treatment to her scalp, her hair began to grow back. The remedy proved to be successful with Sarah's friends as well, and she began selling her "Wonderful Hair Grower" door-to-door in the African-American community. An enterprise was born.

Sarah moved to Denver, Colorado, in 1905 and continued to develop new products. Her "Glossine" hair oil, "Temple Grower," "Tetter Salve," and hot comb—redesigned to better accomodate African hair—enabled black women to style their hair more easily.

In 1906 Sarah married Charles Joseph Walker, whose newspaper background presented new advertising and promotional opportunities. The marriage did not last, but it did provide a new professional name for Sarah and her company: the Madame C. J. Walker Manufacturing Company.

After the East St. Louis Race Riot in 1917, Madame Walker committed to help fight against the oppression of African Americans. She was a major fund-raiser for the NAACP and its antilynching campaign. She donated to all kinds of black organizations and causes. She even gave the largest contribution to save the home of abolitionist Frederick Douglass.

This cosmetic empire—the largest black-owned company in America—made Walker the first female African-American millionaire and one of the first self-made American women millionaires. By the time she died in 1919, Walker had heavily promoted black businesses, supported numerous civil rights causes, and contributed to black education—particularly for black women.

Denise. Carole. Cynthia. Addie Mae

32

Birmingham Bombing of the Sixteenth Street Baptist Church

SEPTEMBER 15, 1963

Denise McNair. Eleven years old.

Three white men, possibly four or even more, planned and carried out the placement of a bomb consisting of anywhere from fifteen to nineteen sticks of dynamite under the stairs leading to the basement of the Sixteenth Street Baptist Church. At 10:21 AM Sunday, September 15, 1963, Sunday school class was wrapping up in the basement. It was Youth Day, and the children would be leading the day's service. Mrs. Ella Demand was encouraging them, soothing their nerves, telling them God would be proud no matter what.

At 10:22 AM the bomb...exploded.

Denise McNair, eleven, was one of four girls to be killed. She was an inquisitive child, bright and prone to smiling. She was the daughter of a photo shop owner and was still struggling to understand the segregation that divided not only the nation, but especially the city of Birmingham, Alabama.

Carole Robertson. Fourteen years old.

Countless men, women, and children were injured in the bombing. Four died. There is an inclination to write *only four died*, but even the death of just one in an act of such pointless hatred and rage is too many. It may be said that God spared lives that day, but the more pressing point is that God should not have had to welcome any little children to his kingdom at all. Four girls died and that is four too many.

Worse still, the bombing only incited a city that always teetered on the brink of self-immolation. Someone with a sick sense of humor dubbed the city "Bombingham." One particular neighborhood into which blacks were moving became known as "Dynamite Hill," there had been so many explosions. Over eighty bombings, of black homes and churches or those of whites who sympathized, added up in less than a decade. We act today as if we have never had terrorists on our soil before, but Birmingham, Alabama, in the 1950s and 1960s shows us something quite different. They lived among us. If we are white and male, they looked like us, only with hatred in their eyes. They liked to see the city rage. And on that day in September, it did.

After the bombing, black citizens took to the streets in frustration and anger. James Robinson, a sixteen-year-old African-American teen, threw rocks at a gang of white teens, turned to run away, and was shot, fatally, in the back by a Birmingham police officer. Later, another teen, thirteen-year-old Virgil Ware, was shot twice in the chest while riding his bike. His murderer, a white teen of sixteen, served seven months in jail.

The city boiled.

But none of it mattered for Carole Robertson, killed during the blast at the church. Carole, fourteen years old, loved music and dance. She had been dressed up that morning, all in white, to take part in the Youth Day program that never took place.

Cynthia Wesley. *Fourteen years old.*

There was no single event that sparked the bombing, just a long resentment and festering hatred manifested in a single act. Sixteenth Street Baptist Church was an unsurprising target, however, for such violence. For many months prior, the church had become planning central for the civil rights demonstrations that Dr. Martin Luther King Jr. and the Southern Christian Leadership Conference were organizing for the city. "The most segregated city in the nation," King called Birmingham, and it was finally time for decisive action to try to break the almost impenetrable walls established by Governor George Wallace and viciously protected by police chief Eugene "Bull" Connor.

Birmingham was different from most cities, though, and the

black men and women of the city weren't interested in protesting. Too scared, perhaps. Too doubtful that anything could change. King and his colleagues were forced to turn to those who still kept hope—and soon the streets were filled with college students, high school students, even middle-school students. The young protesters would gather across the street from the Sixteenth Streeth Baptist in Kelly Ingram Park and begin their march downtown. On May 3, three months before the bombing, one enormous demonstration became infamous when the crowds were met with overwhelming force by the police using angry police dogs and fire hoses to disperse the mob. That the protesters were mostly children seemed not to matter.

Cynthia Wesley may very well have marched in one of those demonstrations. Many of her classmates certainly had. The enormous weight of the movement fell too heavily on small shoulders in Birmingham, a price paid first in beatings and jailings and then in four deaths.

Cynthia certainly didn't feel that weight the morning of September 15. In fact, she was most likely still preoccupied by a small quibble she'd had with her mother that morning. She'd been late and after rushing to get dressed, she tried to leave the house with her slip showing below her skirt. Her mother wouldn't let her take even a step toward church looking that way. You had to look your best for church. After all, God was looking.

Addie Mae Collins. *Fourteen years old.*

In the wake of the bombing, the Birmingham Police Department did almost nothing to solve the case. Some estimates claim that about one-third of the force belonged to the KKK, so it surprised no one. But then the FBI came in and took over the investigation. They got almost nowhere as well, or at least pretended not to. Behind the scenes, the truth was far more complicated.

The FBI at that moment was under the direction of J. Edgar Hoover, a man who felt that the civil rights movement was a puppet being maneuvered by Marxists and Communists. At the time in

Birmingham, the FBI had numerous informants deep within the Ku Klux Klan. Their failure to act on the bombing, they said, was in part to protect these informants.

So for fourteen years the case sat unsolved even though most everybody knew the parties who likely were involved. In 1977 William Baxley, a new district attorney, reopened the case and soon arrested Robert Chambliss. The man went by the name "Dynamite Bob" in public, had been a member of the Klan, was counted a good friend of local police, and still harbored an abiding hatred of blacks. He was convicted mostly on decades-old evidence that should have come to light much sooner, but also on new eyewitness testimony of his niece. He was sentenced to life in prison and died while serving his time.

Evidence was less strong against three other men assumed to be part of the bombing, and Baxley didn't want to risk going to trial and having them walk. Again the case sat dormant, this time until 1997, when the FBI reopened the case, coincidentally just before Spike Lee's documentary *Four Little Girls* aired. With the FBI's renewed involvement, crucial evidence "rediscovered" from their investigation would help convict two other men. (A third implicated in the crime, Herman Cash, had died before any charges could be brought.)

The two men were Thomas Blanton and Bobby Frank Cherry Jr. Both were convicted on four counts of first-degree murder and sentenced to life in prison, Blanton in 2001, Cherry in 2002. After almost forty years, the four girls finally received at least a measure of justice.

Addie Mae Collins would have been about fifty-three years old by the time the case of her murder was finally brought to a close. An outgoing girl who loved her family, her death proved almost unbearable for her sisters, particularly Junie Collins, who suffered panic attacks and depression for many years following both the bombing and having to identify the remains of her sister.

Years later, however, through prayer and counseling and the passing of time, Junie Collins Peavy came to see the bombing with new eyes. Many who look back on it now, even those who lost children or friends, say the same thing: God did not let the four girls die in vain.

The bombing of the Sixteenth Street Baptist Church galvanized the civil rights movement in Birmingham and finally showed the nation the true face of racism and hatred for blacks in this country. It was not an issue about to go quietly into the night. Those who would kill children would not be changed by time, as many whites in the nation had hoped. The movement against racism had to grow stronger, the cause had to be amplified. And it was. And in the words of Junie Peavy: "There is hope for healing in America. I know, because I have been healed. . . . And so God took a day which was meant for evil and turned it around for the good of all."

The struggle is not over. Nearly always, what is meant for evil is turned to good. People of faith trust more fully in God; the church is drawn in need to each other and to caring strangers. Perhaps someday soon, however, no churches will be burned and we can simply live according to what God intends for us, putting the evil days behind us.

* * *

There are six things the Lord hates, seven that are
detestable to him: haughty eyes, a lying tongue,
hands that shed innocent blood, a heart that devises
wicked schemes, feet that are quick to rush into evil,
a false witness who pours out lies and a man who
stirs up dissension among brothers.

PROVERBS 6:16–19 NIV

Martin Luther King Jr. *delivered the eulogy at the funeral for three of the girls. (The fourth was remembered a day earlier at a separate ceremony.) During the most powerful portion of the speech, King found deep significance in the deaths of those little girls, significance for every person listening there, for every man and woman in the country, and significance that transcends time and meets us even now.*

And yet they died nobly. They are the martyred heroines of a holy crusade for freedom and human dignity. And so this afternoon in a real sense they have something to say to each of us in their death. They have something to say to every minister of the gospel who has remained silent behind the safe security of stained-glass windows. They have something to say to every politician who has fed his constituents with the stale bread of hatred and the spoiled meat of racism. They have something to say to a federal government that has compromised with the undemocratic practices of southern Dixiecrats and the blatant hypocrisy of right-wing northern Republicans. They have something to say to every Negro who has passively accepted the evil system of segregation and who has stood on the sidelines in a mighty struggle for justice. They say to each of us, black and white alike, that we must substitute courage for caution. They say to us that we must be concerned not merely about who murdered them, but about the system, the way of life, the philosophy which produced the murderers. Their death says to us that we must work passionately and unrelentingly for the realization of the American dream. And so my friends, they did not die in vain.

Stand Up
Martin Luther King Jr.
1929–1968

*I have a dream that one day this nation will rise up
and live out the true meaning of its creed: "We hold these
truths to be self-evident: that all men are created equal."*

Things seemed to be getting better for Martin Luther King Jr. The boycott on the Montgomery, Alabama, bus system had been a "miracle." He was more comfortable in his role as head of the Southern Christian Leadership Conference and as the unofficial leader of the civil rights movement that was growing stronger every day.

Now here he was in a department store in Harlem, New York, signing copies of his first book, *Stride Toward Freedom: The Montgomery Story.* He heard someone ask, "Are you Martin Luther King?"

Stabbed. He was stabbed right in the middle of the crowded department store by a mentally unstable woman.

The pain was overwhelming. He learned later that if he had so much as sneezed he would have died. Thoughts raced through his mind. . . . Will I make it? Who will watch over my family? Who will carry on the with the work we have started? We have so much more to do. . . .

This was not the first time, nor would it be the last, that King and his family would face the kind of hatred that raises its ugly head to do lasting and permanent damage to people.

*We know through painful experience that
freedom is never voluntarily given by the oppressor;
it must be demanded by the oppressed.*

On January 30, 1956, a bomb was thrown onto the porch of King's home in Montgomery. Fortunately, no one was injured. A year later an unexploded bomb was discovered again on the Kings' front porch.

Detractors also tried to keep him locked up several times. Dr.

King was arrested for loitering, trespassing, obstructing a sidewalk, parading without a permit, driving thirty miles per hour in a twenty-five-mile-per-hour zone, and other trumped-up charges. His opponents even tried to have him arrested for improperly filing his taxes.

Bull Connor, the Director of Public Safety of Birmingham, Alabama, went so far as to order the use of police dogs and fire hoses against marching protesters, including young adults and children.

When they couldn't take out Dr. King, they assassinated one of his long-time companions, Medger Evers, right in his driveway.

Like King David, Martin Luther King Jr. was not a man without faults. What set him apart was his understanding of the special calling that God had placed on his life. He realized the position he was suddenly thrust into as a young twenty-six-year-old pastor; it was a solemn responsibility that he struggled with because of all the trials that he would face. It was not, however, one that he could pass up. God would be with him each step of the way. It was a position he would be able to use for the betterment of millions of African Americans then and in the future.

Dr. King talked about this unique position in a sermon he once gave:

> And I sat at that table thinking about [my daughter] and thinking about the fact that she could be taken away from me any minute. And I started thinking about a dedicated, devoted and loyal wife, who was over there asleep. . . . And I got to the point that I couldn't take it anymore. I was weak. . . .
>
> And I discovered then that religion had to become real to me, and I had to know God for myself. And I bowed down over that cup of coffee. I never will forget it. . . . I prayed a prayer, and I prayed out loud that night. I said, "Lord, I'm down here trying to do what's right. I think I'm right. I think the cause that we represent is right. But, Lord, I must confess that I'm weak now. I'm faltering. I'm losing my courage. . . .
>
> And it seemed at that moment that I could hear an inner voice saying to me, "Martin Luther, stand up for righteousness. Stand up for justice. Stand up for truth. And lo I will be with you, even until the end of the world.". . . I heard the voice of

Jesus saying still to fight on. He promised never to leave me,
never to leave me alone. No, never alone. No, never alone. He
promised never to leave me, never to leave me alone.

"Let justice roll down like waters and righteousness like a
mighty stream." Somehow, the preacher must say with Jesus,
"The spirit of the Lord is upon me, because he hath
anointed me to deal with the problems of the poor."

God was with Dr. King, and he did face many struggles in a cru-
sade that seemed insurmountable at the time. Through those times
God was able to bring victory. Victories like winning the 1964 Nobel
Peace Prize.

The boycott of the Montgomery bus system was originally supposed to last one day. It turned out to be a success and ended up lasting for more than a year. In addition, the U.S. Supreme Court ruled
that having nonintegrated buses was unconstitutional.

The August 28, 1963, March on Washington was one of those
events that will be forever linked with Dr. King. More than 250,000
people gathered near the Lincoln Memorial in Washington, D.C., for
a rally urging Congress to pass civil rights legislation. There were several speakers that day, but as Dr. King was about to sit down, gospel
singer Mahalia Jackson called out, "Tell them about your dream,
Martin! Tell them about the dream!" He then proceeded to deliver one
of the most famous speeches in American history: "I Have a Dream."

More important, he was able to stand up and take the call of God
on his life and run hard with it because God was with him. He was able
to impart to his followers that the only way they were going to see true
victory was not by fighting back but by peaceful nonviolence. That
message was able to get him into the pulpits of America as well as the
Oval Office. On April 3, 1968, Dr. Martin Luther King Jr. gave his
last speech to a sparse crowd in terrible weather conditions in
Memphis, Tennessee. He was in town getting ready for a march that
would take place on April 8 for striking African-American sanitation
workers. Dr. King was distressed, because in a previous march the
month before, violence had erupted and at least one of the marchers
was shot and killed.

In this famous "I've Been to the Mountaintop" speech, given on

April 3, he once again discussed the importance of nonviolence, but he also ended his speech by touching on his own mortality:

Well, I don't know what will happen now. We've got some difficult days ahead. But it doesn't matter with me now. Because I've been to the mountaintop. And I don't mind. Like anybody, I would like to live a long life. Longevity has its place. But I'm not concerned about that now. I just want to do God's will. And He's allowed me to go up to the mountain. And I've looked over. And I've seen the promised land. I may not get there with you. But I want you to know tonight that we, as a people, will get to the promised land. And I'm happy tonight. I'm not worried about anything. I'm not fearing any man. Mine eyes have seen the glory of the coming of the Lord.

The next evening Dr. King and his associates were getting ready to head out for dinner. At 6:01 p.m. Dr. Martin Luther King Jr. was fatally shot at the Lorraine Motel in Memphis, Tennessee, as he stepped out of his hotel room.

★ ★ ★

When we let freedom ring,
when we let it ring from every tenement
and every hamlet, from every state and
every city, we will be able to speed up
that day when all of God's children,
black men and white men,
Jews and Gentiles, Protestants and Catholics,
will be able to join hands
and sing in the words of the
old spiritual, "Free at last, free at last.
Thank God Almighty,
we are free at last."

—MARTIN LUTHER KING JR.

Chinese Labor and the Transcontinental Railroad

Progress is sometimes measured in metal and miles. Such was the case when, on May 10, 1869, the Union Pacific and Central Pacific Railroads joined at Promontory Point, Utah, and for the first time ever, Americans could travel with relative ease from Atlantic to Pacific shores. A trip that used to take four to six months was suddenly reduced to four days, four hours, and forty minutes. Leave New York on Tuesday and arrive in San Francisco in time for Sunday services!

Of the men who made the transcontinental railroad a reality, many have been virtually forgotten. Of course, remembered are the "Big Four" railroad leaders, Collis P. Huntington, Charles Crocker, Leland Stanford, and Mark Hopkins, whose companies funded and executed the grand project. But of the thousands of men who actually built the railroad with pick, blasting powder, spike, and hammer, more than ten thousand—about 80 percent of the entire workforce—were young, male Chinese immigrants seeking work in America.

Due to a lack of white labor, in 1865 Central Pacific General Superintendent Charles Crocker hired fifty Chinese immigrants who were eager to work. At first, the railroad overseers were skeptical. How could these slightly built men, who averaged four feet ten inches tall and 120 pounds, possibly do the job? But do the job they did—even making their white co-laborers look slow. The skills the Chinese had learned building roads in the mountainous regions of China proved invaluable to the great transcontinental enterprise.

In spite of their enormous contribution to the expansion of the nation, Chinese workers in the nineteenth and early twentieth centuries suffered extreme prejudice and mistreatment. Amazingly, it was not until 1943 that Chinese immigrants were allowed American citizenship—nearly seventy-five years after helping America bridge its landmass from sea to shining sea.

When a Sport
Is Something More
Jackie Robinson
1919–1972

It was October 1955, and in what was becoming almost a biennial event, the New York Yankees and the Brooklyn Dodgers were battling for the World Series. They'd met each other in 1947, 1949, 1952, and 1953, with the Yankees of DiMaggio and Berra and this new kid Mantle winning each time. Something had to change this time around or the results would be exactly the same.

Jackie Robinson was in his eighth season as a Dodger and was no longer the star or MVP. Those honors belonged to Gil Hodges, Duke Snider, and Roy Campenella. He'd had a tough season overall, and it seemed unlikely that he'd return to the level of that spectacular athlete who'd amazed so many since his Rookie of the Year season in 1947. His knees and ankles ached now; he'd gained weight: He'd made the simple and unforgivable mistake of aging.

But in the first game of the World Series, Robinson decided to set the tone from the start. If this was to be his last shot (although it turned out he had one more season and one more World Series), he would go down with the same guts with which he'd started.

In the eighth inning, with his team losing 6-3 and a man on first base, Robinson slapped a ball at the Yanks' third baseman and, with all the hustle he could manage, found himself on second after an error. Two men on. One out. Yankee Stadium began a worried murmur. He took a long lead, but the pitcher, Labine, didn't even do him the courtesy of glancing. "Old Man" Robinson wasn't going anywhere.

Only eight years he'd been playing major league baseball. It seemed more like fifteen. It wasn't just that his hair was graying;

that was just an outward sign. He'd aged the most on the inside. Hearing what he'd heard, seeing what'd he seen, and bottling up any response—it changes a person. Especially one never used to staying quiet.

Growing up in Pasadena, California, as one of five children and raised by only his mother, Mollie, Jackie felt he and his siblings were like baby birds, each raising his or her voice louder and louder to get attention. Finally it started to seem like a waste. He skipped out on home, happy to roam the street with his friends. They called themselves a gang, but mostly they just made mischief. Still some of it got the attention of the cops, and when Jackie mouthed off to them, he found himself facing the worst trouble of his life.

Which is exactly when Rev. Karl Downs stepped in. Scanning the crowd after ball two, Robinson wished Downs could be there, sitting in the stands, maybe next to Jackie's own boy. He'd died too young, had Rev. Downs.

When they first met, Karl Downs had just been assigned the pastorship of the Robinsons' church: Scott United Methodist. Jackie didn't know they made pastors so young—Downs was perhaps only seven years older than he. But that was seven years and a lifetime of maturity. He transformed Scott United Methodist and challenged the area's youth with the need for change. In Jack Robinson he saw some of the greatest potential ever.

His message was simple: Live a life of courage. Be fearless in the face of worry. Be thoughtful and rational in the face of raging emotions. Be prepared to give up everything for the fight. Do everything with the will of God in mind and the spirit of Christ in your heart. Fatherless Jackie Robinson thrived under the attention of the man, turned back to the church, and set for himself the model Downs prescribed.

At the plate, Don Zimmer sent a shot to deep center. The crowd gasped, but Robinson knew the smart play was to tag up. He made it to third easily, and Carl Furillo scored in front of him.

Now it was 6-4. In the Yankee dugout, players shouted for their pitcher to finish off the inning. Times were not too long ago that at least a few of them would've been screaming at Jackie, no matter what the score, no matter what the inning.

It was Branch Rickey, the Dodger owner at the time, who'd seen the path they would take. Rickey talked God and money and the future as though they were one thing, so Jackie never knew if it was a holy vision or not. But the old man certainly had thought the thing through.

"I've spent years looking for you," Rickey told Robinson during one of their first meetings while Jackie was still playing for the Negro League's Kansas City Monarchs. Jackie had returned after three years in World War II without a college degree, and baseball seemed his quickest hope at earning a decent salary. Now he was being handed the hopes and dreams of his race. Rickey didn't understate the moment. "This great experiment lives and dies with you."

In fact, Rickey had shown Jackie six factors that needed to be addressed. First was the support of ownership. Now that Rickey owned the Dodgers, that was no problem. Next was the actual nuts-and-bolts details of the thing. Would cities allow a black player onto their ball fields? Third was tempering the response of the Negro race. Fourth was the acceptance of things by other ballplayers. Fifth and sixth were the man's conduct, both on the field and off. Rickey thought he had a handle on the first three. The fourth rested out of his hands. And now he'd answered his search for the perfect man. Jackie Robinson would break the color barrier.

In the Dodgers dugout, Jackie saw his teammates clapping their hands to keep warm and talking in small groups. Many hadn't been with the team when Jackie had come up. There were even two more blacks—catcher Roy Campanella and pitcher Don Newcombe—on the team now. Back then it had just been Jackie.

Branch Rickey had described the man he wanted on his Brooklyn Dodgers, and Jackie heard Rev. Downs' words and the man's description of the courageous life. They were almost exactly the same. Jackie would take any and all abuse without retaliation or even response. He would win people over with his excellence on the field. He would be courageous and level-headed and sacrifice it all for the opening door. On October 23, 1945, he signed the first professional baseball contract ever offered to a black ballplayer. After a year tearing up the minor leagues in Montreal, Jackie was invited to spring training with the Dodgers and pencilled in as their starting first baseman. Ed Stanky played second.

Jackie scanned his teammates' faces and thought of those who were no longer there. Kirby Higbe. Bobby Bragen. Dixie Walker.

None of them had wanted to be teammates with "the great experiment." Even Pee-Wee Reese, a purebred Kentucky shortstop who'd eventually become Robinson's good friend, wasn't crazy about the idea at first. A petition was considered. Rickey gave his players two options: play with Robinson or be traded. That petition died, but around the league similar protests arose. The St. Louis Cardinals said they'd strike. Commissioner Ford Frick offered a not-so-subtle reply: "You will take the field or you will be suspended for the year." With the game's highest powers behind them, Robinson took the field in 1947 as the first black baseball player ever.

It was a lonely life. His teammates, though they loved his play, were still leery around him. Few talked to him in the clubhouse and none socialized with him outside the game. From the diamond, pitchers threw at him—in an era without helmets—and he was forever standing back up and dusting himself off. Umpires squeezed the plate and made sure many close plays went against him. Players, managers, coaches, and fans tormented him with racial epithets and curses and a litany of hatred. Robinson still snarled at the mention of Philadelphia—the "cradle of liberty," the "City of Brotherly Love"—whose Phillies had been worst of all. Abuse and profanity streamed out at him from the manager and the dugout without ceasing from before the game even started. Finally, when it seemed like Jack wouldn't be able to tolerate a single insult more, a voice rang out in reply: "Listen, you cowards, why don't you yell at someone who can answer back?" It was Eddie Stanky, a man who'd barely spoken fifteen words to Jackie. Other Dodgers grumbled in kind. It would still be lonely, it would still be almost unbeatably difficult to turn the other cheek, but from that moment on Jackie knew, at least on the field, he'd always have the support of his team.

The country would take longer. Death threats and hate mail arrived. He was told in Cincinnati that if he took the field, he'd be shot. Hotels refused to serve the team if Robinson was with them. "White-only" taxis wouldn't take him to the game. Everywhere, the stigma of breaking the color barrier surrounded him. He might have been "Jackie Robinson," but Jim Crow only looked at the color of your skin. It was only on the field, in the game, that he could find any moment of escape.

Jackie took his typical three-step lead and then, in a burst of inspiration, danced another step and a half off the bag. The pitcher barely glanced at him, but a buzz sounded in Ebbets Field. They remembered Jackie flying down the basepath, challenging the very speed of a pitch before sliding in a cloud of dust, the umpire pausing a second before screaming, "Safe!" They remembered what he'd been like when he first came up.

That first year Jackie was a "great experiment" and a great ballplayer. He shook off an early season slump and won the Rookie of the Year award. Two years later he was named Most Valuable Player, leading the Dodgers to National League championships both years. Other former Negro League players joined squads throughout baseball. Branch Rickey took Jackie aside and told him, "The experiment is over. We did it." Freed from his vow of restraint, Jackie had argued and bellowed and challenged his way through the next seasons. He'd kept it pent up so long.

Ninety feet to home plate now. Jackie edged further down the line. At the plate was the right-handed Frank Kellert. Another half-slide and now Jackie was eighty-four feet from home. The pitcher had been busting Kellert down and low. It was now or never. Jackie watched the pitcher take his sign from Berra, come to set, and then lift his leg.

Jackie pivoted and exploded down the line. The crowd stood as one, shocked. *He's stealing home!*

Down the line Jackie raced. It felt for that moment like it was 1947 again. All he had to do was be the best ballplayer he could and the nation would learn, Rickey had said. It had sounded so simple and had proved to be so very hard because nothing about that year had been about baseball. It was about race and prejudice and the hopes of his people and the bitterness of others and the insanity of some who wrote him letters wishing him dead and the invective of a few and the color of skin and the battle for equality. Baseball had been merely the stage, but he'd played it then as he did now. With speed and stealth and a blur of legs.

The pitch snapped down and in, like Robinson knew it would. Kellert bailed, and Jackie veered across to the far side of home, crooking his left leg and lowering himself into a slide. Berra backhanded the ball and swept out with his glove. Jackie's right foot crossed home and Berra caught only air with his tag.

"Safe!" screamed the ump, and the crowd, stunned by what they had seen, sat mute. Jackie always did have a knack for silencing critics.

It didn't even matter that the Dodgers lost the game. If there was one thing Jackie had learned, it was that a single game wasn't important. It was the big picture that mattered, and spurred on by his daring, "Dem Bums" would finally win the World Series against their great rivals. In 1957 the Dodgers were moved to Los Angeles and Robinson was traded. Rather than play for another club, he hung up his cleats.

His fight for civil rights continued, stronger than ever, working for the NAACP, marching in many of the protests, working for the National Conference for Christians and Jews, and serving as president of the United Church Men, a denominational movement of the United Church of Christ that called for racial integration long before it was popular or "safe" in the church. And it all went back to what he'd learned those years ago as a nineteen-year-old in California.

Live the courageous life with God's will in mind and Jesus in your heart. It helped Jackie survive. It forged his future. It helped him transcend sports to impact a nation. He opened eyes. Changed hearts. Made this country better. That lesson allowed him to survive baseball's great experiment and forged his future.

That was Jack Roosevelt Robinson.

★ ★ ★

When the blazing light of truth is focused on this marvelous age in which we live—men and women will know and children will be taught that we have a finer land, a better people, a more noble civilization—because these humble children of God were willing to suffer for righteousness' sake.

—MARTIN LUTHER KING JR.

in his Nobel Peace Prize speech

Lifting a People
Richard Allen
1760–1831

Stokeley Sturgis, a Delaware farmer, called out to the young black man, "Richard, come here."

Richard put down his rake and trotted over to the porch of the "big house" where his master stood. "Yes, sir?" he asked.

"It's Thursday. Isn't this the night you and your brother go to that church meeting?" Stokeley asked.

"Yes, sir," Richard replied. "But we wanted to finish raking the vegetable patch first. We're almost finished—I think we can still make the meeting on time."

Stokeley smiled and shook his head. "You have worked enough for today, Richard. Go on to your meeting—you can finish the rest in the morning."

"Thank you, sir, but we would rather stay and get our crops ahead." Richard hurried back to join his brother. Before long they finished and hurried off down the dirt road to their meeting at a nearby farm.

Stokeley remembered how his white neighbors had warned him not to let his slaves attend the church meetings because "religion promotes discontent and laziness among slaves."

Stokeley smiled. If anything, Richard worked harder than ever! He decided to ask Richard about it in the morning.

Richard Allen had become a Christian in his late teens, when a white itinerant Methodist preacher named Freeborn Garretson preached to a group of slaves in a clearing in the woods. Richard had just lost his mother and three younger siblings—sold to a plantation so far away that he had no hope of seeing them again. As he heard the Gospel, he experienced the love of God in a way that changed his life forever. Here was a love—God's love—that could never be cut off.

After this powerful spiritual experience, Richard began going from house to house, telling other slaves about Christ. As Richard continued to grow in Christian character, his master became more and more impressed with the genuineness of his faith and let him conduct prayer services for the slaves.

Stokeley also started asking Richard questions. When asked about working harder, Richard replied, "God's Word says to obey our masters from the heart, the same way we would serve the Lord Jesus himself. When we do that, God makes sure we are rewarded—even if we are slaves."

Richard paused, then added, "Sir, I could ask Rev. Garretson to come and preach right here at your house. He can answer your questions much better than I can."

Stokeley cheerfully agreed. Soon afterward, Rev. Garretson came and preached. When Stokeley heard the Gospel, he, too, became a Christian. A few months later Garretson preached that the sin of owning slaves was so offensive to God that on Judgment Day, slaveholders would be "weighed in the balances, and found wanting" (Daniel 5:27 NKJV).

The next day, Stokeley told Richard, "I can see in the Bible that owning slaves is wrong. Yet I am too deep in debt to just give you your freedom. I believe God has given me an idea: You can leave the farm, go to work for other people, and earn money to buy your freedom from me."

Richard jumped at the chance, believing that God had made a way for him to fulfill this lifelong dream. They agreed on the amount—two thousand Continental dollars.

Richard immediately faced a problem that abolitionists would work on for years to come: Finding a job was not easy for a young black man. "When I left my master's house, I didn't know what to do.... I wondered what business I should follow to pay my master and get my living."

His first job was to cut firewood, and sometime later he took a job making bricks. Then, during the Revolutionary War, he got a job he enjoyed: driving a wagon and delivering salt. Along the way, Richard would stop and preach. "I had my regular stops and preaching places on the road. I enjoyed many happy seasons in meditation and prayer while in this employment." Wherever he went, Richard would preach to anyone who would listen, just as he had seen Freeborn Garretson do.

Once peace was declared in 1783, Richard became a "licensed exhorter" and began to travel and preach the Gospel extensively. His anointed, fiery delivery greatly appealed to his listeners, many of whom had never heard the simple Gospel message that Richard brought. He started in Delaware, then went to New Jersey. He preached the Gospel in the evenings and on Sundays; by day, he cut wood for a living.

In Pennsylvania he had several weeks of glorious meetings. He recalls, "Many souls were awakened, and cried aloud to the Lord to have mercy upon them. It was a time of visitation from above—many were slain of the Lord. Some said, 'This man must be a man of God; I never heard such preaching before.'"

For the next six years Allen traveled the Methodist circuit throughout New York, Maryland, Delaware, and Pennsylvania, preaching to black and white congregations alike. Meanwhile, he worked at a variety of jobs, saving every extra penny until he was able to pay his master in full. Finally he was a free man!

In 1785 Richard's preaching and Holy Spirit–fueled services caught the attention of Francis Asbury, the first American Methodist Bishop. Asbury asked him to travel and preach with him, and although Richard considered it a great honor to be asked, he felt God had other plans for him.

About this time Allen was asked to preach to the black congregation at Saint George's Methodist Church in Philadelphia. This city had become a haven for free blacks and escaped slaves from neighboring slave states. Most of these new residents were uneducated and did not attend church regularly. Richard saw "a large field open in seeking and instructing my African brethren, who had been a long forgotten people."

His constant prayer was, "Lord, how do I lift my people?" Richard began preaching to African Americans whenever and wherever he could. He was given the 5:00 AM services at Saint George's and also preached four or five times a day in parks near where black families lived.

Richard Allen and Absalom Jones, one of the prominent black members at Saint George's, often discussed how to best help their community. "It is one thing to be free from slavery. It is another thing to find your place in society," Richard observed. "These people are like sheep without a shepherd."

Absalom agreed: "The slave system has kept them ignorant. But look what God is doing! The Methodists are taking the Gospel to the slaves on the plantations."

Richard concurred, "I remember how God's love transformed me as I learned His commandments and His ways. Forgiveness, diligence, honesty all became part of my life."

"God's power transformed my life," Absalom said.

"That is the key to lifting our people. It is done one heart at a time."

The number of blacks attending Saint George's increased rapidly as word spread of a church that ministered powerfully to African Americans. Richard's style of preaching was simple, practical, and often spontaneously delivered as the Holy Spirit instructed him. His Spirit-directed approach was a great contrast to the carefully constructed, scholarly orations of other ministers of his day.

In time the large number of African Americans joining the church caused overcrowding—and interracial tensions. The church began a building program and constructed a new balcony to accommodate their new members. No one had told the black members of the congregation, but it had been decided that blacks would no longer be allowed to sit next to white church members on the main floor as they had been doing. From now on, they were to sit only in the new balcony. Segregated seating was now mandatory in the house of God.

In November 1787, on the first Sunday service after the balcony was finished, an usher pointed Richard, Absalom, and William White, another prominent black church member, to seats in the new balcony. But as the three men were a little late, they instead took seats on the lower level, near where they always sat. The service started and the congregation dropped to their knees in prayer.

During the prayer a church trustee grabbed Absalom and tried to pull him to his feet. Absalom did not know what was going on but was shocked to be disturbed during the prayer. He said to the trustee, "Wait until the prayer is over, and I will get up and trouble you no more."

Another trustee came and tried to pull William White from his knees.

When the prayer was over, Richard, Absalom, and William stood up and left the building, followed by every black person at the service. "We all went out of the church in a body," Richard wrote in his memoirs. "They were no more plagued by us in the church." Richard realized his people must have a place of their own to worship, a place where they would be honored and lifted up, not pressed down and degraded.

Already a gifted preacher and teacher, Richard now had a chance to develop yet another gift from God—that of pastor. He soon started to build Bethel Methodist Church. Bethel grew quickly. In its first two years, membership grew to 121; a decade later it had grown to 457, and by 1813 it had reached 1,272.

Bethel's rapid expansion showed that the unique spiritual needs of African Americans were being met. "The plain and simple Gospel suits best for the people—for the unlearned can understand and the learned are sure to understand."

Newly freed blacks welcomed the spontaneity and exuberant atmosphere of the Methodist services. They were attracted as well by the church's strict system of discipline—its sanctions against drinking, gambling, and infidelity—which helped them bring order to their lives.

Allen's preaching also played a role. Sensitive to the Holy Spirit, he could exhort the people with passionate preaching or, with equal ease, carefully teach from the Scriptures, line upon line, showing them how to live godly, peaceful, fruitful lives. The excellence of his sermons was recognized in 1799, when Bishop Asbury ordained him as the first black deacon of the Methodist Church.

From the start Allen recognized the importance of education to the future of the African-American community. In 1795 he opened a day school for sixty children and in 1804 founded the "Society of Free People of Colour for Promoting the Instruction and School Education of Children of African Descent." By 1811 there were no fewer than eleven black schools in the city.

By 1816 Allen realized that to fully meet the needs of his people and lift them up to the place where God wanted them to be, he would need to break with the white establishment and start a new denomination. Representatives from four other black Methodist congregations met with Bethel to organize the African Methodist Episcopal Church, the first fully independent black denomination in America. Allen was named the first bishop.

At the core of Allen's beliefs was his trust that as the lives of church members were transformed by God, they would forge a new identity for their people and would lift the prospects for all blacks. Throughout his life, Richard exhorted all freed blacks to help their enslaved brethren by being exemplary citizens:

> *If we are lazy and idle, the enemies of freedom plead it as a cause why we ought not to be free, and that giving us our liberty would be an injury to us. By such conduct we strengthen the bands of oppression, and keep many in bondage. Will our friends excuse—will God pardon us—for the part we act in making strong the hands of the enemies of our color?*

As Richard sought God for a way to bring his people out of poverty and shame, God guided him through a process that made a tremendous difference in many lives—not only of the citizens of Philadelphia in the 1790s and early 1800s, but also of many black heroes to come. Sojourner Truth, Harriet Tubman, Frederick Douglass, and Biddy Mason all attended the AME church.

★ ★ ★

But this is a people plundered and despoiled . . . a prey with none to deliver them . . . none to say, "Give them back!" Who among you will give ear to this?
ISAIAH 42:22–23 NASB

The religion which has introduced civil liberty is the religion of Christ and His apostles, which enjoins humility, piety, and benevolence; which acknowledges in every person a brother, or a sister, and a citizen with equal rights. This is genuine Christianity, and to this we owe our free Constitutions of Government.
—NOAH WEBSTER

Negro Spirituals

Slaves sang for many reasons—to cheer one another, establish a common rhythm to coordinate efforts in a strenuous task, pass along coded instructions on how to escape, spread word about a secret prayer meeting... or simply to pour out to God their deepest emotions. Out of these often spontaneous expressions grew our country's first uniquely American music—the Negro spiritual.

The Gospel of Christ was embraced by slaves, who identified with the sufferings of Jesus and of the ancient Jews. Though Christianity was usually modeled quite hypocritically by their masters, slaves saw past the dichotomy to the redeeming power found in a life of faith. Still, the hypocrisy was not overlooked in spirituals:

> Everybody talkin' about
> Heaven ain't goin' there . . .

The sophisticated structure and melodies of Negro spirituals' belied the composers' lack of education. Most were drawn from the rhythms that had been passed down from the first generations to be brought in chains from Africa. The popular call-and-response format encouraged exuberant participation by all.

Some songs served as musical roadmaps for the Underground Railroad. For example, the lyric "Follow the drinking gourd" instructs a slave to follow the Big Dipper north to freedom. Other spirituals like "Wade in the Water," "The Gospel Train," and "Swing Low, Sweet Chariot" directly refer to the Underground Railroad.

The original composers of African-American spirituals are unknown, so they have assumed a collective ownership by the whole community. Many spirituals have found their way into today's hymnals, including "Go Tell It on the Mountain," "Amen," "He's Got the Whole World in His Hands," "There is a Balm in Gilead," and "Lord, I Want to Be a Christian."

The Birth and Second Coming of a Message of Hate

Ku Klux Klan

1866–1915

36

What's nearly impossible to fathom is that the KKK, one of the most loathed, feared, and destructive groups ever in the United States, began with six friends retiring from war to a life of idleness and boredom.

In Pulaski, Tennessee, after Appomatox and the South's bitter surrender, a half dozen men returned from the war. Their names are like those you'd find anywhere. They were normal men, disappointed at the defeat but weary and glad to be home.

James Crowe.

Richard Reed.

Calvin Jones.

John Lester.

Frank McCord.

John Kennedy.

All fought and lost for the Confederates. All had seen their share of pain and horror. All were in their twenties and returned home to find perhaps the most unexpected of frustrations: complete boredom. After the crack of musket and rifle, the constant echo of mortar shells, and the furious rush of terror and adrenaline, nights of cicadas and bullfrogs nearly drove them insane. The only excitement—a freak December cyclone that leveled much of Pulaski and seemed like God adding insult to injury.

Sometime after that—legend has it on Christmas Eve 1865, perhaps with the hymns of the season fresh off their lips, though the date is merely speculation—the six decided to form a club. More educated than most for the time, they chose the Greek word for circle—*kyklos*—and threw in a nod to their Scottish roots and their clans to come up with the Ku Klux Klan. The supposed goals of the group: mischief and amusement.

Perhaps this is giving the men too much leeway. From the first, they draped themselves in sheets and masks, pretending to be ghouls. Death was a part of their union from the beginning, even if at first they merely rode about hollering or scaring those out too late. Nor was it long before the now growing membership found their favorite targets to be the newly emancipated blacks of the area. The path from trying to frighten someone to death to actual murder was a short one.

And it was fueled almost entirely by a growing resentment not only for the newfound status of the blacks but for the tide of Northerners coming into the South to make sure things were run "properly." As resentment grew, the Klan, which now had chapters throughout Tennessee, swelled too. In April 1867, as a key election approached, top members of the Klan gathered under the auspices of a political rally to establish control and structure over the autonomous KKK cells that had become a vibrant but unruly mess. At the top of this new ghostly army—for that's what the white robes symbolized, the return of slain Confederate soldiers—was an actual military general: Nathan Bedford Forrest, who'd just years before served under Robert E. Lee. Regrouped and reenergized, the Klan now prepared to truly flex its muscles.

With the passing of the Fourteenth Amendment, black citizens of the state now had the right to vote. As the election approached, the Klan marched and paraded and made noise but did little in threatening the vote. Slaveholders assumed, after talking with their former black slaves, that *status quo* seemed the best for everyone. Blacks could enjoy their new freedom, but power should obviously still be maintained by those prepared to use it.

The freed black men and women did not agree.

At the time, the ruling political party in the South was the Democratic Party. These Democrats—mostly Southern white males—were soundly defeated and a progressive group of

Republicans—whites and blacks—gained control. Blacks were blamed for the Democrats' loss of control, but more so were white activists, particularly the Union League, accused of brainwashing blacks in order to win their vote.

The election, however, broke the last bit of restraint the silent army would have. They now became a deadly army. Lynchings and cross burnings and midnight rides. The Klan at its worst.

Their ferocity would rage from 1868 to 1871. Untold lives—black and Jewish and Catholic and Republican and liberal—were claimed in the name of restoring white, Protestant rule to a chaotic South in the throes of Reconstruction.

Grown too powerful, too destructive, they found themselves under the scrutiny of Washington, D.C., and President Ulysses S. Grant, who eventually signed the Klan Act and Enforcement Act. These acts designated the Ku Klux Klan as an illegal terrorist group, against which the use of force was authorized. This silent, terrible army now rode as enemies of the state. In the face of such terrifying odds, the white robes of the KKK dissolved into the darkness like the spectres they dared to mimic. But they would not stay buried forever.

★ ★ ★

Doc Simmons—William Joseph Simmons—was a man of the cloth. A licensed, though thoroughly unsuccessful, Methodist pastor, Simmons prayed and called to the heavens with the expectant pleading of one who hears things in return. One such night of prayers in 1910 found him at his window, drunkenly entreating the platinum moon that rose cold and unyielding above. On the sill, Simmons' bottle of bourbon cast a long shadow across his apartment floor. Around him the world grew still.

Somewhere a nickering sounded. Simmons instinctively looked to the street, but the gas lamps showed nothing. Yet still it grew louder. And hoofbeats now as well. Simmons looked up.

There, on steeds that frothed in fury, rode four cloaked horsemen. Ghostriders galloping across the sky, over clouds, and against the very surface of the moon. Simmons watched transfixed as in their wake he saw etched, as though by the finest engraver in all of Georgia, a map of the United States.

"What, Lord? What does it mean?" he slurred. "Are they your four riders coming to bring the end? Is the world to perish?"

Nothing.

"What does it mean, God?"

His cry went unanswered.

Five years later, he found his revelation in the wake of the rape and murder of a fourteen-year-old girl.

On April 27, 1915, in Marietta, Georgia, Mary Phagan was found in the basement of a pencil company owned by Leo M. Frank. Jewish and originally from New York, Frank was tried, convicted, and sentenced to death. His case, prosecuted under sketchy circumstances at best, drew outrage from across the nation, and soon the Georgia governor commuted his sentence to life.

On August 16, 1915, twenty-five men stormed a Georgia prison and abducted and hung Leo M. Frank. They called themselves the Knights of Mary Phagan, and on October 16 of that year, they set fire to an enormous cross atop Georgia's Stone Mountain.

Simmons, who'd been thinking about the Klan more and more through the years, found his inspiration. He decided that the riders he'd seen were the reborn clan, galloping with power and glory through both Georgia and the entire South. On October 26, he and thirty-four others applied as a fraternal order to the state of Georgia. A "purely benevolent" fraternal order. The Knights of the Ku Klux Klan.

He timed the Klan's launch to coincide perfectly with the Atlanta premier of D. W. Griffith's racist epic, *The Birth of a Nation*. In its wake the city stood divided: those horrified by what they'd seen on screen and those to whom it seemed the gospel truth. Almost one hundred people joined Simmons his first week. Failed as a minister, he had a new flock to tend and saw it as a spiritual call.

The message he and many like him preached was a disgust with the slipping morality of the nation and a call to decency and uprightness. He felt a passionate belief in the inspired founding of the nation and a desire to return to that idyllic past. An uneasiness with anything that strayed from their interpretation of the literal truth of the Bible.

With nationalism running high in the wake of World War I, many agreed with the Klan's "pro-America" stance, and the lingering bitterness after Reconstruction fueled the hatred not only of blacks but other minority groups as well. And so the Klan grew and grew. At its peak in the mid-1920s, membership reached over four million people. They truly were an army now, and they marched through the night in a reign of terror.

The Tuskegee Institute of Alabama counted more than seven hundred documented lynchings from 1915 to 1935, and those were only the murders that made the newspapers. Hundreds more black men simply disappeared. Churches were burned as well as homes, and many blacks were beaten or terrorized. They were a terrorist organization whose goal was white supremacy over America. They had members in local and state government, the police force, the church—spread over the entire nation. For nearly thirty years they marched undaunted until two events—a terrible scandal involving a murder by one of their highest members and a lawsuit by the IRS for huge amounts of back taxes—combined to gut the organization's resources and silence it. But only temporarily.

A few years later another cross burned at the top of Stone Mountain—always a rallying spot for the Klan—this time ignited by Dr. Samuel Green, a former Klansman desperate to see the group come back to power.

This time the Klan found itself faced with a sweeping social movement that they vowed to destroy. Whether it was the end of school segregation in *Brown v. Board of Education* in 1954 or any of the countless civil rights marches, the KKK found fresh outrages to spur their growth, and the group had not lost any of its viciousness. Klan members murdered civil rights workers, bombed churches and homes, beat protesters to unconsciousness, and desperately tried to restore their rule to Southern America.

This time, however, their efforts met stiff opposition, and the tide of law and of public perception began to change. More and more, politicians and citizens distanced themselves from the Klan. Their membership dropped and they became a splinter group—still capable of terrible tragedy, still promoting hatred and violence, but now loathed throughout the country.

The KKK continues to exist today in every state of the Union. The deep stain of hatred, the lingering sin of fear, will likely always be a part of America's fabric. Only God can change hearts embittered and stony, and still men—thinking they are following His will—march blindly against Him. They continue to take the cross, a Christian's symbol of grace and hope, and purposefully set it on fire hoping to cause fear but not realizing that they are burning a symbol of the one thing, the only thing, that can ever truly save this country.

★ ★ ★

Be still before the Lord and wait patiently for him;
do not fret when men succeed in their ways,
when they carry out their wicked schemes.
Refrain from anger and turn from wrath; do not fret—
it leads only to evil. For evil men will be cut off,
but those who hope in the Lord will inherit the land.
PSALM 37:7–9 NIV

"It Is All So Terribly True"

37 ★ Woodrow Wilson and *The Birth of a Nation*

1915

Whenever you try to reduce a historical event or personage to its essence, you will leave things out. Edges are smoothed. Controversy is left to places better suited to in-depth study. These glimpses are not meant to be the final word, but an inspiration to learn more. Because if at the essence of Martin Luther King Jr. and John Adams and others there shines a powerful example of living as a Christian in the light of history, then the full story is that much richer and fuller.

Sometimes, though, no matter how hard we try, a portion of America's spiritual battle will simply refuse to fit at all, and trying to reduce it to a single sum becomes a kind of lie. This is one of those stories.

Here are two facts:

In 1920 Woodrow Wilson was honored with the Nobel Peace Prize for his efforts on ending World War I and rallying for peace throughout the world.

On February 18, 1915, Woodrow Wilson screened D. W. Griffith's film *The Birth of a Nation* at the White House, perhaps the first motion picture ever shown there, and said of the film, "It is like writing history with lightning and my only regret is that it is all so terribly true."

Which of these does one put at the center of a glimpse of Woodrow Wilson? In most of our lives, our sins and triumphs occur on such a small scale, affecting those few around us. With Wilson, however, at such a critical moment in history, his actions were magnified beyond imaginable scope. A personal belief in the right to self-determination helped shape the end of World War I and led to the forerunner of the United Nations. The simple act of watching a film, however, helped spark a firestorm of racial hatred that still burns today.

The first blockbuster film in America, D. W. Griffith's *The Birth of a Nation* was a tribute to the KKK. It ranked as our country's highest grossing film until 1934, when it was surpassed by tamer fare: Disney's *Snow White and the Seven Dwarfs*. It was simultaneously lauded for technical innovations and revolutionary cinematic techniques and loathed for its inflammatory depiction of American "history"—one of its sources actually being the very man whose "thumb's up" would open a floodgate of criticism.

Woodrow Wilson was born in Staunton, Virginia, in 1856, before the first shots were ever fired in the War for Southern Independence. He was raised a devoted Presbyterian and graduated from the College of New Jersey, soon to become Princeton University. He earned a law degree from the University of Virginia and his Ph.D. from Johns Hopkins, which led to a professorship back at Princeton. Here, in 1902, he wrote a five-volume work titled *The History of the American People*, which celebrated the achievements of white Protestant Americans, frowned at the entire Southern Reconstruction, and relegated blacks to second-class citizens. Selections from this work actually made it into *The Birth of a Nation* as intertitles—words shown on screen during a silent film—making Wilson's affinity for the movie all the easier to comprehend, if not understand.

His thinking on such matters had not changed much, if at all, by the time he was elected president in 1912. Under Wilson's Democratic administration, segregation was reinstituted at the U.S. Post Office and countless other departments and branches. When confronted on the issue, he claimed it was actually done as a favor for blacks, who otherwise would have been unable to compete with superior white co-workers. His domestic policy toward all things of race was an implicit understanding that no further federal interference would dictate how states, particularly those in the South, should handle such matters.

This stands in such stark contrast to Republican Ulysses S. Grant's swift denouncement of the KKK just forty years earlier. Faced with their rise, Grant enacted legislation that made them an enemy of the country and ran them out of business. Wilson welcomed them to his very hearth and gave them a plug.

It is not a coincidence that the rebirth of the KKK occurred in 1915. A great many factors were in place, including a sweeping religious fervor that yearned for the good old days and the lunatic vision of William Simmons, who would relaunch the KKK. But *The Birth of a Nation* became a rallying point in every southern city it visited.

Based on the novel *The Clansman* by southern novelist Thomas Dixon, this three-hour epic followed two families—one Southern, one Northern—from Antebellum South, through the Civil War, Lincoln's assassination, and eventually Reconstruction as well. In the film, blacks—often white actors in blackface—are portrayed in vicious stereotype, or worse, as base and vicious animals. The heroes of the film are the KKK, who ride, like sheeted superheroes, to protect white citizens—especially women—from the marauding violence perpetrated by the freed slaves.

And each time the film was shown—very often as a recruiting tool for the KKK—so too were the words of the president himself, "It is like writing history with lightning. . . ." Instead of cutting hatred off at its knees, he had opened the floodgates instead.

As governor of New Jersey, Wilson said this in a speech celebrating the translation of the Bible into English: "I ask every man and woman in this audience that from this night on they will realize that part of the destiny of America lies in their daily perusal of this great book of revelations—that if they would see America free and pure, they will make their own spirits free and pure by this baptism of the Holy Scripture."

Had Wilson lived a life such as he encouraged others, he might very well occupy another place in this book. He might be held up as an example for men and women, boys and girls, to live out the Christian life. Instead, his chapter ends as a warning.

We all live lives of influence. How many we touch is beside the point. Instead, we need to realize just how important our lives are as examples to others.

★ ★ ★

If the power of the Gospel is not felt through the length and breadth of the land, anarchy and misrule, degradation and misery, corruption and darkness will reign without mitigation or end.
—DANIEL WEBSTER

"BIRTH OF A NATION" BANNED IN WEST VA.

CHARLESTON, W. Va., June 22.—The Executive State Council of Defense, Wednesday, placed a ban on the exhibition of "The Birth of a Nation" and all similar plays in this state during the period of the war.

The action of the state council came as a sequel to the passage of a resolution by the McDowell County Auxiliary Council of Defense protesting against the showing of "The Birth of a Nation," the McDowell Co. Council, composed of Colored citizens of that county, and one of the units of the state Auxiliary Advisory Council, of which J. C. Gilmer is secretary, set forth that the attraction is one "calculated to arouse hatred and prejudice between the white and Negro races of state, and likely to hinder and retard the proper co-operation between races in promoting the greatest efficiency in war work of all kinds."

OPPOSE "BIRTH OF NATION."

Washington, D. C.—Officials of the N. A. C. P. say they will resist to the utmost any effort on the part of the managers here to show "The Birth of a Nation," which it is said is headed this way. With a failure to suppress the film in Boston, New York, Chicago, Atlantic City and Philadelphia, the lawyers in this city are dubious about the course that should be taken to keep the vile production out of Washington. No objection was raised to "The Nigger," which was played here to such large audiences that it had

★ 215 ★

"God Save These People!"
John Witherspoon
1776

No great undertaking happens without setbacks, and so it was with the colonies' pursuit of independence as well. Opinions varied as to what our nation should look like, and for a time, prevailing opinion felt that our domain should extend into Canada as well. On December 31, 1775, a colonist battalion pushing all the way north to Quebec were routed by combined Canadian and British forces at the Battle of Quebec. Their resigned retreat back into upstate New York marked the notable effort to expand the colonial territories and served as a sharp warning to many throughout the colonies that their God-granted vision to freedom might be in trouble. And the threat to all their grandest dreams? It wasn't danger from the Crown but the colonists' own pride.

Ministers from Massachusetts to Virginia preached in warning against trusting too much in their own strength, their own plans. A path without God could only lead to peril and calamity. Not only pastors felt the urgency. The fledgling Congress sensed the need to rededicate themselves to God's vision, and on March 16, 1776, they put forth a proclamation setting May 17, 1776, as a "day of Humiliation, Fasting and Prayer." A day of national repentance to obtain God's "pardon and forgiveness." When May 17 arrived, Dr. John Witherspoon, a Presbyterian minister, president of the College of New Jersey (later to become Princeton University), and one of the eventual fifty-six signers of the Declaration of Independence, gave a sermon that was the most widely reprinted of all those delivered on that day.

As Witherspoon stood in his pulpit, ready to begin, he gave his head the slightest shake of disbelief. *Eight years I've been in this country. Just eight years. There are children with more claim to God's vision for America than I.*

The doubt passed in the same instant. Yes, it had been eight years, but he still recalled his first steps onto American soil in 1768 and the sense that he had finally found his home. Forty-two years he'd spent in Scotland, studying theology and preaching, and yet when the call had come to serve as president for the floundering college, something in him had resonated. He knew what it meant to follow God's will for his life, remembered how amazed and humbled he felt that God might guide his steps. If he could only impart a little of that awe, that wondrous thanks that he felt, to those around him. He looked once to heaven and then to his waiting congregation.

"While we give praise to God, the supreme disposer of all events, for His interposition on our behalf, let us guard against the dangerous error of trusting in, or boasting of, an arm of flesh...."

The words bit as he said them. It was, after all, the daily temptation that met him in the admiring eyes of his students and the grateful thanks of his colleagues who'd asked him to represent the people of New Jersey. His reputation for wisdom, virtue, and scholarship had been what brought him to America. The College of New Jersey had heard of him, and in their desperate plight to raise funds, they sought him as their president. When your name is known across oceans, isn't it your right to boast?

Witherspoon's voice hesitated. He remembered the apostle Paul. *No. I will boast only in the Cross.*

"I look upon ostentation and confidence to be a sort of outrage upon providence, and when it becomes general, and infuses itself into the spirit of a people, it is a forerunner to destruction...."

> **John Witherspoon** was very late in coming to the debates about independence, taking his seat in Congress on June 29, 1776. He did not wait long in making his opinion known, however, when, on July 1, in response to one member's assertion that perhaps the colonies were not ripe for independence, Witherspoon rejoined, "In my judgment, sir, we are not only ripe, but rotting." Three days later was Fourth of July and the turning of history.

Eight years in America and Witherspoon felt God's staggering vision for this country as deeply as anything but his faith in God itself.

He saw it in the hopes and dreams of his peers—no, his brothers—in Congress. They were statesmen rather than politicians—men whose private morality and public discourse were true to each other, and true to God.

He felt it in the passion of the words of his students as they spoke of their future. He encouraged them to become leaders by explaining the three indispensable elements of a statesman and patriot. First, you had to be an active and sincere promoter of "true and undefiled religion." Second, one must "bear down profanity and immorality of every kind" because if the people were profane and immoral, then the government would be profane and immoral. Finally, he declared that if an individual opposed what God stood for, he opposed the very foundation upon which America had been built. How, then, could he be a true patriot?

But most of all Witherspoon felt God's bracing vision for the future in the hymns of his church, a promise of virtue and blessing out from under the rein of tyranny. It was all so clear and yet so very fragile. And the path led only in the footsteps of the God who led them. A single step off, and it might all to come to ruin. They couldn't risk laziness or despair or doubt. They couldn't toil with arrogance.

"But observe," he said as if answering himself, "that if your cause is just, if your principles are pure, and if your conduct is prudent, you need not fear the multitude of opposing hosts.

"What follows from this? That he is the best friend to American liberty who is most sincere and active in promoting true and undefiled religion...."

Witherspoon continued his sermon. He saw the men in his congregation sitting bolt upright in their pews and could not know how many would lose their lives in the coming war. The women beside them. How many would bury husbands, bury sons, watch their houses be burned to the ground? And yet God's call for the country would move forward. If their vision was true. Witherspoon spoke and he did not know that in just three scant months, he'd make himself a traitor to the crown with an ink-stained quill, scrawling his name alongside Hancock and the others. Or that in a year his own son would be killed at the Battle of Germantown, that his property would be destroyed, that his beloved college would be ruined almost beyond recognition. And if he had known, he would not have stilled his tongue. He would have spoken the same words, called for the same humility, and stayed the same path.

His sermon ended, Witherspoon stepped from the podium, and as the service ended and his church cleared, he found himself alone. In the last pew he found one of the printed copies of Congress's proclamation that had been distributed to every hand that would accept one. A day of fasting and repentance. Who knew if it would be enough? He scanned the page and came to the final words: *God Save These People!*

Not *God Save the King!* as across the ocean. Not *People Save Yourselves* as so many seemed to want. But *God Save These People!* It was the best and only hope, and Witherspoon clutched the paper to him as though it were God's promise itself.

★ ★ ★

May I never boast except in the cross of our Lord Jesus
Christ through which the world has been crucified
to me, and I to the world.
GALATIANS 6:14 NIV

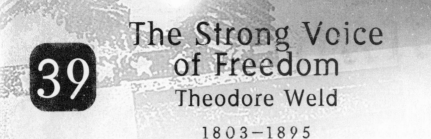

The Strong Voice of Freedom

39

Theodore Weld

1803–1895

Theodore Weld was the most unstoppable voice for abolition the country had ever seen, if only because so many had failed to stop his words. Traveling from small town to small town, he would preach, for days if necessary, on emancipation and God's call to Christian benevolence, and usually his words of peace and holy kindness were greeted with threats and violence wherever he went.

Much of his work in 1835 focused on the state of Ohio, and in town after town Weld arrived, secured a location to speak, and would stay until the area caught hold of the vision for the work God would do. Each night the mob would grow smaller, the shouts quieter, and soon men and women would listen to him. Communities throughout the state accepted his message and, in his wake, formed antislavery societies to carry on the work.

But Weld knew the impact of many small groups would never equal the power of a larger unified group, so in the fall of 1835, he called for a convention of the new-sprung societies to form a larger, more powerful organization. For a location, he felt God leading him to the very lion's den itself, the town of Zanesville, notorious for being the most anti-abolition area in Ohio.

Arriving early to begin preparations, Weld found not a single room or hall for his purposes. If the convention was to be hosted there, hearts would need to change. So, shut out but unbowed, he set up camp across the Muskigum River in Putnam, Ohio. But that was not far enough away for the citizens of Zanesville.

As Weld spoke, his powerful voice filling the hall, a growing murmur could be heard outside. There was a flickering light that could be seen through the space's windows as though of torchlight, and soon the din of angry voices nearly drowned Weld out. On he spoke, fierce and unyielding amid the sound of rocks smashing windows and the great wrenching crash of a fence being destroyed. Windows broken, the chants and threats were even more ominous, but Weld continued through to his end. Then he gathered himself and his few belongings and headed out to meet the mob.

He had done this before, always praying for God's protection. Often he would pass as if unnoticed through angry mobs that had been almost supernaturally stilled. Tonight, God only kept him from death as angry men hurled rocks and swung at him with elm branches they'd made into rude clubs.

Beaten and battered, Weld refused to yield. When the Putnam hall's owner refused to let him return, he found another location. With bruises across his face and a voice raw from a wounded throat, Weld preached God's word of freedom for all. Again the mobs came and the rocks rained down and blows were landed. Night after night, Weld faced the wrath of Zanesville until he wore them out. Subdued by his perseverance, they finally listened to his words and soon welcomed him into their own town. Sixteen days after he'd first arrived, hundreds answered his call to join the abolition movement, and the town, with days to spare, readied itself for Ohio's great antislavery convention. Just as God had promised.

It is important to note that Theodore Weld's work in abolition was not preached in the South. Instead, it was the Northern states who first needed to be converted. Northern citizens were fine without slavery, but the true number who fully opposed it on moral grounds was not overwhelming. They thought about it little and rarely as a sin. It was simply a necessary evil that the Southern states needed to maintain their plantation commerce. Only small groups of men and women saw it not as a necessary evil but simply as evil, a sin in God's eyes.

At the heart of this antislavery movement stood Theodore Weld. A powerful orator and debater, Weld had dedicated himself to the cause after seeing a friend, Charles Stuart, find success in abolishing slavery in the British West Indies. Financed by a group of wealthy New York abolitionists, Weld's first job before heading out to do his speaking was to help establish a seminary where students, many recent converts from Charles Finney's revivals, would be schooled in spreading the truth of God's Word and the Christian call to fight for the rights of all.

Weld chose a newly started school, Lane Seminary, and when the backers were able to secure Lyman Beecher, perhaps the most famous religious mind of the time, as president, success seemed destined.

But the complexity of the abolitionist cause became clear soon after, when Weld discovered that one person's definition of abolition was not necessarily shared by all. Beecher, for instance, opposed slavery. At the same time, he felt that blacks shouldn't be American citizens. He favored returning them to Africa to establish colonies. Weld's fight was for the integration of freed slaves, and the two began a focused though respectful battle that led to eighteen days of discussion that would change the nation.

Called the "Lane Debates," what occurred was more like a revival. Speaker after speaker rose to give their points on slavery, abolition, colonization, and every other aspect of this thorny problem. As the days wore on, a theme emerged. The students and the hearts of those who listened were being won over by Weld and others like him who spoke so eloquently and without denunciation on their view. A vote was put to the students, and they favored "immediate abolition, gradually accomplished." The board of directors for the school and Lyman Beecher disagreed, creating a rift. Weld soon left the school with his protégés and turned to speaking and preaching, in the example of Charles Finney, throughout New York, Ohio, Rhode Island, Massachusetts, and Pennsylvania. Ohio occupied most of his attention in 1835, and he was now notorious wherever he went. The voices who opposed him grew more threatening, more dangerous. Friends feared for not only his safety but also his life. The pinnacle of resistance met Theodore Weld in Troy, New York, June 1836.

In Troy, the mayor himself opposed Weld's presence and sent a message to every citizen in the town that they should meet at the courthouse if they wanted to protest against Weld. The turnout was large and agitated. Weld had his own supporters too, however, and the clash between the groups soon turned from melee into full riot. Stones rained down on Weld as he was escorted to safety and in the following days as well. Bruises covered him, one stone had nearly crushed his larynx, damaging his voice, and he limped terribly. Still he would not leave, prepared to sacrifice even his life. He was never given the option. The town fathers of Troy had had enough and wanted no blood on their hands. They refused to let him return.

Weld continued on, his voice little more than a whisper, but the message of abolition was gaining ground. Thousands would sit in silence, listening to him speak, and thousands converted to the cause. The state of New York soon became a stronghold for abolition societies.

When his voice finally gave out on him, the American Anti-Slavery Society enlisted Weld to serve as trainer, teacher, discipler, and mentor. Following the early church, they selected seventy men and women who would be trained to spread the cause of abolition in campaigns similar to those he'd led. One of these women would include his soon-to-be wife, Angelina Grimké. At the same time he continued in his writing, including *American Slavery As It Is*, which served as a primary source for Harriet Beecher Stowe's *Uncle Tom's Cabin*. In a twist of irony, Stowe, who considered herself a disciple of Weld, was the daughter of Lyman Beecher, Weld's former adversary from their days at Lane Seminary. Stowe had attended the Lane Debates as a child.

The cause of abolition spread westward, and leading the charge was usually a voice converted by Weld or taught by him. He was the shining light for the cause of freedom and God's will that would not be darkened, the voice that would not be stilled, the unstoppable force who changed the perception of a nation.

Weld's entire life is a tribute to perseverance and devotion to God's truth. For him, slavery was not a secondhand issue but a national sin that had been institutionalized. Today as well, there are contradictions to God's Word that have been written or are about to be written into law. How do we stand opposed from them? Do we march once and consider our part done? Do we shout until our voices give out or those oppose us shout louder? Or do we, with discipline and fervor, speak until we are heard?

★ ★ ★

Yet the hour of emancipation is advancing.... This enterprise is for the young; for those who can follow it up, and bear it through it's [sic] consummation.
—THOMAS JEFFERSON

THE REPUBLICAN PLATFORM.

ADOPTED BY THE PHILADELPHIA CONVENTION, JUNE 17TH, 1856. A GOOD DAY FOR THE ADOPTION OF SUCH PRINCIPLES.

THIS Convention of Delegates, assembled in pursuance of a call to the people of the United States, without regard to past political differences or divisions, who are opposed to the repeal of the Missouri Compromise—to the policy of the present administration—to the extension of slavery into free territory; in favor of the admission of Kansas as a free State—of restoring the action of the Federal Government to the principles of Washington and Jefferson, and for the purpose of presenting candidates for the offices of President

The Missouri Compromise
and the Fugitive Slave Law

The Old Testament book of 1 Kings tells a powerful story of two women who claim ownership of the same baby. King Solomon, in his wisdom, decrees that he will simply cut the baby in half, but the real mother pleads with him to let the baby live, even if it means giving up the child. Knowing this, Solomon gives the baby to the true mother.

In 1819 the territory of Missouri finally had a large enough population to qualify for statehood. The problem: Would it be a slave or free state? Choosing political compromise, in 1820 Congress decided Missouri would be a slave state, while Maine would be admitted as a free state, thus retaining the balance of slave v. free states twelve to twelve.

Essentially, the baby was cut in half.

For more than thirty-five years the Missouri Compromise ripped open the midsection of the nation. Additionally, it decreed that above the 36° 30' parallel, freedom for blacks was the law. Below it, slavery reigned. This dark dichotomy, however, only created an atmosphere for the Underground Railroad to grow and thrive. Perhaps more than any other issue in the early 1800s, the Missouri Compromise awakened the nation to the divisiveness of slavery.

In 1850, in an attempt to appease the Southern states, the Democrat-controlled Congress once again cut the baby in half. That year the Fugitive Slave Law was passed—a law requiring all citizens in free states to report escaped slaves to the authorities, upon threat of fine and imprisonment. Bent on profit, dishonest slave hunters were known to kidnap free-born Northern blacks and sell them into slavery. Fear and suspicion reigned, and even African Americans whose families had been free for generations were unsafe.

In 1857 a pro-slavery Supreme Court, via the Dred Scott decision, declared the Missouri Compromise, which restricted slavery in certain states, unconstitutional. It also decreed that slaves were not U.S. citizens and therefore were ineligible to bring a suit to federal court. This delighted Southern slave owners and enraged Northern abolitionists, accelerating the day when the divided nation would clash in civil war.

40 The Repentant Slaveholder
Angelina Grimké
1805–1879

I stand before you as a southerner, exiled from the land of my birth, by the sound of the lash, and the piteous cry of the slave.

Angelina Grimké spoke in a voice that had never been heard before in the State House of Boston. It wasn't her words themselves, as many in the legislature were sympathetic to the abolitionist cause, but her very presence. It was a cold day, February 21, 1838, sixty-two years after independence had been declared, and finally a woman was addressing a legislative body in the United States.

Angelina Grimké was indeed not only a Southerner, raised in Charleston, South Carolina, but part of an aristocratic slave-holding family. When she spoke of the sound of the lash, the cry of the slave, those images came not from a neighboring plantation but from her own upbringing.

I stand before you as a repentant slaveholder.

It was her sister, Sarah, who brought the light of abolition first to Angelina's eyes. Sarah had traveled north in 1819 with her ailing father to help him find rest and care, and the journey opened her eyes. Befriending Quakers, she soon decided to stay in Philadelphia, even after her father died, returning to her home only long enough to convince Angelina of slavery's ills before traveling north again.

Angelina did not at first join her. Instead, she felt called to protest within the system itself. Her radical stance found few open ears and drove a deep wedge between Angelina and her own family. In 1829 things had gotten so bad that she moved north to join her sister in Philadelphia.

In 1835 Angelina joined the Philadelphia Female Anti-Slavery Society, and her world soon changed forever.

I stand before you as a moral being, endowed with precious and inalienable rights, which are correlative with solemn duties and high responsibilities....

For Angelina, her abolitionist views were not just an emotional feeling or a reasoned opinion; they were fully derived from her faith as a Christian woman. Slavery was appalling to God, a sin from which our country needed cleansing and possibly even saving. Revolutionary in her thinking, however, was the notion that it was the nation's women who were duty-bound to end it. In 1836 she penned her *Appeal to the Christian Women of the South*, a sermon-like pamphlet that spelled out her evangelical call. The pamphlet's epigraph was taken directly from the book of Esther and the peasant queen's decision to ask for the deliverance of her people. It was the core scriptural example at the heart of her ministry, her voice, her cause.

And as a moral being I feel that I owe it to the suffering slave, and to the deluded master, to my country and the world, to do all that I can to overturn a system of complicated crime, built up upon the broken hearts and prostrate bodies of my countrymen in chains, and cemented by the blood and sweat and tears of my sisters in bonds.

Following her pamphlet, Angelina, joined by her sister, Sarah, began speaking on slavery

On May 14, 1838, Pennsylvania Hall opened in Philadelphia. It had been built to champion the freedom of speech. The abolitionist cause had become so controversial that finding a location to hold their rallies was nearly impossible. What they needed was their own space, so two thousand people, a majority being women, bought twenty-dollar shares in the building to fund its construction. On May 16 and 17, 1838, Angelina Grimké, joined by Lucretia Mott and Abby Kelley, led a rally opposing slavery, while an angry mob protested throughout the event and long after the speeches had ended. The mayor ordered the men to disperse but provided no force to make them, and when he left, the building was ransacked and eventually burned. The beautiful tribute to free speech, America's greatest freedom, lasted four days.

with groups of women throughout New York. As former eyewitnesses, their provocative accounts were hugely engaging, and soon, what had been planned as merely small gatherings became something more. The women toured the Northern states appealing with ever-growing boldness for not only the abolition of slavery but the cause of the nation's women to bring it about.

Their notoriety, fame, and boldness soon brought not only criticism of their antislavery message but a rising tide of sexism as well. Women were not supposed to behave this way. They were overstepping their bounds. They were, many from the pulpit cried, violating the role of the submissive woman so obviously spelled out in the New Testament.

Their cause now became twofold. Defending the cause of freedom on one side and the rights of women on the other, the Grimké sisters were now constantly attacked, even from within their own abolitionist ranks. They had been too bold. Sarah Grimké's *Letters on the Equality of the Sexes*, which demanded equal rights and education and drew parallels between the treatment of women and slaves, was almost universally detested.

At the same time, Angelina managed to find a ray of happiness in all the tumult. For years she had privately loved one of her abolitionist mentors, Theodore Weld, and he finally took the bold act of confessing that he shared her feelings. United in their common cause, they discovered a unity much deeper and were eventually married.

Just two days after the wedding, Angelina Grimké gave her final speech on May 16, 1838, in Philadelphia. Great protests greeted her, and in the middle of her speech an enormous mob shattered windows and threw rocks. The crowd looked concerned but Angelina pushed on:

"We often hear the question asked: 'What shall we do?' Here is an opportunity for doing something now. Every man and every woman present may do something by showing that we fear not a mob, and, in the midst of threatenings and revilings, by opening our mouths for the dumb and pleading the cause of those who are ready to perish."

Following this speech, Angelina Grimké and Theodore Weld, joined by her sister, Sarah, began a new phase of their abolitionist efforts. In 1839 Weld, with his wife's assistance, wrote *American Slavery As It Is: Testimony of a Thousand Voices*, a chilling, honest, and brutal look at the deep horrors that slaves faced daily. This foundational book for the antislavery movement inspired *Uncle Tom's Cabin*, by Harriet Beecher Stowe, motivating even more men and women to the cause. Now seen as mentors for the upcoming generation, Grimké and Weld turned their strengths to teaching others and equipping many for the spreading of both God's Word and the cause of freedom. Together this couple never wavered in leading the cause of abolition. They faced abuse and threats and beatings but continued to find their strength in God's cause, living with a tenacity that continues to inspire.

★ ★ ★

Then Queen Esther answered, "If I have found
favor with you, O King, and if it pleases your majesty,
grant me my life—this is my petition. And spare
my people—this is my request."
ESTHER 7:3 NIV

41

"As a Mother... As a Christian"
Harriet Beecher Stowe
1811–1896

It came to her in a flash. One minute Harriet Beecher Stowe was taking communion in her home church in Brunswick, Maine, surrounded by her six children. The next minute she was somewhere else, transported in a vision to another time, another place. Before her eyes, as real as life, came a scene of a black man being brutally beaten and dying under the lash because he would not act against his conscience nor deny the existence of his true master, Jesus Christ.

That afternoon Harriet went to her room and wrote down exactly what she had seen. As she wrote, the words flooded out, taking a form and a life of their own.

Later, as she read the vision to her husband, Calvin, they could both feel the power of the Holy Spirit in the words.

Calvin was quiet for a moment, then said, "Harriet, that is by far the best thing you have ever written."

"Calvin, I wish I could explain how I could see every detail—the angle of the sun through the trees, the sounds, the smells. All I had to do was write it down. I remember reading an article about this—I know it really happened." She paused. "But this was so much more real than any article. It was as if I were really there."

"Harriet, the details were there because God himself was there, an unseen witness of the tragedy. He knows everything that happened, the thoughts and feelings of everyone involved. He let you see the scene through His eyes."

"Yes!" Harriet replied. "It was as though God was speaking through me, telling me exactly what He wanted to say."

"You must go on with it, Hattie. You must write a story with this as the ending. It's what the Lord wants you to do."

Harriet agreed. For a long time she had felt God wanted her to use her writing talent to turn the tide against slavery. The abolitionist cause had first come to her attention in 1834, during debates on the slavery question sponsored by Theodore Weld at Lane Seminary.

Then in 1850 Harriet saw firsthand the effects of the new Fugitive Slave Act, which required Northern citizens to offer assistance to slave catchers from the South. She was visiting her brother Edward and his wife, Isabella, in Boston, when the first instances of free blacks being returned to slavery under the new law outraged the local residents.

Harriet later told her son Charles Edward, "My heart was bursting with anguish excited by the cruelty and injustice our nation was showing the slave, and praying to God to let me do a little and cause my cry to be heard." Writing articles was not what Harriet did best; her strongest gift was writing fiction. But she felt inadequate, unable to handle the theme she was tackling.

The Sunday morning vision changed all that. Harriet was convinced that God had shown her how to write a book that would not talk about the evils of slavery but show it through a series of vivid pictures. Supporting characters and stories that she would weave around her hero and his tragic death began to take shape.

The stories in *Uncle Tom's Cabin* are based on actual events. Harriet did extensive research to make her story of slavery and its horrors as authentic—and convincing—as possible. Some of the events, such as the scene Harriet saw in her vision, she had read of in the book *American Slavery As It Is*, a collection of journalistic accounts drawn entirely from the Southern press and published in 1839 by fellow abolitionists Sarah Grimké, Angelina Grimké Weld, and Theodore Weld. She also drew on firsthand accounts collected by Josiah Henson, an escaped slave who pastored a church comprised of escaped slaves in Canada, where British law protected them from arrest and return to slavery.

Other stories were drawn from Harriet's own life experiences. Looking back, Harriet could see how God had been preparing her heart and mind for this task. For several years Harriet had lived in Cincinnati, Ohio, just across the river from Kentucky, a slave state. She employed black women to help her cook, clean, and do the washing. As she worked together with them, she carefully questioned them about their lives as slaves in the South. From these years of conversations, Harriet learned endless details that showed the impact slavery had on the lives of ordinary people.

Harriet and her husband were also active in helping fugitive slaves escape, giving aid and shelter to runaways who passed through their town. Every day she heard new stories of the hunger for freedom, of the separation of families, of cruel brutality. Years later she would write about these fugitives whose suffering and distress she had witnessed with her own eyes. At the same time, she had befriended slaveholders in neighboring Kentucky and had come to understand many of the slaveholders' concerns.

Harriet investigated stories and talked with eyewitnesses. One of the most memorable moments in the book is the true story of Eliza Harris's escape over the frozen Ohio River. It was March, and Eliza expected to be able to walk across the frozen river to the free state of Ohio without a problem. After walking all night, carrying her child, she finally reached the river, only to find that an early thaw had caused the ice to break up. Large blocks were now drifting downstream. For a whole day she waited on the bank, hoping to find some way to cross to freedom. As night fell, she heard the bloodhounds closing in on her and saw the slave catchers not far behind. With courage born of desperation, she decided to cross over on the ice—or die trying. Holding her child tightly with one hand, she leaped from block to block, slipping and scrambling.

An unknown man watched Eliza's progress from the Ohio shore. Deeply moved by the young mother's courage, he pulled her up the riverbank and directed her to a Rev. John Rankin's house, her next stop on the Underground Railroad.

Upon hearing the account of Eliza's escape, Harriet interviewed Rev. Rankin and asked him question after question.

Drawing on such personal experiences, Harriet was able to give slavery a human face and turn fact into powerful fiction. Readers could not easily ignore the way slavery degraded both blacks and whites: floggings and murder; escape and pursuit of fugitives; separation of husbands and wives, parents and children, brothers and sisters; repeated rapes of slave women by their masters, and the damage done to the master's own marriage because of his infidelity. Slavery corrupted the morals of whites and victimized the blacks, damaging everyone who came in contact with it.

Early in March 1851 Harriet wrote to Dr. Gamaliel Bailey, publisher of *The National Era*, a weekly antislavery paper, asking if he would be interested in publishing a story about slavery in serial form. "My vocation," she told Dr. Bailey, "is simply that of *painter*, and my object will be to hold up [slavery] in the most lifelike and graphic manner possible."

Bailey agreed to pay three hundred dollars for the set of stories, which Harriet thought would run for a few weeks. Eventually, Harriet wrote forty installments that ran between June 5, 1851, and April 1, 1852. Despite *The National Era*'s small circulation, the suspenseful episodes reached a large audience through worn copies that were passed from family to family.

Harriet's stories attracted the attention of Boston publisher J. P. Jewett, who published the work as a novel in March 1852. *Uncle Tom's Cabin* immediately broke all sales records of that time. On the first day three thousand copies of the book were sold; within a few days ten thousand copies were gone; by the first of April, the book was in its second edition. Eight presses running day and night were barely able to keep pace with the demand for it. By the end of 1852, three hundred thousand copies had been sold in the U.S. alone. One and a half million copies of the book were sold in Great Britain and the British colonies. Eventually the book was translated into twenty-five languages.

The secret of the book's immense success was that Harriet did not lecture, did not condemn. She let the stories speak for themselves, in pictures so vivid and compelling that even a child could understand them. The unavoidable conclusion: Slavery violated the most basic Christian law: "Do unto others as you would have them do unto you."

Harriet made a personal appeal to the mothers of America: "By the sacred love you bear your child...by the prayers you breathe for his sacred good, I beseech you: pity the mother who has all your affections and not one legal right to protect, guide, or educate the child of her bosom!...Is this a thing to be defended, sympathized with, passed over in silence?"

As Frederick Douglass later pointed out: "Its effect was amazing, instantaneous and universal." Supporters of slavery were furious, and Harriet received hundreds of hostile letters.

Uncle Tom's Cabin made Harriet an international celebrity and a wealthy woman and enabled her to meet the most famous people of her day. When Harriet was introduced to President Abraham Lincoln in 1862, he greeted her with the words, "So you are the little woman who wrote the book that started this great war!"

Stowe believed that a transformation through Christian love must occur before slavery could be abolished successfully.

It was said that with one book Harriet Beecher Stowe created two million abolitionists. Inspired by God, Harriet's stories touched the heart, cut through arguments and debate, and accomplished more for the cause of abolition than one hundred years of sermons had been able to do. Historians have said, "After *Uncle Tom's Cabin*, objective analysis of the slavery issue was almost impossible." Truth, now embodied, was a force that could not be stopped.

★ ★ ★

The Lord replies, "I have seen violence done to the
helpless, and I have heard the groans of the poor.
Now I will rise up to rescue them, as they have
longed for me to do.

PSALM 12:5 NLT

I wrote as I did because as a woman, as a mother,
I was oppressed and broken-hearted with the sorrow
and injustice I saw, because as a Christian I felt the
dishonor to Christianity, because as a lover of my
country I trembled in the coming day of wrath.
It is no merit in the sorrowful that they weep,
or in the oppressed and smothering that they grasp
and struggle, nor to me that I *must* speak for the
oppressed—who cannot speak for themselves.
—HARRIET BEECHER STOWE

The Power to Get Wealth

Arthur and Lewis Tappan were millionaires back in the days when a million dollars was an unthinkable sum of money. Engaged in the silk business in New York City, their company made more than a million dollars every year. Yet Arthur and Lewis chose to live modestly, as they believed God had entrusted them with wealth so they could help their fellow humankind.

Deeply touched by the ministry of Charles Finney, they financially supported his revival work. Later they joined Theodore Weld in founding Lane Seminary and Oberlin College, to prepare Finney's converts for the ministry.

In 1833 the Tappan brothers organized the American Anti-Slavery Society. In those days it took courage to speak out against slavery, and Arthur and Lewis suffered for their convictions. Pro-slavery mobs burned Lewis's home to the ground in 1834. Lewis wrote that he wanted his house to remain "this summer as it is, a silent antislavery preacher to the crowds who will see it." In 1835 a church built by the Tappans was set on fire. Later that same year, fire destroyed a building that housed much of the brothers' business. Undeterred, the brothers continued their work. Lewis wanted to eliminate the "black pew" and caused an uproar in upstate New York when he and his family sat in the pews reserved for blacks.

In addition to their antislavery causes, the Tappans supported the American Bible Society, the American Tract Society, the American Home Missionary Society, the American Education Society, the American Temperance Society, and the American Sunday School Union.

By 1849 Lewis had accumulated enough wealth to retire. Instead he decided to devote the rest of his life to humanitarian causes. When he was sixty-four, Lewis was instrumental in a project that finally broke through the nation's complacency concerning the plight of African Americans. In 1852 one of the publications he financed, the *National Era*, published a series of stories titled *Uncle Tom's Cabin* by Harriet Beecher Stowe, stories God used to forever change how Americans viewed slavery.

Inspiration From a Slave

Josiah Henson experienced and witnessed much abuse in his thirty years as a slave, but perhaps the worst was his father's torture when he attempted to defend his mother from a plantation overseer. Henson's father was whipped one hundred times before his ear was nailed to a post and cut off with a knife. He was sold to another plantation owner and was never heard from again.

Henson's own experiences were not ideal, as his workload was straining and living conditions were poor. Cracks in the log huts allowed the rain and snow to come in, and a dirt floor soaked up the moisture, creating a muddy ground unsuitable but unavoidable for sleeping.

After being abused, lied to, and cheated by his masters, Josiah Henson escaped slavery with his wife and four young children. They traveled north through difficult and unsafe conditions and finally settled in Canada, where Henson immediately set to work assisting others in their escape from slavery, risking his life while using the resources of the Underground Railroad.

Only a few years after farming in Ontario, Canada, Henson created the Dawn Settlement, a self-supporting black colony in northern Canada. He was well-known for lecturing and preaching and teaching other ex-slaves to be successful farmers. While Henson liked the relative fame he had found, his main goal in life was to improve the living conditions for Canada's black population.

Josiah Henson's autobiography, titled *The Life of Josiah Henson*, was published in 1849. The heart-wrenching story inspired Harriet Beecher Stowe, who later based her character Uncle Tom on Henson in her 1852 book *Uncle Tom's Cabin*.

A Cycle of Service and Love
John Perkins
1930—PRESENT

42

John Perkins escaped a life that might have beaten him to nothing. He escaped, but he never forgot that there were others like him who might not be so fortunate—so he did the unthinkable. He returned to that life, looking for a way to change it for others.

Born in 1930, Depression-era Mississippi, John Perkins knew sorrow, heartbreak, and hunger. His mother died from malnutrition; his father abandoned the family trying to find work. John was raised by a grandmother and other extended family. He survived, but barely. He did not thrive; the whites would not allow it. Jim Crow reigned in Mississippi and a black boy learned his place quickly: head bowed, eyes downcast. You never looked a white man in the eye.

John's brother, Clyde, forgot that lesson fighting for the world's freedom during World War II. Returning to New Hebron, Mississippi, after the war, Clyde Perkins chafed at the segregation and second-class treatment. He was a war hero, honored with a Purple Heart. One night he made small trouble with the wrong man and ended up being shot for little reason other than that he was black and had dared to speak up. John was with his brother that night and cradled him in his arms in the backseat of a car as friends rushed them to the hospital. Clyde died before reaching the hospital, his blood staining John's hands and shirt.

It was the future of too many young men in Mississippi, and John Perkins, now bitter and depressed over the loss of his brother, seemed on a path to the same end. His relatives swore it wouldn't claim another of their own. John, just seventeen now, was handed a bus ticket and urged to head to California. Opportunities existed there—though it wasn't easy for a black man anywhere. So John escaped.

He found good work with a steel foundry but never forgot Mississippi. First it was his sweetheart, Vera Mae, whom he arranged to come out from Mississippi so they could marry. Still he couldn't put his past behind him. Success followed him now—he had a house and a growing family with son Spencer—but something still seemed amiss.

In 1957 Spencer Perkins, just three years old, led his father to God because of verses the boy memorized at a children's Bible class. John Perkins, who barely knew his earthly father, found a heavenly one because of his own son. His conversion, cultivated by a pastor friend, was not halfhearted. He soon became part of a prison ministry, and in the stories of the anguish, hurt, anger, and frustration that he heard from the inmates, John Perkins was given a glimpse of the nagging need of his heart. These were not new problems, he realized. They weren't California problems. The anger and pain he heard could be traced back to the unresolved and devastating divide still tearing the South apart. White and black were separate, blame and anger and hatred on both sides. John Perkins felt a call to step in, offer whatever healing he could. And he knew it had to be back in Mississippi. His escape had only freed him to try to bring freedom and help to others.

In 1960, near the very height of the civil rights era, John, his wife, and his son moved to Mendenhall, Mississippi. Here he established Mendenhall Ministries, a multifaceted ministry that grew over the next dozen years to include a day-care center, a youth program, a church, an adult education program, a health center, and more. Perkins long believed that ministry needed to be two-pronged. Not only must God's saving grace be preached, but hurting and desperate people needed to be fitted with tools and education to become productive in society so that the Lord's work regenerates itself, passed on in service from those who have been helped to those who need help.

Not everyone looked on empowering blacks as a good thing, particularly when Perkins and many of his colleagues and followers participated in boycotts, marches, and protests around the state. White officials had their eye on John for a long time, and in early February 1970, they tried their best to break Perkins, the work he was doing, and everything for which he stood.

But they didn't come after him like men. Instead, they arrested a van full of students to whom Perkins was close, along with their white driver, John's good friend Doug Huemmer, as the group drove away from a demonstration. The night of February 7, John received a frantic phone call saying that the group had been arrested in Brandon, Mississippi.

John knew Brandon. The sheriff there enforced the Jim Crow laws as if they'd been brought down from Sinai, beating blacks for daring to register to vote. The arrest of the students was incredibly dangerous, and every moment the kids spent in jail was one more moment to be beaten or worse. John, together with his friends Rev. Curry Brown and Joe Paul Buckley, raced toward Brandon, hoping to post bond for the entire group. They never got the chance.

At the jail, John Perkins, after asking to see the sheriff, was instead met by a dozen highway patrol officers who'd obviously been waiting for his arrival. Before even bringing them into the building, the police were already swinging fists and kicking the defenseless men. Inside, the sheriff showed himself, but only to participate in the beatings.

"During the beatings," Perkins wrote in his autobiography, *Let Justice Roll Down*, "I tried to cover my head with my arms, but they just beat me anyway till I was lying on the floor. Even then they just kept beating and stomping me, kicking me in the head, in the ribs, in the groin. I rolled up in a ball to protect myself as best I could. The beatings just went on and on."

Perkins slipped in and out of consciousness. At some point in the night, the violence waned and officers actually arrived in the cell to mop up the blood. A rumor spread through the students that the FBI was on its way. The police needed to rid themselves of the evidence. Freedom would come soon.

But no help came, and the scare seemed to enrage the police even further. They moved past beating into torture. A fork, its tines sharp, was shoved up John's nose and down his throat. An officer put a gun to Perkins' head and pulled the trigger. John still doesn't know if the gun was loaded or not. They mocked him, made him read aloud the demands for equal rights his Mendenhall community had developed, and never stopped beating him.

"They were like savages—like some horror out of the night. And I can't forget their faces, so twisted with hate. It was like looking at white-faced demons. Hate did that to them."

But John Perkins would not hate them back.

If he'd learned anything in his days, it was that hate offered no freedom. It would only corrupt, turn you into the same spiteful savage. John Perkins took his beatings and pitied those who lashed out at him until darkness swam in at him and he could remember no more.

Students nursed him through the night. Most didn't think he'd make it to morning. His friends outside of prison, however, knew what was happening, and they scoured the county gathering money to post bond for all those incarcerated. Some even put up their property as bond. A day later John Perkins regained his freedom—bloodied, bruised, and more determined than ever to seek not only equal rights and common dignity for blacks but a reconciliation between whites and blacks that needed to start within the Christian church.

"Christian discipleship at its finest is when a person recognizes that he'll never, in and of himself, be complete enough. His completeness comes in relation to other people. As he opens his life to a small group of people, his gifts and skills are released for serving others."

This statement went to the heart of every ministry and outreach program John Perkins established. After Mendenhall, he and his family moved in 1972 to Jackson, Misisissippi, where they bought a former slave plantation and established the Voice of Calvary Ministries. Very similar to his work in Mendenhall, which continued to thrive under some of Perkins' disciples, Voice of Calvary was a Christian community with low-income housing, a church, health center, thrift shop, and leadership development program.

In 1982 the Perkinses returned to California to found the Harambee Christian Family Center in a Pasadena neighborhood that had one of the highest daytime crime rates in the state. Through Bible camps, afterschool programs, and intern programs, the Center helped transform the neighborhood, bringing hope to the youth of the area.

Finally, in 1989, Perkins continued his desire to reach across racial divides by starting the Christian Community Development Association. This group of Christian leaders from across the country were united only by their commitment to reaching out to the poor and needy face-to-face, within communities.

John Perkins was esteemed as a hero of the civil rights movement, but also as a true revolutionary in the cause of service to the needy and his vision for bridging racial divides. Nationally recognized for his vision and leadership, he served on the boards of organizations like World Vision and Prison Fellowship and was awarded honorary doctorates from Wheaton College, Gordon College, Huntington College, and other universities.

Today, Perkins lives in Mississippi with his wife, Vera Mae, where he continues to speak and work on behalf of his twin causes of racial reconciliation and working within communities to train needy men and women to not only support themselves but take the help they've received and use it to help others. The Perkinses have eight grown children, though their eldest, Spencer, died unexpectedly of a heart attack in 1998. Many of their children follow in the Christian work of their parents, ensuring that their legacy will live on for generations. The cycle of service and God's love will reach through generations and change lives as long as God's Word finds willing ears and God's Spirit reaches tender hearts.

★ ★ ★

Blessed are the peacemakers, for they will be called sons
of God. Blessed are those who are persecuted because of
righteousness, for theirs is the kingdom of heaven.

MATTHEW 5:9–10 NIV

1857–1858 Noonday Prayer Meetings

The elders of the North Dutch Reformed Church of New York City hoped to reverse a decline in Sunday attendance, so in June 1857 they enlisted Jeremiah Lanphier as a lay missionary to launch an ambitious visitation ministry. Within weeks attendance increased, most notably among men—quite the departure from what churches of that time were accustomed to.

Lanphier's endeavors were not without discouragement and frustration. But his regular habit of seeking the Lord's renewed strength did not go unanswered. It thus ocurred to Lanphier that perhaps the businessmen of the congregation would also benefit from such a practice, and he set about to organize a weekly prayer meeting held between noon and one o'clock.

The first meeting was held on Wednesday, September 23, 1857, in the church's Consistory building at the corner of Fulton and William Streets—within a stone's throw of where the World Trade Center would one day stand and fall. Only six men came that day, but a week later there were twenty, and the third week there were forty. Almost immediately it was decided that the meetings should be held daily. As the weeks passed, attendance continued to increase and the meeting was moved from room to room as their numbers required. Women began to join the meeting as well, and within six months the entire Consistory building was filled.

Soon noonday prayer meetings sprang up throughout the city. The press caught wind of it and began covering the "Progress of the Revival." With the press coverage came increased awareness, and congregations in cities across the country started their own Noonday Prayer Meetings.

More than one million people across the country came to Christ, and in many recorded cases, the time of conversion was traced back to the exact day of prayer for the individual.

The Noonday Prayer Revival took place three years before the Civil War. One cannot help but think that God was preparing a country for its darkest hour. Many who went into battle were no doubt prepared for the prospect of death as a result of their Noonday Prayer encounters.

An Impassioned Defense

43

John Quincy Adams and the *Amistad*

1839–1841

For abolitionists, one of the most galvanizing moments of the nineteenth century did not even involve American slaves. Instead, it involved thirty-nine African men, kidnapped and sold as slaves to plantation owners in Spanish Cuba. The fate of these men, and their leader Joseph Cinque—born Sengbe Pieh in Sierre Leone—captured the nation's attention in 1839 when their ship docked in Long Island and their dramatic and violent story became public.

Accounts vary, but what we know is that on a rainy night around July 1, en route to the plantations where they would work, the slaves, hands still chained, led a revolt, killing the ship's captain and a cook who had been taunting them. A slave was killed by the captain, and two other sailors were either killed or escaped.

The Africans did not kill the two remaining Spanish captains on board, Pedro Montez and José Ruiz, instead commanding them to sail the ship back to Africa. The two men, who knew the sea far better than their would-be captors, instead sailed for nearest land: the port at Long Island. Officials investigated the suspicious vessel, learned of the deaths, and placed the Africans in custody.

Spanish officials, as represented by Martin Van Buren's administration, demanded that the Africans be extradited so they could be charged with murder. Abolitionists, led by Lewis Tappan, refused to let that happen without a fight and soon had Ruiz and Montez arrested for kidnapping and assault, enraging Spain further but eliciting great interest from many citizens in the North.

These men, after all, weren't slaves. They lived free in Africa. Had families. Joseph Cinque was married with three children. Against their will and usually by great violence, each had been captured and sold into slavery. Where they were blind to the plight of the slaves in their own country, Northerners saw the injustice in this case and soon backed the abolitionist cause.

A district court heard the case first and ruled in favor of the Africans. The prosecution—the United States of America itself—appealed and took the case to a circuit court and then to the Supreme Court.

At each stage, the Africans were represented by Roger Baldwin, but as the Supreme Court case approached, worries broke out among Tappan and other supporters. Perhaps they needed another weapon this time. Lewis Tappan thought through the issue and went to one of his long-standing abolitionist friends he knew: John Quincy Adams.

Adams, now in his seventies, was a man of honor and deep faith who'd even published a volume of Bible studies. Adams had served four years as president of the United States and later was elected as a congressman for Massachusetts. Tappan recalled the speech Adams had given just a few years before on the Fourth of July. He was one of the few men old enough in Congress to have actually witnessed the fight for independence firsthand, and his speech that day in 1837 was bold in linking the cause of independence with faith: "Is it not that the Declaration of Independence first organized the social compact on the foundation of the Redeemer's mission on Earth?"

But nowhere in God's mission did Adams ever acknowledge any acceptance of slavery. Notorious for his outspokenness and labeled the "Hellhound of Slavery," he'd taken many opportunities, often risking his very reputation, career, and safety, to speak on the cause of abolition. Famed for his fire and passion, as well as his sharp tongue, Adams seemed the perfect man to balance Roger Baldwin's exceptional but perhaps dry strategy in the *Amistad* case.

Adams did not accept quickly. He felt himself too old. Too long from the field of practicing law. Tappan reminded Adams that he seemed to manage arguing nearly every day in Congress and that it was more than just words on paper passing this bill or that proclamation that stood at stake here. These were men's lives.

Adams pondered the case. He thought of the fights he'd have over such matters in Congress. How in 1836 his colleagues had grown so weary of the issue that they'd passed a gag rule tabling all talk about abolition and slavery. On that day he'd fought. He stood up and shouted, "I hold the resolution to be a direct violation of the Constitution of the United States, the rules of this house, and the rights of my constituents." Few men were willing to risk such outspokenness. Adams knew he had to take the case.

"By the blessing of God, I'll do it," he told Tappan.

The case was, if there can be such a thing in law, a blowout. The prosecution had not yet been able to muster any kind of attack based on more than the color of the men's skin and the fact that Spain continued to pressure for their conviction.

Roger Baldwin expertly dismantled what little smokescreen they put up, showing how, according to the laws of both the United States *and* Spain, these men were free and their revolt on the *Amistad* an act of self-defense. He then turned the defense over to Adams.

Tentative and nervous at first, Adams soon found himself caught up in the spirit of the men he was defending, and the words came quickly and with great fire. He spoke for four hours the first day and another four when the hearing restarted a few days later after the unexpected death of one of the justices.

His targets included not only a defense of the men but an indictment of Van Buren's administration, an attack on Spain for their slave trade practices, and a challenge of the very nature of slavery itself—which is always about the degradation of a person's rights.

On March 6, 1841, in one of the most lopsided rulings in its history, the Court voted 7 to 1 in favor of the defense, and the African men were finally freed. It was almost a year and half since their revolt and subsequent imprisonment. They were free but with nowhere to go. The abolitionists, who'd stayed with them through all the madness, helped raise funds for their journeys back to Africa, and in November of that year, Joseph Cinque, Sengbe Pieh, finally returned to his native land. His return, however, was bittersweet, as he soon discovered that his wife and children had been killed. Sengbe did not stay long in the mission after arriving. He was a free man—a sad and tired man. One day he left to do some business down the coast and never returned. Nothing more was heard about him.

John Quincy Adams, for his part, received many congratulations, the great satisfaction at having spoken so eloquently for those who couldn't, and also a small gift from Lewis Tappan. It was a Bible, signed by Joseph Cinque and two other of his shipmates on behalf of all the Mendian Africans of the *Amistad*.

John Quincy Adams lived for his service to his country, and he died in his service as well. Common practices of the time held that witnessing how a man faced death gave you the only true sense of the depths of his faith. On February 21, 1848, in the midst of a session in the Old House Chamber, Adams collapsed. His colleagues attended to him as best he could, and in their midst he never showed the smallest fear or regret. His final words, spoken only after he regained himself a little, were, "This is the end of the earth; I am content." Then he was carried into the speaker's room, where he lay two days, and died on February 23. Even in death John Quincy Adams modeled his faith to those who knew him, and his passing reassured many of his devotion to the cause of God.

★ ★ ★

I, the Lord, have called you in righteousness; I will take
hold of your hand. I will keep you and will make you to be
a covenant for the people and a light for the Gentiles, to
opens eyes that are blind, to free captives from prison, and
to release from the dungeon those who sit in darkness.

ISAIAH 42:6–7 NIV

A Father's Advice

John Quincy Adams, sixth president of the United States, was a devout reader of the Scriptures. Adams frequently sent letters to his family when work called him away from home, and these letters were later published in the *New York Tribune*. The following excerpt comes from a letter written by John Quincy Adams in 1811, while ambassador in St. Petersburg, to one of his sons.

In your letter of the 18th January to your mother, you mentioned that you read to your aunt a chapter in the Bible or a section of Doddridge's Annotations *every evening. This information gave me real pleasure; for so great is my veneration for the Bible, and so strong my belief, that when duly read and meditated on, it is of all books in the world, that which contributes most to make men good, wise, and happy.*

I advise you, in whatever you read, and most of all in reading the Bible, to remember that it is for the purpose of making you wiser and more virtuous. I have myself, for many years, made it a practice to read through the Bible once every year.

In your infancy and youth, you have been, and will be for some years, under the authority and control of your friends and instructors; but you must soon come to the age when you must govern yourself. You have already come to that age in many respects; you know the difference between right and wrong, and you know some of your duties, and the obligations you are under, to become acquainted with them all. It is in the Bible, you must learn them, and from the Bible how to practice them. Those duties are to God, to your fellow-creatures, and to yourself.

The Dark Side of Lincoln's Home
Springfield Riot
AUGUST 1908

44

Most of what we once knew about the Springfield Riot is wrong. For years historians looked at the evidence before them in written and oral accounts and made assumptions based on what might seem like commonsense premises.

The riot occurred because the lower-class white population became frustrated by jobs being taken away from them.

The riot occurred because there had been an influx of Southerners who already burned with prejudice against blacks.

The riot occurred because there had been a large influx of black residents into the city, causing unrest and even a housing shortage.

The riot occurred because poor, often drunk, roustabout whites were looking to cause trouble.

Wrong. Wrong. Wrong. Wrong.

Springfield, capital city of Illinois and hometown of Abraham Lincoln, in August 1908 had a healthy economy that felt no effects yet from the recession that gripped other areas. The black population had actually decreased in recent years, and those blacks who did live in the area lived within very specific neighborhoods, barely competing at all for homes and less so for jobs. Freedom did not mean an end to prejudice, and there were many positions for which no person of color would be hired. At the same time, the demographics of those involved in the riot show them to be mostly single men in their mid-twenties, gainfully employed, and of Illinois birth, not Southern blood. They were young men who'd never been in trouble with the law before, who very well may have gone to church every week. But on that August weekend, none of that made any difference. A spark struck and a city nearly collapsed in rage and anger.

The first tinder to be placed was the murder of a railroad engineer, Clergy Ballard, a month earlier. The suspect, a nonresident black man named Joe James, had been arrested and was awaiting trial. Added to this was a horrific tale of rape and assault on Mabel Hallam, who pointed the finger at black caretaker George Richardson.

"Dragged From Her Bed and Outraged By a Negro" screamed the headline of the *Illinois State Journal*.

But Mrs. Hallam was lying. She'd been having an affair with a white man and, caught in her web of fabrication, did the only thing she could think of to free herself. She mixed race and rape into a Molotov cocktail that exploded on the steps of the local jail on Friday, August 14, 1908.

Faced with an innocent man and a bloodthirsty crowd that would not hear the truth, the sheriff tried to escort Richardson out of town in a borrowed car. Once the mob caught wind of the plan, the gathering turned violent. They destroyed both the car and the restaurant owned by the man who'd loaned the car. They moved through the city, assaulting blacks and their businesses, moving forward with unstoppable rage.

They reached the Levee, the black business district, and destroyed almost twenty businesses, owned by either Jews or blacks. Then they turned to Badlands, filled with African American–owned homes.

On their march, a black barber, Scott Burton, tried to defend his shop and was shot to death, his corpse then taken, hung from a tree, and pockmarked with bullets.

Only the eventual arrival of the militia, called in by the Illinois governor, broke the day's violence. It was a calm that would not last.

The next night, the mob gathered again, this time making their way toward the capital. Word had reached them that many of the black residents had taken shelter in the State Arsenal across the street. The building, however, was guarded by a portion of the five thousand National Guard troops who'd been called in. Frustrated by their defeat, one in the crowd suggested an easier victim who lived not too far away.

William Donnegan, a fair-skinned black man, was now eighty years old. He was a cobbler by trade and had made shoes for Abraham Lincoln himself. The two were even known to have become friends. Wealthy, quiet, and unassuming, Donnegan had lived in Springfield for years.

The mob took him from his house, slashed his throat, and hung him from a tree in the local school.

It was to be the final atrocity for the mob. Enough troops marched in to finally disperse the crowd for good. The Springfield Riot, though random violence and destruction occurred for weeks afterward, was over.

Two black residents had been killed.

Four white residents also.

Hundreds were wounded.

More than forty houses of blacks had been burned to nothing.

An all-white jury convicted one rioter. The charge? Theft. His sentence was thirty days.

It is a faceless throng in which the basest hatreds of men can come to life and cowards can scream, "Lincoln freed you. Now we'll show you where you belong" without a single reproach. That Abraham Lincoln's name was raised is perhaps the bitter irony in this. It is an interesting dichotomy to think over the links Lincoln had with the city. The Great Emancipator who, in the end, sacrificed his life in the cause of freedom for all was now forever coupled with a populace known for their prejudice, blood-thirstiness, and violent anger. The two sides of America's past could not be more clearly delineated.

If any good came from the riot, it was that the violence of Springfield prompted a meeting in New York in January 1909 among concerned blacks and white reformers on the topic of race. From this gathering grew what would become the NAACP: the largest and most powerful organization for the fight against racial discrimination and for equal civil rights. Its birth, forged in the blood of victims and the ashes of destruction, was a mere foreshadowing of the long fight they would wage through the years. A fight that would take many more lives and leave our nation forever scarred. And although much progress has been made since the 1960s, the fight against predjudice continues.

★　★　★

America will never be destroyed from the outside. If we
falter and lose our freedoms, it will be because
we destroyed ourselves.
—ABRAHAM LINCOLN

SECOND LYNCHING IN
SPRINGFIELD RIOTS

Brigade of Militia Fails to Check
Mob in Race War.

STRUNG UP NEAR CAPITOL

Lincoln's City Scene of the Bitterest Race War Seen in
Years—Governor Orders More Troops to Re-
store Quiet and Protect Negroes From
Whites Stirred by Two Crimes.

The Price of Fear

Race riots in America occurred in basically three major waves. The third wave produced the greatest number of race riots during and just after World War I, and they were caused by a number of social, political, and economic factors. Typically the riots were sparked by rumors of an African American's criminal activity, and white mobs perpetuated the violence. In almost every situation, the police sided with the whites and either participated in or failed to put an end to the attacks. Hundreds of people—both black and white, but mostly black—were killed in the riots and thousands more were wounded. In most cases "massacre" would be a more appropriate term to use.

The summer of 1919, referred to as the Red Summer, consisted of twenty-six race riots, which was more interracial violence than the nation had ever witnessed.

Some of the most deadly riots occurred in East St. Louis (1917), Philadelphia (1917), Houston (1917), Chicago (1919), Washington, D.C. (1919), Tulsa (1921), and Rosewood, Florida (1923).

The first wave of riots occurred during Reconstruction. Southern white Democrats in power were desperate to regain the control they had lost due to their defeat in the Civil War. Black Codes were passed and the Ku Klux Klan was formed and launched vicious attacks on African Americans and white Republicans. New Orleans had three such major occurrences (1866, 1868, 1874), as well as Memphis (1866), Vicksburg, Mississippi (1874), and Meridian, Mississippi (1870), to name just a few.

The second wave began in 1898 when the white citizens of Wilmington, North Carolina, threatened African-American voters and workers of the town. Dozens of blacks were killed, but the whites remained unharmed. The Jim Crow Era was at full strength at this time. Black Codes, segregation laws, and a reckless media contributed greatly to the oppression of African Americans. As African Americans continued to advance politically, socially, and economically, more outbreaks occurred. Some of the most signifcant riots were in New Orleans (1900), New York City (1900), Atlanta (1906, Greensburg, Indiana (1906), and Springfield, Illinois (1908).

Riots occurred well into the twentieth century, many of them a result of false accusations against a black man for the rape of white woman. In 1921, when a white girl from Tulsa, Oklahoma, charged a black boy with attempted rape—a race war broke out. More than ten thousand whites attacked the black district with machine guns and bombs. In the end almost two hundred blacks were killed as well as fifty whites.

Just a few years later in Sumner, Florida, a white woman claimed that an African-American man had assaulted her. Her bruises proved an attack, but it was never confirmed whether they came from a black man of if it was her own white boyfriend abusing her. An army of white men ganged up to destroy the town of Rosewood, which was a nearby black town. Nobody knows exactly how many people were killed, but the town was completely destroyed and abandoned, with survivors left to flee into the Florida swamps. There are a few survivors still living today.

An amazing attempt to rectify the situation occurred in 1994, when the state of Florida passed the Rosewood Claims Act, a document claiming that state and local officials had had sufficient time and opportunity to prevent the tragedy but failed to act. The Act determined to compensate any survivors of the riot as well as provide scholarships and payments to descendants who could prove property damage.

White violence has destroyed many black communities throughout the U.S. While race riots were the product of the southern power structure's intentions to maintain superiority over blacks, the riots ended in needless deaths and destroyed towns. In most cased blacks fought back, and while there were casulties on both sides, African Americans had by far the greatest losses.

45 The Right Man at the Right Time
Dwight D. Eisenhower
1890–1969

One of the most moving things Dwight D. Eisenhower wrote never saw the light of day in its intended form.

On June 5, 1944, by Eisenhower's own command, Operation Overlord, what would come to be known as D-Day had begun. For months he and other military officials had worked on the plan. On charts and paper and maps, he saw the projected movements of men and equipment and ships. It had been so easy on paper. Nobody dies in the planning. There is no name attached to the first boot to hit the shore, a boy/man most likely about to be torn down by German machine guns.

But Eisenhower and the others agreed the command must come and so it did. Streaming across the English Channel were 5,000 ships and 150,000 men—Americans, British, French, Polish. One would be the first to step onto Normandy. He would most likely be one of the first to die. He would not be the last.

Eisenhower, supreme commander of the Allied forces, was not in a boat with the men. He was waiting now, and though his waiting was nothing compared to what his men faced, it was its own kind of difficult. In the quiet the doubts came. They had talked about the things that could go wrong, and in the end it was on Eisenhower's shoulders to make the decision. They would attack.

And if they failed? Eisenhower held his breath a long moment at the thought. For a second it almost overcame him. *If we fail?* Intuitively, he knew that should the operation not succeed, everyone would be looking for someone to blame, a place to point the finger, and in the tumult that might follow, there would be no time to explain where that place might be. So Dwight Eisenhower took a single sheet of paper and an old pen and in language terse and straightforward said that all blame should rest on him. It was not the troops or the field commanders. Blame would rest on him. He wrote the release, folded it, and stuck it away. If used, it would come in the wake of a devastating defeat and the loss of countless lives. If used, the Germans might never give up Europe. To be willing to take responsibility for those things coming to pass said as much about Dwight D. Eisenhower as almost any other moment in his life.

As general and as president, Eisenhower was not flawless. There are no saints who have held the office. But unlike so many noted heads of state or industry, especially today, he did not pass the blame, split rhetorical hairs, or flat-out lie. He took responsibility for his actions and decisions, particularly in the wake of their failure when so many of the people who would share in victory were nowhere to be seen.

Perhaps it was the day-to-day morality and faith in which he was brought up by his mother and father. Raised in Texas and Kansas, he was brought up in the church by strict but loving parents who struggled to make ends meet with seven sons in the house. Self-control and self-discipline were demanded and stayed with Eisenhower long after he left the quiet fields of his small town.

Faced with slim funds for college, Eisenhower applied to the military academies and was accepted at West Point, launching his military career. He served in World War I but did not see battle. Years following he continued his military training and schooling and slowly began to ascend through the ranks of the army. He studied under Generals McArthur, Patton, and Marshall, eventually becoming a five-star general himself, and his planning and organizational skills made the ideal choice to plan and carry-out D-Day. American and British troops joined forces with French and Polish units for one of the most unprecedented and bloody assaults in human history.

"There are times when you have to put everything you are and everything you have ever learned on the line," Eisenhower said in the hours of waiting for any news from Normandy. Finally word came. Success! The plan, though incredibly costly in the toll of human lives, had worked and the German lines were broken. The march to Paris was underway, and on June 12, Eisenhower landed at Normandy to begin planning the liberation of France and the push toward Berlin.

Following the war he served first as president of Columbia University in New York City and then supreme commander of the newly formed NATO forces. In 1952, after many years of declining any interest, Eisenhower accepted the Republican nomination as their presidential candidate and was elected with Richard Nixon as his vice-president.

Over the next eight years he was president during some of the keystone moments—for good and bad—of America's history.

America left World War II and the Korean War behind but gained a new enemy in the Soviet Union as the two superpowers began the Cold War.

Thirteen-year-old Dwight D. Eisenhower never expected a scrape on his knee would turn out so bad, but one day his leg was so bad he could hardly stand. Dwight tried to work through the pain, but that night his shoe had to be cut off his foot and his mother summoned the doctor, who saw the spreading infection and feared the worst. "We'll amputate," he said. Dwight would hear none of it. A man without a leg in that country was useless, and he knew God wouldn't let him be maimed. Enlisting a brother to help, Dwight locked himself in his room, a wooden fork to bite for the pain, and prayed for his leg. His fever grew and the discoloration of infection marched up Dwight's leg, but his brother would not relent in allowing the doctor in, "It's murder!" Dr. Conklin shouted. "Nothing but a miracle can save the boy!" And so that's what Dwight's parents prayed for all night and what his brothers prayed for as well. The second night passed, and in the morning, the doctor arrived once more. He expected the end of the line. Instead, he found the swelling down and the infection lessened. The doctor could only shake his head and murmur an amazed prayer of his own. That night Dwight roused for the first time in days, and within weeks he was back up and standing. On his own two feet. God had been faithful to his prayers and the prayers of his family, and Eisenhower would never forget that miraculous healing.

Tensions escalated when the Russians launched *Sputnik* in 1957, a clear sign of their missile capabilities.

Whatever goodwill remained between the nations vanished when a United States U2 spy plane Eisenhower had said didn't exist was shot down over the Soviet Union and its pilot captured.

Eisenhower responded to the arms race with quiet resolve and took a measured approach. He also presided over the formation of NASA in the late 1950s

Eisenhower oversaw countless famed international and domestic moments, such as the halt of the McCarthy hearings and the quelling of the Little Rock Central High School crisis. His term also included perhaps lesser-known spiritual moments.

He became the first president to offer his own prayer at his inauguration. His words, in part, called for God to give his administration "the power to discern clearly right from wrong, and allow all our words and actions to be governed thereby, and by the laws of the land. Especially we pray that our concern shall be for all the people regardless of station, race, or calling. May cooperation be permitted and be the mutual aim of those who, under the concepts of our Constitution, hold to differing political faiths; so that all may work for the good of our beloved country and Thy glory."

Under Eisenhower, the Pledge of Allegiance gained the words that helped inspire this book.

As well, he participated in the American Legion's Back-to-God program, giving a speech that was broadcast nationwide. "Without God," he said in his speech, "there could be no American form of Government, nor an American way of life."

A man of principle. A man of God. A man of honor and his word. A man who stood by his decisions, accepted responsibility for his failures, and led by quiet example. A man who upheld the law above his own personal feelings. Dwight Eisenhower may not have been the perfect president, but he was all you could want in a leader and the right man at the right time for our country.

★ ★ ★

There's growing divide in how we look back at the 1950s today. Many people, especially older people, say, "Things were better then." Others point to the struggles for civil rights and the lack of equality for women and shake their heads, saying, "How could they be?" Our need for things to be one or the other sometimes blinds us to the fact that history is rarely that simple. As Dickens said, "They were the best of times, they were the worst of times."

History is not a mathematical equation. You can't add up the positives, subtract the negatives, and be left with the sum of a decade. How do you subtract terrified black students, with armed uniform escorts, walking a gauntlet of venom and abuse? They don't cancel each other out. We must hold on to them both, learn the lessons of both, and we must more strictly follow the example of taking responsibility for the way we shape our future.

★ ★ ★

The fear of the Lord teaches a man wisdom,
and humility comes before honor.
PROVERBS 15:33 NIV

The Pledge of Allegiance

The Pledge of Allegiance was formed largely from the vision of three men: Daniel Ford, James Upham, and Francis Bellamy.

Daniel Ford was the publisher of a popular family magazine, *The Youth's Companion*. Ford's belief in Christ was a great influence on the content of his magazine, and he guided his life and business by Christian principles. With a circulation of nearly half a million, *The Youth's Companion* was the nation's most-read weekly magazine in the late 1880s and early 1890s.

James Upham, head of the magazine's premium department, was disappointed that most public schools did not have their own flags, so he launched a campaign wherein schoolchildren raised funds to purchase a flag from the magazine. As a result, about thirty thousand flags were sold and flown for the first time in front of America's schools between 1888 and 1891.

In 1892, the country prepared to celebrate the four hundredth anniversary of Columbus's arrival in America. President Benjamin Harrison declared Columbus Day, October 12, a national holiday for the first time. Upham wanted children across the country to participate, so he began planning the National Public School Celebration that would center on raising a school flag.

First, a proclamation from the president would be read, followed by prayer and Scripture reading, the singing of "America," and patriotic speeches. Wanting the children to participate more fully, Upham determined that they should recite a salute to the flag. He enlisted the talents of another magazine employee, Francis Bellamy, who had been pastor at the Boston church Daniel Ford attended. Bellamy labored for weeks and finally brought his composition to Upham: *I pledge allegiance to my Flag and to the Republic for which it stands: one Nation, indivisible, with liberty and justice for all.* It was published in

The Youth's Companion on September 8, 1892. Thirty-four days later, twelve million schoolchildren across the country recited the Pledge of Allegiance for the first time.

In 1923 and 1924 the words *my Flag* were changed to *the Flag of the United States of America*. In 1948, a man named Louis A. Bowman proposed to his fellow Sons of the American Revolution that the words *under God* be added after *one nation*—following a precedent set by Abraham Lincoln, who had extemporaneously added those same words to the end of his Gettysburg Address. Then, in 1952, William Randolph Hearst caught wind of the idea and began a campaign in his newspapers that helped bring about legislation to officially add *under God* to the Pledge. President Dwight D. Eisenhower approved this change on Flag Day, 1954, and proclaimed, "In this way we are reaffirming the transcendence of religious faith in America's heritage and future; in this way we shall constantly strengthen those spiritual weapons which forever will be our country's most powerful resource in peace and war."

I pledge allegiance
to the Flag of the
United States of America,
and to the Republic
for which it stands,
one Nation under God,
indivisible, with liberty
and justice for all.

"We Need the Storm, the Whirlwind, and the Earthquake"

Frederick Douglass

1818–1895

The matter is up for debate, but it can at least be put forward that the most eloquent speaker and writer of the Civil War era was a man who literally had no right to do either. Slave by birth, Frederick Douglass might never have learned to read or write and might never have been given any forum other than a meeting of slaves before which to give a speech. Yet by the age of twenty-three, three years after escaping, he was in Massachusetts reading the *Liberator*, William Lloyd Garrison's controversial antislavery newspaper. (Garrison's teachings alleged that the Constitution contained pro-slavery passages.) Young Douglass addressed thousands of abolitionists on what it was like to have been raised in slavery and the ever-more-urgent need to end the abomination that corrupted this country.

To most it seemed amazing, almost incomprehensible. To Douglass himself it was the fulfillment of a divine promise he'd felt in his heart for years.

"From my earliest recollections," he once wrote, "I date the entertainment of a deep conviction that slavery would not always be able to hold me within its foul embrace; and in the darkest hours of my career in slavery, this living word of faith and spirit of hope departed not from me, but remained like ministering angels to cheer me through the gloom. The good spirit was from God, and to him I offer thanksgiving and praise."

Frederick Douglass was born Frederick Bailey to slave Harriet Bailey and an unknown white father. His earliest recollections of the abuse and inhumanity of slavery sealed in him the deepest desire to see freedom come to all slaves. Foremost in his thoughts was a plantation overseer named Mr. Gore of whom Douglass recalled: "He was cruel enough to inflict the severest punishment. . . . He was, of all the overseers, dreaded by the slaves." Douglass saw the man shoot a disobedient slave dead with a musket on the basis that the man had become unmanageable and was setting a bad example. Gore was brutal and calculating; he showed no remorse.

Only Providence kept Douglass from growing too old under such a yoke, and at the age of six he had the good fortune to be sent to more kindly owners, the mistress even teaching the obviously bright young child to read and write—though without the knowledge of her husband, Master Thomas Auld. For five years Douglass studied in secret until he was found out. Master Auld, though a decent man, still feared the "educated" slave and lent the fourteen-year-old Douglass off to Edward Covey, a man with a reputation for "breaking" slaves' spirits through backbreaking work.

Frederick was worked to exhaustion and beaten nearly to death. He tried to run back to the Aulds', but they would not listen to his pleas. They returned him to Covey, but the next time Covey tried to beat Frederick, the boy struck back. Without recourse, he would fight for his life. The scuffle lasted hours, according to legend, and at the end of it Douglass had found that while still "a slave in form" he no longer felt that he could be a "slave in fact." Covey saw the change in the young man too and never raised his hand against Douglass again.

For the next six years he moved between masters until finally he and his new wife, using forged documents, escaped north in 1838 to Massachusetts. Here he was told to change his name so his owner would have a more difficult time tracking him down. Taking inspiration from a literary work he'd been reading, Frederick Bailey became Frederick Douglass, and his career as abolitionist spokesman loomed just around the corner.

Throughout his life two tenets stood as pillars of Douglass's beliefs and actions: The first was his Christian faith, the second his call to stand against the atrocity not only of slavery but of discrimination and oppression in general, be it of women, immigrants, or the working class. "All great reforms go together," he stated. He believed that to be the case because he took as his measuring rod the model of the Bible, in which in the eyes of Christ all were equal—there being neither Greek nor Jew, slave nor freeman, man nor woman. And he hated what some Americans had done in the name of Christianity, distorting and perverting religion to meet their own needs.

In an appendix to his *Narrative of the Life of an American Slave*, Douglass with fierce eloquence writes, "I love the pure, peaceable, and impartial Christianity of Christ: I therefore hate the corrupt, slaveholding, women-whipping, cradle-plundering, partial and hypocritical Christianity of this land. Indeed, I can see no reason, but the most deceitful one, for calling the religion of this land Christianity. I look upon it as the climax of misnomers, the boldest of all frauds, and the grossest of all libels...."

He would never rest in his crusade, not against the church but against the religion of a country that would stand, at all, for slavery. For years his voice thundered those words from stages, platforms, and podiums across the country, but rarely did they reach with such eloquent vehemence or stun such an unprepared audience as in his hometown of Rochester, New York, July 5, 1852.

Douglass, officially a free man now after his friends paid his old master more than twelve hundred dollars for his manumission, was renowned for his speaking, and the organizers of an event for the Rochester Ladies Anti-Slavery Society commemorating the seventy-sixth anniversary of the signing of the Declaration of Independence asked him to make one of the addresses.

This was not necessarily supposed to be an antislavery rally. This certainly was not a liberal church hoping to be scalded and challenged by the words of a former slave, their bit of penance for the atrocities other Christians enacted down South. This was an event that would appeal to the whole town, part of the Fourth of

July celebrations. It was supposed to be an honor, given to him as a resident of Rochester.

But Douglass, pacing his study back home, couldn't overcome the sense that he was being patronized, trotted out on stage so folks could hear a black man and—even better!—former slave talk about the inherent greatness of the country. They weren't asking for that reason, of course. Douglass knew the organizers who asked him greatly respected his oratory skills, always complimenting his eloquence. They considered him, in many ways, their equal or even their better when it came to rousing a crowd with grand words. They had tried their best to act color-blind. But this was one time they should have thought through the matter a little more.

Douglass tried not to hold their good intentions against them, but still he seethed. America. The Fourth of July. Independence. As ideas he loved each one, but each only barely applied to his life and applied not at all to one seventh of the country's population. Pacing now, he began to speak the words aloud.

"Pardon me, allow me to ask," he boomed, "why am I called upon to speak here today? What am I, or those I represent, to do with your national independence?" He paused, moved to his writing desk, and set the words down. "To drag a man in fetters into the grand illuminated temple of liberty, and call upon him to join you in joyous anthems, were inhuman mockery and sacrilegious irony. Do you mean, citizens, to mock me, by asking me to speak today?"

Douglass stood, heart burning. He closed his eyes. Part of him dearly wanted to scratch out the words. It was an honor. They expected platitudes, a strong hammering against slavery, and an obeisance to the founding few. And yet the words burned in him. He had so much to say to a country that continued to be blind and lazy and unwilling to do the hard work of ridding itself of this dreadful, appalling sin. His hesitation lasted a full minute. His quill stood raised over his words, then lifted. He would not bend. God had called him to deliver a message not only to those who wanted to hear it but especially to those who didn't. God hated slavery;

hated that Southerners hid behind His Word; hated that some pastors in the North refused to call it a moral evil; hated that His Creation—men and women made in His image—were treated like chattel. That was the message Douglass knew he needed to deliver.

"Whether we turn to the declarations of the past, or to the professions of the present, the conduct of the nation seems equally hideous and revolting. Standing with God and the crushed and bleeding slave I will…dare to call in question and to denounce, with all the emphasis I can command, everything that serves to perpetuate slavery—the great sin and shame of America."

Douglass turned to his writing paper, settled himself, and went back to the beginning. They had asked him to celebrate freedom and independence and he would do it, if not in words then in spirit. For what could be more American than standing for what was right against all odds, and employing the freedom of speech enacted by law to challenge a nation to look hard at itself?

Days later Douglass took the stage in Rochester's Corinthian Hall to cordial applause, began with some witty self-deprecation, but soon turned grave. The audience hesitated, almost nervous. Their day had been going so pleasantly. They looked up at Douglass in alarm, and he offered no safe haven. For the next hour Douglass spoke with the passion of a man consumed. He did not relent.

He called out the names of Northern politicians who had failed the cause of slavery. He rebuked, by name, famed Northern reverends and pastors who taught that the law of man should be obeyed before the law of God.

He upbraided the hypocrisy of the church as a whole, castigated the slaveowners of the South who knew they stood opposed to God and the Constitution and yet continued to do so, and generally put forth as powerfully as ever before the whole awful mess that was slavery in the United States. There would be no celebration in his speech. He had a specific goal that day.

"It is not light that is needed," he said, "but fire; it is not the gentle shower, but thunder. We need the storm, the whirlwind, and the earthquake. The feeling of the nation must be quickened; the conscience of the nation must be roused; the propriety of the nation must be startled; the hypocrisy of the nation must be exposed; and its crimes against God and man must be proclaimed and denounced."

Every person listening, perhaps even despite themselves, leaned forward. Douglass had come to his central point. He steadied his gaze, lowered his voice to a low rumble.

"What, to the American slave, is your Fourth of July?" he asked. "I answer: a day that reveals to him, more than all other days in the year, the gross injustice and cruelty to which he is the constant victim. To him, your celebration is a sham; your boasted liberty, an unholy license; your national greatness, swelling vanity; your sounds of rejoicing are empty and heartless;...your prayers and hymns, your sermons and thanksgivings, with all your religious parade, and solemnity, are, to him, mere bombast, fraud, deception, impiety, and hypocrisy....

"There is not a nation on the earth guilty of practices, more shocking and bloody, than are the people of the United States, at this very hour."

Frederick Douglass did not and would not back down on the issues of slavery and equality. It was a different time, when public speeches meant something and men and women could offer more than just a sound bite on a news show. Given the podium, Douglass spoke God's anger.

In later years Douglass realized that Garrison's claims that the Constitution was an anti-black document were false. While early in his days of public speaking Douglass criticized some of the Founding Fathers, he later realized that the Constitution was, indeed, a wonderfully inspired document that trumpeted the pursuit of equality.

* * *

We might be a country formed under God, but we were not living up to His standards. He reigns over us and we are called, at all times, to follow His path.

We need Christians today willing to stand for truth no matter what. We need to look beyond the party affiliations of donkeys and elephants to the more lasting truth.

FIRST AFRICAN AMERICANS IN CONGRESS:
Seated: Hiram Rhodes Revels, Benjamin S. Turner,
Josiah T. Walls, Joseph H. Rainey, Robert Brown Elliot.
Standing: Robert C. DeLarge, Jefferson H. Long.

First African Americans in Congress

With the end of the Civil War and the enacting of the Thirteenth, Fourteenth, and Fifteenth Amendments came the guarantee of civil rights and voting privileges for all former slaves. The sudden addition of millions of black voters resulted in a number of African Americans being voted into Congress.

The first African American elected to the U.S. Senate was Hiram Rhodes Revels, who in 1869 filled the seat vacated by Confederate President Jefferson Davis.

Also in 1869, fellow Republican Joseph H. Rainey became the first black member of the U.S. House of Representatives.

Others soon followed, but they were not without opposition. For example, Robert Brown Elliott, elected to the U.S. House in 1871, faced off in a debate over a civil rights bill. After giving a most eloquent and effective speech, his opponents, as reported in the *American Methodist Episcopal Church Review*, "denied his authorship... upon the general principle that the Negro, of himself, could accomplish nothing of literary excellence."

Others among the first African Americans elected to Congress included Benjamin S. Turner, Josiah T. Walls, Robert C. DeLarge, and Jefferson H. Long.

In the history of Congress, 105 black Americans have been elected—101 to the House and 4 to the Senate.

What Four Hundred Dollars Can Buy

47

George and Lewis Latimer

1842, 1880, 1928

Choices, large and small, made in an instant today often resonate through history, a sounding echo that can magnify even the simplest of actions done in the name of freedom and decency and God's Word. That is the mystery of God working through His people in their flaws.

If you knew, for instance, that four hundred dollars—a lot more money back in 1842—could not only buy a man's freedom and likely save his life but open the door of opportunity, a generation later, to one of the finest minds of the late nineteenth century, would you spend it? Of course.

What if you had no such foresight? What would be the price you'd be willing to pay for life, for freedom?

Dr. Rev. Caldwell, a black pastor, and the Tremont Temple Baptist Society understood that, when faced with such a choice, the price could never be too high to intercede. Four hundred dollars from the congregation deprived many of food, maybe even clothing for a season, but it bought the freedom of George Latimer, an escaped slave who had known only days of liberty after his flight north.

George Latimer chafed at the shackles of his slavehood. Owned by James B. Gray, an abusive master who owned a store near Norfolk, Virginia, but who made money mostly through the exchange of stolen goods and by selling liquor to black men, Latimer often stared at his bare arms and thought, *Can this flesh belong to any man as horses do?* On October 4, 1842, Latimer and his wife, Rebecca, finally had their opportunity. Latimer had tried to escape before, even making it to Baltimore once, but was always caught. This time proved just as perilous.

After managing to stow away on one ship headed north, Latimer and his wife later had to board a second ship that would take them to Baltimore. Cramped and worn already from the stress, he knew they had no hope of stealing onto this ship. They'd have to come up with another plan. In an instant Latimer had it. "Hide in plain sight," he told his wife. She just bit her lip.

George Latimer was a "high yellow" slave, almost as light-skinned as any sun-darkened sailor. Approaching the vessel, Latimer knew his best option would simply be to pretend he was white and to use part of the money they'd saved to buy a cabin compartment. Black Quaker hat perched on his head and cloak drawn up to his neck, he and Rebecca walked as tall as they could to the gangway. Nobody even glanced their direction. This might work.

Suddenly, atop the entrance, a broad-shouldered man draped in a cloak as black as charcoal stood facing the gathering passengers as though searching for someone. Latimer saw his face and almost froze. It was a liquor salesman who'd sold rum and whiskey and rye to Latimer's master. And so close to freedom!

George and Rebecca had no option. Part of the surging crowd, they mounted the gangway, and Latimer simply pulled his hat low across his brow and passed on to the ship safely. They hadn't been spotted. Half an hour later anchors were raised and George and Rebecca sat in their first-class cabin, free as they had ever been in their life. In Baltimore, Latimer continued to pose as a white gentle-men—Rebecca as his servant—and they maintained the charade until Philadelphia, after which they went forth as free citizens of the United States, man and wife. Anxious to be as far from Virginia as they could, the Latimers found themselves in Boston. But their dream of freedom ended quickly.

They had been spotted during their escape, and James Gray arrived in Boston shortly after George and Rebecca. With Rebecca hidden away, George still had to try to find work, and during one excursion he was spotted and arrested on a false charge of larceny, without any legal process. He was placed in prison, and James Gray began securing their transportation back to Virginia, never expecting the firestorm of protest to follow.

Over the next days and weeks, the town of Boston exploded with indignation. White abolitionists held meetings and demanded that legislation be enacted to protect fugitive slaves. Free black men, almost three hundred in total, surrounded the courthouse to demand that Latimer not be taken from the state unless due justice was performed.

The judge and the police alike were in a quandary. James Gray would not leave without Latimer. Latimer swore that he'd rather die than return to slavery. The charge of larceny had been dropped as being completely without basis, yet Latimer was still incarcerated. More protests arose. Threats were made by every side until finally a compromise was reached and James Gray agreed to return to Virginia *without* his slave for the sum of four hundred dollars. One generous congregation had come through with a sacrificial donation, and as Latimer was released and left prison, he enjoyed his first true steps as a free man.

George Latimer's incarceration sparked one of the key turning points in the abolitionist movement. With the city still at full voice, more than sixty thousand citizens signed a petition calling for the protection of fugitive slaves. The legislature soon picked up the cause and passed a law calling for the same. Massachusetts had deepened its separation from the South, and the inevitable march toward the Civil War took one more step forward.

But the Latimer case was more than just a benchmark for black freedom. The price of four hundred dollars also enabled George Latimer to stay in a place of opportunity and freedom while starting a family—he and Rebecca had three sons. Not that life was simple or easy by any means. Slave hunters prowled the Northern states, capturing blacks and "returning" them to a South they may have never lived in. As a well-known freed slave, George Latimer was particularly nervous and tried his hardest to keep his wife and three sons safe. His youngest boy, Lewis, was born in 1848, six years after George's escape, but it would be another ten years until George felt secure enough to send the obviously intelligent boy to his first schooling in fifth grade.

When Lewis turned twelve, the first shots rained down on Fort Sumter and a new era rose in the United States. Following his older brothers, Lewis enrolled in the Union forces as soon as he could, serving in the navy on a blockade ship. His service and the sacrifice of thousands of other blacks who fought and died for the cause of freedom convinced Lewis that all races needed to be treated equally in the sight of God. As well, Lewis believed that the place of African Americans was not to be segregated or isolated but to serve and live alongside all races as Americans.

He lived out his philosophy upon his return to Boston after the war. Employed by the patent solicitors Crosby & Gould, Latimer soon discovered his natural passion and talent for drafting. His unparalleled skill eventually placed him in partnership with Alexander Graham Bell. Working together with the inventor, Latimer crafted the patent drawings that filled Bell's applications. As other groups rushed to secure similar technology, it was the proficiency, hard work, and dedication of the two men that helped Bell place his patent mere hours ahead of his competition. Lewis Latimer's star was on the rise.

Employed by some of the brightest minds of the era, Latimer soon found himself in the electric light industry working for Hiram Maxim. Here it wasn't only his technical skills that were displayed but his creative genius as well. Latimer invented and patented a process by which the carbon filaments for incandescent lamps could be made to last exponentially longer—and thus reduced the cost of running electric light. Soon he was traveling the world, bringing electricity to the street lamps of major cities, including New York City, Philadelphia, and London.

Latimer's proficiency, knowledge, and hard work soon caught the eye of the foremost inventive mind of the time, Thomas Edison. Latimer was hired as chief draftsman and patent expert. The only African American in a group of twenty-four men known as "Edison

Pioneers," Latimer often served as the primary witness in the prosecution of Edison patent infringement cases. Just years before, his own father had been unable to gain even a voice in the justice system, and now major legal copyright decisions were being made based on the words of the son. It was in Latimer's own hand that a great many of the Edison patents were submitted for approval.

Lewis Latimer's life of hard work, common sense, and devotion to his family, his community, his call, and his nation served as an inspiration for the great things this country could truly accomplish if freedom were accorded to all men and women, regardless of race. In Lewis Latimer, whose future was bought with four hundred dollars by an unheralded pastor following the will of God, all could see the realization of why the battle over slavery was one worth fighting.

Lewis Latimer helped cities shine with a light created by men. His own life, including a church he founded in his community, shone with a light of the Creator who values men far more than any price one could put on them.

★ ★ ★

Each time a person stands up for an ideal, or acts to improve the lot of others, or strikes out against injustice, he sends forth a tiny ripple of hope, and crossing each other from a million different centers of energy and daring, these ripples build a current that can sweep down the mightiest walls of oppression and resistance.
—ROBERT F. KENNEDY

Their Contributions Many

Americans tend to have a Western view of history, over-looking significant contributions African Americans and Native Americans have made to the development of this country. Though some details may remain obscure, each of the following people played an important role in U.S. history.

African Americans and Native Americans have played a role in all of this country's wars, beginning with America's first, the Revolutionary War. As tension increased between British soldiers and the colonists, conflicts erupted in Boston, culminating in a riot on March 5, 1770. **Crispus Attucks,** a runaway slave of both African and American Indian ancestry, attempted to break up the riot but was instead shot and killed instantly—becoming one of the first martyrs of the American Revolution. The deaths of Attucks and four other men who were killed that day are known as the Boston Massacre; a monument in the Boston Common honors the men, the heroes of the massacre.

Two African-American men, **Peter Salem** and **Salem Poor,** became heroes at the Battle of Bunker Hill when they were each credited with killing a high-ranking British officer. Though Salem and Poor's valiant deed did not end the battle, the men's courageous stand raised the morale of the whole country. Peter Salem and Salem Poor reflect the remarkable character of African-American men who were willing to fight for their country.

James Armistead, a freed slave, provided crucial information to the Continental army, helping to bring a victori-ous end to the American Revolution. Armistead was stationed at the British camp of traitor Benedict Arnold, where he posed as an escaped slaved looking for work. Arnold accepted Armistead, plac-ing the spy in a great position to hear vital information from

British officers. When Armistead provided the British plans to the Americans, an ambush was set up, beginning what would be known as the Battle of Yorktown. Because of the amount of information Armistead fed to the Americans, the ex-slave helped put an end to the war, making him one of the most important American spies during the Revolution.

Many non-European explorers made significant contributions to the developing America, such as **Jean Baptiste Pointe DuSable,** an African-American man who set out to explore the Mississippi River. In 1772 DuSable married a Potawatomi Indian woman, and the two established their home in a village called Eschikagou. There, DuSable built a house and several guesthouses and his wife planted crops. When DuSable invited his wife's tribe to join them on their land, the couple opened a trading post. Soon other settlers were making their homes on this piece of land in midwest America, building up what would eventually be the city of Chicago.

Lewis and Clark, some of the greatest explorers of all time, traveled with an African American and Native American, both indispensable to the expedition. **Sacajawea,** a northern Shoshoni Indian, was young when she began the expedition, but she played a large part in its success. The young girl spoke a number of languages, and when she wasn't able to communicate through voice she used sign language. When the expedition amazingly met up with Sacajawea's brother, he was able to provide the travelers with horses and an American Indian guide. Even when Sacajawea and her husband produced a child, the new mother did not hesitate to continue the trip with her new baby strapped to her back.

York, William Clark's servant, was on hand to help Sacajawea through her final months of pregnancy. The African-American man had joined the Lewis and Clark expedition as

Clark's personal slave, carrying heavy loads, freezing himself while fishing, and hunting for food. Many of the men on the expedition entrusted York with their possessions to trade with the Indians. And he was encouraged to voice his opinions and vote on different issues of the expedition. He was devoted to Clark and well-liked by the explorers, who named geographical features after the black man just as they did with other members of the expedition. The expedition had formed an important and essential family of which York had gladly been accepted a member.

Matthew Henson was the lone African American among the explorers who discovered the North Pole. He was an invaluable member on the journey and served well as a blacksmith, carpenter, dog trainer, hunter, and interpreter, as he was the only member from the crew to learn the Eskimo language. In 1909, when he reached the point of the North Pole forty-five minutes before the crew's commander, Robert Perry, Henson was told to remain silent about the discovery. Perry then returned home to awards and honors while Henson struggled to find work. Matthew Henson was a man to be honored, but because of the racial prejudice of the time, it would be decades before the country would hear of the advancements made by this intrepid explorer.

Benjamin Banneker is responsible for the layout of the beautiful city of Washington, D.C., as he was able to reproduce the plans for the city when the French engineer of the project, Pierre L'Enfant, walked out. Banneker, also a mathematician, descended from both English and African blood, taught himself how to predict the exact hours of sunrise and sunset as well as times and dates for eclipses of the sun and moon, phases of the moon, and tide tables. As an African American of great integrity, Banneker believed he could influence Thomas Jefferson to abolish slavery, making the point in a letter to the Founding Father that the same freedoms American patriots fought for were being denied to African Americans.

Norbert Rillieux's invention of the vacuum pan revolutionized the sugar-refining industry, which helped to revitalize Louisiana's economy after the Civil War. Rillieux's new system increased the production of sugar while it lowered the price, allowing sugar to become a common household product. When Rillieux, an African American, worked out a complete sewerage system for the city of New Orleans, the city officials would not credit a black man for designing a major city project; white men created a near-identical system only a short time later.

Garrett Morgan built several inventions used today, most notably the gas mask and the traffic signal. Morgan's traffic light—today's equivalent to the flashing yellow light—warned drivers to slow down and proceed with caution, which protected many pedestrians. When Morgan invented the gas mask in 1914, the product was extremely useful to fire fighters and U.S. soldiers in World War I, but he was not able to promote the mask himself, as he ran into racial prejudice. When it was discovered that a black man had been the inventor of the gas mask, many people stopped using it.

Elijah McCoy is one of the most notable African-American inventors in the United States. He acquired patents for products such as the ironing table and scaffold support, but McCoy is best known for his invention of the graphite lubricator for steam engines, which was designed to eliminate difficulties in oiling the superheater engine. Those looking for the new device asked for the "real McCoy," and some folklore traces the evolution of the popular American expression back to the new invention.

So many of America's African-American and Native American heroes remain nameless and faceless; had it not been for these and many like them, who have made significant contributions to the development of America, this would not be the great country it is today.

Forever Fourteen
Emmett Till
1941–1955

As soon as she heard the phone ring, Mamie Till knew something was wrong. It was barely daylight on that Sunday morning, August 28, 1955—much too early for a friendly call. As she hurried to answer it, fear gripped her heart. All week she had been worried about her only son, her only child, who was visiting relatives in the South.

Fourteen-year-old Emmett—the family called him "BoBo"—had begged and pleaded with his mother to let him go with his cousin Wheeler Parker and great-uncle Papa Mose to visit family in the Mississippi delta. Mamie had not wanted to let him go. She told him, "Chicago and Mississippi are two very different places, Bo. White people down South can be very mean to blacks, even to black kids. Don't start up any conversations with white people. Only talk if you're spoken to. Then say, 'Yes, sir,' 'Yes, ma'am.' 'No, sir,' 'No, ma'am.'

"If you're walking down the street and a white woman is walking toward you, step off the sidewalk and lower your head. Don't look her in the eye. Wait until she passes by, then get back on the sidewalk, keep going, and don't look back."

Mamie was trying to make Emmett see that he had to watch everything he did. She wanted to make it look as bad as she could. "If you have to humble yourself," she said, "then just do it. Get on your knees if you have to."

It all seemed so incredible to Emmett. He had never known anything but Argo, a solid, middle-class black neighborhood on Chicago's South Side. "Oh, Mama," he said, "it can't be that bad."

Emmett, with the confidence of a fourteen-year-old, thought he understood everything he needed to understand. But there were basic things he couldn't possibly have understood, things that ran deep in the awareness of those who lived in the South. Southern blacks knew where the lines were, knew not to cross them. For outsiders, things weren't that obvious.

Despite her misgivings, Mamie finally agreed to let Emmett go with his cousin. The two boys would be joining another cousin, Curtis Jones. All three would stay at Papa Mose's house in Money, Mississippi. Mose Wright, a sixty-four-year-old cotton farmer, promised Mamie that the boys would not be going off to town alone. "Town" in Money, Mississippi, meant a post office, a filling station, and three stores clustered around a school and a cotton gin, set in the middle of endless cotton fields.

Wednesday, August 24, was the third day of Emmett's visit. That evening, while Papa Mose was at church, Emmett and his cousin Wheeler went to Bryant's grocery store to buy some candy. Emmett struck up a conversation with a group of black teenagers outside the store. Before long Emmett pulled out his new wallet to show pictures of his Chicago friends. Purchased for the trip, the wallet had come with a studio shot of actress Hedy Lamarr.

"That's my girlfriend," Emmett announced, pointing to the white actress.

The Mississippi boys were sure that this was the empty boasting of a city boy from Chicago. One of them challenged Emmett, "If you are so good with white women, I dare you to talk to the woman in there running the cash register."

Emmett went into the store and bought some bubble gum from Carolyn Bryant. Some say Emmett whistled at the twenty-one-year-old white clerk. Others say he said, "Bye, baby," as he left. Mrs. Bryant testified later that Emmett grabbed her and said, "Don't be afraid of me, baby. I been with white girls before."

Whatever Emmett said or did, it broke the "rules" that his mother had tried so hard to warn him about and started a chain of events that would focus the eyes of the nation and the world upon Money, Mississippi.

Emmett and Wheeler decided not to tell Papa Mose about the incident. Nothing had happened, really, and they didn't want to make Papa

Mose angry with them. By the end of the week, the kids weren't even thinking about the incident anymore.

But word spread quickly. Roy Bryant, the store clerk's husband, returned to town on Saturday night and heard what had happened. He and his half-brother, J. W. "Big" Milam, knocked on Papa Mose's door about two in the morning, Sunday, August 28. Big Milam had a flashlight in one hand and a Colt .45 automatic in the other. The two white men told Papa Mose they were looking for "the boy from Chicago, the one who had done the talking." They started searching the house for Emmett. Both Uncle Mose and Aunt Lizzy pleaded with the men—but they took the boy, threatening to kill Uncle Mose if he told anyone.

The family waited until daylight, then called cousin Curtis's mother, Willie Mae, who also lived in the Chicago area. Willie Mae called Emmett's mother with the news: "Emmett is missing. In the middle of the night, white men came and took him from Uncle Mose's house."

It was the call Mamie had feared. She had so many questions: "What men? Why had they come? Where have they taken my boy? What is being done about it?" But Willie Mae was crying so hard she couldn't answer.

On August 29, Milam and Bryant were arrested and held without bond on kidnapping charges in connection with Emmett's disappearance. The two men said they had taken Emmett but had let him go.

On August 31, the body of the fourteen-year-old from Chicago was found by fishermen in the Tallahatchie River. It had been weighted down by a heavy gin fan tied around Emmett's neck with barbed wire. Emmett's face was so mutilated that his uncle could only identify the body by a ring Emmett was wearing.

On September 2, Emmett Till's body arrived in Chicago. At the sight of her son's coffin, Mamie's grief overwhelmed her. She cried out, "Oh, God. Oh, God. My only boy." Newsmen flashed her picture as her grief and fears poured out. People tried to comfort her as she knelt to pray, "Lord, take my soul. Show me what you want me to do, and make me able to do it." Mamie remembers, "Suddenly, everything, everyone, the entire yard fell silent."

Getting Emmett's body sent home had been a legal battle. Officials in the South wanted to bury him in Mississippi, "to get the body in the ground as soon as possible." They finally released the body but had strictly forbidden the funeral director in Chicago to open the officially sealed coffin. But Mamie was determined to see her son. Once the coffin was unsealed, the smell of death was overpowering. This was the sixth day since Emmett's murder, and his body had been in the river for three days. To make matters worse, Southern officials had packed the body in lime so it would deteriorate even faster.

Despite the stench, Mamie wanted to examine the body. She wanted to be sure it was Emmett and have the closure, the finality, of seeing he was really dead. She also wanted to see what the killers had done to her son. She steeled herself for what she would see; like a forensic doctor, she had a job to do. Starting with Emmett's feet, she carefully examined the body. Until she reached Emmett's chin, there were no scars, no signs of violence. There was no question in her mind—this was her son. But Emmett's head was horribly disfigured: The right eye was dangling out of its socket, the left eye missing completely. All but two teeth were broken off and his nose was mutilated. A deep cut ran across the top of his head from ear to ear. The last thing she noticed was the bullet hole that went through his scull and out the other side.

Although she was horrified by the mutilation, Mamie Till courageously decided to have an open-casket funeral, saying, "Everybody needs to know what happened to Emmett Till." She later stated, "There was nothing more we could do for my baby, but we could honor him by recognizing that we all had a responsibility to work together for a common good. I could not accept that my son had died in vain....

"With God's guidance, I made a commitment to rip the covers off Mississippi, USA—revealing to the world the horrible face of race hatred."

For the next three days, more than fifty thousand people waited in line to view Emmett's brutally beaten body. Photos of the young victim's mutilated face stunned the nation and the world.

In fact, Emmett's death was the spark that set off the modern civil rights movement. The Supreme Court decision to integrate schools the year before (*Brown v. Board of Education*) marked a *legal* turning point in the war against racism. But the murder of Emmett Till was the *emotional* turning point. His death and his mother's courage shook the nation and awoke it to action. Putting the struggle for emancipation above her personal privacy and allowing Emmett's disfigured body to be displayed in an open casket resulted in the largest civil rights demonstration of its day. Those who saw Emmett's face were forever changed. Many who had once been content to stay safely on the sidelines now entered directly into the struggle between racists and rights activists.

On September 23, the two white men charged with Emmett's murder were acquitted by an all-white jury after only an hour of deliberation. Their defense: The body found in the river was not Emmett Till. They admitted that they had taken Emmett but said they had let him go. They claimed that the NAACP and Mamie Till had dug up a body and pretended it was Emmett. According to their defense, Emmett was hiding out in Chicago.

Newspapers across the U.S. and in six European countries expressed shock and outrage over the Till verdict.

On December 1, one hundred days after Emmett's murder, Rosa Parks refused to give up her seat to a white passenger on a city bus in Montgomery, Alabama. When asked, "Why didn't you go to the back of the bus after such threats?" she said she thought of Emmett Till and knew she couldn't give in. Soon after this, Martin Luther King Jr., called for a city-wide bus boycott that lasted 381 days. The civil rights movement was born.

A few months later, *Look* magazine offered Emmett's murderers four thousand dollars for an exclusive interview. The graphic account of how and why Roy Bryant and J. W. Milam killed Emmett Till was published in January 1956. Because they had already been tried and acquitted for this crime, they knew they could not be tried again.

On May 10, 2004, almost fifty years after Emmett's death, the U.S. Justice Department announced it was reopening the investigation into his murder. Both of the murderers have since died.

"This brutal murder and grotesque miscarriage of justice outraged a nation and helped galvanize support for the modern American civil rights movement," said R. Alexander Acosta, assistant attorney general for civil rights. "We owe it to Emmett Till, and we owe it to ourselves, to see whether after all these years some additional measure of justice remains possible."

★ ★ ★

Usually death stops everything. That is the calculation
of the enemy. But here, death started everything.
The murderers of Emmett Till miscalculated the power
of people who have faith in God.... If the men
who killed Emmett Till had known his body would free
a people, they would have let him live.

God had the last answer. Even death cannot stop our
God. Mamie turned a crucifixion into a resurrection.
Well done, Mamie, well done.
—REV. JESSE L. JACKSON SR.

Be strong and courageous, and do the work.
Don't be afraid or discouraged by the size of the task,
for the Lord God, my God, is with you.
He will not fail you or forsake you.
1 CHRONICLES 28:20 NLT

It is curious that physical courage should be
so common in the world and moral courage so rare.
—MARK TWAIN

Medgar Evers

When Medgar Evers applied for and was denied admission to the University of Mississippi Law School, the NAACP took notice of Evers' attempt to integrate the oldest public university in the state, leading Evers to become the first field secretary for the NAACP in the state of Mississippi. While in the honored position, Evers insisted that the state enforce the 1954 Supreme Court decision declaring segregation in public education unconstitutional. Because of Evers' firm stance, he and his family endured many threats and other acts of violence.

Medgar had several jobs while on the board of the NAACP, one of which was the responsibility to investigate murders of African Americans throughout the state. When fourteen-year-old Emmett Till was murdered in Money, Mississippi, Evers was sent to investigate the case and find evidence to provide for the prosecution. After hearing about the Emmett Till murder, Evers started to become frustrated and feel hopeless about the situation with blacks in the South. As a result, Evers pushed more intensely to promote understanding and equality between the two races.

Evers' highly public persistence for integration of public facilities, schools, and restaurants, as well as his encouraging blacks to vote, caused his life to be in danger twenty-four hours a day. Constant violence and threats forced neighbors and friends to watch over Evers' house, in attempts to deter some of the vandalism. But an assassin's bullet in the back killed Evers in 1963; his wife and children found him bleeding to death on their front doorstep. Medgar Evers thus became the first major civil rights leader to be assassinated. Evers was a prominent voice in the struggle for civil rights in Mississippi, and he wasn't afraid to die for his cause. His death was a milestone in the hard-fought integration war in America in the 1950s and 1960s, and his legacy is present everywhere in Mississippi today.

A Legacy of Freedom
John Jay
1745–1829

Christmas brought both the best moments and some of the loneliest for John Jay. His retirement to Bedford, New York, was supposed to have been a time for quiet reflection on a long and varied career, the woman he loved by his side. But Sally died just a year after he'd promised to spend more time with her, and he felt that loss most keenly when the rest of the family came home. John let the infectious laughter of their grandchildren cheer him as much as he could and spent the rest of the time needling his son, William, for news of the fight.

Of all his children, it had been William who had understood John's passion and drive best. The same unwavering intensity and steady character had, time and again, placed him at the highest levels of influence and responsibility.

Elected to the First Continental Congress in 1774, Jay would later become the group's fifth president. He was one of three Americans who negotiated the Treaty of Paris that helped end the American Revolution and later, as Secretary of Foreign Affairs (1784–1789), his Jay Treaty helped avoid a second war between England and the United States. During this crucial period of American history, Jay played other important roles. Together with Alexander Hamilton and James Madison, Jay helped pen the *Federalist Papers*, a series of passionate and reasoned letters defending the Constitution that were published in newspapers and helped turn public opinion toward this powerful document.

Later he would serve as First Chief Justice of the United States Supreme Court (1789–1795), and he even spent two terms as governor of New York. Trusted by many to fill crucial positions during our nation's founding, Jay was known as a man of honor and his word. He was a man of God's Word, too, as he'd also been the president of the American Bible Society. And nowhere in God's Word could he find any defense for upholding the practice of slavery. Yet still it remained, a lawful policy of the land. For the time.

"We're closer now than ever, Father," William assured his father. They shared the same glinting eyes that saw to the marrow of difficult issues. William had followed his father's path into law and now sat on the New York Supreme Court. Just last year, in 1826, he'd managed to use the plight of Gilbert Horton, a free black about to be sold as a fugitive slave, to point out the peril in such a policy and led a petition to have slavery revoked in Washington, D.C. In every protest, in every piece of writing and call to action, William always remembered his father's simple eloquence: *We have the highest reason to believe that the Almighty will not suffer slavery and the Gospel to go hand in hand. It cannot, it will not be.*

John was still staring at his son, but his eyes were vacant as though staring at something miles away or years past. "We had the chance," John said, voice hushed with regret.

William knew his father regretted not pushing harder during the framing of the Constitution to formally declare an end to the hateful institution. His antislavery group, the New York State Society for Promoting the Manumission of Slaves, had been prepared to petition the Constitutional Convention, but when colleagues as sympathetic as Benjamin Franklin—who presided over the Pennsylvania Antislavery Society—warned that such a move would jeopardize the group's brittle unity, Jay held his sharp pen and the Constitution moved forward with slavery still intact.

William, who'd seen his father too weary and worried these last years, struggled to find anything to change the subject. "Da, read us the story," he said at last, almost in the same words he'd used as a child. "Tell the kids about their ancestors."

John's eyes sharpened again. He flashed his son a wry grin. He knew it was only a ploy to shake him from his lethargy, but it worked nonetheless. John instructed William to gather the family.

The story started quietly—his family were Huguenots who'd settled in La Rochelle, France. Henry IV's Edict of Toleration still held the land, and despite their Catholic neighbors, they practiced their religion in freedom, in quiet peace. But then came Louis XIV, whose wife insisted that the heretics living in her country be punished. In 1685 the Edict crumbled. John's eyes flashed in the telling. Now came the exciting part.

As he told of Pierre Jay, his great-grandfather, who'd helped his family escape, been imprisoned, and just made it out of the country alive, or of Auguste Jay, his grandfather, whose tale of peril included escaping from a fortress one stormy evening, Jay saw the wonder and awe in his own grandson's eyes. Even in his son William's eyes after all these years. This, he knew, was the power of legacy. He'd felt it in hearing it from his own father's words, felt it deeply in every part he'd played in the fight for America's freedom. Once, men with the same blood as his had nearly died because of their faith and had found freedom here on these shores. God had led them here. Not that it was a blessed land, but rather a chance for a new beginning. For man to worship God without shackles. And John knew that would be his legacy as well.

Already his son was spoken of as one of the greatest minds and voices in America's abolitionist movement. Revolution might not always come in the flash of a musket as it had at Bunker Hill. Sometimes it might take generations. But if the legacy was strong and the cause was of God, who could stand against such a turning of the tide?

John Jay could only hope that turning tide would come swiftly.

★ ★ ★

I hope I shall always possess firmness and virtue
enough to maintain what I consider the most enviable
of all titles, the character of an honest man.
—GEORGE WASHINGTON

Robert Gould Shaw and the 54th Massachusetts

Robert Gould Shaw was born into an affluent Boston abolitionist family and wandered through his early years searching for purpose. When the Civil War broke out, Robert found himself in the Union army. He distinguished himself as a brave soldier and respected officer, participating in the battles of Antietam and Front Royal, suffering minor wounds in both.

Soon after the Emancipation Proclamation in January 1863, the Union army, its ranks depleted by two years of withering warfare, began to accept black men as enlistees in volunteer regiments. The governor of Massachusetts soon issued a call to all blacks to join the newly formed 54th Massachusetts Regiment. Though there existed a handful of black Union regiments in the occupied South, the 54th was the first formed in a Northern state. Shaw, just twenty-five years old, was tapped to lead the 54th Massachusetts as its colonel. At first hesitant to accept command of men so different from himself, Shaw agreed and slowly began to realize the strength and courage of the men serving with him.

After proving themselves in two successive battles in South Carolina, the 54th was ordered to march to Fort Wagner, an indomitable Confederate stronghold and coveted Union prize. Tired and hungry from two sleepless days of marching, Shaw and the 54th nonetheless accepted the honor of leading the assault. The consequence of a white officer or black soldier being taken prisoner: summary execution.

On the night of July 18, Shaw led the men of the 54th and two brigades of white soldiers in a frontal assault on Fort Wagner. In a final push to take the fort, Shaw was killed as he reached the top of the parapet. Though the 54th had fought bravely, they were repulsed. The Confederates, outraged that the Union would arm black soldiers, sought to insult Shaw by burying him with his men, instead of in a whites-only grave. Upon hearing the news, Shaw's parents were gratified, knowing that was how their son would have wanted it.

Abraham Lincoln credited black volunteer soldiers for turning the tide of the war. From 1863 to 1865, some 180,000 black soldiers fought for the Union.

Shaw's story was depicted in the epic film *Glory*.

50 "I Will Fight No More Forever"
Chief Joseph and the Nez Percé War

OCTOBER 5, 1877

In-mut-too-yah-lat-lat, known to the whites as Chief Joseph, fought the desire to escape in his spirit to a quiet place. He closed handsome black eyes and envisioned his favorite meadow hundreds of miles west in the Wallowa Valley of northeastern Oregon—his ancestral homeland. He imagined lying down with the summer wind upon his face, cool grass beneath him, shade of the pines above him.

But there had been no rest for many months. Years it seemed. Instead, he was here, huddled in a makeshift camp at the foot of the Bear's Paw Mountains in northern Montana, fleeing for his life, the October chill reaching into his bones on this sorrowful morning. The tepees were gone now; the fierce battle and then the rushed flight from the Big Hole in southern Montana, some two months and many miles ago, had given the Wallowa Band of Nez Percé no choice but to leave their dwellings behind. The fortunate ones now slept in temporary wickiups, wrapped in buffalo hides; the unlucky ones suffered the elements with little more than the filthy, trail-torn garments on their backs.

His people. How many yet lived? How many would live to see the Old Woman's Country, Queen Victoria's Canada? *Just forty miles to go—we are so close*, he told himself. Chief Joseph shook himself free of this haunting thought and struggled to focus on the situation at hand. Sitting with him were the remaining chiefs. *So few left now—too few.* Joseph gathered himself, his mind racing with so many heavy impressions.

He recalled how in 1855 his father, Old Chief Joseph, had signed a treaty with the U.S. government that helped the Nez Percé retain most of their traditional lands—roughly two thirds of their original territory, encompassing western Idaho, northeastern Oregon, and southeastern Washington. In 1863, with the discovery of gold and the arrival of endless groups of settlers, however, another treaty—known to many Nez Percé as the "steal treaty"—was created, reducing Nez Percé lands to a reservation approximately one-tenth the size of what the 1855 agreement had allotted.

The fateful words of his father came to him as he sat on the cold hardscrabble: *Always remember that your father never sold his country. You must stop your ears whenever you are asked to sign a treaty selling your home. A few years more, and the white men will be all around you. They have their eyes on this land.* While many Nez Percé chiefs reluctantly signed the 1863 treaty and moved onto the reservation, located at Lapwai, Idaho, Old Chief Joseph would not sign. With the slaughter of the Son of the Morning Star, whom the blue coat soldiers called Custer, at Little Big Horn just the year before, the mood had grown increasingly hostile toward the Indians.

Just months before, Young Chief Joseph and several other Nez Percé chiefs were prepared to leave their beloved land to search for a new home—perhaps in Canada. But on June 14, before the "non-treaty" Nez Percé could begin their peaceable exile, three rash young warriors killed a white settler as retribution for the death of one warrior's father. More settlers soon died, and the conflict quickly escalated. Much to his dismay, Joseph and his fellow chiefs had little choice but to flee. The Nez Percé War, or more accurately, the Flight of 1877, had begun.

Joseph stared across his camp at some women and children huddled together in a shallow pit, hides of buffalo covering them against the cold, cloudless morning. His heart was pierced with sorrow as he recalled the long, desperate 113-day retreat that had covered more than eleven hundred miles and had decimated his warriors' numbers in numbing fashion. From the beginning, his fighting men had been outnumbered nearly ten to one by their pursuers. Around 750 Nez Percé women, children, and men had begun the flight; just over half now remained. Many had died, and others had escaped already into Canada with Chief White

Bird. Their enemy, the U.S. army, civilian volunteers, and Indians from a handful of rival tribes, numbered about two thousand. They were led by General Oliver O. Howard, whom the chiefs called Cut Arm, in reference to his missing right appendage, removed after being shattered by two rifle balls during the Civil War battle of Fair Oaks.

Looking Glass, the group's best war leader, was dead, inauspiciously shot just three days earlier by an army sniper. So too was Chief Toohoolhoolzote. How had he and the other headmen misjudged the blue coats? Joseph was certain he was many days' march ahead of the army. But then, the soldiers had descended upon their camp. The warriors had fought bravely, but the battle had settled into a siege—and it was now Joseph's time to make a decision. He was the leader now, mainly because most of the other chiefs were dead. For three days they had held out, but now there were so many wounded, so many starving. Even if he wanted to escape to Canada, where Sitting Bull, the fabled Lakota/Sioux leader, was waiting to receive them, he could not. He would not leave the old and sick behind.

Only one choice left. Joseph wrapped the gray, black-striped blanket tightly around his tall frame, black braids falling over tired shoulders. A hush fell over the camp. He raised his head to speak as Nez Percé interpreter, "Captain" John, prepared to carry Joseph's message across the field to the white soldiers:

> *I am tired of fighting. Our chiefs are killed. Looking Glass is dead. Toohoolhoolzote is dead. The old men are all dead. It is the young men who say yes or no. . . .*
>
> *It is cold and we have no blankets. The little children are freezing to death. My people, some of them, have run away to the hills, and have no blankets, no food; no one knows where they are— perhaps freezing to death. I want to have time to look for my children and see how many of them I can find. Maybe I shall find them among the dead.*
>
> *Hear me, my chiefs. I am tired; my heart is sick and sad. From where the sun now stands, I will fight no more forever.*

This now-famous speech was delivered on the morning of October 5, 1877. Later that day, Chief Joseph surrendered his rifle to Captain Nelson Miles, who had engaged the Nez Percé throughout the campaign. It is estimated that approximately 175 U.S. soldiers and citizen volunteers were killed, while as many as 200 Nez Percé lost their lives, and 90 were wounded—a casualty rate exceeding 30 percent.

Some survivors were able to escape to Canada, most joining the Sioux of Sitting Bull. Those who surrendered believed they would be returned to the Nez Percé reservation, but instead they were relocated to Oklahoma's Indian Country. Joseph later commented: "General Miles had promised that we might return to our country with what stock we had left. . . . I believed General Miles, or I never would have surrendered."

Chief Joseph was never allowed to live again in his ancestral homeland in the Wallowa Valley. His final years were spent at the Colville Indian Reservation in northeastern Washington. He died on September 21, 1904, at age sixty-four, of what the agency doctor determined was "a broken heart."

In 1805, during their push to the Pacific, Lewis and Clark stumbled upon a peaceable people they called the Chopunnish, or Pierced Nose Indians, a misleading name given them by the expedition for a practice that was never a large part of their culture. The Nimíipuu, or Nee-Me-Poo, came to be called the Nez Percé (pronounced nez purse) by the whites. That fall, with provisions running low and the expedition faltering, the Nez Percé came to the aid of Lewis and Clark, providing food, shelter, and honorable hospitality.

In 1986 the Nez Percé (*Nimíipuu*) Trail was established by the U.S. Congress as a National Historic Trail. The trail traces the 1,170-mile journey of the 1877 flight, stretching from Wallowa Lake, Oregon, to the Bear's Paw Battlefield near Chinook, Montana. Today, some Nez Percé make their home on the reservation at Lapwai, Idaho. Others, including some descendants of the 1887 Nez Percé, live in and around Chief Joseph's beloved Wallowa Valley, Oregon.

It does not require many words to speak the truth.
—CHIEF JOSEPH

Do not let kindness and truth leave you;
Bind them around your neck,
Write them on the tablet of your heart,
So you will find favor and good repute
in the sight of God and man.
PROVERBS 3:3–4 NASB

America's First Nations People

In his powerful book *One Tribe, Many Nations* (Regal Books, 1997), Lakota/Sioux Richard Twiss writes:

America has often been referred to as the melting pot of the world. A Native man once said about Native people and their place in this supposed culturally homogenized melting pot, "Whatever it is that Indian people are made out of, we don't melt too easy."

The First Nations [Host People, or Native Americans] have often been viewed as obstacles to the civilization, development and cultivation of the land. L. Frank Baum, author of the classic children's story *The Wizard of Oz*, wrote in South Dakota's *Aberdeen Saturday Pioneer* in 1890:

> *With his fall the nobility of the Redskin is extinguished, and what few are left are a pack of whining curs who lick the hand that smites them. The whites, by law of conquest and by justice of civilization, are master of the American continent, and the best safety of the frontier settlements will be secured by the total annihilation of the few remaining Indians.*

The "total annihilation" of Native people was once considered a legitimate approach to solving the Native problem. And it almost happened.

Estimates of the pre-Columbus Indian population range from 1 million to 30 million, depending upon the criteria used. Many historians use a conservative figure of 10 to 12 million. If this is true, then the following facts are most disturbing:

* By 1900 only 237,000 native people were left in the United States.

* In the early 1800s, California was home to an estimated 260,000 Indians. By 1900, there were 20,000.

* Today nearly 2 million self-declared Native Americans live in the United States. Another 1.3 million live in Canada.

* According to the 1990 census, 23 percent of the Native population live on reservations; 77 percent live in urban areas.

* There are 562 federally recognized tribes, or nations; 220 of those are in Alaska. Another 150 tribes are in the process of petitioning for federal recognition.

* Approximately 200 Native tribes have become extinct.

* There are 250 different Native languages and dialects spoken on a daily basis. (Apache and Lakota are as different from Navajo and Mohawk as Norwegian is from Japanese.)

* Fewer than 10 percent of contemporary Indians speak their Native languages.

* The federal government recognizes 300 reservations, which take up less than 4 percent of the land in the continental United States.

* About 11 million acres of land within reservation boundaries (20 percent) are owned by non-Indians.

* Nearly one-half of reservation populations are non-Indian.

[The above list quoted in *One Church, Many Tribes* from *American Indian Facts of Life* by George Russell.]

Moral evil infects every culture, and during the eighteenth and nineteenth centuries, white-on-Indian violence was almost incomprehensible. However, over the past four hundred years of our national history, atrocities occurred on both sides—white on Indian (most prominently in the nineteenth century, when the pioneer push west was at its height), and Indian on white (most incidents occurring in the seventeenth and eighteenth centuries). What we remember, of course, are the dark stories. But let us not forget Squanto and the benevolent tribes that rescued the early colonists from starvation and death. Or the Nez Percé, who provided critically needed stores to Lewis and Clark in the midst of a bleak winter. Or the William Penns, Benjamin Franklins, Plymouth colonists, and others who treated the Host Peoples in a dignified, honorable manner.

God has a heart for those who weep, and as we strive to heal the wounds of the past, let us never forget the Native Americans and the price they paid as this nation was forged. Their contributions have been many—may they be recognized and honored, under God.

The Smuggled Patriot
John Adams
1778

Captain Samuel Tucker stood in the bitter February wind, watching through the gathering gloom and the blowing snow for the small boat carrying a most-important passenger, Mr. John Adams. As the newly-assigned captain of the Continental navy's frigate *Boston*, Captain Tucker had been given the task of smuggling the well-known patriot to France, where Adams would join Benjamin Franklin in securing France as an ally in the war against Great Britain.

Secrecy was vital to completing this mission. British spies abounded in Boston and British warships waited just off the coast, ready to capture any American vessel. How delighted they would be to capture the famous Mr. Adams. To maintain secrecy, Mr. Adams did not board the *Boston* in the harbor with the other thirty-four passengers; instead the captain arranged to meet him on the shore near his home. The *Boston* had waited in a snowstorm and gale-force winds for two days before they could drop off sailors in the ship's boat to pick up Mr. Adams, his ten-year-old son, and his servant.

Even now the winds were high, and the sea was very rough. Finally Captain Tucker saw the ship's boat returning. Crewmen hurried to help the statesman and his party on board. But high winds, steep seas, and more snow caused further delays—it wasn't until three days later, on Tuesday, February 17, 1778, that the *Boston* finally put out to sea.

But their difficulties were not all behind them. The three-thousand-mile voyage on the North Atlantic in its most treacherous season held great risks. If one could get past the shoals of Cape Cod, known as the "graveyard of ships," there was the sheer terror of winter storms at sea—the violently pitching deck and the freezing spray that coated the sails, making them so heavy the ship could capsize. And there was the difficulty in navigation, as storms hid the sun and stars, often for days at a time. Under ideal conditions the trip to France could be made in about three weeks; in winter it usually took eight to ten weeks. Even in peacetime no one put to sea from Boston in winter if it could possibly be avoided.

After the first full day on the rough seas, all the passengers and half of the crew were seasick. On their second day out, three British frigates spotted the *Boston* and gave chase. The *Boston* was quick for such a heavily armed vessel and outran two of the ships, but the third chased them for three days.

Then a violent storm struck suddenly in the night. The ship was tossed so violently that John Adams and his young son had to hold on to their beds with both hands as they braced their feet against the walls. There was a terrifying crash as lightning hit the main mast—and injured twenty seamen. Captain Tucker wrote, "One thing and another continually gave way on board. Pray, God, protect us!"

John Adams and his son prayed continually. Young John Quincy Adams displayed "manly courage and patience," and Adams noted, with some surprise, that he himself had remained "perfectly calm."

After the storm came many days of smooth sailing, and the voyage settled into a routine. John Adams had plenty of time to reflect on his past and future as a public servant. He had been there for the birth of the new nation, as a delegate to the first and second Continental Congress. He had signed the Declaration of Independence.

Whenever John and his wife, Abigail, were separated, he wrote her letters—hundreds of them over their lifetime. On the day they signed the Declaration of Independence, John wrote Abigail twice. John knew Abigail was proud of him—she knew how important it had been for the new nation to have such a godly voice among the top leaders.

John Adams was known for his shrewd judgment of character and was one of the most persuasive members of Congress, exerting decisive leadership and often turning the tide of public opinion. For example, on July 1, 1776, when Congress entered what John called "the greatest debate of all," John Dickinson, a delegate from Pennsylvania, spoke long and eloquently against independence. When he finally finished, there was a lengthy silence. John waited and waited for someone to speak up for independence. But when no one else did, he rose and gave a powerful speech that touched every heart in the room.

> *Before God, I believe the hour has come. My judgment*
> *approves this measure, and my whole heart is in it. All that*
> *I have, and all that I am, and all that I hope in this life, I*
> *am now ready here to stake upon it. And I leave off as I*
> *began, that live or die, survive or perish, I am for the*
> *Declaration. It is my living sentiment, and by the blessing of*
> *God it shall be my dying sentiment, Independence now, and*
> *Independence for ever!*

But in 1777 John Adams retired from Congress, feeling it was time to step down from public life. He wrote, "I see my brothers, as lawyers, easily making fortunes for themselves and their families. . . . I see my own children growing up in something very like real want, because I have taken no care of them." He was home to stay.

Then came a packet of letters from Congress naming Adams as a commissioner to France, to work with Benjamin Franklin and Arthur Lee. One of the letters noted the extreme importance of the negotiations with France, expressed concern over Franklin's age, and stated, "We want one man of inflexible integrity on the embassy."

The packet arrived in mid-December, about the time General George Washington was moving his army to Valley Forge. John Adams was out of town on law business. Abigail opened the package, thinking it was urgent. She was stunned as she read it and asked herself, "How could these congressmen contrive to rob me of all my happiness?" She immediately wrote in a letter:

> *And can I, sir, consent to be separated from him whom*
> *my heart esteems above all earthly things, and for an unlim-*
> *ited time? My life will be one continued scene of anxiety and*
> *apprehension, and must I cheerfully comply with the demand*
> *of my country?*

When John returned home, he and Abigail sat down to seek God's guidance, knowing it would be a turning point in their lives. They rose from prayer with a decision: This was God's will. John would accept this "momentous trust"—he would go to France.

Abigail wanted to go with him, despite her fear of sailing. But the risk of her, a woman, being captured by the enemy, the expense of setting up a household in Paris, and the need for someone to run things at home caused John to decide against it. Ten-year-old John Quincy Adams also wanted to go—and his parents agreed. It was the chance of a lifetime "for acquiring useful knowledge and virtue, such as will render you . . . an honor to your country, and a blessing to your parents."

There was also time and opportunity on the trip for both father and son to work on their French, as many of the other passengers were French officers returning after service in the Continental army.

There was also time on the trip to appraise the Continental navy firsthand. Mr. Adams found many things to correct: There was too much informality, too little discipline, a "detestable" use of profanity, and a dangerous indifference to sanitation that, if not corrected, could lead to death from disease. "I am constantly giving hints to the Captain concerning order, economy and regularity," Adams wrote, "and he seems to be sensible of the necessity of them, and exerts himself to introduce them." The ship took on a new look—things were swept, washed, and hung out to dry and purify in the sunshine. Captain Tucker took all of Adams' suggestions in good spirit—after all, he couldn't have his esteemed passenger dying from a fever.

The trip afforded time for John Adams to wonder about *why* he was going to France. He felt ill suited for the position. He knew nothing of European politics or diplomacy, he could not speak French, and he had never even seen a king or queen. All he had to offer was courage, a passion for freedom and the American cause, and a sensitivity to the will and timing of God.

His friend Benjamin Rush had assured him, "Your abilities and firmness are much needed at the Court of France, and though dressing fashionably, powdering one's hair, and bowing well may be seen by some as necessary accomplishments for an ambassador, I maintain that knowledge and integrity with prudence are of far more importance."

John prayed he was right.

Just as life at sea was becoming too predictable, the crew spotted a hostile sail on the horizon. Captain Tucker consulted Mr. Adams, and they both felt they should attack. Captain Tucker, ever aware that his foremost duty was to deliver his highly important passenger safely to France, respectfully suggested Adams go belowdecks, as "hot work" was about to begin.

Giving chase, they discovered the other ship was a heavily armed merchantman flying the British flag. The *Boston* fired one shot, the merchantman fired three. When Captain Tucker turned to survey the damage, he saw to his horror that there stood John Adams—the man he had been working so hard to preserve and protect—his head just inches away from where the cannonball had split the mizzen yard! With musket in hand, and with no thought for his own life, John Adams had taken his place in the heart of the action. He stood with the other marines in defense of the ship, ready to fight in hand-to-hand combat.

Captain Tucker rushed to his side. "My dear sir, what are you doing here?" he asked incredulously.

John Adams smiled. "I thought I ought to do my share of the fighting!"

Captain Tucker later spoke warmly of Adams, saying, "This was sufficient for me to judge the bravery of my venerable and patriotic Adams."

After six weeks and four days at sea, the *Boston* reached harbor. John was to remain in France for a little more than a year.

The American diplomatic mission was a great success. While John Adams was in Paris, the French declared war on Great Britain. Historians agree that America had little chance of winning the war without France's help, as France was *the* major source of military supplies to Washington's army. They also provided us with trained soldiers and a fleet of warships.

Once France's help was secured, John sailed for home, only to be sent back across the Atlantic—to England this time—to begin negotiating peace. The British were not interested in negotiating peace, however, as they still thought they were going to win the war. John worked alone, as the sole negotiator, for almost two years until Benjamin Franklin, Thomas Jefferson, and two others joined him on June 11, 1781.

Then, in the fall of 1781, General George Washington defeated Cornwallis at Yorktown. Cornwallis surrendered on October 19. Five days too late, on October 24, seven thousand British reinforcements arrived under General Clinton. They turned back when they found Cornwallis had already surrendered.

Although the war was over, England did not officially declare an end to hostilities for sixteen more months.

After the treaties were all signed, John Adams assumed his new post as American ambassador in London, where he lived until his return to America in 1788. Once again, he tried to retire from politics, but before too long he was involved again. In 1789 he was elected vice-president and served two terms with George Washington. After this, he was elected as the second president of the United States.

John Adams had an overriding sense of duty and a need to serve, and he was passionate about America. He did the right thing, even when it made him unpopular. He took a long, historical view of the decisions that faced the young nation. He is famous for saying things like "Think of your forefathers! Think of your posterity," and "I must study politics and war that my sons may have liberty to study mathematics and philosophy."

A patriot's patriot, John Adams had the humble heart of a servant, saying, "If we do not lay out ourselves in the service of mankind, whom should we serve?"

★ ★ ★

I always consider the settlement of America with
reverence and wonder as the opening of a grand scene
and design in providence, for the illumination of the
ignorant and the emancipation of the slavish part of
mankind all over the earth.
—JOHN ADAMS

Suppose a nation in some distant region should take the
Bible for their only law book, and every member should
regulate his conduct by the precepts there exhibited!
Every member would be obliged in conscience, to temperance, frugality, and industry; to justice, kindness, and
charity towards his fellow men; and to piety, love, and
reverence toward Almighty God. . . . What a Utopia,
what a Paradise would this region be.
—JOHN ADAMS

Fifty Years Later

Adams and Jefferson are no more. On our fiftieth anniversary,
the great day of national jubilee, in the very hour of public rejoicing,
in the midst of echoing and reechoing voices of thanksgiving,
while their own names were on all tongues, they took their flight
together to the world of spirits.
—DANIEL WEBSTER

How appropriate that two of our nation's most cherished and respected Founding Fathers would pass away on July 4, 1826, just a few hours apart of each other. What makes it even more appropriate is that they died exactly fifty years to the day after the Declaration of Independence was voted on and approved by the Continental Congress.

Daniel Webster described the day of their passing:

> *Until within a few days previous, Mr. Adams had*
> *exhibited no indications of rapid decline. The morning of*
> *the fourth of July, 1826, he was unable to rise from his*
> *bed. Neither to himself, or his friends, however, was his*
> *dissolution supposed to be so near. He was asked to sug-*
> *gest a toast, appropriate to the celebration of the day.*
> *His mind seemed to glance back to the hour in which,*
> *fifty years before, he had voted for the Declaration*
> *of Independence, and with the spirit with which he*
> *then raised his hand, he now exclaimed, "Independence*
> *forever." At four o'clock in the afternoon he expired.*
> *Mr. Jefferson had departed a few hours before him.*

Looking back at this twist of fate of the two beloved leaders, one might say that it was just a coincidence. Taking a step back, however, we can see that it actually represents something truly interesting.

Adams and Jefferson differed on many things, although they believed in an independent nation. Politically Adams, a Federalist, was at odds with Jefferson, who would become the leader of the rival Democratic-Republicans. After George Washington left the presidency, a bitterly fought battle ensued between Vice-President Adams and Secretary Jefferson. Adams defeated Jefferson by a three-vote margin (seventy-one to sixty-eight electoral votes), becoming the second president in America's short history. In 1800 another rough campaign occurred again between the two men, except Jefferson ended up the winner. It was even reported that, on the day of Jefferson's inauguration, John Adams was on a carriage headed out of the city. His son had recently passed away in New York, giving him a convenient excuse not to attend the inauguration of the incoming president.

The two also didn't agree on religion. But as they say, "time heals all wounds," and in this case that might be true. For as the two men took a step back from the public, their friendship was reconciled by Benjamin Rush in 1812. They became very good friends, writing to each other quite often on topics like philosophy and religion.

What makes this such a fascinating story is that even though Adams and Jefferson were from virtual opposite ends of the political spectrum, they were cordial and complimentary of each other. They served on the committee that drafted the Declaration of Independence, and despite their differences they worked together to draft one of the greatest documents in our history. Politicians today ought to take a peek into the past and catch a glimpse of these two stalwarts and see how divergent personalities can work together for the greater good.

John Quincy Adams, son of John Adams, said it best when he wrote about his father and Thomas Jefferson:

> *Then, glancing through the same lapse of time, in the condition of the individuals, we see the first day marked with fulness of vigour of youth, in the pledge of their lives, their fortunes and their sacred honour, to the cause of freedom and of mankind. And on the last, extended on the bed of death, with but sense and sensibility left to breathe a last aspiration to heaven of blessing upon their country; may we not humbly hope, that to them, too, it was a pledge of transition from gloom to glory; and that while their mortal vestments were sinking into the clod of the valley, their emancipated spirits were ascending to the bosom of their God!*

"Remember the Ladies"
Abigail Adams
1776

52

Though it was spring, in the mornings Abigail Adams felt March all the way through her bones, and much of her constant chill she attributed to John not being near to warm her as he had so often when they were newly wed. She'd known when she and John married a dozen years ago, the busy course his life might take as both farmer and talented lawyer. His hard work and devotion were two of the qualities that had drawn her so close to him. What she hadn't managed to foresee was the cataclysm that now loomed larger every day.

Citizens shot dead by muskets on the streets of Boston. Tea dumped into the harbor. Skirmishes and volleys, first only occasionally but now almost nightly. And, at the very marrow of the conflict, her husband, whose sharp mind, skilled tongue, and patriot's heart had made him almost a forgone choice for the Continental Congress in Philadelphia. Now the long weeks and months apart became almost too much to bear. There were days she couldn't remember the line of his jaw or the weight of him lying beside her.

Rousing herself, Abigail sat still in her bed, goose down comforter pulled up about her shoulders, and listened to the silence of dawn. The cock's crow never woke her any longer—the churning of her thoughts, the occasional nightmare of what might happen in John's absence, they all seemed to crowd in at her just at night's last breath, waking her to look out her leaded windows at the silver of coming day. The children—Nabby, John Quincy, Charles, and Thomas—still slumbered, so Abigail made ready to occupy herself the way she did whenever loneliness fell heaviest. She planned her day's letters.

Without quill and ink, nib and paper, Abigail did not know how she would have survived her separation. Today she needed to send off a reply to her sister, Mary, and take up her most recent missive to Mercy Warren. Then there would be her latest letter to John.

Abigail spent days, sometimes weeks, thinking through her letters. They were as close as she could come to talking to her dearest in person, and she wanted her correspondence to be sustaining and uplifting to him. But he'd also encouraged her to challenge him. He treated their marriage, unlike too many couples she knew, as one of equals. John had a brilliant mind that did not fear challenge but craved inspiration. So Abigail had taken his challenge to heart, and their letters were filled with both the daily business of life as well as news and thoughts about the momentous future just around the corner.

This morning, as Abigail finally heard the rooster shatter the morning with its beckon, she would begin putting to words a thought that had troubled her—and other women, like Mercy, as well. All this talk going around about freedom, independence, and sovereignty from under the shadow of tyranny—why was it only being spoken by men and for men? Shouldn't the call to liberty from tyrants at home be just as important? Did not the apostle say that "In Christ there is neither man nor woman"? If any man should carry forth the rights of women to the same freedoms as men, her husband, John, who lived a life of Christian service and sacrifice, seemed the best situated to take the message to the very heart of Congressional debate.

No letter from wife to husband could start so bold, though, and as Abigail lit a candle and moved as quietly as she could through the saltbox house in Braintree, downstairs to her writing desk in the parlor, she knew she should tackle less controversial ground first. It was so hard being away from him, though, and his letters home were often so brief that her emotions got the better of her.

I wish you would ever write me a Letter half as long as I you, she pleaded. It was chide enough. His next letter, she was sure, would be half and again as long as previous. She moved onto the topics of the defense of Virginia, her esteem for George Washington, and an idea she'd been thinking through lately.

I have sometimes been ready to think that the passion
for Liberty cannot be Eaquelly Strong in the Breasts if those
who have been accustomed to deprive their fellow Creatures
of theirs. Of this I am certain that it is not founded upon that
generous and christian principle of doing to others as we would
that others should do unto us.

It was a statement she thought her husband would agree with vehemently, and she hoped that it might lay the ground for her letter's later call to freedom for women as well. Now, though, she heard the creaking of floorboards above and knew that either Charles or Thomas had roused. Nabby and John Quincy wouldn't have raised themselves so early had a cock been crowing perched on a pillow next to their very ear. Either way, it was time to be "Mother."

The day's chill soon broke and glorious spring seemed to fully take hold of the Massachussetts countryside. The farm's first growth already showed above the soil, and nature seemed clothed in its most splendid attire. Perhaps it was two weeks without atrocities. She'd been warned about smallpox in Boston and had put off visiting the family home in the city, but friends and neighbors mostly came by with good news over the next few days. All of it made her letter when she finally returned to her writing on the last day of March 1776. A post would be leaving for New York and Philadelphia tomorrow, and if she wanted her letter on it she needed to finish tonight. Which meant finally asking the question she'd been toiling through in her heart.

I long to hear you have declared an independancy—and
by the way in the new Code of Laws which I suppose it will
be necessary for you to make I desire you would Remember
the Ladies, and be more generous and favourable to them
than your ancestors. Do not put such unlimited power into the
hands of the Husbands. Remember all Men would be tyrants
if they could.

Once started, she could barely contain herself. Would John scold her for calling all men tyrants? Would he hear her passion in the words, or would the letter be read only halfheartedly in the midst of one of Franklin's digressions or Jefferson's eloquent speeches?

> *Men of Sense in all Ages abhor those customs which treat us only as the vassals of your Sex. Regard us then as Beings placed by providence under your protection and in immitation of the Suprem [sic] Being make us of that power only for our happiness.*

She signed, as she always did, *Portia*, dated the letter, and sealed it with wax. She had put forth the question with eloquence and even-handedness to one of the best men in the colonies. That women should stand equal and free, as God himself intended, alongside their husbands, seemed only natural to Abigail, and she thought John might feel the same way.

But even the best men in the Union could not change centuries of customs overnight. Nor did they feel particularly inclined. One revolution, it seemed, was more than enough at the moment for John, who responded to his wife's sincere call for equality as though she might be jesting.

> *As to your extraordinary Code of Laws, I cannot but laugh. We have been told that our Struggle has loosened the bands of Government every where. That Children and Apprentices were disobedient—that schools and Colledges were grown turbulent—that Indians slighted their Guardians and Negroes grew insolent to their Masters. But your Letter was the first Intimation that another Tribe more numerous and powerfull than all the rest were grown discontented. — This is rather too coarse a Compliment but you are so saucy, I won't blot it out.*

Abigail's disappointment in her husband was sharp but focused. On so many things he followed God's leading, and the cause of emancipating the colonies was vast and great. Yet on this single issue he had failed to see what her eyes could. He would not budge, and so she chastised him wryly in her next letter, warning of the coming days when the *next* revolution would come and women would subdue their masters.

That letter was posted May 7, 1776.

In 1869, ninety-three years later, Susan B. Anthony helped form the Women's Suffrage Movement.

Fifty-one years after that, in 1920, the Nineteenth Amendment to the Constitution—the Constitution John Adams himself helped draft—was ratified and women gained the right to vote.

Abigail Adams returned to her empty bedchamber the evening after her letter found its way south, weary and already chilled. Great things, it seemed, were coming, her husband at their very fulcrum. And yet even great men can be blinded or need reminding of their true cause from time to time. It was not the goals of men for which they were fighting, but for God's own purpose—a design that included all his faithful, men, women, and children. All called to Him.

★ ★ ★

There is neither Jew nor Greek, slave nor free, male
nor female, for you are all one in Christ Jesus.
GALATIANS 3:28

The Construction of the U.S. Capitol

The great dome of the United States Capitol is one of the most instantly recognizable architectural landmarks in the world. To countless people it is a symbol of liberty, democracy, and the promise of opportunity for which the United States of America is famous. Even in its building, however, it tells a more complicated story of our country's history, for many who built it were black slaves, hired from their masters' Virginia and Maryland plantations.

The intention at first was to import workers from Europe; however, response to opportunity was slim. Faced with the enormity of the project and an unexpected lack of inexpensive labor, the commissioners turned to the surrounding landowners. And so from 1790 to 1863, more than half the workers on the U.S. Capitol—and the White House too—were slaves.

Perhaps in the greatest irony, the famed Statue of Freedom was cast by a slave by the name of Philip Reid, at a local foundry in Bladensburg, Maryland. Reid actually earned his emancipation through his work, but it was his master who was compensated for the loss of his "property."

On December 2, 1863, as an enormous crowd cheered, the head and shoulders of the Statue of Freedom were finally set atop the Capitol. The story of those who helped build the home of Congress was kept mostly quiet and continues to remain a little-known fact today.

The Voice of Reason
Roger Sherman
1721–1793

53

It was summer in Philadelphia, June 11, 1787, and the heat made it almost impossible to think, let alone be reasonable and accommodating to debate. Yet hour after hour, Roger Sherman and his Constitutional Convention colleagues toiled away, charting the course of freedom in a document that would govern the nation.

The hard work of forging the future of the country by quill and ink went in fits and starts. On certain topics—the issue of import and export taxes—it seemed that discussion went smoothly. On many others, though, each representative had an opinion and few shared any common ground. One such battle was being fought on the issue of congressional representation as Roger Sherman of Connecticut stared, blinking at the ceiling. They had gotten nowhere on Saturday with the issue; in fact, tempers flared so high that there had been threats of leaving the Convention, maybe even leaving the Union. Hours in such humidity could make a man say almost anything, and thankfully they'd taken off the Sabbath and were giving it one more go.

Of any in the room, Sherman truly could claim to have seen it all. He'd played a part in the creation of all four major founding documents the country had yet seen—the Articles of Association in 1774, the Declaration of Independence in 1776, the Articles of Confederation two years later in 1778, and now this, the Constitution. He had watched these great men whom he considered brothers go gray under their powdered wigs.

Sherman himself did not stand on such ceremony. A cobbler by birth and without much in the way of education as a young man, he'd nevertheless worked diligently at bettering himself and eventually earned an honorary degree at Yale University, even serving as the school's treasurer. His common background, though, showed in his speech, his dress, and even the clipped style in which he kept his hair.

Now, however, was one of those times he wished for a wig, if only to pull it over his eyes. He couldn't stand any more of the bickering.

It all came down to voice. Whose voice would stand out strongest in Congress? Delegates from Pennsylvania, Massachusetts, and Virginia argued that since their states contained the lion's share of the people, shouldered the lion's share of the tax burden, and would carry the weight of the new republic on the backs of their cities and citizens, they should have the most say.

"Representatives based on population," one began, in yet another redundant summary.

He was quickly followed by Delaware's representative, who pointed out that the lion's share of struggle and sacrifice was technically born equally *per capita*. They paid in less as a whole, but the individual obligation of their citizens was no different than in any other state. Why should their people be punished for living on one side of an imaginary line? "We've always stood as equals before," he said. "We'll stand as equals always!"

Sherman could take it no longer.

"Gentlemen," he addressed his colleagues and they all quieted. Sherman hadn't spoken during this debate, a rarity as he was one of the Convention's most loquacious delegates, and from New Hampshire to Georgia his peers respected his commonsense approach to difficult impasses. "Gentlemen, my fellow statesmen from Pennsylvania and Virginia are correct."

The room fell silent. By siding with the large states, he'd effectively taken equal voice away from his own people. But he wasn't finished.

"Gentlemen, my fellow statesmen from Delaware and Rhode Island are correct, too. Every point each makes is undeniably true. And therefore we must heed them all."

What followed was the proposal of a bicameral system by which Congress would consist of two halves: the Senate, which put all states on equal footing, and the House of Representatives, which gave states with larger populations greater representation. In the end, a system nearly exactly as he proposed made it into the final draft of the U.S. Constitution, and we continue to see the results of his thinking today.

Roger Sherman's voice was heard not only on political matters but on religious topics as well. Sherman took the same insightful, straightforward, commonsense approach to faith as he did to politics. A member of the White Haven Church pastored by Jonathan Edwards Jr., son of the famed Puritan theologian, Sherman once penned a creed in his own words, spelling out the core beliefs he held so dear. So eloquent were his words that White Haven adopted the creed.

At Sherman's death, Rev. Edwards gave the eulogy, reaffirming what all who knew him understood: Roger Sherman had lived God's calling in his life.

It is most fitting that this man, with God-given talents to serve as a politician in the truest sense as a wise representative of his people's common good, was the only man to sign all four founding documents of America's birth. Called to serve his faith and his country, he did both beyond reproach. A true patriot, a true Christian, Roger Sherman is a powerful example of a man of God doing great, and often unseen, things for this country.

★ ★ ★

Your fathers, the fathers of this republic, did,
most deliberately, under the inspiration
of a glorious patriotism, and with a sublime faith
in the great principles of justice and freedom,
lay deep a corner-stone of the national superstructure,
which has risen and still rises in grandeur around you.
—FREDERICK DOUGLASS

We the People of the United States,

in Order to form a more

perfect Union, establish Justice,

insure domestic Tranquility,

provide for the common defense,

promote the general Welfare,

and secure the Blessings of Liberty

to ourselves and our Posterity,

do ordain and establish this

Constitution for the United States

of America.

PREAMBLE TO THE CONSTITUTION
OF THE UNITED STATES OF AMERICA

54

"Turned Loose to the Whirlwind"
Compromise of 1877

MARCH 1877

See if this sounds familiar:

With the sitting president not running for reelection, a Republican and a Democrat square off for the job. The last administration is coming off a tidal wave of moral failure, making his party's job of holding the office far more difficult. As well, the nation is becoming increasingly fractious, splitting down party lines on a number of key issues.

The election season is contentious and the vote is close. Very close. Too close, in fact, to call. At least in the electoral college.

The popular vote anoints a clear winner; however, that's not how we elect a president in the United States. And so, amid charges of voter fraud and election mishaps, in Florida among other places, the new president isn't so much elected as appointed and a lot of people aren't happy with the results.

This isn't the election of 2000, however. It's the election of 1876, between Rutherford B. Hayes for the Republicans and Samuel J. Tilden for the Democrats, one of the clearest examples in American history of how the past quite often repeats itself. The social circumstances surrounding the election and the aftermath, though, teach their own lessons about our country and the difficulty it was having in moving past slavery and recovering from the Civil War.

In 1876 Ulysses S. Grant still held the office of president, though most of the country, Republicans and Democrats alike, were tired of him. Corruption ruled during Grant's terms, and the great job of pulling together a fractured nation seemed lost in Washington's clamor for lined pockets and the fight for self-interest. If bribes were going to be paid anyway, they might as well be coming to you.

On the national agenda stood the issue of Reconstruction. It was now eleven years since the Confederate Army surrendered, and yet the work was still not done.

See if this sounds familiar:

When a war, which seems to have been started for just reasons, ends, the winning nation finds itself faced with a land torn in two. On one side stand the liberated, who have never held power, land, or even basic human rights. On the other side are the conquered forces who seethe at someone coming in and telling them how to run their nation. Worse, they're now expected to just accept edicts from the country that just defeated them, allow a population of men and women they hate to live free, and submit to it all under threat of military action.

There has never been an easy or simple solution to such problems. There isn't one today and there wasn't one back in 1866. Union troops roamed the South, Southern states were forced to accept new amendments to the U.S. Constitution to be let back into the country, and a powerful Congress overrode President Johnson's veto by passing the Reconstruction Acts, dividing states into military districts.

The Freedman's Bureau, created in 1865, was given the enormous task of tackling the transition at a practical level. The jobs included finding work for freed slaves, setting up schools and educational systems, and much more. The Bureau had the power to enact laws to meet their goals and helped establish new state constitutions and governments for each reconstructed Southern state. Southerners, who watched their states be handed over to blacks and newly arrived "carpetbagger" Yankees, hated the Bureau with a passion, and it's not surprising that members were often targeted by the newly emerged Ku Klux Klan.

Take all this unrest, let it fester for a number of years, and then add the Hayes-Tilden Election of 1876, and you have a rough idea of the state of the country at that time. Angry voices, pointing fingers, and outright threats filled the public discourse. We were still a nation divided.

The problem with the election was this:

Democrat Samuel Tilden, champion of the white South, had won the popular vote, 4,282,020 to 4,036,572, and the day after the election the electoral returns stood at 184 for Tilden and 165 for Hayes. But the winner needed 185 votes, and four states' votes still remained—Oregon, Florida, South Carolina, and Louisiana.

Oregon's three votes soon went to Hayes, but the other three states were a debacle. In the end, under reciprocal charges of voter fraud, both parties produced their own sets of electoral results and sent the results to Washington, D.C. All the numbers contradicted each other, and when the government turned to the Constitution for help they found none. No manner of resolution for such a problem had ever been spelled out.

Days turned into weeks turned into months. It was now March 1877, and the inauguration, now merely theoretical, was just days away. A bill was passed calling an Electoral Commission consisting of five members of the Senate, House, and Supreme Court to review the election and vote for the winner. There would be seven Republicans, seven Democrats, and one Independent. Shortly after the bill, however, the one Independent left the Supreme Court for a Senate seat. In filling the remaining spot from the Supreme Court, the commission had no choice but to select a Republican; there were no Democrats left.

The Commission's vote, eight to seven, made Rutherford Hayes president of the United States. But Congress still needed to accept the decision. Securing the majority vote necessary to carry the measure seemed almost an impossibility until a compromise was reached. In return for accepting Hayes as president, his first tasks would be to provide more federal funds for rebuilding ruined Southern infrastructure and also to end Reconstruction by officially removing federal troops and recognizing Democrat governors elected to numerous Southern states. The Republicans agreed. Their man took office, but in return for the Republicans' win, the Democrats, over the next decade, were able to erase most of the civil rights laws that had been passed in the preceding fifteen years. And so among blacks, the Compromise of 1877 became known as the Great Betrayal.

The South celebrated as if they'd actually won the war. As Northern troops boarded ships home, Southern citizens fired guns and rang bells. Meanwhile black citizens, free but unequal, watched in silence. The war that was fought seemed to have been won in vain. They were emancipated, but that freedom now seemed worthless as their other rights soon vanished without protection.

After the Civil War, Southern states had been forced to accept laws declaring blacks and whites equal, but when that threat of force vanished, segregation became enacted into law with the *Plessy v. Ferguson* decision calling for "separate but equal" treatment. And it was easy to ignore the "equal" part of that ruling. Poll taxes, literacy tests, and brutal force kept blacks from voting. Courts turned a blind eye to justice—often rendering convictions without trials or throwing out complaints made by blacks without even considering evidence—and with the eventual rise of the KKK, segregation turned into something more than separation. It turned brutal and violent. The KKK reigned with terror, and the rope noose struck terror for decades. More than three thousand blacks would be lynched over the next forty years, and that doesn't even mark the tip of the mountain of those who were beaten, tortured, abused, stolen from, and treated as insignificant. In many ways, during Jim Crow a black southerner's life was, arguably, worth less now than during slavery.

As Frederick Douglass put it: "You have emancipated us. I thank you for it. You have enfranchised us. And I thank you for it. But what is your emancipation—what is your enfranchisement if the black man having been made free by the letter of the law, is unable to exercise that freedom? You have turned us loose to the sky, to the storm, to the whirlwind, and worst of all, you have turned us loose to our infuriated masters. What does it all amount to if the black man after having been freed from the slaveholder's lash is subject to the slaveholder's shotgun!"

There is no denying Douglass's words. The North, tired and frustrated by the political quagmire in which it had become entangled, bailed when expedience called for it. For the sake of the executive office they traded the burgeoning rights of a race of men and women. What might have been won over the next five years now took blacks nearly a century. There are no easy answers, but there are certainly bad choices—and the Compromise of 1877 stands as one of the worst in our nation's history. For it compromised very little that affected the people making the choices. It wasn't *their* freedoms they were surrendering, their rights they were chaining down. Our call is to look out for the powerless, not to sell them out for power.

★ ★ ★

Whenever I hear anyone arguing for slavery, I feel a strong impulse to see it tried on him personally.
—ABRAHAM LINCOLN

A Purposeful Life
George Washington Carver
1861–1943

George Washington Carver was alone in the biology lab at Iowa State College when the student brought him the letter that would change his life.

It had been a wonderful morning—summer break meant he was free from his teaching duties, free to do what he loved best: commune with God by examining the plant life around him.

His work with plants had so impressed his teachers at Iowa State that they had invited him to teach there while he finished his master's degree. Yet he had this feeling there was more. Why had God given him such an ability to unlock the secrets of nature?

He examined the letter: *That's curious*, he thought. *It's from Booker T. Washington.* Washington was the founder of Tuskegee Institute in Alabama, a school dedicated to helping Southern blacks through vocational training and teaching the biblical virtues of hard work and thrift.

Washington wrote:

> *Our students are poor, often starving. They travel miles of torn roads, across years of poverty. We teach them to read and write, but words cannot fill stomachs. They need to learn how to plant and harvest crops. . . .*
>
> *I cannot offer you money, position or fame. The first two you have. The last, from the place you now occupy, you will no doubt achieve.*
>
> *These things I now ask you to give up. I offer you in their place work—hard, hard work—the challenge of bringing people from degradation, poverty and waste to full manhood.*

Suddenly George knew. This was God's plan for his life, the purpose God had been preparing him for: He would teach his people to grow food.

He traveled to Tuskegee, where, during the interview with Washington, he had a "mighty vision." He saw how, with God's help, he would turn the dusty campus into an oasis of hope and promise for the burned-out South.

For the next forty-six years George Washington Carver lived and worked at Tuskegee Institute as the director of agriculture. He was a popular teacher—his students felt they were truly important to him. He called them his children.

He was also passionate about his topic. He inspired his students to use the gifts of nature for the betterment of mankind. He was convinced that God had given mankind everything necessary, telling his students, "To solve any shortage or problem, all we need is to set the creative mind to work."

It was an era of exciting inventions: Edison invented the light bulb in 1910. In 1913 Henry Ford perfected the assembly line, making automotives available to the common man. These great inventors were attracted by George's prolific creativity, and both offered him high-paying jobs. But Carver turned them down, choosing to remain in the service of "his people."

In everything he did, George merged the worlds of science and religion. Locking the door to his laboratory, Dr. Carver confided: "Only alone can I draw close enough to God to discover His secrets."

On November 19, 1924, Carver spoke at New York City's Marble Collegiate Church, where he attributed his success as a scientist to divine revelation:

> God is going to reveal to us things He never revealed before
> if we put our hands in His. No books ever go into my laboratory.
> The thing I am to do and the way of doing it are revealed to me.
> I never have to grope for methods. The method is revealed to me
> the moment I am inspired to create something new. Without God
> to draw aside the curtain I would be helpless.

This was an unpopular notion at the time, and George was scorned by scientists who were turning from the Bible and embracing the theory of evolution. Two days after his speech, the *New York Times* ran an editorial titled "Men of Science Never Talk that Way," in which they attempted to discredit Carver, his race, and the Tuskegee Institute, saying that he revealed "a complete lack of the scientific spirit."

In his rebuttal Dr. Carver wrote: "I understand that there are scientists to whom the world is merely the result of chemical forces or material electrons. I do not belong to this class."

As far as using books to help him in his research, he wrote, "The master analyst needs no book: he is at liberty to take apart and put together substances, compatible or non compatible to suit his own particular taste or fancy. . . ." As an example of his creativity, he reported he had noticed a bin of exotic taro roots in a New York market and that dozens of ideas for products came to him. He wrote: "I know of no book from which I can get this information, yet I will have no trouble in doing it. If this is not inspiration and information from a source greater than myself, or greater than any one has wrought up to the present time, kindly tell me what it is."

Rejection was not new to George Washington Carver. Throughout his early life, racism had thrown roadblock after roadblock in George's path. But he never grew bitter, saying, "If I used my energy to fight every wrong done to me, I would have no energy left for my work."

George was born into slavery just before the Civil War on a plantation owned by Moses Carver in southwest Missouri. Outlaws kidnapped baby George and his mother, but only George was found. George's father had already died in an accident, so the little orphan boy was raised by the Carver family. George showed unusual intelligence and a great desire to learn, but the only school nearby was exclusively for white children. So George learned to read at home, practically memorizing the Carver family's only book, *Webster's Elementary Speller*.

When he was ten years old, a white neighbor boy told him about Sunday school and prayer. George remembers: "As soon as he left I climbed up into the 'loft' of our big barn, knelt down by a barrel of corn and prayed as best I could. I do not remember what I said, I only recall that I felt so good that I prayed several times before I quit. . . . God came into my heart that afternoon while I was alone in the loft."

Soon after that, the Carver family agreed to let George attend the Lincoln School for Colored Children. The little boy walked the eight miles to Neosho, Missouri, by himself. He reached Neosho too late at night to find a friendly family to stay with, so he found a comfortable spot in a barn where he could sleep. In the morning he discovered that God had guided him to the perfect place. The barn was owned by a childless black couple, Andrew and Mariah Watkins, who took him in. "Aunt Mariah" gave George his first book, a Bible. He was eager to learn and began to read the Bible—which he read every day for the rest of his life. Mariah also gave young George a purpose: "George, you must learn all you can. Then go out in the world and give your learning back to our people. They're starving for a little knowledge."

After learning all he could at the Lincoln School, George began a decade of traveling from one midwestern community to another, earning a living and attending school whenever he could. During this time, he lived wherever he could—for a while he slept under a porch. When he finally graduated from high school, he wrote to Highland College in Kansas, where he was accepted sight unseen. But when he tried to register at the all-white college, they refused to let him in, saying, "We didn't know you were a Negro."

George gave up all hope of going to college until he met Dr. and Mrs. Milholland, who were convinced that God had special things in store for him. They finally persuaded him to enroll at Simpson College, a Methodist school, where he was the only black student. George remembers, "The kind of people at Simpson made me believe that I was a human being." He began to study art, his first love. Then in a vision, God showed him that he would be a teacher of blacks. Soon afterward, he changed his major to agriculture and transferred to Iowa State College.

After accepting Booker T. Washington's offer to work at Tuskegee, Carver set about to use the discoveries of science to transform southern agriculture. He said, "The primary idea in all of my work was to help the farmer and fill the poor man's empty dinner pail. . . . My idea is to help the 'man farthest down.' This is why I have made every process just as simple as I could to put it within his reach."

Carver noticed the soil was worn out due to years of growing nothing but cotton. So he introduced techniques of crop rotation, soil improvement, and erosion prevention. He showed the farmers how planting legumes such as peanuts would put nitrogen back into the soil.

Then he went to the laboratory to invent products that used the crops he was encouraging Southern farmers to grow, including peanuts, sweet potatoes, and soybeans. Over the years he developed hundreds of food items; nine medicines; twelve animal feeds and fertilizers; twenty cosmetic items; dozens of dyes, paints, and stains; and synthetic cotton, synthetic plastics, and synthetic rubber, which was used widely during World War II.

He wrote, "As I worked on projects which fulfilled a real human need, forces were working through me which amazed me. I would often go to sleep with an apparently insoluble problem. When I woke the answer was there. Why should we who believe in Christ be so surprised at what God can do with a willing man in a laboratory? Some things must be baffling to the critic who has never been born again."

In 1921 he was invited to Washington, D.C., to speak to the House Ways and Means Committee as an expert on the peanut. They had planned to give him just ten minutes, but his presentation was so fascinating that the chairman said, "Go ahead, brother. Your time is unlimited."

He showed them "milk" extracted from peanuts that looked just like cow's milk. He showed them buttermilk, cheese, and ice cream. He showed them breakfast food, coffee substitutes, meat substitutes, cosmetics, and ink—all made from the peanut. (Today much of Carver's research has been applied to making the same products from soybeans, as fewer people are allergic to soybeans than to peanuts.)

George ended up speaking for one hour and forty-five minutes to his captivated audience. At the end of his address, the committee chairman asked, "Dr. Carver, how did you learn all of these things?"

Carver answered, "From an old book."

"What book?" asked the chairman.

Carver replied, "The Bible."

The chairman asked, "Does the Bible tell about peanuts?"

"No, sir" Dr. Carver replied, "but it tells about the God who made the peanut. I asked Him to show me what to do with the peanut, and He did."

Speaking before the Congressional Committee brought Carver national recognition both as a scientist and as a Christian. In the 1920s, when the Commission on Interracial Cooperation and the YMCA were looking for someone who could bridge the gap between blacks and whites, they chose George Washington Carver. His audiences—comprised of young white males—were deeply touched by his life's story, his strong faith, and his intimate relationship with God. They wrote to him, addressing him as "Dad Carver," "Dear Father," "Daddy," and "My Only Dad."

George, a bachelor with no children, welcomed these young men into his heart, just as he did his students at Tuskegee. He ended up mentoring many of these young Christians—whom he called "my boys"— through the trials of growing up, encouraging their own creativity, and helping them discover their own purpose in life.

Meanwhile, Dr. Carver's fame as a botanist was spreading around the world. Leaders of nations such as Mahatma Gandhi of India and Joseph Stalin of the USSR sought out his advice on building agricultural systems for their countries. Educators from all over the world came to study his methods. And Dr. Carver's peanut milk saved the lives of hundreds of babies in West Africa.

Among the heroes of American agriculture, there has been no one more creative or more productive than George Washington Carver, the "Wizard of Tuskegee." Carver dedicated his work to improving life for African Americans, and his scientific applications helped feed hungry populations worldwide. He introduced new cash crops for Southern farmers that would enrich the depleted soil. His innovations stimulated demand for those crops, greatly benefiting the Southern agrarian economy. New industries were sparked by his genius. By the early 1940s, George's research and agricultural contributions resulted in a five-hundred-million-dollar peanut industry, with more than five million acres planted in peanuts. His life—from his humble beginnings as a sickly, orphaned slave to becoming a scientist of international reputation—is a testimony of what God can do through someone who is totally yielded to His purposes.

★ ★ ★

I am simply trying as best I can and as fast as
God gives me light to do the job I believe
He has given me in trust to do.
—GEORGE WASHINGTON CARVER

The singing birds, the buzzing bees, the opening flower,
and the budding trees are the little windows through
which God permits us to commune with Him, and to see
much of His glory, majesty, and power by simply lifting
the curtain and looking in. I love to think of nature as
unlimited broadcasting stations, through which God
speaks to us every day, every hour and every moment of
our lives, if we will only tune in and remain so.
—GEORGE WASHINGTON CARVER

Forty Acres and a Mule

As the Union Army marched through Georgia in 1865, they were followed by a band of freed slaves, some working as laborers for the Union, but all of them homeless and hungry. They had nowhere to go, and no one had any immediate answers.

When President Lincoln became aware of the situation, he ordered Major General William T. Sherman to organize a meeting with twenty other men, some of them also freed slaves, to discuss how to resolve the situation of having thousands of freed slaves with nowhere to go. Sherman soon discovered that the freed slaves really just wanted their own land with their own independence, a feat that was unattainable under the current conditions. As an offer of assistance, General Sherman drew up some plans to set aside hundreds of miles of land along the southern coast to be used as a settlement for blacks. According to Sherman's Special Field Order No. 15, each family would receive no more than forty acres of land and an animal that was no longer of use to the army. By June of 1865, approximately forty thousand ex-slaves had settled on about 400,000 acres of land. The soil had been tired from years of raising nothing but cotton, but the plots of land ensured freedom and independence for the black families tired of traveling.

But the feelings of independence lasted only a few months, as President Andrew Johnson, Lincoln's successor, pardoned former Confederates and ordered the land the freedmen were homesteading to be restored to their owners. The blacks truly believed they had earned that land as an acknowledgment of their unpaid labor, and when federal troops arrived to forcibly evacuate the ex-slaves, riots were common. This was the first bitter taste of the promised land of freedom for freed slaves.

Remembering Everyone at the Alamo

In the early 1800s, Texas was populated by a variety of peoples, including Mexican nationals, European settlers, Americans, and Tejanos—men and women of Mexican and Hispanic descent who considered themselves Texans (Tejanos) first and Mexicans second. Under the heavy rule of Mexico, these varied Texas peoples united in what has come to be known as the Texas Revolution.

During the revolution, the fight for the Alamo mission became the stuff of legends. In March 1836, several hundred men, women, and children barricaded themselves inside the mission fort, anticipating the arrival of brutal Mexican president General Santa Anna and his large army. After a thirteen-day siege, Santa Anna's forces stormed the mission. In all, 189 men died defending the Alamo.

Davy Crockett. Jim Bowie. William Travis. James Bonham. These are the names remembered by our history books.

But mostly forgotten are the eight Tejano patriots who died alongside Bowie and Crockett: Juan Abamillo, Juan Badillo, Carlos Espalier, Gregorio Esparaza (one of the only defenders whose body was not burned, but given a proper Christian burial), Antonio Fuentes, Damacio Jiménez, José Losoya, and Andrés Nava. Most of these men were born in Texas, and they bled for their homeland alongside their Anglo brothers-in-arms.

Scores of other Tejano patriots played a critical role in the Texas Revolution. There was Juan Seguín, rebel leader who later helped defeat Santa Anna, and José Antonio Navarro, one of only three Tejano Mexicano signers of the Texas Declaration of Independence (along with José Francisco Ruiz and Lorenzo de Zavala).

Let us remember the Alamo. But when we do, let us not forget the Tejanos.

56

A Soldier's View
The Sand Creek Massacre

1864

Silas Soule was a white abolitionist whose family had moved from Massachusetts to Kansas in 1854 to help usher the territory into the Union as a free state. A devout man, Amassa Soule established their home near Lawrence as a stop along the Underground Railroad. By age fifteen young Silas was helping escaped slaves from Missouri find freedom in the North. Ten years later Silas found himself on the Colorado frontier, an officer of the Colorado Third Regiment, fighting for a different kind of justice. . . .

★ ★ ★

Silas could not sleep. He felt as if his mind were on fire. He raised a small light in his lantern and wrote, knowing that if he did not record his terrible memories now, the facts would fade with each passing day.

Silas considered Colonel John Chivington to be a man looking for attention in dangerous ways. With no more battles to fight against the defeated western Confederates, Chivington, a former Methodist preacher with political ambitions, itched for an Indian campaign in which to distinguish himself. After all, Chivington had said, the Dog Soldiers, a renegade band of northern Cheyenne, were known to have committed atrocities against the white settlers of Colorado. Justice was demanded, Chivington had told Soule and other officers at Fort Lyon. But the sort of justice the colonel was about to exact was a kind born in hell. . . .

Silas was tired from a long night's ride. As dawn arrived, word came down the line that they had reached their destination: Sand

Creek. Silas eased his horse to the edge of the bluff, peering over the escarpment at what lay below. "Chief Black Kettle's people," he said to Lieutenant James Cannon, a junior officer. "Old men, women, children—the braves are probably off hunting buffalo. No sign of any Dog Soldiers, either." Below them lay the quiet winter camp of Black Kettle, White Antelope, Left Hand, and other friendly southern Cheyenne and Arapaho chiefs, about 550 people total.

Suddenly Silas heard the order from Chivington: "Attack! Attack!" Silas paused, not wanting to accept what he had feared for days. "We can't attack," he said to himself. He was thinking out loud, more than he was giving a command. But he realized, reflexively, that he could not follow Chivington's order.

"No one attacks!" Soule shouted to his company. "I am ordering you to stand your ground." All around him, however, Silas saw the majority of the other 725 cavalry soldiers indeed attacking as chaos erupted. Chivington himself approached Soule, red faced, demanding he attack—Chivington knew that Soule preferred peace with Black Kettle. But Soule refused Chivington's direct order. "This is murder!" yelled Soule. Chivington reared his horse and thundered down the embankment, cursing Soule.

Black Kettle, the peace-seeking Cheyenne chief who had personally met President Lincoln, had been told by a white officer to always fly the American flag while encamped. "If you do, no one will harm you," he had been promised.

Silas could hear the screams of the women and children and the look of realization as the old men and chiefs scrambled into action. "Come to the flag," yelled Black Kettle. "You will not be harmed if you do!" Hundreds of terrified souls heeded the chief's words and ran for his tepee, panic beginning to give way to relief. But their hopes were short-lived. Chief White Antelope hailed the approaching soldiers, raising his hands and imploring them to stop. He was shot dead. Chief Left Hand stood before his tepee, arms crossed, refusing to take up his rifle against the soldiers, whom he called his friends. He was shot dead. Chivington's troops ignored the American flag flying over Black

Kettle's lodge, as well as the white flag fluttering below it. Indiscriminate killing ensued. As he ran with his people away from the soldiers, Black Kettle saw his wife, Medicine Woman, fall, her body pierced by bullets. Women and children fell around him. Many dead.

Silas paused, wiping moisture from his bloodshot eyes. He wrote, "You would think it impossible for white men to butcher and mutilate human beings as they did there, but every word I have told you is the truth that they do not deny."

The attack continued for about six hours, Silas recorded, over a distance of four miles up the creek bed. The massacre took place as a running engagement. In all, 163 Cheyenne and Arapaho were slaughtered, two thirds being women, children, and infants. The soldiers lost fewer than ten men.

"It is hard to see little children on their knees have their brains beat out by men professing to be 'civilized,'" wrote Silas. "One squaw was wounded and a fellow took a hatchet to finish her, she held her arms up to defend her, and he cut one arm off and held the other with the one hand and dashed a hatchet through her brain. I saw two Indians hold one another's hands, chased until they were exhausted, when they kneeled down, and clasped each other around the neck and were both shot together." Silas hesitated, barely able to continue. "One woman was cut open and the child inside of her taken out, and scalped." Silas buried his face in his hands then, ashamed.

Silas placed his pen on the desk and raised his eyes to stare out the small window at the rising quarter moon. Was there more I could have done to stop the slaughter? he thought. The only reply was the sound of the cruel December wind blowing down from the Front Range.

The only known photograph of Chief Black Kettle (second row, left), taken two months before the Sand Creek Massacre. Foreground: Major Edward Wynkoop (in hat) and Captain Silas Soule.

The preceding quotes from Silas Soule referencing the atrocities at Sand Creek are taken from a letter to commanding officer Major Ned Wynkoop, which, along with other witness accounts, has since been entered into the Congressional Record. Miraculously, Chief Black Kettle survived the massacre, as did his wife, though she suffered nine gunshot wounds. More amazing, perhaps, is that Black Kettle continued to advocate peace against a rising tide of Cheyenne rage. In 1865, while still pursuing peace with the U.S. government, he said, "Although the troops have struck us, we throw it all behind and are glad to meet you in peace and friendship. . . . We are different nations, but it seems as if we were but one people, whites and all. . . . Again, I take you by the hand, and I feel happy."

Three years later, Black Kettle's band was ambushed, and the chief was killed at the Washita River, in Oklahoma, by George Armstrong Custer. Dead was the last Cheyenne chief who had held out for peace. In 1876, the bitterness of Sand Creek and Washita still fresh in their hearts, an overwhelming force of Cheyenne, Arapaho, and Lakota/Sioux annihilated Custer on the grassy hillocks of Little Big Horn.

In the days following Sand Creek, the *Rocky Mountain News* hailed Chivington and his men as heroes in the "battle." Upon their return to Denver, "trophies" of the slaughter—scalps, fingers, ears, and other body parts—were displayed in public. Due to the mounting evidence provided by eyewitnesses such as Silas Soule, Lieutenant Joseph Cramer, who also refused to take part in the massacre, and Robert Bent, who was an unwilling guide for Chivington that day, the truth soon surfaced. A few months later a congressional investigation was launched, and in a rare admittance of guilt for that time, the government recognized the incident as a massacre. Financial reparations were promised, but not a single Indian was ever paid. Likewise, neither Chivington nor any other participant was ever prosecuted.

On April 23, 1865, Charles Squiers, purportedly hired by Chivington's men, shot and killed Soule near his home in Denver, shortly after Soule had testified against Chivington. Soule had been married just weeks earlier. When Chivington took the stand just one day after Soule's burial, he tried to brand Soule a coward and drunkard. But men who served under Soule could stand it no longer and came to his defense, praising Soule for his unwavering courage in the face of the treacherous order to attack. First Lieutenant James Cannon, loyal to Soule, tracked down Squiers in New Mexico and brought him back to Denver to stand trial. Squiers escaped, and Cannon was poisoned. Squiers was never recaptured.

Black Kettle. White Antelope. Left Hand. These and other peace-seeking Cheyenne and Arapaho chiefs were heroes in that they sought peace, even in the face of death and betrayal. In the 140 years since Sand Creek, other heroes have emerged—men such as Silas Soule and James Cannon, who also gave their lives for fighting against injustice. Soule, son of devout abolitionists, took the narrow road, choosing to serve God, not man.

★ ★ ★

In 1996, at its national convention in Denver, the United Methodist Church, carrying the burden of Chivington's deeds, formally apologized to the Arapaho and Cheyenne Indian tribes for the Sand Creek Massacre.

For the past twenty years, descendents of the Sand Creek victims have attempted to buy the land upon which the massacre occurred. In December 2003, a businessman bought the site and has donated it to the Cheyenne and Arapaho. The tribes have leased the area to the National Parks Service, which is in the process of creating the first national historic site dedicated solely to a massacre. The site, encompassing some 12,500 acres, is projected to open in 2007.

Mariano Guadalupe Vallejo

Native Californian: In the early 1800s, when California was still part of Mexico, it was rare for a Mexican military officer to claim this distinction.

Such was the case with Mariano Guadalupe Vallejo. Born in 1808 to a respectable Monterey, California, military family, Vallejo quickly rose through the ranks of California's provincial military. General Vallejo served Mexico skillfully, eventually becoming the senior commander in the northern half of the province, charged with keeping order and peace in the isolated outposts of *Alta* (upper) *California*.

In the 1840s, as more and more American settlers poured into California in search of gold, Vallejo was known to be a gracious and fair host. Because of his geographic isolation from Mexico, Vallejo learned to think for himself, raising his own, privately funded army garrison, serving as foreign minister to the Russians who occupied Fort Ross on the coast, and overseeing the American immigrants and merchants.

By the mid-1840s, Vallejo realized that the future of California rested with the cause of the United States. But despite their support for independence from Mexico, General Vallejo, and his brother Salvador Vallejo, were arrested by American zealots during the 1846 Bear Flag Revolt, and imprisoned for two months in Sacramento. While in prison, Vallejo lost the majority of his vast wealth and land.

Yet despite this injustice, Vallejo remained devoted to the American cause and went on to become the only Mexican-American delegate to the state's first constitutional convention. Brother Salvador became a major for the Union army and served in the Civil War, while Mariano's son, Platon, served as a doctor on the Union front lines. After the Civil War, General Vallejo was invited to the White House, where he met President Lincoln, a meeting arranged by Vallejo's acquaintances, Generals Sheridan, Sherman, and Grant.

The Vallejo men played a critical role in helping California make the monumental transition from Mexican rule to American statehood, and should aptly be named among California's founding fathers.

A Growing Awareness
Benjamin Franklin
1706–1790

57

"**Ben, in your heart** you know I'm right!" George Mason, the delegate from Virginia, let his voice rise with passion. "We must introduce the question of slavery! We cannot let the government of this great nation, the land of the free, continue with the blotch of slavery upon it."

Benjamin Franklin closed his eyes and let his head drop. It was a hot July day and he was tired. The delegates to the 1787 Constitutional Convention had come with such hopes. Many felt that this convention would be as momentous as the one that produced the Declaration of Independence. But putting the final form to American democracy, the noblest social experiment ever devised, was proving difficult. "George, we've been at this for months—and have accomplished so little. Opening up the issue of slavery at this point would only bring more delays and controversy."

"But we must address it, Ben. Slavery is wrong! It will bring the judgment of heaven upon our country."

Benjamin nodded in agreement. Over the course of his eighty-one years, he had experienced a complete change of heart on this issue. In his younger days he had not questioned the institution of slavery. In fact, he was a slave owner. He and his wife purchased household slaves in the late 1740s. And while he argued that owning slaves took the edge off a man's work ethic and "educated children in idleness," he owned slaves while raising his own son, William.

During the years leading up to the American Revolution, such double-mindedness was common among white colonists. The colonists intellectually believed that all men were created equal and given the same rights by God—rights of life, liberty, and the pursuit of happiness. Many whites grew to dislike slavery, but not enough to sacrifice their investments and comforts. Thomas Jefferson, in his will, arranged for the emancipation of his own slaves upon his death. George Washington emancipated his slaves after Martha Washington died. In 1786 Washington wrote, "I never mean to possess another slave by purchase, it being among my first wishes to see some plan adopted by which slavery in this country may be abolished." Franklin arranged for his two remaining slaves to be freed at his death—but he had outlived them.

Scenes began to play through Franklin's mind. . . . There was the time his manservant, King, had escaped while he and William were living in England. King was found later in the service of a lady who had taught him to read and write and to play the violin and the French horn. It was an eye-opening experience for Franklin, who, though a great champion of literacy and education, had never considered teaching his slaves to read.

Then there was the day he visited an Anglican school for blacks in Philadelphia. Again he was surprised. Afterward he wrote, "Their apprehension [comprehension] seems as quick, their memory as strong, and their docility in every respect equal to that of white children."

His thoughts flashed back to July 1773. Coming home from a visit with Miss Phillis Wheatley, he couldn't stop muttering to himself, "Truly remarkable!" He could readily see why the black teenager was causing such a sensation among the Boston intellectuals. He later told his wife, Deborah, "What a mind young Miss Wheatley has! It is a joy to talk to her. She's translated Ovid's poem, 'Metamorphoses,' from Latin—and it's one of the best translations I have ever seen." His interview with Phillis Wheatley finally convinced him that any racial differences were a result of a lack of learning opportunities, not "natural capacities."

As a man who had spent his life fighting for freedom, Franklin's growing awareness of the inhumanity of slavery was now, at the end of his life, moving him to take action.

"George, as you know, I've recently been asked to be president of the Pennsylvania Abolition Society," Franklin answered. "I have with me an exhortation that members are urging me to present to the Convention." He reached into his desk drawer and pulled out a sheet of parchment. "You'll like this part: 'the Creator of the world made of one flesh, all the children of men.' It goes on to ask the Convention to arrange for the abolition of slavery in the new government, just as you desire."

George nodded his agreement. "Ben, you *must* speak out against this evil. All the Convention delegates honor you. They will listen! We must push for what's right. If we do our part, God will move on their hearts. He will do His part!"

"George, at the beginning of the Convention, I had planned to present this petition. But things have dragged on so, and such great rifts have split the states between North and South, that I have reconsidered. To tell the truth, at this point, I will be happy to get the new Constitution ratified, with all thirteen states included. Congress can hammer out the issue of slavery later. George, I know it's not the perfect solution. But it's the best we can hope for."

A fellow congressman had come in while Franklin was speaking and said, "George, perhaps you are worrying too much about this issue. Slavery is gradually dying out. It is almost gone in Virginia, except in the Tidewater country, and the world trend is decidedly against it. No progressive, civilized Christian society will condone it much longer."

"I have to agree with Benjamin. We need a strong federal government, and we need it now. The feeble Confederation just isn't working—there's way too much jealousy and petty bickering between the states. Better to get the Constitution ratified, and sort out the slavery issue later."

At the Convention the next day, thirty minutes before they were to adjourn, Franklin caught General Washington's eye just as one speaker sat down and before another took his turn. Franklin motioned that he wished to speak. With permission, he rose, leaning upon his walking stick. Every eye was upon the most senior delegate.

George Mason's heart leaped. Had his words changed Franklin's mind? Was he about to introduce the issue of abolition?

But Franklin did not read the petition from the Abolition Society. Instead he made a most remarkable speech acknowledging that the delegates needed God's help to design the new government and requesting that prayer be made each morning before they started their business for the day, just as the Continental Congress had done in the days of the American Revolution.

Everyone was stunned by Franklin's words. It was clearly the most amazing speech they had heard in the entire convention. There was a long silence. General Washington was delighted. Many of the delegates nodded their agreement. Others were hesitant to introduce prayer after so many days had passed without it, thinking it might cause the public to think they were failing at their task.

Virginia's Edmund Jennings Randolph offered a counter proposal. He recommended that a special "sermon be preached at the request of the convention on the Fourth of July, the anniversary of Independence, and thence forward prayers be used in ye Convention every morning." Franklin seconded this motion. The delegates did not decide on the prayer issue, but did agree to take a two-day recess over the Independence Day holiday to let tempers cool.

The mood of the delegates was much different when they reconvened on July 5. A compromise on how to count slaves when determining the number of congressional representatives for each state was proposed and accepted (five slaves were to equal three free men). In actuality, this "Three Fifths Clause" was not an anti-black addition, but rather an attempt to weaken the power of pro-slavery states. Previously, despite the fact that the slaves had no voting voice, slaveholders had counted their slaves in the push to increase their number of congressional representatives. By reducing the equation to three-fifths, it made it more difficult for pro-slavery states to increase their numbers in Congress.

In the end, the delegates were able to come up with a Constitution and a Bill of Rights that has lasted longer than any other constitution in modern history, and has been a model for national governments around the world for more than two hundred years.

★ ★ ★

True to his intention, Benjamin Franklin presented a petition asking for the abolition of slavery to the first U.S. Congress in February 1790. No action was taken, however.

Meanwhile, the Quakers and Abolitionists of the Pennsylvania/West Jersey area had already enacted an abolition of their own. An informal network was organized to hide and assist escaping slaves. It proved so effective that George Washington commented, "Once slaves get to the Pennsylvania/West Jersey area, they become nearly impossible to find, capture and return to their masters." This network later became the foundation of the Underground Railroad.

Benjamin Franklin helped the Pennsylvania Abolition Society develop a plan to overcome one of the practical difficulties with abolishing slavery: how to integrate a freed slave into society. Franklin's *Plan for Improving the Condition of the Free Blacks* included setting children in families and placing young apprentices; unsegregated education, especially in "the most important and generally acknowledged moral and religious principles"; and employment for working-age freedmen (including apprenticeships as needed).

A Brief History of Abolition in America

1780—Pennsylvania takes steps to gradually outlaw slavery by the "Act for the Gradual Abolition of Slavery." It provides that no child born in Pennsylvania can be a slave and that any person that is currently a slave will be freed at the age of twenty-eight.

1783—Massachusetts abolishes slavery.

1784—Connecticut and Rhode Island abolish slavery.

1784—Thomas Jefferson introduces a law in the Continental Congress to abolish slavery in every state in America. His proposal states, "that after the year 1800 of the Christian era, there shall be neither slavery nor involuntary servitude in any of the said States, otherwise than in punishment of crimes, whereof the party shall have been duly convicted to have been personally guilty." Unfortunately, Jefferson's law fell one vote short of passage.

1786—Vermont abolishes slavery.

1787—Provision is made in the U.S. Constitution for the end of the slave trade by 1808.

1789—Congress prohibits slavery in any new state entering the Union as well as in all American territories held at that time.

1792—New Hampshire abolishes slavery.

1794—Prohibition of American slavers taking slaves abroad.

1799—New York passes law to gradually abolish slavery by 1827.

1804—New Jersey abolishes slavery.

1808—Slave ban enacted. It was now illegal to import slaves. The South accelerates domestic and black-market slave trading.

1861—Civil War breaks out.

1863—President Lincoln issues the Emancipation Proclamation.

1865—The end of slavery in America.

58

"Before We Proceed to Business"
Congressional Prayer

1787

It was hot and humid in Philadelphia in the summer of 1787. At General Washington's personal, urgent appeal, delegates from all thirteen colonies had come to Philadelphia to "form a more perfect union." Instead they were discovering their differences—and tempers flared. Just as they were about to adjourn in confusion, Benjamin Franklin stood to address General Washington and the assembly:

> *How has it happened, Sir, that we have not hitherto once thought of humbly applying to the Father of lights to illuminate our understandings? In the beginning of the contest with Great Britain, when we were sensible of danger we had daily prayer in this room for the Divine protection.*
>
> *Our prayers, Sir, were heard, and they were graciously answered. All of us who were engaged in the struggle must have observed frequent instances of a Superintending Providence in our favor. . . . And have we now forgotten that powerful Friend? Or do we imagine we no longer need His assistance?*
>
> *I have lived, Sir, a long time, and the longer I live, the more convincing proofs I see of this truth—that God governs in the affairs of men. And if a sparrow cannot fall to the ground without His notice, is it probable that an empire can rise without His aid? We have been assured, Sir, in the Sacred Writings, that "except the Lord build the house they labor in vain that build it." I firmly believe this. I also believe that without His concurring aid we shall*

succeed in this political building no better than the builders
of Babel; we shall be divided by our little partial local
interests; our projects will be confounded, and we ourselves
shall become a reproach and byword down to future ages.
And what is worse, mankind may hereafter from this unfor-
tunate instance, despair of establishing governments by
human wisdom and leave it to chance, war and conquest.

I therefore beg leave to move that henceforth prayers
imploring the assistance of Heaven and its blessings on our
deliberations be held in this Assembly every morning before
we proceed to business.

★ ★ ★

Franklin's proposal was never adopted in the proceedings of
the Constitutional Convention. However, when the first
Constitutional Congress convened in April of 1789, they imple-
mented Franklin's recommendation. Two chaplains of different
denominations were appointed, one to the House and one to the
Senate, with a salary of five hundred dollars each. This practice
continues today with prayer offered at the beginning of each daily
meeting when Congress is in session.

What Happened to the Signers of the Declaration of Independence?

For a representation of the actual painting, see the inside front cover.

1. William Whipple was appointed Brigadier General of the New Hampshire militia by General Washington.

2. Josiah Bartlett became the first governor and first senator of New Hampshire.

3. Thomas Lynch Jr. and his wife set sail on a ship bound for the West Indies; the ship was never seen again.

4. Benjamin Harrison served as governor of Virginia before being elected to the state convention to discuss the new U.S. Constitution.

5. Richard Henry Lee put forth the motion in the Continental Congress to create the Declaration of Independence. He later served as a U.S. senator.

6. Samuel Adams was chosen governor of Massachusetts and was re-elected for three years until his retirement.

7. George Clinton (did not sign) was prevented from signing the Declaration because of military duties for the Continental army.

8. William Paca contributed from his private wealth to the American army. He was appointed as a United States district judge by President Washington.

9. Samuel Chase served in the Supreme Court as associate justice during a period that became one of the stormiest times on record for the Court.

10. Lewis Morris's house was ransacked, his family driven away, his livestock captured, and the entire property ruined.

11. William Floyd's family fled their home when a company of British horsemen occupied it. Floyd and his family were refugees from their home for nearly seven years.

12. Arthur Middleton's plantation was raided by the British, who destroyed everything. His family escaped unharmed.

13. Thomas Heyward Jr. was taken prisoner by the British. After the war he continued to serve as a judge.

14. Charles Carroll was the last surviving signer of the Declaration and was considered the wealthiest citizen in America; he was the only Roman Catholic signer of the Declaration.

15. Robert Morris provided $10,000 of his own money to the war. He put the rest of his fortune at risk for the American cause.

16. Thomas Willing (did not sign), a member of the Continental Congress, voted against the Declaration because he felt it was premature and unnecessary.

17. Benjamin Rush became treasurer of the U.S. Mint, the "Father of Public Schools," and, as a physician, the "Father of American Medicine." He also founded and managed the Philadelphia Bible Society.

18. Elbridge Gerry was elected vice-president of the United States under President James Madison and died in office at the age of seventy.

19. Robert Treat Paine, a lawyer, was a founder of the American Academy of Arts and Sciences, established in Massachusetts in 1780.

20. William Hooper, a lawyer from North Carolina, lost his estate when the British burned it down; his family was saved.

21. Stephen Hopkins, founder of the town library of Providence, was the first chancellor of Rhode Island College—now Brown University.

22. William Ellery, an abolitionist, was the first customs collector of Newport, Rhode Island, under the Constitution.

23. George Clymer's house was destroyed when British soldiers attacked. Fortunately his family was able to escape.

24. Joseph Hewes served as the Secretary of the Naval Affairs Committee of Congress until 1779. He died during the Revolution.

25. George Walton, a prisoner of war during the Revolution, became the governor of Georgia for several years.

26. James Wilson served as Associate Justice of the U.S. Supreme Court and was the first professor of law at the College of Philadelphia.

27. Abraham Clark suffered the capture and torture of two sons by the British.

28. Francis Hopkinson's home was invaded and destroyed during the Revolution. Later he was appointed Judge of the United States for the district of Pennsylvania.

29. John Adams helped develop and sign the Treaty of Peace with Great Britain, ending the Revolutionary War. Adams became the second president of the United States.

30. Roger Sherman is the only American to sign four important historical documents: The Continental Association of 1774, The Declaration of Independence, The Articles of Confederation, and The Federal Constitution.

31. Robert Livingston, one of the writers of the Declaration, retired from Congress before he was able to sign.

32. Thomas Jefferson, the country's third president, extended the country's boundaries with the Louisiana Purchase. He created the Library of Congress, donating his own books to start.

33. Benjamin Franklin edited the Declaration of Independence and negotiated the Treaty of Paris. Later in life he promoted the abolition of slavery.

34. Thomas Nelson Jr. lost his house when a British general made it his headquarters. He used his remaining wealth to pay the debts of the new nation.

35. Francis Lewis's home was destroyed by the British army, who then took his wife prisoner. She died within a year or two after her release.

36. Rev. John Witherspoon's library was burned by the British. Several years later Witherspoon lost a son in battle.

37. Samuel Huntington served two terms as president of the Congress during the adoption of the Articles of Confederation.

38. William Williams offered his home to the American army. He abandoned his business and went from house to house soliciting private donations to supply the army.

39. Oliver Wolcott was appointed one of the commissioners of Indian affairs and negotiated a treaty of peace with the Six Nations.

40. Charles Thomson was one of only two people to actually sign the Declaration on July 4, 1776. When the rest of the Founding Fathers gathered a month later to sign a fresh copy, Thomson was not present.

41. John Hancock, a prominent Revolutionary general, became president of the Continental Congress and was the first man to sign the Declaration. He retired soon after signing.

42. George Read was twice elected Delaware state senator and was later appointed Chief Justice of the State of Delaware.

43. John Dickinson (did not sign) opposed the Declaration because he believed the colonies were not yet ready for a complete separation from Great Britain.

44. Edward Rutledge was taken prisoner by the British during the Revolution. He later became the governor of South Carolina but died in office.

45. Thomas McKean was elected governor of Pennsylvania, filling the office by popular reelection for nine years. The British hounded his family, forcing them to move constantly.

Signers Not Pictured:

Carter Braxton lost his fortune when just about every shipping vessel in which he held an interest was either sunk or captured by the British. He was forced to sell his land.

Button Gwinnett was shot in a duel over political differences. He died during the Revolution.

Lyman Hall's plantation was destroyed during the Revolutionary War, but Hall's family managed to escape. Hall then served as governor of Georgia for one year.

John Hart lost his wife shortly after his farm was destroyed by British troops. He and his children were forced into hiding. Hart died shortly after.

Francis Lightfoot Lee became a member of the Virginia Senate before retiring with his wife.

Philip Livingston, a congressman, succumbed to failing health during the Revolution and died within two years of signing the Declaration.

John Morton, a professor of religion, had the responsibility of casting his vote to an equally divided delegation. In the spirit of true patriotism, he voted in favor of the liberty of the country.

John Penn, a lawyer, became the Receiver of Taxes from North Carolina before resigning to return to life as a private citizen.

Caesar Rodney was the war governor during a large part of the Revolution. He sacrificed his private interests for the public good.

George Ross was appointed Pennsylvania's Judge of the Court of Admiralty but passed away within a few months of gaining the esteemed position.

James Smith, a professor of religion, suggested a boycott of British goods and organized a volunteer militia company in York.

Richard Stockton was imprisoned and abused by British soldiers and his home was destroyed. His ailments and devastation caused an early death.

Thomas Stone was a member of the committee that framed the Articles of Confederation.

George Taylor was not present on the Fourth of July when the Declaration was proclaimed, but he signed it at a later date. Taylor died during the Revolution.

Dr. Matthew Thornton returned to New Hampshire and his medical practice after signing the Declaration of Independence.

George Wythe became the first professor of law at the College of William and Mary, the second oldest college in the U.S. (established 1693).

59 The Interesting Narrative
Olaudah Equiano
1745–1797

To the ten-year-old boy from a small village in the interior of Nigeria, the sights, smells, and sounds of the harbor were overwhelming. Olaudah Equiano had never even heard of such a place—with water that went as far as you could see and a slave ship riding at anchor.

Years later, writing in his autobiography, he recalled his feelings: "These sights filled me with astonishment, which was soon converted into terror, when I was carried on board the ship." Suddenly surrounded by European sailors, their unfamiliar features added to his fears. He remembered them as "ugly, horrible-looking men, with pale, reddish faces and long, loose hair."

The white sailors, surprised to see such a young child all alone, playfully picked him up and tossed him in the air.

> Terrified, I knew now that I had somehow gotten into a world of evil spirits, and that they were going to kill me. The language they spoke, (which was very different from any I had ever heard) confirmed this belief.
>
> I looked round the ship, and saw a large copper pot of boiling water, and a multitude of black people of every description chained together, every one of their countenances expressing dejection and sorrow. I no longer doubted of my fate; and, quite overpowered with horror and anguish, I fell motionless on the deck and fainted.
>
> When I recovered a little, I saw the black people who had brought me on, who were receiving their pay. They tried in vain to cheer me.

I asked them, "Are we going to be eaten by these ugly white men?"

They told me I was not. Soon after this, the blacks who brought me on board got off the ship and left me abandoned to despair.

I was soon put down under the decks, and there I received such a greeting in my nostrils as I had never experienced in my life. With the loathsomeness of the stench, and crying together, I became so sick and low that I was not able to eat, nor had I the least desire to taste anything. I now wished for the last friend, death, to relieve me. Soon, to my grief, two of the white men offered me food. When I refused to eat, one of them held me fast by the hands, laid me across a beam, and tied my feet, while the other flogged me severely. I had never seen among my people such instances of brutal cruelty.

The closeness of the place, and the heat of the climate, added to the number in the ship, which was so crowded that each had scarcely room to turn himself. This produced much perspiration.

The air soon became unfit to breathe, from a variety of loathsome smells, and brought on a sickness among the slaves, of which many died. The wretched situation was made worse by our chains and the filth of the necessary tubs. The shrieks of the women, and the groans of the dying, rendered the whole a scene of horror almost inconceivable.

After several months at sea, the ship landed at Bridgetown, Barbados. About half of the slaves had died during the trip. The traders sold the surviving slaves to merchants and sugar planters. Since no one bought little Equiano—he was too young to provide much labor—they put him and other unsaleable slaves on a boat bound for the American colony of Virginia. There he worked on a plantation, pulling weeds and collecting stones. Not long after, a lieutenant in the

Royal Navy, Michael Henry Pascal, bought him. Pascal commanded a merchant ship trading between the colonies and England. For several years, Equiano sailed with Pascal.

When they returned to England, Equiano lived with some friends of Pascal's, the two Guerin sisters. They sent him to school, where he learned to read and write. They also arranged for his baptism in Saint Margaret's Church, Westminster, in 1759.

When Pascal went to sea again, Equiano became his steward, a position he says he enjoyed because he had free time to improve on his reading and writing skills.

While a slave, Equiano learned the trade of merchant seafaring, traveling up and down the coast of America. On the side, he was able to raise enough money to buy his freedom.

Equiano soon found, however, that the life of a freed man in the West Indies was fraught with danger. Blacks had no protection under the law and might easily be kidnapped and taken away on a ship as a slave. To protect himself, Equiano signed on as a sailor on a ship going to England.

Equiano continued as a sailor for several more voyages. Once he had to command the ship himself as the captain and first mate took ill. The captain died on board the ship, and Equiano successfully sailed the sloop safely into harbor. He also survived a shipwreck in the Bahamas caused by a self-assured captain who steered an incorrect course.

Although Equiano was baptized as a youth and heard the fiery preaching of George Whitefield in Savannah, Georgia, in 1765, Christianity did not deeply influence his life until he faced death during a nearly disastrous Arctic expedition in 1773. After profound soul searching, he committed his life to Jesus Christ in 1774. In 1775 he traveled to Nicaragua as a Christian missionary, accompanying Dr. Irving, who wanted to establish a plantation on the Mosquito Coast and take the Gospel to the Indian population there.

As a youth, Equiano had been blessed with the opportunity to learn to read and write at a time when very few slaves were so allowed. As a sailor, he had the time to continue to read and to improve his writing skills. As a Christian, he saw how God could use his communication skills and his personal experience to give the world a glimpse of how horrific the life of a slave was.

In January 1777, Equiano traveled to England, where he became involved in the antislavery movement and spoke in a large number of public meetings, describing the cruelty of the slave trade. About this time, Equiano began writing his autobiography, *The Interesting Narrative of the Life of Olaudah Equiano, or Gustavus Vassa, the African*, which was published in 1789.

His autobiography gives a dramatic account of his life from his childhood in Africa to his passage on the slave ship to his life as a slave and then a free man. It provides unique insight into the nightmarish experiences of an African slave.

His book was famous in its time, running into seventeen editions in Great Britain and the United States, and was translated into Dutch and German. Equiano spent the next few years traveling throughout England promoting the book and making speeches against slavery.

Although Equiano did not live to see the abolition of slavery in America, his narrative made the public aware of the horrors of the trade and the problems a freed slave faced. The book became a bestseller in both England and America and fueled the antislavery movement on both sides of the ocean.

Kettle Prayers
Lake Providence, Louisiana
1860s

60

Mattie knew what it meant when all the slaves were called to the barnyard like this. Someone was going to be whipped—as an example to the rest. How she dreaded these times! The twelve-year-old slave girl always cried for the one being whipped—and she hoped she would never do anything wrong to upset the master.

All the slaves waited silently in the yard. Finally Master came out with the one to be punished. It was her uncle Charlie! Mattie could not believe it. Uncle Charlie was a strong Christian—he would never lie or steal or slack off from his work. As Master chained him to the post, he told the slaves, "Charlie here was caught praying. Slaves are not allowed to pray on my plantation. Let this be a lesson to y'all."

Finally the whipping was over and the slaves went quietly back to their work. Mattie, the oldest daughter in her family, was still too small to work in the fields with her mother and father. Her job was to watch the younger children and help her grandmother with the cooking and cleaning.

Once they were back in the safety of their cabin, Mattie had a lot of questions. "Gramma," she whispered, "why does Master say it's wrong to pray?"

Gramma whispered back, "'Cuz he thinks the only thing we ever pray about is to get free from him!"

"But why does he let us go to church?"

"'Cuz it makes us better workers. The preachers he hires always say the same thing, 'Obey your master, or you won't go to heaven.' Child, that's enough talk about this, now. You don't want Master to whip you, do you?"

No more was said about the matter for a year. Then, late one night after the younger children were asleep, her parents said, "Mattie, we're gonna tell you a secret. We have secret prayer meetin's whenever we can, an' you're now old enough to come. But never, ever talk 'bout our meetin's to anyone, anywhere. Not even one of us here at home. You never know when someone might hear an' tell Master."

Mattie was excited. "When do we go? Tonight?"

"No, not tonight. We never know much ahead of time—it's safer that way. Now go to sleep. No more questions."

Mattie was so excited she couldn't sleep. Just thinking about being invited made her feel proud. It meant everyone thought she was growing up—you would never tell little kids secrets this important. If someone found out, everyone would get whipped. She suddenly realized. . . *she* could get whipped! Did she really want to do this? Mattie argued back and forth with herself, tossing and turning until finally she dozed off.

The next afternoon the chores seemed to go slower than ever—she kept thinking about the secret prayer meeting. She had decided she would go, no matter what. It was wash day, so as always, she helped by carrying water from the well—bucket after bucket, trip after trip—until the family's big cast-iron kettle was full. Mattie and her grandmother then worked together—soaping, scrubbing, and rinsing the clothes. After that, Mattie would hang them on bushes to dry.

By then it was time for supper, and Mattie had to hurry to rinse the big kettle clean so her grandmother could use it to cook the family meal. As Mattie cut up vegetables for the stew, she couldn't stop thinking about the prayer meeting.

Just then a group of slaves walked past, returning from a long day in the fields. They were singing a song Mattie had heard many times: "Steal away, steal away, steal away to Jesus." Gramma caught Mattie's eye and then winked. Mattie had never seen her grandmother wink before—at first she wondered what it could mean. Then Gramma started singing, still looking intently at Mattie, watching for her response. "Steal away, steal away, steal away to Jesus."

In a flash of insight, Mattie realized that particular song was the secret invitation to a prayer meeting that night.

As they were washing up the supper dishes, Gramma told her,

"Mattie, be sure an' clean the smoke off the outside real good. We'll be takin' the kettle with us tonight."

"Gramma," Mattie asked, "how does our secret prayer meetin' have anything to do with our big ol' kettle?"

Her grandmother looked up at her sharply. She whispered, "Hush, girl!" then nodded toward Mattie's little sister.

Oops! Mattie thought to herself. *I've gotta get better at keepin' secrets, or they won't let me come for 'nother year!*

Mattie looked over at Gramma. Gramma started singing again softly, "Steal away, steal away, steal away to Jesus." And again she winked at Mattie. Now Mattie knew that Gramma still believed she was big enough to be trusted and still wanted to include her. She joined in singing and winked back at Gramma.

Finally it was dark, and Mattie helped put the younger children to bed. She tried to stay awake but kept dozing off. Sometime in the middle of the night, her father whispered, "It's time!"

Silently, they opened the door to their cabin. By the moonlight, Mattie could see small groups of two or three adults stealing away to the barn. Mattie's father and one of the other men carried the large iron kettle. Others carried large rocks.

So they do *use the kettle!* Mattie thought to herself. *But what does a kettle have to do with prayin'? Will we need water? And what are the big rocks for?* Mattie was full of questions, but this time, she knew better than to ask.

The men carefully opened the big barn door, moving it so slowly that it made no sound. They slipped into the barn carrying the kettle and shut the door behind them. Once inside, they turned the kettle upside down so the rim of the kettle was on the dirt floor of the barn, then placed four rocks under the rim to prop it up and create an opening.

One by one, Mattie's family and neighbors lay on the ground around the kettle, their mouths close to the opening. Gramma motioned for Mattie to come lie beside her. Soon Mattie's father began to pray softly, the kettle muffling his voice. Taking turns, others joined in. They prayed and sang softly long into the night.

As Mattie watched, her questions were answered—except for one. Whenever she prayed, Mattie asked God for help with something she faced that day. But as she listened, she noticed her family and neighbors were not praying for themselves. They didn't think they would see freedom in their time, so they prayed for the freedom of their children and their children's children. Mattie realized they were risking their lives to pray for her freedom and for children who would one day be born to her. She now had new questions: *How long do prayers keep? Do they last forever? Where does God keep them?*

Mattie dozed off wondering how many prayers it would take to fill the big kettle. She woke as the big folks were quietly getting up off the dirt floor. She was quickly alert, knowing that this would be her only chance to ask about all that she had seen.

Just then her favorite uncle, Robert, came over and gave her a hug. He whispered, "I betcha got a lotta questions. I did! Like, how does this thing work?"

Mattie nodded. "Yeah, how does it work?"

"I asked a lotta folks, and I got a lotta answers," Robert said. "Folks say God catches the sound of the prayin' and the singin' and keeps it in the kettle so the white folk can't hear us.

"You know, some families don't get down on the floor like we do. They just put the kettle on the doorstep to keep the sounds from escapin' out the door. They say that works just as well.

"Some say it don't matter *where* you put the kettle, 'cause the kettle is just a sign that shows God we're trustin' Him to be with us and protect us."

Mattie nodded. "Gramma says God can do anythin' if we trust Him."

At that moment Gramma joined them. Uncle Robert asked, "Mama, where did folks learn about prayin' into the kettle?"

"I don't know where they learned it," Gramma answered. "I kinda think the Lord put these things in their minds to do for themselves, just like He helps us Christians in other ways." She paused. "Don't ya think so?"

Robert smiled. "All I know is it works! I talk with folks from other plantations, and I never heard tell of anyone caught prayin' since our people started using them kettles."

Mattie noticed that most of the folks had left already. "Gramma, I got some more questions," she said. "How long do prayers keep? Do they last forever? Where does God keep 'em?"

The old woman smiled. "I heard a preacher once tell that in heaven there was bowls full of the prayers of the saints. Them bowls sit right in front of the throne of God where He can see them all the time."

Mattie watched as her father and his friend picked up the big family kettle. "And our kettle is like our own secret bowl of prayers for our family forever."

Gramma reached out to hug Mattie. "I'm so proud of you, Mattie. Someday you'll be free, an' you will be able to pray wherever and whenever you want. Be sure to keep prayin' for your children. And be sure to tell your children how we prayed for them under the kettle."

Gramma noticed the men were waiting for them to leave so they could close the big barn big door. "Now hush, Mattie. No more questions about prayin' until next meetin'!"

★ ★ ★

Intercessor and author William Ford III owns the prayer kettle used by his ancestors to pray for his freedom. He writes:

One day, freedom did come. While many of those who prayed did not live to see freedom, their prayers were answered for the next generation. The young girl ["Mattie" in the above story] who passed down these stories attended these prayer meetings until slavery was abolished. . . . . As a young teenager, she was set free. Can you imagine being that one that freedom fell upon, having listened to others pray for your freedom for many years?

I believe this teenage girl saw fit to pass down this kettle because she knew that not only was she standing on the sacrifice of others' devotion to Christ, but so was everyone born after her in our family. She was careful to preserve and pass on both the kettle and its history. She passed it to her daughter, Harriet Locket, who passed it to Nora Locket, who passed it to William Ford, Sr., who passed it to William Ford, Jr., who gave it to me, William Ford III. It has been in our family for 200 years.

As Will continued to study generational prayer, he came to realize:

I could agree with the prayers made under our family's kettle by those who had gone before me. I thought, "Lord, I can agree with the prayers of my ancestors for the freedom of today's and the future generations in America." God was showing me in a new way that He is powerful, yesterday, today, and forever.

In his book, *History Makers* (Regal Books, 2004), which he coauthored with Dutch Sheets, Will speaks of the "synergy of the ages." He writes:

In God's kingdom, the prayers of Abraham are as immediate and relevant today as they were the day he prayed them. And so with the prayers of our forefathers. In other words, God is bringing together all the prayers of the saints to bear on the condition of America today. Connecting with this heritage can strengthen our prayers and heal our land, bringing revival and great societal change. No prayer is wasted. Our prayers count.

Will then includes the following prayer:

Father, John Quincy Adams said it best when he wrote, "Posterity—you will never know how much it has cost my generation to preserve your freedom. I hope you make good use of it." Help us to make good use of what You started in America. Thank You for those who sacrificed yesterday so that we can have freedom today. Thank You for the sacrifice of Your Son, Who died and rose again and Who ever lives to make intercession for us. We thank You that the same God who broke the power of slavery, can break the power of every stronghold in our day. Connect us with the past revival power that moves the chain forward for future generations. Unite Your Church! Make us repairers of the breach, the restorers of many generations. Teach us to pray. In Jesus' name, Amen.

America's Underground Church

By the late 1840s many slaves belonged to what we would today call an underground church. It was similar in many ways to churches in today's "closed" nations. In the South before emancipation, there were independent black churches with slave members, as well as racially mixed churches, where it was not uncommon for slaves to outnumber masters in attendance at Sunday services.

But outside of these visible, Sunday morning meetings, the slave community worshiped in their own manner. Hidden from the eyes of their masters, slaves gathered in slave quarters or out of doors in the woods or swamps for informal believers' meetings.

The persecution was real. Because of the fear of a slave revolt, many areas would not allow blacks to congregate. Slaves often faced severe punishment if caught attending secret prayer meetings. One escaped slave told how he was threatened with five hundred lashes for attending a prayer meeting—without permission—that was conducted by slaves on a neighboring plantation. His master, incidentally, was a deacon of the local Baptist church.

Despite these dangers, slaves continued having their own meetings because they liked them better—they could pray and sing freely, as the Holy Spirit led them. They were willing to risk punishment by their earthly masters in order to worship their Heavenly Master as they saw fit. Peter Randolph, a slave in Prince George County, Virginia, until he was freed in 1847, gave the following description of a secret prayer meeting:

The slaves assemble in the swamp, out of reach of the patrols. They have an understanding among themselves as to the time and place of getting together. This is often done by the first one arriving breaking boughs from the trees, and bending them in the direction of the selected spot. . . . The speaker usually. . .talks very slowly, until feeling the Spirit, he grows excited, and in a short time, there fall to the ground twenty or thirty men and women under its influence. . . .

Their deep love for God and their desire to feel His embrace and experience the amazing peace that comes from His presence caused these believers to risk all to gather for corporate worship.

What Is Freedom For?

★ ★ ★

Freedom is not an ideal, it is not even a protection,
if it means nothing more than freedom to stagnate,
to live without dreams, to have no greater aim
than a second car and another television set.
–ADLAI STEVENSON, AMERICAN STATESMAN

What if Patrick Henry had not made his fiery speech at Saint John's Church and let the vote pass to continue to appease Great Britain?

What if General George Washington had returned to Mount Vernon after the war and not accepted the presidency?

What if Harriet Tubman had made a new life for herself cleaning houses in Pennsylvania instead of returning to the South again and again, risking her life to bring others to freedom?

What if the citizens of Boston had obeyed the Fugitive Slave Act instead of protecting William and Ellen Craft?

What if John Ray had stood strong and insisted on a fair trial for C. J. Miller?

What if George Washington Carver had taken a high-paying job with Ford or Edison instead of seeking God for supernatural insight into how to grow crops to give the poor farmers of the South a way to recover from ruin and destruction?

What if Mamie Till had quietly buried Emmett, her only child, brutally murdered at age fourteen by racists in Mississippi?

What if Rosa Parks had gotten off that segregated bus in Montgomery, Alabama?

Our generation is at the end of a long chain of men and women who have sacrificed pleasure, personal comfort, and sometimes even their lives to make sure we have the freedoms we enjoy today. They searched the scriptures to find God's plan for our nation. They "did the next right thing" that God placed in their own personal path—acting to end social injustice and prejudice. This sometimes involved prayer and acts of repentance and reconciliation, sometimes helping a single individual, sometimes acts of government involvement, sometimes acts of civil disobedience and protest.

These Americans took their place and proved, over and over, that "One person acting with God can make a difference."

Can we do less?

Some Closing Thoughts

★ ★ ★

FROM TOBY...

As you were reading all these stories, most likely you encountered a lot of different thoughts and feelings like I did. Honor. Shame. Inspiration. Guilt.

Knowing the past is crucial in dealing with the present. History proves to be an invaluable part of having a vision for the future. We can learn a lot from those who have gone before us.

It is easy to live in America today and develop an air of superiority because of all of our success and wealth. We dominate the world on so many different levels.

By and large, we have no idea how we got here, and we certainly have no vision for where we should go. Our forefathers could look into the future and see the consequences of their actions and the course that this nation would take. The fruit of liberty and freedom looked awfully sweet. It was why they were willing to risk so much.

Today we live in a world that gorges itself on the spoils of the American Revolution, and our only vision is that which leads to self-gratification. One area that reflects this is education. Many of our forefathers realized that the goal of education was to obtain wisdom, knowledge, and understanding so that one could better serve his fellowman. Today, education is about acquiring skills and information so that we can get a good job. We want a good job so we can afford a comfortable life. All means lead to the same end: self. The servant's heart has been long lost in this journey. As society crumbles, our forefathers' words come back to haunt us.

But there is hope. We can rediscover our history and gain a vision for the future. Our forefathers used the Bible as a resource as they searched for answers on how to structure this new government.

It holds the same power today that it held back then. Repentance is a theme in the Bible that also occurs throughout our nation's history. Our forefathers recognized that we as a nation were subject to a higher judgment and we would have to answer as a nation for our actions. Abraham Lincoln recognized this as well as he repented for the sins of the nation during one of our darkest hours. In the Bible, Nehemiah is one example, where the people identify with their nation and repent, not only for their sins but also for the sins of their forefathers and the sins of their nation. Today I believe we Americans are in need of repentance.

It is my hope that this book serves as an encouragement to help you seek out your history and to discover more about the heroes who sacrificed their lives so that we could have better ones. I also encourage you to seek out the wounds of injustice that still might need healing today. Many times, the anger of today is a result of the wounds of yesterday, and our nation still carries many open wounds. I suggest you start with prayer and ask God to lead you. Much research can be done just by doing a word search on the Internet or at your local library. We have also provided a list of resources (see page 384), and there are more at *www.undergodthebook.com*. It is my hope that you will embark upon this great journey. I can tell you it will be a most rewarding one.

—TOBY MAC

FROM MICHAEL...

As I discovered the stories in this book, I couldn't help but think of my father, who gave me such a rich heritage, for which I will be forever grateful. Nathel Tait was born in 1922, deep in the heart of Alabama. Anybody who knows anything about Southern history knows that a black man growing up in the Deep South in the 1920s and 1930s saw some of the worst racism this country had to offer. He lived in a world where the lines were drawn clearly and there was no crossing them. The Ku Klux Klan killed his grandfather. His mother died when he was a child. He had to work hard labor in levee camps as a young boy. All in all, he faced what you would expect from Jim Crow and the Deep South.

If anybody had a right to be bitter, it would be my father. If anybody should have distrust for the white man, it would be him. But that was not the case. My father had a love for all people, and he passed that on to his family. Our home was always full of people of all different races. He would always say, "Racism is not a skin problem; it's a sin problem." He taught us to appreciate our differences and to see a man for who he really is, not what he looks like. He taught us that love is more powerful than hate and that the real victims of hate are those who possess and exercise it. It is because of my father I was able to break out of the stereotypes trying to constrain me and enter into relationships with those who were different than myself.

One of those relationships was with Toby, and I am thankful for what God has done through that relationship. While I agree with my brother that America is in great need of repentance and I do not brush over that lightly, I must add that our country is also in great need of forgiveness. As a black man, when I discover the stories of all the injustices that occurred in the past as well as all the injustices that take place today, many times I become angry. It is unfathomable to comprehend all the injustices that have been committed. The more you study, the worse it gets. It is understandable to be angry. It is okay to be angry.

But it is what you do with that anger that matters. When anger turns to hate, it becomes a vicious poison that creates its own form of imprisonment. There is a supernatural power that is needed to overcome hate. It is the same power that is needed to forgive. It is a supernatural love that comes only from God. It is the same love that my ancestors of slavery found as they cried out to God in their secret prayer meetings. It is the same love that found my father as he searched for the answers to his difficult life. Only love, real love in the form of Jesus Christ, will truly set you free.

—MICHAEL TAIT

A Call to Prayer

★ ★ ★

When national tragedy struck America on September 11, 2001, people cried out, "Where is God? How could He let something like this happen?" Perhaps, as some have speculated, it was because we as a nation had taken so many steps to remove Him from our government, our schools, our very lives. But the truth is, we don't really know why God allowed it to happen. Instead, we can only turn to Him, open our hearts to Him, put our trust in Him.

In fact, that was the response of many Americans in the wake of 9/11. In a nation that had become more and more closed to God, suddenly there was an openness to Him, a seeking after His comfort, His protection, His guidance. Church attendance increased and Bible sales went up.

Now, however, only a few years later, most Americans have returned to a pre-9/11 sense of spiritual ambivalence. "One nation under God" we say in our pledge. "In God we trust" we print on our coins. For many these are just words of tradition with no real meaning. But for the heroes of faith in this book, those words spoke of a covenant with the God who promised to fight for them as they acknowledged and obeyed Him.

The spiritual battle raging over America concerns this covenant— will our nation serve God or not? God-fearing people ask, "How do we turn our nation around?"

THE FIRST STEP IS INDIVIDUAL REPENTANCE AND HUMILITY.

Individual repentance requires an unveiling, a revelation, so we can really understand things from God's perspective. Once we see the difference between our opinion and His truth, we can admit when He is right and we are wrong. We put our trust in Him and not our own good works. Then His power and His grace begin to transform us, to make us like Christ. We can now hear His voice and can do "the next right thing."

Individual repentance establishes our individual covenant with God, the first step in turning our nation around. We must first be "God's people" before we can effectively pray for our nation.

THE NEXT STEP IS TO RENEW OUR NATIONAL COVENANT WITH GOD.

Our national covenant began with the Pilgrims and the Mayflower Compact. There is no greater or more powerful thing we can do as individuals, as Americans, than pray for the revival of our nation and our culture. Political activism has its place and is needed, but it is not primary. Government programs are good and helpful, but governments cannot love. Only people can love.

Prayer for revival is different from petitional prayer ("list praying") in that we are not praying for ourselves but interceding for our country. In this sense we "stand in the gap," identifying with the sins of our nation (even if they are sins we, ourselves, did not commit), and ask for forgiveness on behalf of our ancestors, our people group, our nation for the dark failings of our national past. We are appealing to our advocate, Jesus Christ, who in turn is pleading our case to the Judge to pardon us as a nation.

Nehemiah prayed for national repentance: "I pray before You now, day and night, for the children of Israel Your servants, and confess the sins of the children of Israel which we have sinned against You. Both my father's house and I have sinned. We have acted very corruptly against You, and have not kept the commandments, the statutes, nor the ordinances which You commanded Your servant Moses" (Nehemiah 1:6–7 NKJV).

Ezra, an Old Testament prophet, was appalled when he saw the sin in his nation. He tore his clothes, pulled his hair, and fell on his knees. Lifting his hands to God, he prayed, confessing the sins of his people and pleading with God for mercy. As he prayed, God moved, and soon "a very great congregation of men and women and children" gathered around him and wept very bitterly. The people decided then and there to undo the wrongs they had done and renew their covenant with God (Ezra 9:3–10:4).

When a great awakening hits America, our hearts will be changed. We will be ashamed of breaking our marriage vows; of sexual perversion; of mistreating our unborn, our children, and our elderly; of turning our backs on the poor and destitute; of not teaching our children about God's beautiful grace and power. Godly voters will vote their convictions and be citizens under God, transformed and motivated to then vote their consciences. Patrick Henry said it well: "Righteousness alone can exalt America as a nation. Virtue, morality, and religion . . . [are] the armor . . . that renders us invincible."

There has never been a spiritual awakening that did not begin in fervent prayer. Human efforts are not sufficient. Only a mighty move of God's Spirit will cause a people to look to Him and be changed.

WE HAVE A COVENANT WITH ONE ANOTHER TOO.

In addition to our national covenant with God, we have a covenant with one another. The Pilgrims mentioned both parts of this covenant in the Mayflower Compact: "We . . . solemnly and mutually in the presence of God and of one another covenant and combine ourselves together . . . for the general good of the colony." The Signers of the Declaration of Independence saw it too: "With a firm reliance on the protection of Divine Providence, we mutually pledge to each other our lives, our fortunes and our sacred honor." Jesus said, "Again I say to you that if two of you agree on earth concerning anything that they ask, it will be done for them by My Father in heaven" (Matthew 18:19 NKJV).

Momentum in Prayer:
Praying Side-by-Side With Others

This principle of agreement is why there is great momentum when the Body of Christ prays together. We've experienced this momentum, this oneness, in such events as the Prayer March on Washington, when thousands of believers came together to pray for our nation, or in youth prayer and fasting assemblies such as The Call. We experience it during citywide or whole-church gatherings when our president calls us to come together for a National Day of Prayer. Modern technology through e-mail and the Internet has added another facet to united prayer, such as the Presidential Prayer Team.

But it is also important to know that this momentum in prayer is not about how many are praying or about praying for praying's sake. Rather, it's about unity in purpose. Though invisible, it is just as real. Next time you feel God asking you to pray for America, say, "I join my faith with all the others you, Lord, are calling right now to pray for this nation." Try it—you will sense the difference. When we pray, we do not pray alone!

Momentum in Prayer:
Praying With Our Forefathers

There is another dimension of momentum and unity in prayer. Just as Will Ford learned how to join his faith with the "kettle prayers" of his ancestors, we, too, are part of a long chain of believers. As God-fearing people, as Americans, we are now "family" with all the godly of the land.

As we enter into our hearts the passions and sacrifices of those who have gone before us, we sense a generational momentum. "Their faith and our faith...come together to make one completed whole, their lives of faith not complete apart from ours" (Hebrews 11:40 THE MESSAGE).

Our Prayers Result
in Divine Intervention

America is in a time of national crisis—in a great spiritual battle between the very forces of heaven and hell. The Bible is full of evidence that the prayers of God's people in times of crisis result in divine intervention. Without exception, when God's people united in specific prayer, God heard, answered, delivered, provided, empowered, conquered. In fact, He did whatever was needed!

What do we pray?

We declare God's Word. When God "highlights" a scripture to you, declare it out loud in the circumstances that you see. This is how God accomplishes His work on the earth—He speaks His Word through the lips of His covenanted people. God's truth will always change "the facts."

First, we pray to release our nation from the curse that comes from disobeying God's law.

We also pray to release the blessings. Generational curses are real, but generational blessings go to a thousand generations (Deuteronomy 7:9).

Pray for your leaders.

Pray for those enslaved by sin. We are to break every enslaving yoke, forgive, and break the power of judgment and unforgiveness (Isaiah 58:6). We stand in the gap for others. We hope in God's mercy.

Pray for your children and your children's children. Tell your children about the God-guided heritage they have as Americans. Give them an example to live up to.

Our God-given past can empower our God-given future. It will ignite something inside; it will move us past a healthy sense of patriotism into our personal destiny.

Moved Beyond Prayer to Action

Prayer is the most important step we can take, but we must also move beyond prayer to action.

A crucial action we must take is to vote. Our forefathers fought and died for the right to choose our leaders. The least we can do is honor them by exercising that right. Inform yourself, pray for God's guidance, and vote as you feel led.

Each person plays a part—some in bigger ways, some in smaller ways—using the gifts God has given them: whether Robert Morris with his financial abilities, Phillis Wheatley encouraging Washington with her poetry, or Harriet Tubman leading slaves through the woods in the dark of night. We, too, can follow God's leading—even if it seems insignificant or we can't preplan it or do it perfectly.

God's supernatural hand was upon our nation at its birth. He wanted a shining example of a nation "under God." He still does. But being a nation under God does not mean pointing fingers or cursing those with whom we don't agree. It starts with pointing our prayers to God, allowing Him to first judge our hearts and then acting in love and grace as we seek to fulfill the specific things He calls us to do. We must first talk to God about our neighbors before we talk to our neighbors about God. Pray, and then act.

If all you can do is pray, then pray. Nothing is more powerful! If you can build houses, build them for the poor in God's name. Or perhaps God will lead you to volunteer to help the less fortunate. He is a creative God. Trust us—if He wants you to do it, He will make it clear.

It is not hopeless—God still has a plan. As we trust Him and one another to do our part, His original plan for this nation will come to pass: a land rich in freedom and justice for all.

1607	Jamestown, the first permanent English settlement in America, is established by the London Company in southeast Virginia.
Winter 1620	A Special Instrument Sent of God: Tisquantum—"Squanto"
November 1620	A Covenanted People: The Pilgrims' Landing at Cape Cod
Spring 1623	Government by the Gospel: Plymouth, Massachusetts
1644–1718	The Holy Experiment: William Penn
1706–1790	A Growing Awareness: Benjamin Franklin
1721–1793	The Voice of Reason: Roger Sherman
1736–1799	Empowered to Persuade: Patrick Henry
1741–1801	With Regrets: Benedict Arnold
1741–1806	Giving Credit Where It's Due: Robert Morris
1743–1813	Benjamin *Who?*: Benjamin Rush
1745–1797	The Interesting Narrative: Olaudah Equiano
1745–1829	A Legacy of Freedom: John Jay
1753–1784	Gifted: Phillis Wheatley

1600   1620   1640   1660   1680   1700

1754–1763	The French and Indian War—an ongoing struggle between the British and French for control of eastern North America.
1755–1776	One Life to Lose: Nathan Hale
July 9, 1755	Bulletproof: The French and Indian War—Account of a British Officer
1760–1831	Lifting a People: Richard Allen
March 5, 1770	Boston Massacre: British troops fire into a mob, killing five men and leading to intense public protests.
September 5–October 26, 1774	First Continental Congress meets in Philadelphia.
September 7, 1774	Into the Presence: Continental Congress Prayer
1775–1783	American Revolution
1776	Saved by the Fog: Evacuation of Long Island
1776	"God Save These People": John Witherspoon
1776	"Remember the Ladies": Abigail Adams
January 21, 1776	A Time for War: Peter Muhlenberg
Summer 1776	A Declaration of Dependence...Upon God: The Signing of the Declaration of Independence
July 4, 1776	Continental Congress adopts the Declaration of Independence in Philadelphia.
1778	The Smuggled Patriot: John Adams
1781	His Sons—Captured!: Abraham Clark
1783–1852	Defender of the Union: Daniel Webster
May–September 1787	Constitutional Convention meets in Philadelphia to draft the U.S. Constitution.
1787	"Before We Proceed to Business": Congressional Prayer
April 30, 1789	Washington is inaugurated as the first President of the United States at Federal Hall in New York City.

December 15, 1791	The first ten amendments to the Constitution, known as the Bill of Rights, are ratified.
1793	Eli Whitney's invention of the cotton gin greatly increases the demand for slave labor.
1797–1883	Turning Point: Isabella Baumfree—"Sojourner Truth"
1803–1895	The Strong Voice of Freedom: Theodore Weld
May 2, 1803	Louisiana Purchase
May 14, 1804	The exploration team of Lewis and Clark set out from St. Louis, Missouri, on expedition to explore the West and find a route to the Pacific Ocean.
1805–1879	The Repentant Slaveholder: Angelina Grimké
1811–1896	"As a Mother...As a Christian": Harriet Beecher Stowe
1812–1814	War of 1812 occurred. The U.S. declares war on Britain over British interference with American maritime shipping and westward expansion.
September 13–14, 1814	Francis Scott Key writes "The Star-Spangled Banner."
1818–1892	Begin Again: Bridget "Biddy" Mason

1740   1760   1780   1800   1820   1840

1818–1895	"We Need the Storm, the Whirlwind, and the Earthquake": Frederick Douglass
1818–1900	Crazy Bet: Elizabeth Van Lew
1820–1913	Freedom's Railroad: Harriet Tubman
March 3, 1820	Missouri Compromise
July 4, 1828	Construction is begun on the Baltimore and Ohio Railroad, the first public railroad in the U.S.
May 28, 1830	President Jackson signs the Indian Removal Act, which authorizes the forced removal of Native Americans living in the eastern part of the country to lands west of the Mississippi River.
March 2, 1836	Texas declares its independence from Mexico. Texan defenders of the Alamo are all killed during a siege by the Mexican Army.
1838	"Trail of Tears": More than fifteen thousand Cherokee Indians are forced to march from Georgia to Indian Territory in present-day Oklahoma. Approximately four thousand die from starvation and disease.
1839–1841	An Impassioned Defense: John Quincy Adams and the *Amistad*
1839–1915	Pirating the *Planter*: Robert Smalls
1840–1883	"Unless You Kill Me": John Prentiss "Print" Matthews
1842, 1880, 1928	What Four Hundred Dollars Can Buy: George and Lewis Latimer
January 24, 1848	Gold is discovered at Sutter's Mill in California.
December 1848 & October 1850	Out of the Jaws of the Wicked: William and Ellen Craft
1852	Harriet Beecher Stowe's novel *Uncle Tom's Cabin* is published.
May 30, 1854	Congress passes the Kansas-Nebraska Act, establishing the territories of Kansas and Nebraska but at the same time repealing the Missouri Compromise of 1820 and renewing tensions between anti- and pro-slavery factions.
1857	Supreme Court renders landmark decision in *Dred Scott v. Sanford* when it says that Congress does not have the right to ban slavery in states and, furthermore, that slaves are not citizens.

1860s   Kettle Prayers: Lake Providence, Louisiana

Spring 1860   "Don't Let Them Have Him!": Charles Nalle and Harriet Tubman

November 6, 1860   Abraham Lincoln is elected president. The next month South Carolina secedes from the Union.

1861–1865   Civil War: Conflict between the North (the Union) and the South (the Confederacy) over the expansion of slavery into western states.

1861–1943   A Purposeful Life: George Washington Carver

April 12, 1861   Confederates attack Fort Sumter in Charleston, South Carolina, marking the start of the war.

April–June 1861   Virginia, Arkansas, North Carolina, and Tennessee secede.

1862–1931   Innocent Blood Cries Out: Ida B. Wells-Barnett

January 1, 1863   Emancipation Proclamation is issued, freeing slaves in the Confederate states.

July 1863   The United Cry of the Nation: Abraham Lincoln

July 1–3, 1863   Battle of Gettysburg

November 19, 1863   President Lincoln delivers the Gettysburg Address.

1864   A Soldier's View: The Sand Creek Massacre

1780   1800   1820   1840   1860   1880

September 2, 1864   General William T. Sherman captures Atlanta.

March 4, 1865   Lincoln's second inauguration.

April 3, 1865   General Ulysses S. Grant captures Richmond, Virginia, the capital of the Confederacy.

April 9, 1865   Confederate general Robert E. Lee surrenders to Ulysses S. Grant at Appomattox Courthouse, Virginia.

April 14, 1865   Lincoln is assassinated by John Wilkes Booth in Washington, D.C., and is succeeded by his vice-president, Andrew Johnson.

June 19, 1865   Juneteenth

December 6, 1865   Thirteenth Amendment to the Constitution is ratified, prohibiting slavery.

1866–1915   The Birth and Second Coming of a Message of Hate: Ku Klux Klan

February 3, 1870   The Fifteenth Amendment to the Constitution is ratified, giving blacks the right to vote.

March 1877   "Turned Loose to the Whirlwind": Compromise of 1877

October 5, 1877   "I Will Fight No More Forever": Chief Joseph and the Nez Percé War

October 28, 1886   The Statue of Liberty is dedicated.

1890–1969   The Right Man at the Right Time: Dwight D. Eisenhower

July 5–7, 1893   No Justice: C. J. Miller

May 18, 1896   *Plessy v. Ferguson*: Supreme Court rules that racial segregation is constitutional, paving the way for the repressive Jim Crow laws in the South.

April 25, 1898   The Spanish-American War begins when the U.S.S. *Maine* is blown up in Havana, Cuba, harbor, prompting U.S. to declare war on Spain.

August 1908   The Dark Side of Lincoln's Home: Springfield Riot

1913–present   Tired of Giving In: Rosa Parks

1914–1918	World War I: U.S. enters World War I, declaring war on Germany on April 6, 1917, and Austria-Hungary on December 7, 1917. Armistice ending World War I is signed on November 11, 1918.
1915	"It Is All So Terribly True": Woodrow Wilson and *The Birth of a Nation*
1919–1972	When a Sport Is Something More: Jackie Robinson
June 15, 1920	They Tried to Forget: Duluth, Minnesota
1929–1968	Stand Up: Martin Luther King Jr.
1930–present	A Cycle of Service and Love: John Perkins
1941–1955	Forever Fourteen: Emmett Till
1939–1945	World War II
October 24, 1945	The United Nations is established.
1950–1953	Korean War
1950–1975	Vietnam War. Last U.S. troops leave Vietnam on March 29, 1973.
May 17, 1954	*Brown v. Board of Education of Topeka, Kansas*: Landmark Supreme Court decision declares that racial segregation in schools is unconstitutional.
1960	In a Class of Only One: Ruby Bridges

1920   1940   1960   1980   2000   2020

August 28, 1963	Rev. Martin Luther King Jr. delivers his "I Have a Dream" speech before a crowd of 200,000 during the civil rights march on Washington, D.C.
September 15, 1963	Denise. Carole. Cynthia. Addie Mae: Birmingham Bombing of the Sixteenth Street Baptist Church
November 22, 1963	President John F. Kennedy is assassinted in Dallas, Texas.
April 4, 1968	Rev. Martin Luther King Jr. is assassinated in Memphis, Tennessee.
June 5, 1968	Senator Robert F. Kennedy is assassinated in Los Angeles, California.
July 20, 1969	Astronauts Neil Armstrong and Edwin "Buzz" Aldrin Jr. become the first men to land on the moon.
January 22, 1973	*Roe v. Wade*: Landmark Supreme Court decision legalizes abortion in first trimester of pregnancy.
August 9, 1974	President Richard Nixon resigns and is succeeded by Vice-President Gerald Ford.
January 28, 1986	Space shuttle *Challenger* explodes seventy-three seconds after lift-off, killing all seven crew members.
August 2, 1990	Iraqi troops invade Kuwait, leading to the Persian Gulf War.
February 1, 1992	Following the breakup of the Soviet Union in December 1991, President George H. W. Bush and Russian president Boris Yeltsin meet at Camp David and formally declare an end to the Cold War.
April 19, 1995	Bombing of federal office building in Oklahoma City kills 168 people.
September 11, 2001	Two hijacked jetliners ram the twin towers of the World Trade Center in the worst terrorist attack against the U.S. in history; a third hijacked plane flies into the Pentagon; a fourth crashes in rural Pennsylvania. More than three thousand people die in the attacks.

Bibliography

Adams, Charles Francis. *Familiar Letters of John Adams and His Wife Abigail Adams During the Revolution With a Memoir of Mrs. Adams.* Boston: Houghton, Mifflin and Company, 1875.

Adams, Charles Francis. *Memoirs of John Quincy Adams: Comprising Portions of His Diary From 1795 to 1848.* New York: AMS Press, 1970.

African Biography. 3 vols. U*X*L, 1999. Reproduced in *Biography Resource Center.* Farmington Hills, MI: The Gale Group, 2004. "Olaudah Equiano."

Allen, William. *An American Biographical and Historical Dictionary, Containing an Account of the Lives, Characters, and Writings of the Most Eminent Persons in North America From Its First Discovery to the Present Time, and a Summary of the History of the Several Colonies and of the United States.* Cambridge: William Hilliard, 1809.

America's Great Revivals. Reprinted from *Christian Life Magazine.* Minneapolis: Bethany House Publishers, 1970.

American Decades. Gale Research, 1998. Reproduced in *Biography Resource Center.* Farmington Hills, MI: The Gale Group, 2004. CD-ROM. "Mary McLeod Bethune," "Rosa Parks," "Woodrow Wilson."

American Eras. 8 vols. Gale Research, 1997–1998. Reproduced in *Biography Resource Center.* Farmington Hills, MI: The Gale Group, 2004. "Benjamin Banneker," "Daniel Webster," "Richard Allen," "Robert Smalls," "Sojourner Truth."

Authors and Artists for Young Adults, vol. 53. Gale Group, 2003. Reproduced in *Biography Resource Center.* Farmington Hills, MI: The Gale Group, 2004. "Harriet Beecher Stowe."

Bardolph, Richard. *The Negro Vanguard.* New York. Rinehart & Company, Inc., 1959.

Bartholomew, Sam with Stephen L. Mansfield. *God's Role in America.* Nashville: Eggman Publishing Company, 1996.

Barton, David. *A Spiritual Heritage of the United States Capitol.* Aledo, TX: WallBuilder Press, 2000.

———. *America's Godly Heritage.* Aledo, TX: WallBuilder Press, 1993.

———. *Education and the Founding Fathers.* Aledo, TX: WallBuilder Press, 1993.

———. *Keys to Good Government.* Aledo, TX: WallBuilder Press, 2000.

———. *Original Intent: The Courts, the Constitution, and Religion.* Aledo, TX: WallBuilders Press, 2000.

———. *The Bulletproof George Washington.* Aledo, TX: WallBuilder Press, 1990.

———. *The Foundations of American Government.* Aledo, TX: WallBuilder Press, 1993.

———. *The Practical Benefits of Christianity.* Aledo, TX: WallBuilder Press, 2001.

———. *The Spirit of the American Revolution.* Aledo, TX: WallBuilder Press, 2000.

———. *The WallBuilder Report.* Aledo, TX: WallBuilder Presentations, Winter, 1998.

Beliles, Mark A. and Stephen K. McDowell. *America's Providential History.* Charlottesville, VA: The Providence Foundation, 1989.

Bellis, Mary. "Lewis Latimer." *Inventors.* About.com. http://inventors.about.com/library/inventors/bllatimer.htm.

Bickel, Bill. "Church Bombing...Birmingham, Alabama...1963." *Crime and Punishment.* About.com. http://crime.about.com/library/weekly/aabirmingham.htm.

Binger, Carl. *Revolutionary Doctor: Benjamin Rush (1746–1813).* New York: W. W. Norton & Company, Inc, 1966.

"Black Kettle—Cheyenne Chief at the Sand Creek Massacre." http://www.lastoftheindependents.com/BlackKettle.html.

Bono. "Because We Can, We Must." Commencement address at the University of Pennsylvania, Philadelphia, May 17, 2004. http://www.upenn.edu/ almanac/between/2004/commence-b.html.

Bridges, Ruby. *Through My Eyes.* New York: Scholastic, 1999.

Bridges Hall, Ruby. "The Education of Ruby Nell." Ruby Bridges Foundation. http://www.rubybridges.org/story.htm http://www.rubybridges.org/story.htm.

Burks, Charles S. "A Class of One." By Charlayne Hunter-Gault. PBS *Online Newshour* (February 18, 1997). http://www.pbs.org/newshour/bb/race_relations/jan-june97/bridges_2-18.html.

Business Leader Profiles for Students, vol. 1. Gale Research, 1999. Reproduced in *Biography Resource Center.* Farmington Hills, MI: The Gale Group, 2004. "Cyrus McCormick," "Madame C. J. Walker."

Carlisle Bigelow, Barbara and Julia M. Rubiner, eds. *Contemporary Black Biographies,* vol. 2. Detroit: Gale Research, Inc., 1992.

Carlisle Bigelow, Barbara, Suzanne M. Bourgoin, Nicolet V. Elert, and L. Mpho Mabunda, eds. *Contemporary Black Biographies,* vol. 3. Detroit: Gale Research, Inc., 1993.

Champagne, Duane, ed. *The Native North American Almanac.* Farmington Hills, MI: Gale Group, 2001.

Chief Joseph. "An Indian's View of Indian Affairs." *North American Review,* 128:269, April 1879.

Christenson, Elise. "Civil Rights: Time to Get Back on the Bus." *Newsweek,* February 3, 2003, 10.

Christian History Institute. http://www.gospelcom.net/chi/. "John Quincy Adams," "Birmingham Bombing," "Nathan Hale," "Francis Scott Key," "Martin Luther King Jr.," "Mayflower," "Harriet Beecher Stowe," "Harriet Tubman," "George Washington—Thanksgiving Proclamation," "Phillis Wheatley," "John Witherspoon."

Coles, Robert. "The Inexplicable Prayers of Ruby Bridges." *Christianity Today,* August 9, 1985, 17–20.

Commire, Anne and Deborah Klezmer, eds. *Historic World Leaders North and South America,* vol. 4. Detroit: Gale Research, Inc., 1994.

Contemporary Authors Online. Gale, 2004. Reproduced in *Biography Resource Center.* Farmington Hills, MI: The Gale Group, 2004. "Ida Wells-Barnett," "Ruby Bridges."

Contemporary Black Biography, vol. 6. Gale Research, 1994. Reproduced in *Biography Resource Center.* Farmington Hills, MI: The Gale Group, 2004. "Jackie Robinson," "Madame C. J. Walker," "Mary McLeod Bethune," "Rosa Parks."

Contemporary Heroes and Heroines, Book IV. Gale Group, 2000. Reproduced in *Biography Resource Center.* Farmington Hills, MI: The Gale Group, 2004. "Dwight D. Eisenhower," "Rosa Parks."

Cushman, Candi. "For John Perkins, It's Black and White." *World Magazine,* June 15, 2002.

Davis, Asa J. "The George Latimer Case: A Benchmark in the Struggle for Freedom." Extracted from "The Two Autobiographical Fragments of George W. Latimer," *Journal of Afro-American Historical and Genealogical Society,* No. 1, Summer 1980.

Davis, Chris. "Jubilation in June: The Story of Juneteenth, America's Other Independence Day." *Weekly Wire,* June 19, 2000. http://weeklywire.com/ww/06-19-00/memphis_socvr.html.

Dawson, John. *Healing America's Wounds.* Ventura, CA: Gospel Light/Regal Books, 1997.

Dictionary of American Biography Base Set. American Council of Learned Societies, 1928–1936. Reproduced in *Biography Resource Center*. "Benedict Arnold," "Benjamin Rush," "Daniel Webster," "Frederick Augustus Conrad Muhlenberg," "George Duffield," "James Caldwell," "John Peter Gabriel Muhlenberg," "Josiah Henson," "Nathan Hale," "Phillis Wheatley," "Roger Sherman," "Theodore Dwight Weld."

DuBois, W. E. Burghardt. *The Suppression of the African Slave-Trade to the United States of America 1638–1870*. Baton Rouge: Louisiana State University Press, 1896.

Eidsmoe, John. *Christianity and the Constitution*. Grand Rapids, MI: Baker Book House Company, 1987.

Eisert, Kevin. "The Missouri Compromise 'A Balance of Power' March 3, 1820." *The War for States' Rights*. http://civilwar.bluegrass.net/secessioncrisis/200303.html.

Ellis, Joseph John. *John Adams*. http://www.ragz-international.com/john_adams.htm.

Encyclopedia of World Biography Supplement, vol. 22. Gale Group, 2002. Reproduced in *Biography Resource Center*. Farmington Hills, MI: The Gale Group, 2004. "Biddy Mason," "Norbert Rillieux."

Encyclopedia of World Biography, and ed. 17 vols. Gale Research, 1998. Reproduced in *Biography Resource Center*. Farmington Hills, MI: The Gale Group, 2004. "Benjamin Banneker," "Roger Sherman," "Sarah Moore and Angelina Emily Grimké," "Tappan Brothers," "Theodore Dwight Weld."

Eskew, Glenn T. *But for Birmingham: The Local and National Movements in the Civil Rights Struggle*. Chapel Hill: University of North Carolina Press, 1997.

Faith Project and Blackside Inc., in association with Independent Television and Broadcast Service. "This Far by Faith: African-American Spiritual Journeys." http://www.pbs.org/thisfarbyfaith/.

Federer, William J. *George Washington Carver—His Life & Faith in His Own Words*. St. Louis: Amerisearch, Inc., 2002.

Feminist Writers. St. James Press, 1996. Reproduced in *Biography Resource Center*. Farmington Hills, MI: The Gale Group, 2004. "Sarah Moore Grimké and Angelina (Emily) Grimké Weld."

Flynt, Wayne et al. *Alabama: The History of a Deep South State*. Tuscaloosa: University of Alabama Press, 1994.

Foner, Eric and John A. Garraty, eds. *Reader's Companion to American History*. Boston: Houghton Mifflin Company, 1991.

Ford III, William and Dutch Sheets. *History Makers*. Ventura, CA: Gospel Light/Regal Books, 2004.

Gado, Mark. "Birmingham Church Bombing." Court TV's Crime Library. http://www.crimelibrary.com/terrorists_spies/terrorists/birmingham_church/index.html?sect=22.

Garrow, David. *The FBI and Martin Luther King, Jr.* New York: Penguin Books, 1981.

Gibson, Robert A. "The Negro Holocaust: Lynching and Race Riots in the United States, 1880–1950." Yale-New Haven Teachers Institute. http://www.yale.edu/ynhti/curriculum/units/1979/2/79.02.04.x.html#c.

Hacker, Carlotta. *Great African Americans in History*. New York: Crabtree Publishing Company, 1997.

Hall, Brian. *I Should Be Extremely Happy in Your Company*. Excerpted in *Time*, June 30, 2002.

Hampton, Bruce. *Children of Grace: The Nez Percé War of 1877*. New York: Henry Holt and Co., 1994.

Henson, Josiah. *Uncle Tom's Story of His Life: An Autobiography of the Rev. Josiah Henson*. London, 1877.

Higginson, Thomas Wentworth. "Negro Spirituals." *Atlantic Monthly*, June 1867.

Historic World Leaders. Gale Research, 1994. Reproduced in *Biography Resource Center*. Farmington Hills, MI: The Gale Group, 2004. "Daniel Webster."

Hull, LeAnne von Neumeyer. "A Story of Bridget 'Biddy' Smith Mason: Her Legacy Among the Mormons." http://ldssocal.org/history/biddymason.htm.

Jackson, Dave and Neta. *Hero Tales Vol. II: A Family Treasury of True Stories From the Lives of Christian Heroes*. Minneapolis: Bethany House Publishers, 1997.

———. *Hero Tales Vol. III: A Family Treasury of True Stories From the Lives of Christian Heroes*. Minneapolis: Bethany House Publishers, 1998.

———. *Hero Tales: A Family Treasury of True Stories From the Lives of Christian Heroes*. Minneapolis: Bethany House Publishers, 1996.

Katz, William Loren. *Eyewitness: The Negro in American History*. New York: Ethrac Publications Inc., 1995.

Kay Wright, ed. *The African-American Archive*. New York: Black Dog & Leventhal Publishers, Inc., 2001.

Kelly, David. "Soothing the Souls at Last." *Los Angeles Times*, February 10, 2004.

Keoke, Emory Dean and Kay Marie Porterfield. *Encyclopedia of American Indian Contributions to the World*. New York: Facts on File, Inc., 2002.

King, Martin Luther Jr.: "Never Again Where He Was." *Time*, January 3, 1964.

Kohn, George Childs. *The New Encyclopedia of American Scandal*. New York: Checkmark Books, 2001.

Larson, Kate Clifford. *Bound for the Promised Land: Harriet Tubman, Portrait of an American Hero*. Harriet Tubman Biography. http://www.harriettubmanbiography.com/.

Lindsay, Rae. *The Presidents' First Ladies*. New York: Scholastic Library Pub, 1989.

Loewen, James W. *Lies My Teacher Told Me: Everything Your American History Textbook Got Wrong*. New York: Touchstone, 1995.

Loewen, James. *Lies Across America: What Our Historic Sites Get Wrong*. New York: Touchstone, 2000.

Logan, Rayford and Michael R. Winston, eds. *Dictionary of American Negro Biography*. New York: W. W. Norton & Company, 1982.

Lossing, B.J. *Biographical Sketches of the Signers of the Declaration of American Independence*. New York: George F. Cooledge & Brother, 1848. Reprinted by WallBuilder Press, 1995.

Madigan, Tim. *The Burning: Massacre, Destruction, and the Tulsa Race Riot of 1921*. New York: St. Martin's Press, 2001.

Marshall, Peter J. and David Manuel. *From Sea to Shining Sea*. Grand Rapids, MI: Baker Book House Company, 1986.

———. *Sounding Forth the Trumpet*. Grand Rapids, MI: Baker Book House Company, 1997.

———. *The Light and the Glory*. Grand Rapids, MI: Baker Book House, 1977.

Math & Mathematicians: The History of Math Discoveries Around the World. 2 vols. 1999. Reproduced in *Biography Resource Center*. Farmington Hills, MI: The Gale Group, 2004. "Benjamin Banneker."

McCullough, David. *John Adams*. New York: Simon & Schuster, 2001.

McDowell, Stephen. *Building Godly Nations: Lessons From the Bible and America's Christian History*. Charlottesville, VA: The Providence Foundation, 2003.

McDowell, Stephen and Mark Beliles. *In God We Trust Tour Guide: Featuring America's Landmarks of Liberty*. Charlottesville, VA: The Providence Foundation, 1998.

McElrath, Jessica. *African American History*. About.com. http://afroamhistory.about.com/od/people/.

Mulford, Karen Surina. *Trailblazers: 20 Amazing Western Women*. Flagstaff, AZ: Northland Publishing Company, 2001.

Murphy, Mabel Ansley. *American Leaders*. Philadelphia: The Union Press, 1920.

Nationmaster.com. "Silas Soule." Nationmaster.com Encyclopedia. http://www.nationmaster.com/encyclopedia/Silas-Soule

NorthStar Network. "A Chronology of Race Riots in America." http://www.thenorthstarnetwork.com/news/othernews/181547-1.html.

Notable Black American Men. Gale Research, 1998. Reproduced in *Biography Resource Center.* Farmington Hills, MI: The Gale Group, 2004. "Crispus Attucks," "Jean Baptiste Pointe Du Sable," "Richard Allen," "Robert Smalls."

Notable Black American Scientists. Gale Research, 1998. Reproduced in *Biography Resource Center.* Farmington Hills, MI: The Gale Group, 2004. "Norbert Rillieux."

Notable Black American Women, Book 1. Gale Research, 1992. Reproduced in *Biography Resource Center.* Farmington Hills, MI: The Gale Group, 2004. "Phillis Wheatley."

Ortner, Mary J. "Captain Nathan Hale." The Connecticut Society of the Sons of the Revolution. http://www.ctssar.org/patriots/nathan_hale_2.htm.

Oursler, Grace Perkins. "A Question of Courage." *Guideposts.* Reprinted from *Readers Digest School Reader,* 1959, condensed and adapted from *Guideposts.*

Parks, Rosa. *Dear Mrs. Parks: A Dialogue With Today's Youth.* New York: Lee & Low Books, Inc., 1996.

PBS Online. "Democracy and Struggles." *Freedom: A History of US.* 2002 Picture History and Educational Broadcasting Corporation. http://www.pbs.org/wnet/historyofus/web13/index.html.

PBS Online. "The Presidents: Dwight D. Eisenhower." *American Experience.* http://www.pbs.org/wgbh/amex/presidents/34_eisenhower/.

Perkins, John. *John M. Perkins Foundation.* http://www.jmpf.org/.

———. *Let Justice Roll Down.* Ventura, CA: GL Publications, 1976.

Ploski, Harry A. and James Williams, eds. *The Negro Almanac: A Reference Work on the African American.* Farmington Hills, MI: Gale Research, Inc., 1898.

Rand, Roberta. "The Amazing Journey of John Perkins." *Focus Over Fifty.* Focus on the Family. http://www.family.org/focusoverfifty/justforyou/a0024302.cfm.

Riedman, Sarah R. and Clarence C. Green. *Benjamin Rush: Physician, Patriot, Founding Father.* New York: Abelard-Schuman, 1964.

Rinehart, Paula. "John Perkins and the Voice of Calvary." *The Navigators,* issue 25, January 1985. http://www.navpress.com/Magazines/DJ/ArticleDisplay.asp?ID=025.01.

Rollins, Charlemae Hill. *They Showed the Way.* New York: Thomas Y. Crowell Company, 1964.

Rush, Benjamin. "Letter to John Dickinson, October 11, 1797" in *Letters of Benjamin Rush,* vol. 2. Edited by L. H. Butterfield. Princeton, NJ: Princeton University Press, 1951.

———. *Medical Inquiries and Observations,* vol. III. Philadelphia: J. Conrad & Co., 1805.

Ryan, Elizabeth A. *The Biographical Dictionary of Black Americans.* New York: Facts on File, Inc., 1992.

Scott, John Anthony. *Woman Against Slavery: The Story of Harriet Beecher Stowe.* New York: Thomas Y. Crowell Company, 1978.

Sheets, Dutch and William Ford III. *History Makers.* Ventura, CA: Gospel Light/Regal Books, 2004.

Smith, Jessie Carney, ed. *Notable Black American Men.* Farmington Hills, MI.: Gale Research, Inc., 1999.

Smith, Kyle, Gail Cameron Wescott, David Cobb Craig. "The Day the Children Died." *People Weekly,* vol. 48, iss. 6, August 11, 1997: 87–89.

Stowe, Harriet Beecher. "Sojourner Truth: The Libyan Sibyl." *Atlantic Monthly,* April 1863.

———. *The Key to Uncle Tom's Cabin: Presenting the Original Facts and Documents Upon Which the Story Is Founded, Together with Corroborative Statements Verifying the Truth of the Work.* Boston: John P. Jewett and Company, 1854. http://www.iath.virginia.edu/utc/uncletom/key/kyhp.html.

Sullivan, George. *Harriet Tubman.* New York: Scholastic, Inc., 2001.

Taylor, Kimberly Hayes. *Black Abolitionists and Freedom Fighters.* Minneapolis: The Oliver Press, Inc., 1996.

Till-Mobley, Mamie and Christopher Benson. *Death of Innocence: The Story of the Hate Crime That Changed America.* New York: Random House, 2003.

Tiner, John Hudson. *The Story of the Pledge of Allegiance.* Green Forest, AR: New Leaf Press, Inc., 2003.

Truth, Sojourner. "Narrative of Sojourner Truth." *Sojourner Truth Biography.* http://www.topicsites.com/sojourner-truth/sojourner-truth-biography.htm.

Twiss, Richard. *One Tribe, Many Nations.* Ventura, CA: Regal Books, 1997.

University of Kentucky. "A Reply from Soujourner Truth (1795–1883)." Speech recorded by Frances D. Gage, Chair Presiding of the woman's convention at Akron, Ohio, 1851. http://www.uky.edu/LCC/HIS/scraps/ideal.html.

U.S. News & World Report. "In New Orleans—It's Crowds vs. Negro Pupils and Legislature vs. Judge." November 28, 1960, 60–61.

Weatherford, Jack McIver. *Indian Givers: How the Indians of the Americas Transformed the World.* New York: Ballantine Publishing Group, 1988.

Webster, Daniel. "Adams and Jefferson." *Daniel Webster: Dartmouth's Favorite Son.* Dartmouth College. http://www.dartmouth.edu/~dwebster/speeches/adams-jefferson.html.

Weld, Theodore Dwight and Angelina and Sarah Grimké. *American Slavery As It Is: Testimony of a Thousand Witnesses Written by Slaveholders (1837–1839).* New York: American Anti-Slavery Society, 1839. http://medicolegal.tripod.com/weldslaveryasis.htm.

Whalin, Terry. *Sojourner Truth: American Abolitionist.* New York: Chelsea House Publishers, a division of Main Line Book Company, 1999.

Wikipedia. "Martin Luther King, Jr." http://en.wikipedia.org/wiki/Martin_Luther_King,_Jr.

Wilson, Vincent Jr. *The Book of the Founding Fathers.* Brookeville, MD: American History Research Associates, 1974.

"Wives of the Signers: The Women Behind the Declaration of Independence," excerpted from *The Pioneer Mothers of America.* Aledo, TX: WallBuilder Press, 1997.

World of Invention, 2nd ed. Gale Group, 1999. Reproduced in *Biography Resource Center.* Farmington Hills, MI: The Gale Group, 2004. "Norbert Rillieux."

Yancey, Philip. *Soul Survivor: How Thirteen Unlikely Mentors Helped My Faith Survive the Church.* New York: Galilee Trade, 2003.

Unless otherwise noted, images courtesy of WallBuilders.

Photo of Chief Black Kettle ("A Soldier's View: The Sand Creek Massacre," p. 333) courtesy of Colorado Historical Society. Negative #WPA 834, Indian Councils—Camp Weld 1864.

Photo of Chief Joseph ca. 1877 ("I Will Fight No More Forever: Chief Joseph and the Nez Percé War," p. 294) courtesy of Smithsonian Institution, National Anthropological Archives. Negative #43.201-A, photographer F. Jay Haynes.

Index

Abamillo, Juan 330
Aberdeen Saturday Pioneer 295
Acosta, R. Alexander . . . 284
Act of Uniformity, The . . 140
Adams, Abigail. 27, 33, 46, 299, 301, 307–311
Adams, Charles 307, 309
Adams, John 16, 19, 27, 30, 33, 44–46, 87, 305–311, 346
Adams, John Quincy 14, 149, 244–248, 299, 301, 306, 307, 309, 359
Adams, Nabby 307, 309
Adams, Samuel. 19, 27, 38, 43, 345
Adams, Thomas. . . . 307, 309
Addison, Joseph 151
African Civilization Society . 62
African Methodist Episcopal Church (AME) 20, 203–204
"Ain't I a Woman" (Sojourner Truth) . 174, 176
Alabama . . . 101, 180, 186, 322
Alamo, The. 330
Alaska 296
Alleged Causes of Lynching in the United States, 1892, 1893, 1894 (Ida B. Wells-Barnett) 104
Allen, Richard 30, 198–202, 204
Allen, William. 38
Alpha Suffrage Club 105
Alta California 336
American Academy of Arts and Sciences. 346
American Anti-Slavery Society 223, 236
American Bible Society 236, 286
American Education Society. 236
American Home Mission Missionary Society 236
American Indian 11, 81, 275–276, 296
American Indian Facts of Life (George Russell) 296
American Legion 258
American Methodist Episcopal Church Review 269
American Methodist Episcopal Zion Church 114
American Red Cross 177
American Revolution7–8, 275, 286, 337, 340, 346, 361
American Slavery As It Is (Theodore Weld) 223, 229, 231
American Sunday School Union 150, 236
American Temperance Society. 236
American Tract Society 236
Amistad 244–248
Anabaptists. 43
André, Major John 000 161–163
Anglican 140, 338
Anna, General Santa 330
Anthony, Susan B. 311
Anti-Lynching Bureau 105
Apache 296, 334
Appeal to the Christian Women of the South (Angelina Grimké) 227
Appomattox Courthouse. 53
Arapaho 206, 333–334
Arkansas. 75
Arkansas Race Riot, The (Ida B. Wells-Barnett) 105–106
Armistead, James . . . 275–276
Army Intelligence Bureau. 130
Army of Northern Virginia 165
Army of the Potomac . . . 165
Army of the West 167
Arnold, Benedict 151, 161–164, 275
Articles of Association . . . 313
Articles of Confederation 313, 347–348
Asbury, Francis. . . . 200, 203
Asia (Asia Minor). 84
Assistant Commissary General 24
Associate Justice 346
Associated Press. 177
Atlanta 209, 254
Atlantic Ocean . . 40, 60, 139, 298
Attucks, Crispus 275
Auburn, New York . . . 112, 118
Auld, Thomas. 263
Azusa Street Revival 112
Badillo, Juan. 330
Bahamas 351
Bailey, Frederick . . . 262–263
Bailey, Gamaliel 233
Bailey, Harriet 262
Baldwin, Roger 245–246
Ballard, Clergy 250
Baltimore 14, 35, 48, 50, 111, 150, 154, 270–271
Banneker, Benjamin 277
Bardwell, Kentucky .94–95, 97
Barnett, Ferdinand L. . . . 105
Bartlett, Josiah 345
Barton, Clara 177
Battle of Bunker Hill. . . . 275
Battle of Germantown . . . 219
Battle of Lexington . . . 37, 168
Battle of Quebec 216
Battle of Yorktown 276
Baum, L. Frank 295
Baumfree, Isabella. . . 172–176
Baxley, William 183
Bear Flag Revolt 336
Bear's Paw Battlefield . . . 293
Bear's Paw Mountains . . 290
Beaufort Jail. 58
Bedford, New York. 286
Beecher, Lyman 222–223
Bell, Alexander Graham . 273.
Bellamy, Francis. 260
Benezet, Anthony 28, 30
Bent, Robert 34
Berlin, Germany 257
Bethel Methodist Church 202
Bethune, Albertus 178
Bethune, Mary McLeod 177–178
Bethune-Cookman College 178
Bible Society 29, 154
Big Hole. 290
Bill of Rights. 21, 340
Birmingham Police Department. 181
Birth of a Nation, The 209, 212–215
Black Codes 99–101, 253
Black Kettle, Chief . . 322–325
Bladensburg, Maryland . . 312
Blanton, Thomas 183
Blue Ridge Mountains . . . 20
"Bobo" (Emmett Till) . . . 279
Bonham, James. 330
Bono (lead singer of U2) 142
Boston (city)39, 41, 44, 46, 51, 172, 215, 231, 233, 271–272, 298, 307, 309, 339, 370
Boston (ship). . . 298–299, 302
Boston Common 275
Boston Massacre . . 38–41, 275
Boston Vigilance Committee 51
Boudinot, Elias. 24
Bowie, Jim 330
Bowman, Louis A. 261
Bowser, Mary 129
boycott 66, 186, 188, 348
Bradford, Governor William. 79, 84–86, 91–92
Bradford, Sarah 112
Bragen, Bobby 194
Brandon, Mississippi. . . . 240
Braxton, Carter. 348
Breedlove, Sarah 178–179
Brewster, William 84–85
Bridges, Abon. 70
Bridges, Lucille 68, 69
Bridges, Ruby 68–74
Bridgetown, Barbados . . . 350
Bristol, England 52
British Parliament 16, 38, 140
British West Indies 222
Brooklyn Dodgers. . . 191–197
Brown University (Rhode Island College). 346
Brown v. Board of Education of Topeka, Kansas. . . 69, 75, 100, 210
Brown, Curry 240
Brunswick, Maine. 230
Bryant, Carolyn 280
Bryant, Roy 281, 283
Bryant's Grocery Store . . 280
Buckley, Joe Paul 240
Bunker Hill. 288
Burke, Edmund 138
Burks, Charles 69
Burton, Scott 250
Bush, George H. W. 122
Caldwell, Dr. Rev. 270
Caldwell, James 24
Calhoun, John. 148
California. . 120, 143, 192–193, 197, 238–239
Campenella, Roy 193
Canada. . . . 117, 216, 231, 236, 291–293, 296
Canassatego 81
Cannon, Lieutenant James 332, 335
Cape Cod 79, 83, 298
Carroll, Charles 346
Carrollton, Mississippi. . . . 55
Carver, George Washington . 322–328, 370
Carver, John. 79, 84
Carver, Moses 324
Cash, Herman 183
Cato (Joseph Addison) . . . 151
Cato the Younger 151
caucus (caucauasu) 82
Central High School . 75, 258
Central Pacific Railroad 190
Chambliss, Robert 183
Chancellorsville. 166
Charles the First 139, 157
Charleston, South Carolina. 49–50, 58–60, 226
Charlottesville 159
Chase, Samuel. 345
Cherry, Bobby Frank, Jr. 183
Cheyenne 331–335
Chicago . . . 105, 215, 253, 276
Chicago Conservator 105
Chicago Evening Post 135
Chief Justice of the State of Delaware 347
Chief Justice of the U.S. Supreme Court. 286
China 154, 190
Chinese 190
Chivington, John. . . . 331–335
Chopunnish (Pierced Nose Indians) 293
Christ Church, Philadelphia . 46
Christian Community Development Association 242
Christmas Day . . 55, 177, 286
Cincinnati, Ohio . . . 195, 232
Cinque, Joseph 244, 246–247
City of Brotherly Love. 41, 194
Civil Rights Act of 1875 100
Civil Rights Bill 99
Civil War . . 52–53, 55, 62, 90, 99, 108, 113, 118, 125–128, 177, 243, 253, 262, 269, 272, 278, 292, 317, 320, 324, 342
Clansman, The (Thomas Dixon) 124
Clark, Abraham 24–26, 346
Clark, William 29, 276–277, 293, 297
Clay, Henry 148
Clayton, Elias 134–135
Clinton, General 303
Clinton, George. 345
Clinton, William Jefferson 67
Clymer, George. 346
Coffin, Levi. 115
Cold War. 257
Cole's Island. 60
Coles, Robert 71–72
College of New Jersey 213, 216–217
College of Philadelphia . . 346
College of William and Mary 348
Collins, Addie Mae . . 180–185
Collins, Junie. 183
Colorado Third Regiment 331
Columbia University 257
Columbus Day 260
Columbus, Christopher . . 261
Colville Indian Reservation 293
Commission on Interracial Cooperation 327
Communists 182
Compromise of 1877. . . . . 100, 219, 321
Concord, Massachusetts 168
Confederate. 58–60, 125, 127–130, 206–207, 269, 318, 329
Confederate States of America 127
Congregationalist 143
Congress 14, 16–17, 24, 27, 33, 35–37, 43–44, 51, 57, 99, 113, 154, 159, 162, 164, 188, 216–219, 225, 245–246, 268–269, 299–300, 312, 314, 339–340, 344, 346–347
Congressional Gold Medal 67
Connecticut. . 43, 151, 168, 313
Connor, Eugene "Bull" 181, 189
Constitution, The . 37, 57, 67, 143, 146–147, 154, 246, 258, 262, 266–267, 286–287, 313, 315–316, 318–319, 339, 342, 345–346
Continental Army . 12, 21, 29, 31, 34, 36, 301, 345
Continental Association. . 347
Continental Congress 15–16, 22, 27, 31, 33–34, 43, 46, 158, 286, 299, 305, 307, 340, 342, 347
convict leasing. 101
Cookman Institute of Jacksonville 178
Copiah County, Mississippi 54–55
Corinthian Hall 266
Cornwallis, General Charles . 36, 303
Countess of Huntingdon . . 41
County Board of Supervisors 55
Court of Admiralty 348
Court of France 301
Covey, Edward 263
Craft, William and Ellen 48–52, 370
Cramer, Lieutenant Joseph 334
Crocker, Charles. 190
Crockett, David. 330
Crosby & Gould 273
Crowe, James 206
Custer, George Armstrong 291, 334
Cut Arm. 292
Dartmouth College 145
Davis, Jefferson . . . 129, 269
Dawes, William. 168
Dawn Settlement. 236
Day of Prayer. 367
Daytona Beach, Florida . . 178
Daytona Normal and Industrial Institute for Black Girls 178
D-Day 255–256
de Grasse, Admiral Count. 36
de Zavala, Lorenzo 330
Deane, Silas 46
Dearborn, Michigan 65
Declaration of Independence 7, 15, 17, 24–26, 28, 31, 33, 37, 143, 171, 216, 245, 264, 299–300, 305–306, 313, 330, 337, 345–348, 366
"Defense of Fort McHenry, The" (Francis Scott Key) 150
DeLarge, Robert C. 264
Delaware . 143, 198, 200, 314, 347

Delaware Indians 141
Demand, Ella 180
Democratic Party 54, 99, 207–208, 213, 225
Democratic-Republicans 305
Democrats 54–57, 99, 207–208, 253, 317, 319
Denver, Colorado . . . 179, 335
Dermer, Captain 77, 79
Detroit, Michigan 67
Dickens, Charles 258
Dickinson, John . . . 299, 347
DiMaggio, Joe 191
Dixiecrats 185
Dixon, Thomas 214
Doddridge's Annotations . . 248
Dog Soldiers 331–332
Dondino, Louis 136–137
Donnegan, William 250
Douglass, Frederick . 172, 174, 204, 234, 262–267, 315, 320, 331
Downs, Karl 192–193
Dred Scott Decision 225
Du Pont, Admiral 60
Duché, Jacob 43–45
Duffield, George 33
Duluth, Minnesota . . 132–138
DuSable, Jean Baptiste Pointe 276
East River 31
East St. Louis Race Riot in 1917 . . . . 179, 253
Ecclesiastes 20, 23
Edict of Toleration 288
Edison Pioneers 273–274
Edison, Thomas 273–274, 323, 379
Edward, Charles 231
Edwards, Al 53
Edwards, Jonathan 125
Edwards, Jonathan, Jr. . . . 315
Egypt 59, 80, 113
8th Viriginia Regiment . . . 22
Einstein, Albert 138
Eisenhower, Dwight D. 255–258, 261
Electoral Commission . . . 319
Ellery, William 18, 346
Elliott, Robert Brown . . . 269
Emancipation Proclamation . 53, 105, 171, 342n
England . . . 17, 28, 38, 40–41, 76–78, 83, 88, 90–92, 142, 156, 162, 164, 286, 303, 339, 351–352
English Channel 256
Episcopalian 14
Equiano, Olaudah . . 349–352
Eschikagou 276
Eskimo 277
Espalier, Carlos 330
Esparaza, Gregorio 330
Esther 227, 229
Europe7, 81, 132, 256, 283, 330
European 8, 11, 82, 344
Evers, Medgar 187, 285
Ezra 366
Fair Oaks 292
FAME Renaissance 122
Faneuil Hall 172
Faubus, Orval 175
Federal Constitution . . 22, 347
Federalist Papers, The . . . 286
Fifteenth Amendment . . . 269
Fifteenth Street Presbyterian Church of Washington, D.C. 62
54th Massachusetts Regiment 289
Finney, Charles . 125, 222, 236
First African Methodist Episcopal Church . . 121–122
First Colored Presbyterian Church in New York . . . 62
First Day Society 29
1 Kings 225
First Presbyterian Church of Elizabethtown, New Jersey 24
Flight of 1877 291
Florida . 60, 143, 254, 317, 319
Floyd, William 345
Ford, Daniel 260
Ford, Henry 323, 370
Ford, William, III 357
Ford, William, Jr. 258
Ford, William, Sr. . . . 358, 367
Forrest, Nathan Bedford 207
Fort Duquesne 12
Fort Lyon 331
Fort McHenry 150
Fort Ross 336
Fort Sumter 59–60, 273
Founding Fathers 16, 18, 81, 141, 305, 347
Four Little Girls 183
Fourteenth Amendment 207, 264
Fourth of July . . 53, 264–265, 267
Frames of Government (William Penn) 141
France 88, 298, 301–303
Franco-Prussian War 177
Francis, Nellie 136
Frank, Leo M. 209
Franklin, Benjamin 16, 18, 22, 29, 40, 82, 142, 153, 287, 297, 299–300, 303, 310, 337–344, 347
Franklin, Deborah 338
Fredericksburg 50, 166
Free Labor Movement . . . 62
Free Speech 102
freedmen 318, 329
Freedmen's Bureau . . 175, 318
French 11, 36, 255–256, 301–302
French and Indian War 11–12
Frick, Ford 194
Fuentes, Antonio 330
Fugitive Slave Act 51, 111, 115, 225, 231, 370
Fulton Street 243
Furillo, Carl 192
Fusion Independent Party 54–55
Gage, Thomas 168
Galveston 53
Gandhi, Mahatma 327
Garnett, Henry Highland 62
Garretson, Freeborn 198–200
Garrison, William Lloyd 174, 262, 267
Gates, Thomas 90
Genesis 79
Geneva Convention of 1864 . 177
Georgia 51, 60, 108–109, 119–120, 209
German(s) . . 22, 255–257, 352
Germany 16, 257
Gerry, Elbridge 18, 346
Gettysburg 166–167, 171
Gettysburg Address 171
Gordon College 242
Gore, Mr. 263
Granger, Gordon 53
Grant, Ulysses S.130–131, 209, 214
Gray, James B. 270–272
Great Awakening . . . 40, 366
Great Britain (British) 16–17, 20, 25–26, 31–35, 38, 43–45, 47, 62, 89, 150, 152, 158, 161, 164, 168–169, 231, 233, 255–256, 275, 298–299, 302–303, 343–348, 352, 370
Great Law of Peace 81
Great Spirit 11, 13
Green, Ernest 75
Green, Samuel 210
Greensburg, Indiana 254
Griffith, D. W. . 209, 212–213
Grimké, Angelina 223, 226–229, 231
Grimké, Sarah 226–229
Grubber, William 30
Guerin 351
Gwinnett, Button 348
Hale, Nathan 151–153
Hall, Lyman 348
Hall, Malcolm 73
Hallam, Mabel 250
Hamilton, Alexander 35, 286
Hammerberg, Carl 136
Hancock, John . . . 17, 42, 219, 310, 331, 333, 334, 347, 351
Harambee Christian Family Center 241
Harlem, New York 186
Harper's Weekly 60
Harriet Tubman Home for Aged and Indigent Colored People 114
Harris, Eliza 232–233
Harrison, Benjamin (signer of the Declaration of Independence) . 18, 260, 345
Harrison, Benjamin (U.S. president) 55
Hart, John 348
Harvard College 47
Hayden, Lewis 51
Hayes, Rutherford B. 317, 318
Hayne, Senator 147
Hazlehurst 55, 57
Headley, J. T. 33
Hearst, William Randolph 261
Henry Ford Museum 65
Henry IV 288
Henry, Mrs. 68–72
Henry, Patrick . 21, 156–159, 366, 370
Henson, Josiah 23, 237
Henson, Matthew 277
Hewes, Joseph 346
Heyward, Thomas, Jr. . . . 364
Higbe, Kirby 194
Highland College 325
History Makers (William Ford III and Dutch Sheets) 358
History of the American People, The (Woodrow Wilson) 213
Hodges, Gil 191
Holland 86
"holy cause" 125
Holy Spirit . 44, 122, 158, 167, 200, 203, 230
Hooper, William 346
Hoover, J. Edgar 182
Hopkins, Mark 190
Hopkins, Stephen 18, 346
Hopkinson, Francis 346
Horton, Gilbert 287
Host People 7, 295, 297
House Ways and Means Committee 326
Houston, Texas 253
Howard, Oliver O. 125
Hudson River 83
Huemmer, Doug 240
Huguenots 288
Hunt, Robert 89
Hunt, Thomas 77
Huntington College 242
Huntington, Collis 190
Huntington, Samuel 347
Idaho 291
Illinois State Journal 250
India 327
Indians (indios) . . 82, 89, 92, 96–97, 310, 331, 333–344, 347, 351
Indies 345
Interesting Narrative of the Life of Olaudah Equiano, or Gustavus Vassa, the African, The 352
Internal Revenue Service (IRS) 210
International Red Cross . . 177
Iowa 120
Iowa State College . . 322–323
Ireland 88, 142
Irving, Dr. 351
Isaiah 124, 247, 368
Israelites 33, 59, 113
"I've Been to the Mountaintop" (Martin Luther King Jr.) 189
Jackson, Andrew 148
Jackson, Elmer 134–135
Jackson, Jesse L., Sr. . . . 284
Jackson, Mahalia 188
Jackson, Mississippi 240
Jackson, Thomas "Stonewall" 125
Jamaica 62
James, Joe 250
Jamestown 8, 89–90
Japanese 296
Jay, Auguste 288
Jay, John . . 35, 154, 286–288
Jay, Pierre 288
Jefferson, Thomas 15–16, 154, 224, 277, 303, 305–306, 310, 337, 342, 347
Jersey 25
Jesus Christ 20, 45, 78, 85–86, 109, 173–174, 176, 199, 205, 230, 311, 354–355, 358, 365–366
"Jesus Shall Reign" (Isaac Watts) 24
Jewett, J. P. 233
Jim Crow . . 99–101, 195, 238, 240, 253, 320, 363
Jimenez, Damacio 330
Job 145–146
Johns Hopkins University 213
Johnson, Andrew 99, 318
Johnson, William 49
Jones, Absalom 201–202
Jones, Calvin 206
Jones, Captain 83–84
Jones, Curtis 280
Jones, J. William 125
Joseph (from Genesis) . . . 79
Joseph, Chief (In-mut-too-yah-lat-lat) 290–294
"Joy to the World" (Isaac Watts) 24
Judy, Milton W. 135
Juneteenth 53
Kansas. 69, 143, 224, 256, 325
Kansas City Monarchs . . . 193
Kellert, Frank 195–196
Kelley, Abby 227
Kelly Ingram Park 182
Kennedy, John 206
Kennedy, Robert F. 274
Kentucky 120, 194, 232
Key, Francis Scott 150
King David 9, 187
King George III . . . 16–17, 33
King Solomon 225
King, Martin Luther, Jr. . . . 66, 71, 74, 138, 181, 185–189, 197, 212, 283
Kingston, Washington . . . 137
Klan Act and Enforcement Act, The 208
Knights of Mary Phagan 209
Knowlton Rangers 152
Korean War 257
Ku Klux Klan . . . 99, 132, 178, 182–183, 206–211, 213–214, 253, 318, 320, 362
L'Enfant, Pierre 277
La Rochelle, France 288
Lake Providence, Louisiana . 353
Lakota/Sioux 292, 295–296, 334
Lamarr, Hedy 280
Langdon, Samuel 47
Lane Seminary 222, 231, 236
Lanphier, Jeremiah 243
Lapwai, Idaho 291
Latimer, George . . . 270–274
Latimer, Lewis 272–273
Latimer, Rebecca . . . 270–274
Laus Deo 154
Lawrence, Kansas 331
League of the Iroquois . . . 81
Lee, Arthur 300
Lee, Francis Lightfoot . . 348
Lee, Richard Henry . . 17, 345
Lee, Robert E. . . 125, 130–131, 165–167, 207
Lee, Spike 183
Left Hand 332, 335
Lelia 178–179
Leni-Lenape Indians 141
Lester, John 206
Let Justice Roll Down (John Perkins) 240
Letters on the Equality of the Sexes (Sarah Grimké) 228
Lewis, Francis 347
Lewis, Meriwether 29, 276, 293, 297
Libby Prison 128–129
Liberator 51, 174, 262
Liberty Street Presbyterian Church 62
Liberty Window 46
Library of Congress 347
Life of Josiah Henson, The 237
Lincoln Memorial 188
Lincoln School for Colored Children 325
Lincoln, Abraham . 53, 55, 61, 165–171, 234, 249–250, 252, 262, 321, 329, 332, 336, 342
Little Big Horn 291, 334
Little Rock Central High School 75, 258
Little Rock, Arkansas 75, 105
Livingston, Philip 348
Livingston, Robert 347
Livingston, William 24
Lizzy, Aunt 281
Lockett, Harriet 358

Lockett, Nora 358
Loe, Thomas 140
London 77, 140, 273, 303
Long Island . . . 152, 174, 244
Long, Jefferson H. 269
Look magazine. 283
Looking Glass 292
Lorraine Motel 189
Los Angeles . . . 120–123, 196
Losoya, José 330
Louis XIV 288
Louisiana 143, 319
Louisiana Purchase 347
Lyman Hall 348
Lynch, Thomas, Jr. 345
lynching(s) 98, 102–108
Macedonia 84
Macon, Georgia 48
Madame C. J. Walker Manufacturing Company. 179
Madison, James 286, 346
Mae, Vera 239, 242
Mae, Willie 281
Maine. 143, 225
Manassas, Virginia 128
Marble Collegiate Church 323
Mardi Gras. 68
Marietta, Georgia 209
Marshall, General 256
Marxists 182
Maryland. . . 109, 112–113, 118, 150, 200, 312
Mason, Bridget "Biddy" 204
Mason, Max. 135
Massachusetts 8, 16, 18, 31, 42, 47, 131, 146–148, 159, 162, 174, 177, 216, 222, 245, 262–263, 272, 309, 314, 331, 342, 345–346
Massasoit, Chief 77–79
Matteson, Harrison Tompkins 46
Matthew. 124, 242, 306
Matthews, John Prentiss "Print" 54–57
Matthews, John Prentiss, Jr. . 55
Mattie (young slave girl in "Kettle Prayers") . . 353–359
Maxim, Hiram 273
Mayflower 83–85
Mayflower Compact 86, 365–366
McArthur, General 256
McCarthy hearings 258
McClellan, George B.. . . . 125
McCord, Frank. 206
McCoy, Elijah 278
McDonogh School No. 19 70
McDowell, Calvin . . 102–103
McGhie, Isaac. 134–135
McKean, Thomas 347
McKean, Toby (Toby Mac) . . 7–9, 363–364
McNair, Denise 180–185
McWilliams, Moses 178
Meade, General George . . 165
Medicine Woman. 333
Memphis, Tennessee . . . 102, 104–105, 188–189, 253
Mendenhall Ministries . . 239
Mendenhall, Mississippi 239, 241
Mendian Africans 247
Meridian, Mississippi. . . . 253
"Metamorphoses" (Ovid) 338
Methodist . . 96, 98, 200–202, 208, 325, 331
Middleton, Arthur. 346
Milam, J. W. "Big" . . 281, 283
Miles, Captain Nelson . . . 293
Milholland, Dr. and Mrs. 325
militia 21, 161, 252
Miller, C. J. 94–97
Miller, William 135
ministry62, 122, 227, 236, 239, 241, 243
Minneapolis Journal 135
Minnesota . . 132, 135–136, 143
missionary . . 62, 178, 243, 351
Mississippi . . 55, 57, 100, 105, 108, 119, 178, 238–240, 242, 279–280, 282–285, 370
Mississippi River 92, 167
Missouri 94, 97, 120, 225
Missouri Compromise . . . 224
Mohawk. 296
Money, Mississippi. . 280, 285
Monongahela River . . . 11–12
Montana 288–289
Monterey, California. . . . 336
Montez, Pedro 244
Montgomery, Alabama. . . 63, 65–66, 186, 188, 283, 370
Montgomery, Colonel James 13
Moody, D. L. 125
Morgan, Garrett 278
Morris, Lewis 345
Morris, Robert 34–37, 346, 369
Morton, John 348
Mose, Papa. 279–281
Mose, Uncle 281
Moses 33, 113, 365
Mosquito Coast 351
Moss, Thomas 102–103
Most Valuable Player . . . 195
Mott, Lucretia. 227
Mount Hope 55
Mount Vernon 370
Mr. Cray 49
Muhlenberg, Pastor Frederick 21
Muhlenberg, Pastor Peter. 20–22
Murphy, Police Chief John 132–133
Muskigum River. 220
Nalle, Charles 116–117
Narrative of the Life of an American Slave (Frederick Douglass) 264
NASA. 258
Natchez, Mississippi 102
National Advisory Committee to the National Youth Administration (NYA) . 178
National Afro-American Council 105
National Association for the Advancement of Colored People (NAACP). 65–66, 70, 105, 196, 218, 252, 283, 285
National Conference for Christians and Jews . . . 196
National Council of Negro Women. 178
National Day of Prayer 367
National Era 233, 238
National Guard. 75, 251
National Historic Trail . . 293
National League Championship 195
National Parks Service. . . 335
National Public School Celebration 260
Native American 7–8, 77, 278, 295–297
NATO 257
Nava, Andres 330
Navajo 296
Navarro, José Antonio . . 330
Nebraska. 120
Negro Fellowship League. 105
Negro League. 193, 195
Negro Spiritual 205
Nehemiah 362, 365
Nelson, Thomas, Jr. 347
Neosho, Missouri. 325
New England. 20, 82, 92, 152, 158
New Hampshire 146, 178, 314, 342, 345, 348
New Hebron, Mississippi 238
New Jersey 24, 35, 200, 214, 342
New Orleans, Louisiana 68–69, 73, 253–254, 279
New World 16, 79, 81, 83, 89, 140
New York (city) . 21, 62, 104, 118, 152, 154, 173, 215, 236, 243, 254, 257, 273, 323
New York (state) . 17, 62, 139, 158, 161, 172, 174, 186, 190, 200, 209, 216, 222–223, 228, 238, 251, 286, 306, 324, 342
New York State Society for Promoting the Manumission of Slaves. 287
New York Supreme Court 286
New York Times 324
New York Tribune 248
New York Yankees 181
Newcombe, Don 193
Newport, Rhode Island . . . 346
Nez Percé (Nimi'ipuu) Trail. 293
Nez Percé War 290–293
Nicaragua 351
Nicholas, Captain. 60
Nigeria. 349
Nimiipuu (Nee-Me-Poo). 293
Ningpo Chekiang Province, China. 154
Nixon, Richard 257
No Cross, No Crown (William Penn). 140
Nobel Peace Prize. . . 188, 212
Noonday Prayer Meeting 243
Norfolk, Virginia 270
Normandy 255–257
North Carolina. 346
North Dutch Reformed Church. 243
North Pole 277
North Star. 110–111
Northampton, Massachusetts 174
Northwest Territories. . . . 29
Norwegian 296
Oberlin College. 236
"O God Our Help in Ages Past" (Isaac Watts). 24
Ohio 174, 220, 222, 232
Ohio River 232
Oklahoma 293, 334
Oklahoma's Indian Country 293
Old House Chamber 247
Old South Church. 41
Old Testament. 225, 366
Old Woman's Country . . 290
Omaha, Nebraska 253
"On America" (Phillis Wheatley) 41
"On Being Brought From Africa to America" (Phillis Wheatley) 41
One Tribe, Many Nations (Richard Twiss) 295
Ontario, Canada 237
"On the Affray in King Street on the Evening of the 5th of March" (Phillis Wheatley) 41
"On the Arrival of the Ships of War and Landing of the Troops" (Phillis Wheatley) 41
"On the Death of Master Snider" (Phillis Wheatley) 41
"On the Death of Mr. George Whitefield" (Phillis Wheatley) 40
Operation Overlord 255
Oregon 290, 319
Overland Trail 120
Ovid 338
Owens, Robert 119–123
Paca, William 345
Paine, Robert Treat 346
Parker, Theodore 52
Parker, Wheeler. . . . 279–280
Parks, Rosa . . 63–65, 283, 370
Pasadena, California. 192, 241
Pascal, Michael Henry . . . 351
Patton, General. 256
Patuxet 76–78
Paul (the apostle) 84, 217
Peavy, Junie Collins. 183–184
Penn, John 348
Penn, William . . 139–141, 297
Pennsylvania . . 12, 22, 28, 33, 110, 139, 141, 158, 200, 222, 227, 299, 314, 341–342, 346–348, 370
Pennsylvania Abolition Society 28, 30, 338, 341
Pennsylvania Antislavery Society 287
Pennsylvania Hall. 227
Pentecost. 157
peonage. 101
People's Grocery Store . . . 12
Perkins, Clyde. 238
Perkins, John. 238–242
Perry, Robert. 277
Peter (the apostle) 157
Peters, Judge Richard 36
Phagan, Mary. 209
Pharaoh 33
Philadelphia 17, 28–30, 33, 35, 44, 46, 48, 50–51, 110, 129, 141, 154, 163, 194, 200, 226, 228, 253, 271, 273, 313, 338, 343
Philadelphia Bible Society 346
Philadelphia Yearly Meeting 28
Philistines 157
Phillips County, Arkansas 106
Phillips Exeter Academy 145
Pieh, Sengbe . . 244, 246–247
Pilgrims . 8, 18, 78–79, 83–86, 89, 91–92, 144, 365–366
Pine Street Presbyterian Church. 33
Pittsburgh. 12
Plan for Improving the Condition of the Free Blacks (Benjamin Franklin). . . 341
Planter 58–60
Planter's Hotel 59
Pledge of Allegiance. . . . 258, 260–261
Plessy v. Ferguson 320
Plymouth Bay. 76
Plymouth Rock. 144
Plymouth, Massachusetts 8, 78–79, 86, 91
Polish 255–256
Polk, James K. 48
Poor, Salem. 275
Portia (Abigail Adams) . . 310
Potawatomi Indian 276
Prayer March 367
Presbyterians 24, 43, 178, 217
Presidential Prayer Team 367
Prince George County, Virginia. 360
Princeton University 213
Princeton's Theological Seminary 62
Prison Fellowship 242
Progress of the Revival . . 243
Promontory Point, Utah. 190
Protestant Huguenots 28
Protestant Reformation . . . 8
Providence (divine) 16
Province of Massachusetts Bay 46
Provincial Congress of Massachusetts 47
Psalms . 13, 43–46, 52, 211, 235
public schools29, 61, 100. 114, 346
Pulaski, Tennessee 206
Putnam, Israel 43
Putnam, Ohio 220–221
Quaker 28, 35, 43, 46, 51, 109, 127, 140, 226, 271, 341
Quebec, Canada. 216
Queen Victoria, Canada 290
Radical Republicans 99
Rainey, Joseph H.. 269
Randolph, Edmund Jennings 340
Randolph, Peter 360
Randolph, Peyton 158
Rankin, John 232–233
Rattoon, Mr. 14
Ray, John 94–97, 370
Ray, Mary 94
Ray, Ruby 94
Read, George. 347
Read, Warren 37
Reagan, Ronald 92
real McCoy 278
Receiver of Taxes from North Carolina. 348
Reconstruction . . 55, 99, 208, 213–214, 253, 307, 318–319
Red Hill 159
Red Record, A. 103–104
Red Summer 253
Reed, Richard. 206
Reese, Pee-Wee 194
Reid, Philip 312
Republican Party. 55, 57, 99, 185, 208, 214, 253, 257, 269, 317, 319
Resolution for Independence . . 17
Revels, Hiram Rhodes . . 264
Revere, Paul 168
Revolutionary War. . . 31, 155, 161–162, 199, 275–276, 346, 348
Rhode Island 18, 222, 314, 342
Rhode Island College (Brown University). 346
Richardson, George. 250

Richmond, Virginia ... to The ... 126-131, 156
Rickey, Branch ... 193-195
Rillieux, Norbert ... 278
Roanoke ... 89
Robertson, Carole ... 180-185
Robinson, Jackie ... 191-197
Robinson, James ... 181
Robinson, Mollie ... 192
Robinson, Pastor ... 86
Rochester Ladies Anti-Slavery Society ... 264
Rochester, New York ... 264-266
Rocky Mountain News ... 334
Rodney, Caesar ... 348
Roman Catholic ... 189, 208, 288, 346
Rookie of the Year ... 191, 195
Rosecrans, General William ... 125
Rosewood Claims Act ... 254
Rosewood, Florida ... 253-254
Ross, George ... 348
Royal Navy ... 351
Ruby Bridges Foundation ... 73
Ruiz, José ... 244, 330
Rush, Benjamin ... 29-30, 301, 306, 346
Russell, George ... 296
Russia ... 258, 336
Rutledge, Edward ... 347
Sacajawea ... 276
Saint George's Methodist Church ... 200-201
Saint John's Church ... 156
Saint Margaret's Church ... 351
Salem, Massachusetts ... 32
Salem, Peter ... 275
Salisbury, New Hampshire ... 144
Samoset ... 77-79
Samson ... 157
San Bernardino, California ... 120
Sand Creek Massacre ... 331-335
Sandy Foundation Shaken, The (William Penn) ... 140
San Francisco, California ... 190
Santa Monica Mountains ... 120
Savannah, Georgia ... 49
Scotia Seminary ... 178
Scotland ... 88, 217
Scott United Methodist ... 192
Second Revolutionary Convention of Virginia ... 150, 158-159
2 Thessalonians ... 92
Secretary of Foreign Affairs ... 286
Secretary of the Naval Affairs Committee of Congress ... 346
Seguin, Juan ... 330
Senegal, Africa ... 40
sharecropping ... 100-101, 105, 178
Sharpe, George ... 130
Shaw, Robert Gould ... 000
Sheets, Dutch ... 358
Sherman, Roger ... 313-315, 347
Sherman, William T. ... 329, 336
Shiloh Church in New York ... 62
Shoshoni Indian ... 276
Sickles, Daniel ... 166
Sierra Leone ... 244
Sikeston, Missouri ... 94-95

Silus ... 84
Simmons, William Joseph ... 208-209
Simpson College ... 325
Sinai ... 240
Sioux of Sitting Bull ... 293
Sitting Bull ... 292
Six Nations ... 347
Sixteenth Street Baptist Church ... 180-184
Skinner, John ... 150
Smalls, Lydia ... 58
Smalls, Robert ... 58-61
Smith, James ... 348
Smith, John ... 76, 90
Smith, Robert ... 119-120
Smithsonian ... 65
Snider, Duke ... 41, 191
Snow White and the Seven Dwarfs ... 213
Society of Free People of Colour for Promoting the Instruction and School Education of Children of African Descent ... 203
Soderberg, Jim ... 138
Soldier Parson ... 24
Solomon, King ... 225
Son of the Morning Star ... 291
Sons of Liberty ... 38
Sons of the American Revolution ... 261
Soule, Amassa ... 331
Soule, Silas ... 331-334
South Carolina ... 60-61, 119, 147-148, 177-178, 319, 347
South Dakota ... 295
Southern Christian Leadership Conference ... 181
Southern Horrors: Lynch Law in All Its Phases (Ida B. Wells-Barnett) ... 104
Soviet Union ... 257-258
Spain ... 77, 246
Spanish ... 244
Spanish Cuba ... 244
Special Field Order No. 15 ... 329
Spring Street ... 123
Springfield Riot ... 249, 251
Springfield, Illinois ... 95-97, 249
Sputnik ... 258
Squanto ... 76-79
Squiers, Charles ... 335
St. Louis Cardinals ... 194
St. Louis, Missouri ... 179, 253
St. Paul, Minnesota ... 136
St. Petersburg, Russia ... 248
Stalin, Joseph ... 327
Stamp Act ... 38
Stanford, Leland ... 190
Stanky, Ed ... 194-195
"Star-Spangled Banner, The" ... 150
State Arsenal ... 250
State House of Boston ... 226
Statue of Freedom ... 312
Staunton, Virginia ... 213
Stephen (the martyr) ... 157
Stephenson, Gilbert ... 136
Stevenson, Adlai ... 370
Stewart, Lee ... 102-103
Stockton, Richard ... 348
Stone Mountain ... 209-210
Stone, Thomas ... 348
Stone's River, Tennessee ... 125
Story, Joseph ... 147
Stowe, Calvin ... 230
Stowe, Harriet Beecher ... 223, 229

Stride Toward Freedom (Martin Luther King Jr.) ... 186
Stuart, Charles ... 221
Sturgis, Stokely ... 198-199
Sumner, Florida ... 254
Superintendent of Finance ... 36
Supreme Judge of the World ... 17
Tait, Michael ... 9, 362-363
Tallahatchie County Courthouse ... 384
Tallahatchie River ... 281
Tallmadge, Benjamin ... 31-32, 162
Tappan, Arthur ... 236
Tappan, Lewis ... 236, 244-247
Tariff of 1832 ... 148
Taylor, George ... 348
Tejanos ... 330
Tennessee ... 125, 206-207
Texas ... 53, 120, 256
Texas Declaration of Independence ... 330
Texas Revolution ... 330
Thanksgiving ... 81
Thirteenth Amendment ... 269
Thomson, Charles ... 347
Thornton, Matthew ... 348
Three Fifths Clause ... 340
Tilden, Samuel J. ... 317-319
Till, Emmett ... 279-285, 370
Till, Mamie ... 279-284, 370
"To Anacreon in Heaven" ... 150
Tonnant ... 150
Toohoolhoolzote, Chief ... 292
Transcontinental Railroad ... 190
Travis, William ... 330
Treasury ... 14
Treaty of Paris ... 286, 347
Treaty of Peace ... 346
Tremont Temple ... 270
Trenton, New Jersey ... 179
Troy, New York ... 116-118, 222-223
True Relations (John Smith) ... 90
Trumbull, Jonathan ... 168
Truth, Sojourner ... 172-176, 204
Tubman, Harriet ... 109-114, 116-118, 369
Tubman, John ... 111
Tucker, Samuel ... 298-299, 302
Tulsa, Oklahoma ... 253
Turner, Benjamin S. ... 269
Tuskegee Institute of Alabama ... 322, 325, 327
Twain, Mark ... 284
Twiss, Richard ... 295
U2 spy plane ... 258
Uncle Charlie ... 353
Uncle Tom's Cabin ... 223, 229, 231, 233-234, 236-237
under God ... 261, 297, 364, 369-370
Underground Railroad ... 51, 109, 111, 114, 205, 225, 232, 237, 331, 341
Union League ... 209
Union Pacific Railroad ... 190
Union Village, New York ... 174
United Church Men ... 196
United Church of Christ ... 197
United Methodist Church ... 335
United Presbyterian Church

of Scotland ... 62
United States Army ... 292
University of Mississippi Law School ... 285
University of Pennsylvania ... 142
University of Virginia ... 213
Upham, James ... 260
U.S. federal marshal ... 51, 68-69, 73, 115
U.S. House of Representatives ... 61, 289
U.S. Justice Department ... 289
U.S. Mint ... 346
U.S. News & World Report ... 70
U.S. Patent Office ... 177
U.S. Post Office ... 213
U.S.S. *Onward* ... 60
USSR ... 327
U.S. Supreme Court ... 66, 100, 106, 188, 245, 284, 319, 345-346
Utah ... 119
Vallejo, Mariano Guadalupe ... 336
Vallejo, Platon ... 336
Vallejo, Salvador ... 336
Valley Forge ... 163, 300
Van Buren, Martin ... 244, 246
Van Lew, Elizabeth ... 126-131
Vassa, Gustavus ... 352
Vermont ... 342
Vicksburg, Mississippi ... 167
Virginia ... 8, 18, 36, 84-85, 88-89, 125, 158-159, 165, 216, 271-272, 308, 312, 314, 337, 339, 350, 360
Virginia Colony ... 76, 83
Virginia Senate ... 348
Voice of Calvary Ministries, The ... 241
Wales ... 16
Walker, Charles Joseph ... 179
Walker, Dixie ... 194
Walker, Madame C.J. ... 179
Wallace, George ... 181
Wallis, Tom ... 54
Walloa Band ... 290
Wallowa Valley, Oregon ... 290, 293
Walls, Josiah T. ... 269
Walton, George ... 346
Wampanoag ... 76
War of 1812 ... 150
Ware, Virgil ... 181
Warren, Joseph ... 168
Warren, Mercy ... 308
Washington (state) ... 143, 291, 293
Washington Monument ... 154
Washington, Booker T. ... 322
Washington, D.C. ... 154, 170, 174, 177, 188, 208, 253, 277, 287, 317, 326, 367
Washington, George ... 12-13, 22, 31-32, 34-37, 39-40, 42, 154-155, 159, 161-164, 173, 224, 288, 300, 302-303, 305, 308, 338, 340, 342
Washington, Martha ... 338
Washita River ... 334
Watkins, Andrew and Mariah ... 325
Watts' *Psalms and Hymns* ... 24
Watts, Isaac ... 24
Webster, Daniel ... 144-149, 214, 305
Webster, Noah ... 87, 204
Webster's Elementary Speller ... 324
Weld, Theodore ... 220-224,

... 228-229, 231
Wells-Barnett, Ida ... 102-107
Wesley, Cynthia ... 180-185
Wesley, John ... 28
West Indies ... 345
West Point ... 161-164, 256
Westminster ... 351
Weymouth, George ... 76
Wheatley, John ... 40, 42
Wheatley, Mary ... 40
Wheatley, Nathaniel ... 40-41
Wheatley, Phillis ... 39-42, 338, 369
Wheatley, Susannah ... 39-40, 42
Wheaton College ... 242
Wheeler, Ras ... 56
Whipple, William ... 348
White Antelope ... 332, 335
White Bird, Chief ... 291-292
White Haven ... 315
White, William ... 244
Whitefield, George ... 40-41, 125, 351
Wiesel, Elie ... 138
Wilberforce, William ... 28
William Street ... 243
William T. Frantz Elementary School ... 68-70, 73
Williams, William ... 347
Williamsburg ... 158
Willing, Thomas ... 346
Wilmington, North Carolina ... 50, 253
Wilson, James ... 346
Wilson, Woodrow ... 212-214
Winslow, Edward ... 91
Winslow, Susanna ... 216-219, 347
Witherspoon, John ... 216-219
Wizard of Oz, The (L. Frank Baum) ... 295
Wolcott, Oliver ... 347
Women's Auxiliary Corps of the U.S. Army ... 178
Women's Suffrage Movement ... 311
Wonderful Hair Grower ... 179
Woodstock, Virginia ... 20
Woolman, John ... 28
World Series ... 191
World Trade Center ... 243
World Vision ... 242
World War I ... 32, 210, 212, 253, 256, 278
World War II ... 193, 238, 257, 326
Wright, Mose ... 279-281
Wright, Theodore Sedgwick ... 62
Wynkoop, Ned ... 334
Wyoming ... 120
Wythe, George ... 348
ale ollege ... 151
Yale University ... 313
Yankee Stadium ... 191, 193
YMCA ... 327
York ... 276
Yorktown, Virginia ... 36-37
Youth Day ... 180
Youth's Companion ... 260
Zanesville, Ohio ... 220-221
Zimmer, Don ... 192

Music projects also available from the authors:

TOBYMAC

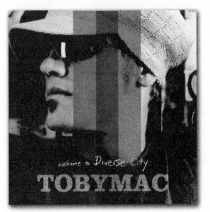

tobyMac
Welcome to Diverse City
The new studio album

tobyMac is a pioneering artist
who communicates life through
spiritually liberating, socially conscious
music. Blurring the boundaries between
rock, pop, hip hop, and urban genres,
tobyMac creates music that is both
entertaining and substantive.
Over the span of a 15-year career,
he has become a relevant voice to
youth culture through consistent
delivery of highly compelling music.

www.tobyMac.com

MICHAEL TAIT

TAIT
Lose This Life

Michael Tait is all about "connection"—
connection with God, with fans, and
with culture. Combining hip sensibilities,
emotional integrity, social consciousness,
and melodic hooks, TAIT's music
challenges listeners with thought-
provoking and emotionally uplifting
songs that reach out with relatable lyrics.

www.taitband.com

Other CDs also available:

dc Talk
Jesus Freak

dc Talk
Intermission

tobyMac
Momentum

TAIT
Empty

FOR MORE INFORMATION

www.undergodthebook.com
WallBuilders: www.WallBuilders.com

American Christian History Institute: www.achipa.com
American Colonist's Library: http://personal.pitnet.net/primarysources
Christian History Institute: www.gospelcom.net/chi
Documents in Law, History and Diplomacy: www.yale.edu/lawweb/
    avalon/avalon.htm
Erace Foundation: www.Erace.com
Harambee Christian Family Center: www.harambee.org
International Reconciliation Coalition: www.reconcile.org
John M. Perkins Foundation: www.jmpf.org
Library of Congress
    Religion and the Founding of the American Republic: www
        .loc.gov/exhibits/religion
    A Century of Lawmaking: http://lcweb2.loc.gov/ammem/
        amlaw/lawhome.html
    Thomas Historical Documents: http://thomas.loc.gov/
        home/histdoxmainpg.html
Providence Foundation: www.providencefoundation.com
Ruby Bridges Foundation: www.rubybridges.org
Wiconi International: www.wiconi.com

★ ★ ★

Additional photograph (see inside back cover, opposite) descriptions:

Medgar Evers' home / Medgar Evers' driveway: Toby visits the home of civil rights leader Medgar Evers and touches the driveway at the spot where he was shot in the back and murdered. Story on page 285.

Grocery store—Emmett Till: Michael visits the former grocery store where Emmett Till, a fourteen-year-old black boy, reportedly whistled at a white woman. Emmett was later dragged out of his bed and murdered for the alleged "offense." Story on page 279.

Tallahatchie County Courthouse: Site of the trial of the two men charged with killing Emmett Till. The two men were acquitted by an all-white jury after only an hour of deliberation. Story on page 279.

MLK Jr. assassination site: Michael points from the assassin's point of view at the balcony of the Lorraine Motel in Memphis, Tennessee, where Martin Luther King Jr. was shot. Story on page 186.

John Prentiss Matthews' gravesite: Toby sits in front of the gravesite of John Prentiss Matthews, a white leader in the interracial Fusion Independent Party. Matthews, who had been threatened and warned not to vote in the 1883 Copiah County, Mississippi, election, was shot and killed just minutes after handing in his ballot. Story on page 54.

Photographs by Eric Welch of Broken Poet Productions.